FIELDING
TRAVEL GUIDES

D1542276

FIELDING'S
SAN DIEGO
AGENDA

The Buzz About Fielding

Fielding Worldwide

"The new Fielding guidebook style mirrors the style of the company's new publisher: irreverent, urbane, adventuresome and in search of the unique travel experience."

—*San Diego Union Tribune*

"Individualistic, entertaining, comprehensive."

—*Consumers Digest*

"Guidebooks with attitude."

—*Dallas Morning News*

"Full of author's tips and asides, the books seem more personal and more credible than many similarly encyclopedic tomes."

—*Los Angeles Times*

"At Fielding Worldwide, adventurous might well be the order of the day."

—*Des Moines Register*

"Biting travel guides give readers a fresh look."

—*Houston Chronicle*

"For over 30 years Fielding guides have been the standard of modern travel books."

—*Observer Times*

Fielding's Las Vegas Agenda

"A concise but detailed look at the capital of glitter and gambling."

—*Atlanta Journal Constitution*

Fielding's Los Angeles Agenda

"…contains much more than the standard travel guide. The lists of theatres, sports arenas and attractions are worth the book's price by itself."

—*Baton Rouge Advocate*

Fielding's New York Agenda

"Loaded with advice…puts the whole of the Big Apple in hand."

—*Bon Appetit*

Fielding's Guide to Worldwide Cruises

"One of the year's ten best books."

—*Gourmet Magazine*

"Perhaps the best single source for unbiased cruise information."

—*New York Times*

"To be all things to all people is impossible, but this book pretty well does it."

—*The New York Daily News*

"You can trust them [Fielding] to tell the truth. It's fun—and very informative."

—*New Orleans Times-Picayune*

"The Bible. If scarcity is any indication of quality, then this book is superb."

—*St. Petersburg Florida Times*

Cruise Insider

"One of the best, most compact, yet interesting books about cruising today is the fact-filled *Cruise Insider*."

—*John Clayton's Travel With a Difference*

Fielding's The World's Most Dangerous Places

"Rarely does a travel guide turn out to be as irresistible as a John Grisham novel. But *The World's Most Dangerous Places*, a 1000-page tome for the truly adventurous traveler, manages to do just that."

—*Arkansas Democrat-Gazette*

"A travel guide that could be a real lifesaver. Practical tips for those seeking the road less traveled."

—*Time Magazine*

"The greatest derring-do of this year's memoirs."

—*Publishers Weekly*

"Reads like a first-run adventure movie."

—*Travel Books Worldwide*

"One of the oddest and most fascinating travel books to appear in a long time."

—*New York Times*

"...publishing *terra incognita*...a primer on how to get in and out of potentially lethal places."

—*U.S. News and World Report*

"Tired of the same old beach vacation?...this book may be just the antidote."

—*USA Today*

"Guide to hot spots will keep travelers glued to their armchairs."

—*The Vancouver Sun*

Fielding's Borneo

"One of a kind...a guide that reads like an adventure story."

—*San Diego Union*

Fielding's Budget Europe

"This is a guide to great times, great buys and discovery in 18 countries."

—*Monroe News-Star*

Fielding's Caribbean

"If you have trouble deciding which regional guidebook to reach for, you can't go wrong with *Fielding's Caribbean*."

—*Washington Times*

"Opinionated, clearly written and probably the only guide that any visitor to the Caribbean really needs."

—*New York Times*

Fielding's Europe

"Synonymous with the dissemination of travel information for five decades."

—*Traveller's Bookcase*

"The definitive Europe...shame on you if you don't read it before you leave."

—*Travel Europe*

Fielding's Far East

"This well-respected guide is thoroughly updated and checked out."

—*The Reader Review*

Fielding's France

"Winner of the annual 'Award of Excellence' [with Michelin and Dorling Kindersley]."

—*FrancePresse*

Fielding's Freewheelin' USA

"...an informative, thorough and entertaining 400-page guide to the sometimes maligned world of recreational vehicle travel."

—*Travel Weekly*

"...very comprehensive...lots more fun than most guides of this sort..."

—*Los Angeles Times*

Fielding's Italy

"A good investment...contains excellent tips on driving, touring, cities, etc."

—*Travel Savvy*

Fielding's Mexico

"Among the very best."

—*Library Journal*

Fielding's Spain and Portugal

"Our best sources of information were fellow tour-goers and *Fielding's Spain and Portugal*."

—*New York Times*

Vacation Places Rated

"...can best be described as a thinking person's guide if used to its fullest."

—*Chicago Tribune*

"Tells how 13,500 veteran vacationers rate destinations for satisfaction and how well a destination delivers on what is promised."

—*USA Today*

Fielding's Vietnam

"Fielding has the answer to every conceivable question."

—*Destination Vietnam*

"An important book about an important country."

—*NPR Business Radio*

Fielding Titles

FIELDING'S SAN DIEGO AGENDA

by
Marael Johnson

Fielding Worldwide, Inc.
308 South Catalina Avenue
Redondo Beach, California 90277 U.S.A.

Fielding's San Diego Agenda
Published by Fielding Worldwide, Inc.
Text Copyright ©1997 FWI
Icons & Illustrations Copyright ©1997 FWI
Photo Copyrights ©1997 to Individual Photographers

FIELDING WORLDWIDE INC.

PUBLISHER AND CEO	Robert Young Pelton
GENERAL MANAGER	John Guillebeaux
OPERATIONS DIRECTOR	George Posanke
ELEC. PUBLISHING DIRECTOR	Larry E. Hart
PUBLIC RELATIONS DIRECTOR	Beverly Riess
ACCOUNT SERVICES MANAGER	Cindy Henrichon
PROJECT MANAGER	Chris Snyder
MANAGING EDITOR	Amanda K. Knoles

PRODUCTION

Martin Mancha   Ramses Reynoso

Craig South

COVER DESIGNED BY	Digital Artists, Inc.
COVER PHOTOGRAPHERS —	
Front Cover	Robert Young Pelton/Westlight
Back Cover	Woody Woodworth/Adventure Photo & Film
INSIDE PHOTOS	James Blank, Bob Yarborough, Bill Robinson, Bob & Carol Culver, Gene Warneke for San Diego Convention & Visitors Bureau; Robert Young Pelton/ Westlight; Zoological Society of San Diego, Baja Tourist Association
CARTOONS:	*The New Yorker,* Cartoonists and Writers Syndicate

Inquiries should be addressed to: Fielding Worldwide, Inc., 308 South Catalina Ave., Redondo Beach, California 90277 U.S.A., ☎ *(310) 372-4474*, Facsimile *(310) 376-8064*, 8:30 a.m.–5:30 p.m. Pacific Standard Time.
Website: http://www.fieldingtravel.com
e-mail: fielding@fieldingtravel.com

ISBN 1-56952-153-0

Printed in the United States of America

Letter from the Publisher

In 1946, Temple Fielding began the first of what would be a remarkable new series of well-written, highly personalized guidebooks for independent travelers. Temple's opinionated, witty, and oft-imitated books have now guided travelers for almost a half-century. More important to some was Fielding's humorous and direct method of steering travelers away from the dull and the insipid. Today, Fielding Travel Guides are still written by experienced travelers for experienced travelers. Our authors carry on Fielding's reputation for creating travel experiences that deliver insight with a sense of discovery and style.

Designed to save travelers time and money, Fielding's *San Diego Agenda* cuts to the chase, telling readers all they need to know to "do" the town. Whether you have a day or a week in San Diego, author Marael Johnson will take you straight to all the right places and off the beaten path.

The concept of independent travel has never been bigger. Our policy of *brutal honesty* and a highly personal point of view has never changed; it just seems the travel world has caught up with us.

Enjoy your San Diego adventure with Marael Johnson and Fielding.

RYP

Robert Young Pelton
Publisher and CEO
Fielding Worldwide, Inc.

ABOUT THE AUTHOR

Marael Johnson is an award-winning freelance writer and poet who works and travels throughout the world. She's written guides to Australia, Hawaii, Louisiana and California for major travel publishers, and has contributed to dozens of other guidebooks.

Before and after taking up travel writing, the author designed and stitched clothing for rock stars, sold love beads outside American Express offices in Europe, worked as a barmaid in Spain, an artist's model everywhere and a set dresser. She has lived in paisley-painted communes in Santa Cruz, elegant Victorians in San Francisco, squats in London, handmade tents in Spain, chateaux in France, monasteries along the Pacific Ocean and currently resides in San Diego County. She has completely disproven her mother's theory that "you can't run away," as well as Thomas Wolfe's, who swore "you can never go home again." She does both—very successfully.

The author is an active member of the Society of American Travel Writers.

Fielding Rating Icons

The Fielding Rating Icons are highly personal and awarded to help the besieged traveler choose from among the dizzying array of activities, attractions, hotels, restaurants and sights. The awarding of an icon denotes unusual or exceptional qualities in the relevant category.

RATINGS

Fielding Award	Author Selection	Money Saver	Expensive	Quality	Warning	Danger	Inexpensive
Spacious	Cramped	Mild Disapproval	Timesaving				

CULTURAL

Museum /Art	Interesting Architecture	History	Book Reference	Artistically Important	Musically Interesting	Cultural Archeology	Crafts
Theater	Festivals						

SIGHTS

Picturesque	Great Scenery	Market	Beaches/ Resorts	Cultural	Fortress	Castles	Church

WHERE TO STAY

Simple	Luxurious	Cottage	Bed & Breakfast	Scenic	Business	Honeymoon	Château

TRAVEL TIPS

Arrival/ Departure	By Air	By Water	By Train	By Car	Bus/Local Transit	Barge	River Boat
Calendar	Itinerary	Compass	Kids				

SPECIAL INTERESTS

Nightlife	Singles	Romantic	Nude Beaches	Lecture	Spectacular Cuisine	Wine Tasting	Shopping
Cafe Stops	Gardening	Pro Sports	Mystery	Gambling	Wildlife		

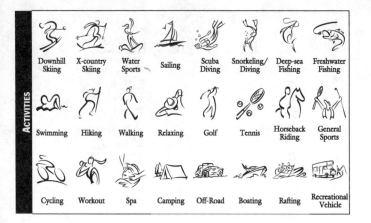

ACTIVITIES

Downhill Skiing	X-country Skiing	Water Sports	Sailing	Scuba Diving	Snorkeling/ Diving	Deep-sea Fishing	Freshwater Fishing
Swimming	Hiking	Walking	Relaxing	Golf	Tennis	Horseback Riding	General Sports
Cycling	Workout	Spa	Camping	Off-Road	Boating	Rafting	Recreational Vehicle

Star Ratings

Fielding rates all hotels, restaurants and attractives (with the exception of sporting activities) with a star system of one to five. Obviously, ratings are highly subjective. Keep in mind that more stars does not necessarily mean more expensive.

★ ★ ★ ★ ★ **Doesn't get any better**

★ ★ ★ ★ **Excellent**

★ ★ ★ **Good**

★ ★ **Fair to middling**

★ **Nothing to write home about**

Map Legend

Essentials

- **H** Hotel
- **†** Youth Hostel
- **✗** Restaurant
- **S** Bank
- **C** Telephone
- **i** Tourist Info.
- **✛** Hospital
- **♟** Pub/Bar
- **✉** Post Office
- **P** Parking
- **T** Taxi
- **S** Subway
- **M** Metro
- **M** Market
- **S** Shopping
- **C** Cinema
- **♥** Theatre
- **✈** Int'l Airport
- **✛** Regional Airport
- **✶** Police Station
- **⚖** Courthouse
- **⛪** Gov't. Building
- **■** Attraction
- **✈** Military Airbase
- **♟** Army Base
- **⚓** Naval base
- **⛫** Fort
- **🎓** University
- **♟** School

Historical

- **∴** Archeological Site
- **⚔** Battleground
- **♜** Castle

Monument

- **🕴** Monument
- **🏛** Museum
- **⚱** Ruin
- **🚢** Shipwreck

Religious

- **✝** Church
- **🛕** Buddhist Temple
- **🛕** Hindu Temple
- **☪** Mosque
- **卐** Pagoda
- **✡** Synagogue

Activities

- **⛱** Beach
- **▲** Campground
- **⛅** Picnic Area
- **⛳** Golf Course
- **🚣** Boat Launch
- **🤿** Diving
- **🐟** Fishing
- **🎿** Water Skiing
- **⛷** Snow Skiing
- **🦅** Bird Sanctuary
- **🦌** Wildlife Sanctuary
- **♠** Park
- **♠♠** Park Headquarters
- **⛏** Mine
- **🗼** Lighthouse
- **🗼** Windmill
- **⚓** Cruise Port
- **✈** View
- **⬭** Stadium
- **▬** Building
- **🐘** Zoo
- **✿** Garden

Physical

- — — — — International Boundary
- – – – – County/Regional Boundary
- **PARIS** ⊕ National Capital
- **Victoria** ◉ State/Parish Capital
- **Los Angeles** ● Major City
- **Quy Nhon** ○ Town/Village
- ===(5)=== Motorway/Freeway
- ---(163)--- Highway
- ═══════ Primary Road
- ═══════ Secondary Road
- — — — Subway
- _ _ 🚲 _ _ Biking Route

- 🥾 Hiking Trail
- ▬▬▬ Dirt Road
- ┼┼┼┼┼┼ Railroad
- **RR** Railroad Station
- _ 🚢 _ Ferry Route
- ▲ Mountain Peak
- ⬛ Lake
- ～～～ River
- ◗ Cave
- 🪸 Coral Reef
- 〰 Waterfall
- ♨ Hot Spring

©FWI 1995

TABLE OF CONTENTS

LIST OF MAPS

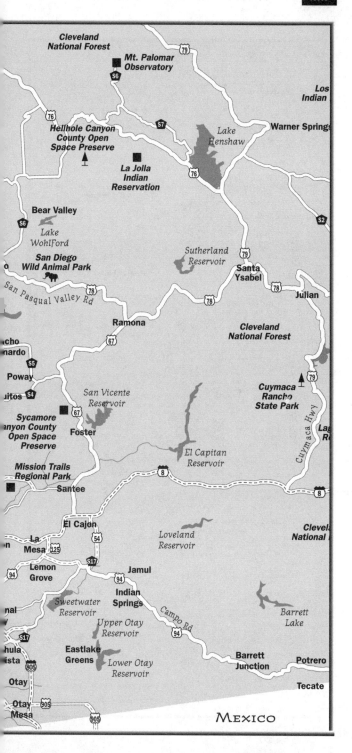

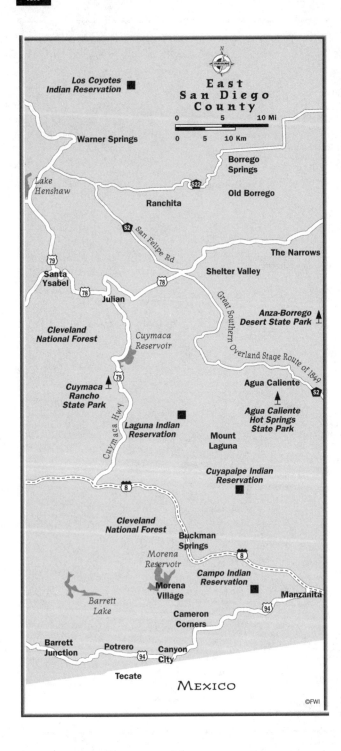

PREFACE

Elaborate sand castles on Mission Beach.

San Diego, bless its sunshiny heart and soul, is America's perennial happy face—golden, smiling, unflinching as a Buckingham Palace guard. Go ahead, tease us (lots of people do), tell us a dirty joke, bare your body parts. You won't even get a grimace, much less a rise—though we'll probably try hard to stifle a yawn. Yes, we've seen it all. But then we've *got* it all (all we *want*, anyway) because, unlike those poker-faced guards in their frou frou garb, our happy face is, by choice, one-dimensional. San Diego is simply, irrefutably, indisputably—almost nauseatingly—*nice*. Nice news, nice weather, nice people, nice beaches, nice food and grog, and nice stuff to do. A nice place for families, sailors, swingles and scientists, as well as for bikers, psychics, hookers and the homeless. Our weather makes us egalitarian. Hey dude, this is the Riviera of the U.S. of A., so put on that happy face. We've got better things to do than worry about the rest of the world. We've got holes to play, balls to toss, waves to ride and rays, z's and fish to catch.

Of course, like any fun-loving normal folk, we thrive on the occasional tawdry, kinky embarrassment or rocking-good high-profile disaster—but that's what freaky L.A.'s for, up the road. We *adore* scandals and round-the-clock CNN reports—we just don't particularly want them in our own backyard. We positively reveled in L.A.'s riots and earthquakes, in Desert Storm's scuds and patriots, so long as we were a safe distance away, that is. And, as a major naval district and aerospace manufacturing mecca, we're pretty generous about providing military might—as long as the fighting is some place *else*. Aside from that, where controversy and combat are concerned, we generally hang out in the closet behind the long dresses, living vicariously like any well-guarded queen.

As I began writing this book's first edition, San Diego's top news item was an on-the-spot interview with an irate man angered that his favorite restaurant would not deliver barbecued ribs to his home. He was crying "discrimination" (everyone involved was the same race and lived in the same neighborhood), he had already consulted a lawyer (yawn) and—even though he'd been a longtime patron—he was never going to eat at that restaurant again. The camera panned the ribs, still waiting down the road—gloriously fatty, juicy and dripping with sauce. The tang penetrated the tube. What was the name of that place again? The interview was lengthy—aired even before the news anchors' introductions. These are the kinds of problems we like—stupid, meaningless, nonthreatening discords. Throw us bones with succulent sauces and let us savor the good life. Bosnia depresses us.

Not even Al and O.J. made it to San Diego. Nope, they turned back before even hitting the county line. Too bad. By my calculations that gas-guzzling Bronco would've emptied its reserve tank precisely at the off-ramp to Torrey Pines Golf Course—they could've coasted down the hill, into the parking lot and gotten in a few rounds, all perfectly timed to the summer sun setting over the Pacific Ocean. Bad planning—they should've packed a travel guide instead of a pistol.

San Diego County may be the only place in the world that can accomplish a perfect segue not just from golf course to pistol range, but to almost any sport of your dreams. We have world-class golf and tennis tournaments, thoroughbred racing, water— *lots* of water—a Super Bowl past and a Super Bowl future and, ahem, we *did* have the America's Cup. And how's this for diversity? Our boundaries stretch from Camp Pendleton all the way south to the Mexican border; from the Cleveland National Forest and Anza-Borrego Desert in the east to the (usually) blue Pacific at the continent's edge. In the span of one day it is possible to swim the ocean, water ski the bay, off-road the desert, climb a mountain, tour the city and end the night in Mexico doing the cucaracha with a painted donkey wearing a sunbonnet. Odds are the weather will never interfere.

This is not to say that San Diego is devoid of Big City problems. After all—this is the sixth largest city in the United States, and the county is home to 2.7 million people (and that's just counting the legal inhabitants). We accommodate not only a thriving city but chic communities, retirement villages, beachy towns, ethnic neighborhoods, prosperous ranches and groves, military enclaves and hippie havens and *plenty* of nondescript'burbs. A melange of ethnic, religious and social groups brush against each other every day. And whether Nobel Laureate, El Norte dreamer or one of the myriad of ants tunneled in between, most of us manage to avoid getting stepped on.

"Well, it certainly explains why everyone's so nice!"

Drawing by Gahan Wilson; ©1995 The New Yorker Magazine, Inc.

Our crimes are more *laid back*, if you catch my drift. *Our* gangs don't cruise, they idle. *Our* homeless population can keep a tan going year-round. *Our* underground clubs are actually advertised in the weekly newspaper. Okay, okay, so there was that messy incident at the San Ysidro McDonald's some years back but, no doubt, it was the result of some planetary realignment (inquire at one of the psychic fairs). For the most part, San Diego is the nice guy on the Big Bad City hot list of stranglers, stalkers, snipers, castrators and cannibals. Again, we're that smileyfaced innocent—a lightweight on the crime scale. San Diego County is home to Dr. Seuss, where the Duke of Windsor met Wallis (no relation to O.J.) Simpson, and where Oprah met Rosey (no relation to Grier). We are home to both Deepak

Chopra and Ravi Shankar, where east-meets-east, and seven-course ayurvedic meals are complemented by exquisite vintage ragas. Most of us are in touch with our feelings and at least pretend that we care about the feelings of others. Bonds, to us, are not a financial matter—they are emotional ties established with our pets, lovers and postal workers. We are sun-kissed, healthy and active. And we like to hug just about *everyone* (in fact, as repugnant as this may sound, you are more apt to seal a business deal with a bear-hug embrace than with a firm handshake). I *know* what you're thinking—this city sounds too good to be true, like some gigantic playground full of grown-up kids. That's precisely why curious tourists and active sports enthusiasts come in droves—then decide to pack up the cat and move here for good. The climate, casual ambiance and healthy lifestyle are a real pick-me-up even in the worst of times. And, yes, there *is* a downside—San Diego is not the most sophisticated, fashion-oriented or culturally stimulating city in the country. In fact, it doesn't even come close. For those pleasures, you'll be happier in New York, San Francisco or even Los Angeles. But if you crave the sweet scents of surfboard resin, SPF 15, ripe fruits, salty air and some damn good barbecued ribs—then you're happily welcome to get in our face.

Fielding's San Diego Fast Facts

Golf courses	83
Tennis courts	1200
Zoo animals	3900
Balboa Park acres	1200
Miles of beach	70
Hotel rooms	45,000
County homicides per year	200+
Passing gray whales	50,000
Price of 1-lb. bunch of bananas	$0.44

Author's Crime Perspective

Visitors from other countries make a big deal out of handgun deaths in San Diego and the entire U.S. Our staggering statistics (about 11,000 deaths per year) are usually pitted against those of Australia (10) and Japan (90). Unfair! Everyone knows the Australians and Japanese kill people with their bare hands and feet—and not gently either. Wouldn't you rather go quickly?

Fielding's Guide to Famous San Diegans

Annette Bening: She's a real actress, really she is. Okay, she's the woman who inspired Warren Beatty to marry, father children and settle down. For now.

Betty Broderick: Overly exhausted, under-appreciated double murderess.

Florence Chadwick: Florence swam the English Channel in 1950 and holds 16 world records for long-distance swimming.

Deepak Chopra: New-age health guru, founder of Mind/Body Institute, bestselling author.

Dennis Connor: Red-faced, non-swimming yachtsman with an attitude–he won the America's Cup, lost it to Australia, won it back, lost it to New Zealand.

Warren Farrell: Consummate sensitive male, author of many emotional treatises on male liberation.

Theodore Geisel: Dr. Seuss.

Francoise Gilot: French-born artist and Picasso model, mother of Paloma Picasso, widow of Dr. Jonas Salk.

Janet Jackson: The youngest-born of the semi-surgically altered Jackson Family, sort-of-topless cover girl, and Grammy winner.

Frankie Laine: Rollin,' rollin,' rollin,' keep them doggies rollin,' Rawhide.

Cleavon Little: Tony- and Emmy Award-winning actor.

Anita Loos: Author of Gentlemen Prefer Blondes.

Greg Louganis: Aids activist and Olympic gold medalist in springboard and platform diving.

Bert Parks: "There she is," former emcee of Miss America pageants.

Gregory Peck: Academy Award-winning actor and cofounder of La Jolla Playhouse.

Carl Rogers: father of humanistic psychology, founder of Center for Studies of the Person, psycho-babble author.

Dr. Jonas Salk: recently deceased savior; developer of polio vaccine, founder of Salk Institute for Biological Studies, Aids researcher, husband of Francoise Gilot and one sharp cookie.

E.W. Scripps: newspaper magnate, developer of United Press International.

Ravi Shankar: sitarist extraordinaire, hippie-era idol, friend and mentor of George Harrison and Eric Clapton.

Tom Waits: singer, songwriter, actor with gravel lodged in his voicebox.

Ted Williams: Triple Crown-winning, baseball-batting great.

SAN DIEGO TRAVEL ADVISORY

Amtrak trains leave eight times a day from San Diego to L.A.

Are We There Yet?

Probably. No matter how you travel to San Diego you'll arrive either in or near the middle of the city. The train, bus, trolley and cruise ship terminals are an easy walk—an even easier cab ride—to the heart of downtown and many nearby attractions.

The major freeways will off-ramp you at convenient locations. Even the airport is *right there.*

Getting around San Diego is not nearly as gruesome as navigating Los Angeles. The city proper measures 320 square miles of land and 73 square miles of water, while the entire county encompasses 4255 square miles. If you're staying put in just one or two areas, then cabs, your feet and public transportation should be adequate. The train will take you up the coast, the ferry will cruise you to Coronado and the trolley will scoot you to the Mexican border. A bicycle, golf cart, skateboard, surfboard, snorkel and a pair of rollerblades will get you anywhere. Cars, of course, offer the most flexibility and freedom to explore.

The Airport

Unless you've flown into Hong Kong, the descent into San Diego International Airport (more commonly known as Lindbergh Field) is likely to scare the pants off you but, take heart—it's scarier watching from the ground. Wide-body jets weave between skyscrapers, shake residential neighborhoods, cast huge shadows over major thoroughfares, narrowly skirt office buildings, mesmerize pedestrians who can bare-eye every crack on the underbellies, practically graze a parking structure and somehow, miraculously—just at the moment you are cursing yourself for passing up that Scotch—roar onto the tarmac. Those fast taxis to the gate are no doubt propelled by all the passengers exhaling in unison.

Our airport is a hotly contested item and usually hits the ballots every other election. Should we or shouldn't we move it farther out of town? Should we give the planes more air space and landing room? Or should we keep those pilots on their toes? So far, the toes have it.

Lindbergh Field, serving more than twelve million passengers annually, has a tad more air traffic than it did in 1927 when Charles Lindbergh—its namesake—took off in his *Spirit of St. Louis.* But it's so *convenient* (especially for conventioneers)—just three miles from downtown with easy freeway access. Face it: cheap cab fare takes precedence over disaster prevention. Anyway, judging from the somewhat chaotic new construction, expansion and renovation taking place at the existing facility, I'd bet on Lindbergh for the long haul.

Private aircraft can use Brown Field, Montgomery Field, Palomar Airport and other small county strips; the Blue Angels and Navy fighter jets (and, soon, possibly helicopters) set down at Miramar Naval Air Station; alien spacecraft usually opt for a desert landing.

Airlines That Serve San Diego

Aeromexico
☎ *(800) 237-6639*

Alaska Airlines
☎ *(800) 426-0333*

America West
☎ *(800) 247-5692*

American
☎ *(800) 433-7300*

Continental
☎ *(800) 525-0280*

Delta
☎ *(800) 221-1212*

Midwest Express
☎ *(800) 452-2022*

Northwest
☎ *(800) 225-2525*

Reno Air
☎ *(800) 736-6247*

Sky West
☎ *(800) 453-9417)*

Southwest
☎ *(800) 435-9792*

Trans World
☎ *(800) 221-2000*

United
☎ *(800) 241-6522*

USAir
☎ *(800) 428-4322*

Considering the size of the city it serves, Lindbergh Field is relatively minuscule. There are two terminals, east and west, side-by-side, simple as that. The airlines are divided somewhat evenly between them, though the West Terminal is in the process of adding eight additional gates. (Note that there is plenty of construction chaos in progress!) Get off the plane, follow the signs to your baggage claim area if you have luggage to collect (there will be rental carts, if needed), and walk out one of the automatic, sliding-glass doors. Voilá! Prepare for your Pavlovian greeting—the endless-loop announcement that warns not to park in the loading zone.

Taxis should be ready and waiting, though *you* might have to be ready and waiting for a shuttle service. Cross at the light to the Ground Transportation Area where a stranger will come up, ask where you're headed and eventually direct you onto the appropriate shuttle when it comes around (if you're in a rush, this isn't the best option). A cab ride into downtown should run about $10; the shuttle goes for $6. Many hotels and motels provide courtesy vans for guests—ask when you book your room, or check the courtesy phones inside the terminal.

Rental Cars

Major car rental agencies have desks at the airport; others can be beckoned via courtesy phone. Avis, Hertz and National have banded together in an unused General Dynamics site near Lindbergh Field, providing customers with more efficient service and expanded facilities. Those companies and most others will pick you up and shuttle you to the car lot.

It's always best to reserve your car ahead, especially during peak holiday times. Weekly rates are the best deal, with economy cars going for around $135 including unlimited mileage. If you're considering a jaunt into Mexico, say so before booking a car. The mandatory Mexican insurance will add about $15 per day to your tab though many companies won't allow you to take their vehicles across for *any* price. Ask first.

Author's Tip

Don't try to sneak a rental car into Mexico–it won't work. Also don't arbitrarily assume that your credit card or auto insurance carrier will cover that somewhat costly Collision Damage Waiver. Check before you rent. If you're covered, great; if not, you should sign up–it'll be cheaper than any body repair.

Car Rental Agencies

Alamo	**Enterprise**
☎ (800) 327-9633	☎ (800) 325-8007
Avis	**Hertz**
☎ (800) 331-1212	☎ (800) 654-3131
Aztec	**National**
☎ (800) 231-0400	☎ (800) 227-7368
Budget	**Rent A Vette**
☎ (800) 527-0700	☎ (619) 238-3883
Dollar	**Rent A Wreck**
☎ (800) 800-4000	☎ (800) 228-8235

(P.S. Don't get too excited about Rent A Vette for that Baja trip.)

You'll probably return to the airport the same way you left. If you already have a ticket in hand, check your bags curbside and proceed to the gate—or the bar.

Author's Tip

Airport shuttles supposedly provide transportation 24 hours a day, every day. Unfortunately they are not always dependable. Sometimes two vans arrive simultaneously, other times they're behind schedule or you're forgotten altogether. Book 24 hours ahead, and reconfirm at least two hours before your scheduled pickup. And always tell them you need to be at the airport at least 30 minutes earlier than necessary. One reasonably reliable company that serves the entire county is Cloud 9. For information, call ☎ (800) 9SHUTTLE.

SAN DIEGO AVIATION FIRSTS

1883 John and James Montgomery made the first controlled-wing flight

1911 Glen Curtiss made the world's first seaplane flight

SAN DIEGO AVIATION FIRSTS

1911 Glen Curtiss made the first amphibian flight

1911 Glen Curtiss made the first ship-to-shore flight

1912 Glen Curtiss received the first radio communication during flight

1912 Lincoln Beachy performed the first aerial hoop

1925 Rayn Airlines began the first daily-scheduled, year-round passenger service

1926 San Diego became the first U.S. city to establish a municipal board of air control

1926 San Diego was the first city to issue a complete set of air ordinances

Cruises

Carnivalesque B Street Pier is the site of San Diego's cruise ship terminal, the country's ninth-largest cruise port and the only West Coast facility that accommodates both one-day and longer-duration voyages. Ships usually are on their way to or from Mexico, and Norwegian Cruise Line's *Southward* swings over to Catalina Island.

If you come to San Diego (or anywhere) by cruise ship, you can expect the one-day, in-and-out, see-all tour bus excursion. San Diego offers a bit of an edge in that its safe, good-part-of-town location offers an escape route (however brief) from the passengers and crew you are probably ready to push overboard. The direct baggage transfer system between the cruise terminal and airport is especially handy if you're picking up or departing the cruise in San Diego. Talks are underway with Mexican *oficiales* to develop new port destinations in Baja. The cruise lines come and go, and also change itineraries. Contact your favorite travel agent to find out who's docking at San Diego.

The Train

AMTRAK chugs eight times daily between San Diego's Santa Fe Depot and L.A.'s Union Station, stopping at the Oceanside Transit Center and the Solana Beach station. The fare to Solana Beach is $7, and to L.A. $25. Special deals are offered for round-trip excursions. Buy tickets before boarding or you'll be liable for a surcharge. For information, ☎ *(800) USA-RAIL.*

The Coaster is a double-decker commuter train that operates six times a day, Monday–Friday (with a couple of extra runs on

Friday nights and Saturday afternoons), between the downtown Santa Fe Depot, Old Town, Sorrento Valley, Solana Beach, Encinitas, Carlsbad and Oceanside. Fares ($2.50–$3.75, half-price for seniors and disabled passengers) are based on zones and include free transfers to connecting San Diego Transit buses, the San Diego Trolley and North County Transit District buses. Purchase tickets from vending machines at each station (they take cash, Visa and Master Card), validate your ticket before boarding the train and hang onto it—authorities make random checks, issuing fines to freeloaders or ticket-losers. A confounding array of discounts and passes are available. For schedules and information, ☎ *(800) COASTER* or *(619) 685-4900.*

Author's Survival Tip

Unsuspecting people are killed on San Diego County's railroad tracks every year. For some unfathomable reason the train screams through built-up coastal towns at 90 m.p.h., yet barely grunts along sparsely populated areas. The speed and distance of a train are very deceptive. Keep clear both of the tracks and the adjacent embankments; cross only at designated intersections and—even then—look both ways. Try to play chicken and you'll end up a dead duck in someone else's tracks.

The Trolley

Efficient, cheap and redder than Madonna's lips, the San Diego Trolley—like the Coaster—is a model of successful public transportation. The South Line offers service from downtown to the Mexican border (where you can walk across *la frontera*), stopping at 21 suburban stations along the way; the East Line covers Bayside stations (Seaport Village, the San Diego Convention Center and Gaslamp Quarter) plus the East County communities of Encanto, Lemon Grove, La Mesa, El Cajon and Santee. Mid-1996 saw the inception of a North Line extension from the Santa Fe Depot to Old Town Historical Park. Another line, with a projected completion date of late 1997, will link downtown with Mission Valley and the San Diego Jack Murphy Stadium—site of the 1998 Super Bowl. Trolleys operate daily, 5 a.m.–1 a.m., every 15 minutes until 9 p.m., and every 30 minutes until 1 a.m. and on weekends. South Line trolleys offer more frequent service during weekday rush hours. Fares are $1-$1.75 and tickets must be purchased before boarding. Ticket-vending machines, located at each station, take only exact change. A variety of discounts and passes are available. For more information, stop by **The Transit Store**, *449 Broadway*, or ☎ *(619) 233-3004;* for 24-hour recorded info, ☎ *(619) 685-4900.*

The clean and inexpensive trolley is a fun way to travel to the Mexican border.

The Bus

Greyhound Bus Lines (☎ *(800) 231-2222)* serves San Diego from almost everywhere. The terminal, *120 W. Broadway,* ☎ *(619) 239-8082,* between Front Street and First Avenue, is centrally located and within walking distance of major hotels. Suburban stations are located in Oceanside, El Cajon and San Ysidro.

Compared to the slick trolleys and Coasters, **local buses** are dinosaurs, basically good for short (slow) journeys. **San Diego Transit** buses serve the city and most routes connect to trolley lines. Fares are $1.50–$1.75 (exact change) and include a free transfer that can be used on the trolley (request it upon boarding). The **Day Tripper Transit Pass** allows unlimited bus, trolley and ferry rides ($5 for one-day, $15 for four-days). For information and passes, contact **The Transit Store** (☎ *(800) 262-7837 or (619) 233-3004)*. The Transit Store can also provide info and schedules for suburban transit systems. For rural bus service, call

Southeast Rural Bus System (☎ (619) 478-5875) or Northeast Rural Bus System (☎ (619) 767-4287).

Waterways

The trusty **San Diego Bay Ferry**, shut down in 1969 when the Coronado Bridge opened, was reinstated in 1987. The fifteen-minute ride affords great views of the city—a treat lost to bridge drivers who must exercise enormous discipline to ignore the hypnotic sight. Catch your ride across San Diego Bay at the Fifth Avenue Landing, next to the Convention Center, Sun.–Thurs. 9 a.m.–9:30 p.m., Fri.–Sat. 9 a.m.–10:30 p.m., on the hour. Return is from Coronado's Old Ferry Landing, on the half hour. Fare is $2 each way an additional 50¢ per bicycle. Tickets must be purchased before boarding. Look for the signs on either end. For information, ☎ *(619) 234-4111.*

San Diego Harbor Excursion's Water Taxi offers regularly scheduled ferry service daily, noon–7 p.m., from Seaport Village on the Embarcadero to several spots in Coronado. On-call service is provided daily, 10 a.m.–10 p.m., to other points of interest such as Harbor Island, Shelter Island, Chula Vista Marina and South Bay. Fare is $5 one way. For information, ☎ *(619) 235-4111.*

FIELDING'S FAVORITE REST STOP THAT'S REALLY NOT

The freeway rest stop on the west side of Interstate 5, between San Onofre and Oceanside, is famous from Europe to Australia. A strange, transient community has been set up there over the years—filled with misfits, runaways, undiscovered talent and foot-long hot dogs. Forget going to the circus, or else join the one here. The atmosphere is vibrant, catchy and dangerous.

The Fast Lane

It's a cinch getting to San Diego on wheels. Interstate 5 cuts through the city on its Canada-to-Mexico odyssey. If you're coming from points east, take Interstate 8; Interstate 15 is the route in from Nevada and outlying mountain regions. Follow the signs leading to downtown, Old Town or other towns. Balboa Park, Lindbergh Field and the Coronado Bay Bridge are also well-marked. Keep a buck handy for the bridge toll if you're alone—two or more in a vehicle get a free ride.

Officially the speed limit is 65 m.p.h. That's the *legal* limit—naturally most vehicles drive much faster or, in some cases, much slower. Like most Southern Californians, San Diego drivers love to scare wimpy drivers by speeding up at on- and off-ramps (cheap thrills, I know). If you're in this category, try to fake it while merging. Other rules to remember: wearing a seatbelt is mandatory; children must be strapped into approved contraptions; and right turns on red lights are permitted if no cars are approaching.

Unless you're out in the 'burbs, the parking situation is dreary. Exhausted and impatient drivers try to outrun and outwit one another for one- or two-hour spaces, metered and monitored by overly eager patrols who delight in giving citations. Large hotels supply expensive on-site parking (with or without the valet), while smaller establishments often offer free lots. Free or validated parking is provided at shopping malls. Good luck finding a space, free or otherwise, at the beach during the summer.

Author's Tip

Many downtown streets are one-way. Before you hit the road, arm yourself with plenty of maps. Thomas Brothers is the best, but the Automobile Club of Southern California is also a valuable source. Study mergers and interchanges as though they were your futures on the stock exchange.

Fielding's Color-Coded Curb Confusion

If your car is missing from where you left it, check first to see if it was heisted by the cops for parking violations. Call ☎ (619) 531- 2844 to find out the ransom.

White: *Three-minute maximum for active loading (no stopping for a smoke or stargaze), enforced 24 hours per day; loading time at hotels is 10 minutes; at the airport, drivers must stay with the car (helping your old aunt inside with her hat box is verboten).*

Green: *Short stints for the time posted, unless you have a visible disabled placard—then it's unlimited.*

Yellow: *Twenty-minute loading zone for vehicles with commercial plates; anyone can park 6 p.m.–6 a.m., and on Sundays and some holidays—check the posted signs.*

Red: *No stopping, standing or parking at any time. Watch, in particular, for marked fire lanes.*

Blue: *For physically disabled persons ONLY; unless you have officially issued license plates or placards, you will be in BIG trouble if parked here. Citations for violators usually run into the hundreds of dollars—and the cops are merciless.*

Fielding's Freeway Rescue Guide

You blew it. You're stuck in rush-hour traffic, at a border-crossing backup or gridlocked near some big event you didn't even know about. Whatever, you're now embroiled in the nightmarish stop-and-go routine—agonizing as a game of charades at a bad party with people you hate.

If you have a cell phone, you're in great shape. Not only can you call friends and business associates or make crank calls, you can take advantage of **Local Talk***, a Pacific Bell service that provides you with an amazing array of information. The catch is that you need the front section of the Pacific Bell Yellow Pages for the listings of four-digit codes to access your desired message. It's worth keeping in the car (of course, if you're desperate—which you probably are—you can always call a friend to look in the book for you). Think of it—you can get updates on news and weather, soap operas and horoscopes, sports events and tourist attractions, vasectomies and chickenpox, IRS audits and weight management— all before your car moves three feet! Dial 569-1000, then press in the four-digit access code. The service is free within the local San Diego calling area but long distance and airtime charges are additional.*

FIELDING'S CAN'T-LIVE-WITHOUT-THESE ACCESS CODES

Did you think I was going to abandon you? After sifting through hundreds of Local Talk choices, I have selected this eclectic mix:

1510	National News
1515	World News
5673	Local News
7777	Lottery Updates
1050	All My Children Update
1970	Book Reviews
1910	Movie Reviews
1980	Entertainment News
9090	Street Blimp Appearances
6170	Local Attractions
6171	Local Festivals
1710	National Sports Report
1715	Sports Scoreboard
5673	Local Sports
2500	Bankruptcy

No cell phone? Try the radio. Besides the San Diego stations, you may be able to pick up L.A. and Baja broadcasts. Catch up on your prayers, reminisce over some blurry backseat romance, wallow in you-done-me-wrong-baby blues, become reborn and brush up on your Spanish.

San Diego Radio

AM		
KKLQ	600	Top 40
KFMB	760	Talk
KSDO	1130	Talk
KCBQ	1170	Oldies
FM		
KSDS	88.3	Jazz
KIFM	98.1	Jazz
KPBS/NPR	89.5	News and Classical
KVCR	91.9	News and Classical
KSON	97.3	Country
KFMB	100.7	News and Talk
KCLX	102.9	Classic Rock
XTLA	104.9	Radio Latina

No cell phone or radio??? Not even a moderately amusing passenger? Sorry, you've been relegated to decoding vanity license plates (probably brain teasers like GOFOURIT or CHILLOUT). This is God's punishment for people who travel without electronic devices.

The Slow Lane

Already dreading the thought of getting behind the wheel? Call a **taxi**. San Diego is **not** New York—you will probably be ignored or run over if you leap into the street to hail a cab. Unless you're at the airport, train depot or a large hotel, you'd better phone ahead if you need a ride. Some established companies include: **Coronado Cab** (☎ *(619) 435-6211)*; **La Jolla Cab** (☎ *(619) 453-4222)*; **Orange Cab** (☎ *(619) 291-3333)*; **Silver Cabs** (☎ *(619) 280-5555)*; and **Yellow Cab** (☎ *(619) 234-6161)*.

Or how about a chauffeur-driven stretch **limo** with TV and full bar? Most hotels will make the arrangements. One well-known local service is **Olde English Livery** (☎ *(619) 232-6533)*.

For those who want air-conditioned comfort and a running commentary, do-the-town-in-a-day **tours** are scheduled daily by **Gray Line** (☎ *(619) 491-0011 or* ☎ *(800) 331-5077, outside California)*.

Exploring **on foot** allows you to glimpse details that you would never catch otherwise—a scrumptious private garden, a magnificent piece of architecture, an impromptu street performance, an original Picasso set out with someone's garbage. San Diego is a great place for striking out on your own—choose the city or beach, mountains or desert.

Author's Tip

Visitors are often amused that San Diegans take those walk/don't walk signs so seriously and never, ever (well, hardly ever) jaywalk. The terrible secret revealed: San Diego police actually screech their cars to a halt, red lights a-flash, prisoners cuffed in the backseat, nearly mowing down pedestrians—just to cite, and often to hassle, jaywalkers. Sheriff's helicopters will swoop from the sky, turn on loudspeakers and publicly humiliate souls brazen enough to step off a curb after "don't" walk" has quit blinking. Amusing?

The Bike Lane

San Diego's miles of bike paths often appear more like other cities' carpool lanes. Everyone gets into the act. On a typical day you might spot sleek Italian racers, old Schwinns with training wheels, shiny trikes, tandem affairs, rigs with homemade sidecars (carrying pets, kids or lovers), chopper wheelchairs, skateboards and rollerblades as well as joggers, sprinters and powerwalkers.

Favorite (flat) bike paths are along Old Highway 101 (through North County beach communities), Mission Bay and Mission Bay Boardwalk. Hotels and resorts usually have bicycles available for guests' use. **Rent-A-Bike** (☎ *(619) 232-4700)* offers daily, weekly and monthly rentals and also provides free pickup and delivery.

A SURVIVOR'S GUIDE TO SAN DIEGO

San Diego's nice weather, beautiful beaches and friendly atmosphere lure many visitors into becoming residents.

Surfing the Web

San Diego is an easy city—hardly any drive-by shootings, minimal graffiti and few of the street-smart scams and cons that pervade *really* hip Bad Guys like D.C., New York and Philly. In comparison our downtown is almost a folksy affair, and probably the most nonthreatening of any major metropolis in America. Follow some simple guidelines, use common sense and try not to trip over any bodies.

FIELDING'S FAVORITE BEFORE-THERE-WAS-O.J. CRIME

San Diego claims Betty Broderick—La Jolla matron, mother of four and Wronged Woman. One night Betty and her gun paid an unexpected visit to ex-husband Dan and his pretty new wife and hot-headedly shot them in cold blood. The mini-series has come and gone. The exposé books are on the bargain rack. Perhaps Betty's biggest mistake was putting Dan through law school and then helping him become one of the most respected attorneys in town. No dream team for Betty—just one long nightmare in jail.

Down and Out and Not Bad Off

You will encounter many bodies during your visit. Some of these will be slumped in doorways, housed under cardboard boxes or at the helm of shopping-cart trains. Others might be standing in the street displaying signs saying they will work for food or need money to visit mom in Kansas. We have a lot of homeless people—the climate is great year-round and the living is easy. Some of them are legitimately down-and-out, others are on the streets by choice. Give offers of work and you'll more than likely be turned down.

The con is obvious: most of the street-dwellers know there's a greater likelihood that you'll throw some change their way rather take them back to your home or office (though each and every one would love to star in a remake of *Down and Out in Beverly Hills*.) Like hookers, they keep the same turf for months or years. They never go back to Kansas. The business community is trying to discourage visitors and residents from giving hand-outs and ask, instead, that people contribute to one of the charities that house and feed the homeless. It's your choice: give the money discreetly, or politely refuse.

Author's Tip

There are people living in some of San Diego's toilets: the airport, Santa Fe Depot, bus terminals, department stores and public libraries are good bets. Sometimes they come out of the cubicles, sometimes you never see them. But they are in there.

Sex and Drugs in the Smiley-Face Badlands

San Diego's namby-pamby red-light district casts more of a pinkish glow. El Cajon Boulevard, east of Park Boulevard, is lined with no-tell motels and is the main strip for those lookin'-for-love. Second to jaywalkers, the cops love to hassle streetwalkers and regularly set up decoys, make undercover busts and rid the city of hookers and johns (well, at least, for a night). As in other cities, rest areas are sometimes hot beds for homosexual encounters with passing strangers. Watch out for the rest stops with ocean views, they're particularly popular at sunset when all parties are facing the same direction.

Yes, we have heaps of drugs (after all, this is a border town), but we probably have just as many avocados. Unless you hang around school yards, you most likely won't notice a thing. The Feds, making another valiant (and expensive) attempt to clean up drug trafficking at the border, have instigated **Operation Hardline**—hardball that will maybe, for once, at least ding the seemingly impenetrable armor of the drugmobile. Since February 1995, the operation has seized millions of dollars-worth of cocaine, marijuana and heroin. Sounds like a lot but really it's a pittance.

Fielding's Basic Survival Kit

1. Don't look like a bewildered tourist even if you are one; even mediocre thieves are fluent in body language.

2. Leave the jewels and Rolex at home or in the hotel safe; if you're too much of a sentimentalist to remove your wedding band or championship ring, at least turn the stone to the inside of your hand.

3. Carry an inconspicuous purse or knapsack—lowbrow thieves can't tell it's not a real Louis Vuitton.

4. Walk purposefully and confidently, even if you have neither purpose nor confidence.

5. Don't go into isolated areas at night, and that includes lonely beaches; always be aware of your surroundings.

6. If driving, plan your route (and lock your doors) before you set off; if you become lost in an iffy-looking neighborhood, get out of the area as quickly as possible.

7. Be wary of using ATM machines, particularly at night—and never hang around after collecting your cash (count it later—it's doubtful the bank shortchanged you).

8. Be alert for pickpockets, especially at airports, hotels and large events; don't hang your bag on the door hook when using public restrooms—purse snatchers love to sweep through and grab the take, catching you (literally) with your pants down.

9. Park in well-lighted areas, do not leave valuables or bags in view, and make sure your vehicle is locked.

10. If you are carjacked or robbed, don't resist. Hand over the goods and you'll probably escape with your life.

Fielding's Guide to Hot and Cool Cars

In San Diego, you're more likely to lose your car than your life. Fast wheels are more fun than dead people.

What's Hot

According to the CHP, the county's top stolen vehicles include Toyota Corollas (from 1980 up), Toyota Camrys, Honda Accords, Acuras and the enormous Chevy Suburban (used for one-time criminal purposes). As for Z-cars and Toyota trucks, and any sport utility...you may as well say your last goodbyes every time you leave them unattended.

What's Cool

Beemers? No. Jeeps? No, no.

The HUMMER. YES!

It's more than just another pretty face though it is a head-turner. It's also a gas guzzler and very, very slow. The Hummer, war hero and veteran of Desert Storm, was given civilian status in 1992. Base price is about $48,000. Enticing options include steel doors, a vehicle-recovery strap and high-quality sound system. And no one is stupid enough to steal it (even border patrol agents might get suspicious). Roads not wide enough? Widen them!

Top 10 Stats of the Coolest Car

Manufacturer: AM General	*Engine: 5.7-liter V-8*
Length: 15 feet, 4-1/2 inches	*Horsepower: 190 at 4000 rpm*
Width: 7 feet, 2-1/2 inches	*Gas Tank: 23 gallons*
Height: 6 feet, 3 inches	*Maximum Speed: 75+ m.p.h.*
Curb Weight: 6100 pounds	*Estimated Mileage: 10–11 m.p.g.*

Floating Down the Highway Without a Log

San Diego has courtesy booths within visitor bureaus within tourist centers. There are books, maps, brochures, hotlines and electronic planners to assist. People in shops and on the street will smile and help you. We're nice to our visitors—unlike that hideously humid Florida place.

Alternative Accommodations

Can't afford to stay at one of the big high-rise hotels or posh resorts? Feel like retching when you see one of those Motel 6 or Super 8 signs? Want to meet other travelers with similar interests, inclinations, and budgets? Along with top-notch accommodations and really boring motel chains, San Diego also offers an interesting and eclectic selection of "alternative" stays.

Youth hostels are the most popular. Despite the word "youth," these budget accommodations welcome all ages. Be prepared to bring, or rent, your own sheet sack, and to share a dorm room with other travelers (semi-private rooms are sometimes available). Bathroom and kitchen facilities are also communal. Some lock the doors during daytime hours, others lock them early at night. And most expect you to help with the daily chores. Inquire at each about restrictions and expectations (and also payment policies—some accept cash or traveler's checks only). Rates range $7–$25 per night, per person, and reservations are advisable during peak periods. **Hosteling International-American Youth Hostels** operates a wide range of well-run establishments throughout the world. For a complete list of hostels, and to obtain a membership card (for cheaper rates and other privileges), contact **Hosteling International-American Youth Hostels** *(733 15th St. NW, Suite 840, Washington DC 20005; ☎ (202) 783-6161)*. The HI hostels in the San Diego area are: **HI-Hostel on Broadway**, in downtown *(500 W. Broadway, San Diego, CA 92101, phone (619) 525-1531)*; and **HI-Point Loma Hostel**, also called 'Elliott Hostel' *(3790 Udall Street, San Diego 92107, ☎ (619) 223-4778)*.

Various **private hostels** also exist, but beware—they can range from great-finds to hell-holes. **Ocean Beach International Hostel** *(4961 Newport Avenue, Ocean Beach, ☎ (800) 339-7263 or (619) 223-7873)*, housed in the old Newport Hotel, offers hostel-type lodging, shared facilities, fun (a little too funsy) environment, and a beach location. **Banana Bungalow** *(707 Reed Avenue, Mission Beach, ☎ (800) 546-7835 or (619) 273-3060)*, is another beach-area location for "adventurous" travelers (i.e. party, party, down and dirty). **Jim's San Diego** *(1425 C Street, San Diego, ☎ (619) 235-0234)*, is a small shared-room hostel near downtown. In Tijuana, **Villas Juvenile Youth Hostel** *(Av. Padre Kino 22320, Tijuana, ☎ 66-84-2523)* offers south-of-the-border dorm beds in a parklike setting.

San Diego is fortunate to have two really fine budget hotels designed by local wonder-boy architect Rob Wellington Quigley. The **J Street Inn** *(222 J Street., San Diego, ☎ (619) 696-6922)* and the **Island Inn** *(202 Island Avenue, San Diego, ☎ (619) 232-4138)* are both situated just outside the Gaslamp Quarter and within walking distance of the Convention Center, Seaport Village, Horton Plaza, and all transportation depots. Both are beautifully designed for tourists as well as locals and feature small private studio apartments with kitchenettes and bathrooms. A reading room, outdoor patios, exercise room, desk clerk, and underground parking are bonuses. Rates run only about $30 per day, single or double, with a discount for weekly guests. You can't beat this deal for clean, comfortable, convenient, private, and affordable housing.

Campgrounds include: **Campland on the Bay** (*2211 Pacific Beach Drive, Mission Bay Park,* ☎ *(619) 581-4200);* **De Anza Bay Resort RV Park** (*2727 De Anza Road, Mission Bay Park,* ☎ *(619) 273-311);* **Silver Strand State Park** (*south of Coronado,* ☎ *(619) 435-5184);* **San Elijo Beach State Park** (*Cardiff-by-the-Sea,* ☎ *(619) 753-5091);* and **South Carlsbad State Beach** (*Carlsbad,* ☎ *(619) 438-3143).* Rates will run $16-$30, and some of the parks permit tents but no RVs, others RVs but no tents. San Elijo and South Carlsbad state parks, both fronting the ocean, are *packed* during summer and holidays. Make reservations for either of those facilities through MISTIX (☎ *(800) 444-7275).*

For a list of private accommodations, contact **Bed and Breakfast Guild of San Diego** (☎ *(619) 523-1300).* For house and condo rentals, try **San Diego Vacation Rentals** (☎ *(619) 296-1000),* or **Beach Connection** (☎ *(619) 456-9411).*

Sweet dreams!

Tourist Information

Stop by the **International Visitor Information Center**, First Avenue and F Street, in Horton Plaza. The multilingual staff hands out multilingual hospitality guides and will load your briefcase or backpack with brochures. Hours are Monday-Saturday 8:30 a.m.–5 p.m. year-round, Sundays 11 a.m.–5 p.m., June through August. For information, ☎ *(619) 236-1212.*

Additional visitor centers include: **Balboa Park Information Center**, *House of Hospitality, 1549 El Prado,* in the park (☎ *(619) 239- 0512);* **Coronado Visitor Bureau**, *111 Orange Ave., Suite A, Coronado* (☎ *(619) 437-8788);* **Old Town State Historic Park Visitor & Information Center**, *2645 San Diego Ave., in Old Town* (☎ *(619) 220-5422;* and **Mission Bay Visitor Information Center**, *2688 E. Mission Bay Dr.* (☎ *(619) 276-8200).*

Emergencies

Dial 911 from anywhere for medical, fire or police emergencies.

Hospital emergency rooms with physicians on duty around the clock include: **Kaiser Permanente Medical Center**, *4647 Zion Avenue* (☎ *(619) 528-5000);* **Mercy Hospital and Medical Center**, *4077 5th Avenue, Uptown* (☎ *(619) 294-8111);* **Scripps Memorial Hospital**, *9888 Genesee Avenue, La Jolla* (☎ *(619) 457-4123);* **UCSD Medical Center**, *200 W. Arbor Drive, Uptown* (☎ *(619) 543-6222);* and **Veterans Administration Hospital**, *3350 La Jolla Village Drive, La Jolla* (☎ *(619) 552-8585).* The rich and special usually go to Scripps Clinic and Research Foundation, up the road from Torrey Pines Golf Course—Mother Teresa went there and was saved; Jonas Salk went there and died.

Fielding's Award for Best Near-Death Kitsch

Members of the Kaiser Permanente medical care system are lucky stiffs in time of emergency. An espresso counter has been installed right outside the hospital's ambulance entrance. Specialty coffees and biscotti brew and crunch as paramedics wheel the bodies by on gurneys. Having a full-on cardiac arrest? Forget the paddles. Kick start your ticker with a double espresso.

Meeting People

The **Personal Ads** are the rage these days. People place ads in local newspapers and magazines, giving a blurb about themselves and the type of person or relationship they're looking for. Ads are categorized (Men-Seeking-Women, Women-Seeking-Men, etc. etc.), and each advertiser is assigned a personal voice-mail box. The calls roll in, conversations ensue and a meeting might be arranged. *The Reader* offers the widest selection of ads in all "categories." Be forewarned: "Young blonde surfer chick" in the ad can translate to "middle-aged couch potato" in person. And the "Tall, dark bodybuilder" you're searching for at the bar is the short, pasty, bald guy over in the corner. Not only do people lie about their appearances, jobs and lives—they seem to have no remorse whatsoever when they're found out. (Are you sure you want to go this route?)

Fielding's Guide to the San Diego Singles Scene

Women With Ticking Biological Clocks: All

Men Who Are Ready to Commit: None

The Press

The *San Diego Union-Tribune* is the daily, *The Los Angeles Times*, *USA Today*, and *Wall Street Journal* are widely available, and you can even find *The New York Times*. Almost every outlying town and community puts out a local rag.

The Reader, San Diego's "alternative press," contains a large section with entertainment and events listings—as well as those Personal Ads. It comes off the press on Thursday and is available at shops, cafes, markets and convenience stores throughout the county.

San Diego magazine and *San Diego Home and Garden* are the city's homegrown 'zines and contain the usual profiles of locals and visiting celebs, sagas of things being grown or built, and the social and party scene (complete with photos of uncomfortable men overshadowed by women with sequined gowns and big hair). Unfortunately over the lean years, both mags have become rather anorexic.

Fielding's Favorite Feed-Your-Head Book Shops

You'll find Crown, Super Crown, Barnes and Noble and Bookstar around town, but literati and many locals favor the smaller specialty shops.

Blue Door Bookstore

> *3823 Fifth Avenue, Hillcrest;* ☎ *(619) 298-8610.*
> Beat and offbeat fiction, literary paperbacks, gay and lesbian titles, poetry, philosophy, hard-to-find mags.

D. G. Wills

> *7461 Girard Avenue, La Jolla;* ☎ *(619) 456-1800.*
> Shelves and stacks packed tightly with used books on every subject imaginable; great browsing; hosts free readings by Allan Ginsburg and local poets and authors.

Esmeralda

> *1555 Camino del Mar, in the Plaza, Del Mar;* ☎ *(619) 755-2707.*
> Bestsellers, new fiction, literature, art, philosophy and a coffee bar; often hosts free readings by authors.

Libros Bookstore

> *2754 Calhoun Street, in Bazaar del Mundo, Old Town;*
> ☎ *(619) 299-1139.*
> California and Latin American fiction, history, art and architecture, as well as philosophy and psychology titles and greeting cards.

White Rabbit

> *7755 Girard Avenue, La Jolla (*☎ *(619) 454-3518.*
> Exclusively children's books—sleepy-time-story babies through junior high readers.

Fielding's Weather Report

Perfect almost all the time. The average high is 70 degrees Fahrenheit, the low is 55 degrees Fahrenheit, and the average annual rainfall is less than 10 inches. Low humidity, lots of sun, hardly any smog—the Riviera of the United States. We do have occasional droughts and floods, but visitors can usually plan any activity without staying glued to the weather channel.

Come mid-December through mid-March for whale-watching or early spring to catch the desert in bloom. For **Weather Information**, ☎ *289-1212; for the* **Beach Report**, ☎ *221-8884.*

AVERAGE TEMPERATURES IN SAN DIEGO

Month	High °F	Low °F	Average Rainfall (inches)	Average Sunshine (percentage)
Jan.	65	48	2.11	72
Feb.	66	50	1.43	72
Mar.	66	52	1.60	70
Apr.	68	55	0.78	67
May	69	58	0.24	59
Jun.	71	61	0.06	58
Jul.	76	65	0.01	68
Aug.	78	67	0.11	70
Sept.	77	65	0.19	69
Oct.	75	60	0.33	68
Nov.	70	54	1.10	75
Dec.	66	49	1.36	73

Author's Tip

Southern Californians do not know how to drive in the rain. If even one minuscule drop of water falls onto the windshield, beware! Every car will, in unison, hit the wipers and the brakes, and many will swerve or skid. In San Diego, a drizzle is treated like a flash flood.

A SURVIVOR'S GUIDE TO SAN DIEGO

June Gloom, Crimson Tides and the Divine Wind

June brides may be "in" but the gloom may be out—that's the month when coastal regions are often caked under the marine layer. Nonetheless you can still count on inland areas to be bright and sunny. Even during the Big Gloom, however, the sun will often make a grandstand appearance by day's end.

Red tides can be a shocking sight. The ocean actually appears red but it's not caused by blood (usually) or some villainous underground testing (usually), but by the microscopic plant *pchytoplankton*. "The so-called "red tide" is something of a misnomer because the *phytoplankton* is not red and it has nothing to do with the tide. It's usually the combination of a lot of fresh water runoff (when there are sufficient nutrients in the water) and low turbulence—for example, a big rainstorm followed by sunny and calm days. February and March are the most common months for this phenomenon but it can also creep around during summer when hot weather and a warm, calm surface layer are sufficient. Even though the "tide" can look rather foreboding, it's almost never toxic and shouldn't scare off swimmers and surfers. **Raw sewage**, however, should scare off *everyone*.

Beaches near the Tijuana River estuary are often hard hit, but even the lagoons in the "good neighborhoods" of North County are occasional targets. Obey the posted warnings and keep out of the water (that includes dipping your tootsies)—a bad case of hepatitis can *really* turn your happy face yellow.

Author's Tip

The so-called Red Tide may look gruesome by day, but at night it turns the beach into a stunning light show. Our little phytoplankton are bioluminescent, creating neon blue lightening flashes across the crests of waves. It's no secret to surfers, who cherish the event. Beach walkers can create their own spectacle on the sand just by treading barefoot–footprints will appear to glow and sparkle. (Courtesy of Dr. Peter Franks, Scripps Institute of Oceanography).

Almost everyone dreads the **Santa Ana winds**—hot, dry gusts that blast 15-40 m.p.h. and occasionally reach hurricane strength. High air pressure buildup over the deserts causes the warmed air to head for the ocean, which is what the locals do as temperatures soar into the hundreds. San Diego ordinarily gets hit once each winter and in late summer. We hate the Santa Anas—they are practically soul mates with ravaging fires. They bestow L.A. smog upon us. They put us into bad moods, burn our eyes and lungs, and ruin our hair. What could be worse?

Drawing by Curtis; © Cartoonists & Writers Syndicate

The Big One Is Never Big Enough

Out-of-state visitors will come to realize that Californians don't lose much sleep over earthquakes—even after the all-too-recent Los Angeles and San Francisco shakers. San Diego, again, has been the lucky player in this regard—living vicariously. We awaken, bump and grind along with the earth-moves, then click on CNN for a fix on the epicenter. No big deal. We remain unscathed except for some broken glass and fallen debris. On the other hand, most of us can't imagine how our compatriots live even one minute in places that get hit by tornadoes and hurricanes. I suppose it's a matter of perspective. Would you rather be blown away or fall into a big crack?

Dateline San Diego

Pre-1000 BC—The La Jolla tribe gathered shells along the same shores as the Armani/Karan tribes of today.

Circa-1000 BC—The migratory Kumeyaay tribe ousted the La Jollans. Compared to their Sioux and Cheyenne brothers and sisters, they were fairly laid-back—the forerunners to today's seize-the-moment-mañana culture.

1542—Crackerjack explorer Juan Rodriguez Cabrillo, a former ragbaby from the nasty calles of Sevilla, landed near the tip of Point Loma—claiming another bauble for the bejeweled Spanish Crown. That harbor—originally named San Miguel—was the birthplace of California but, like an unwanted babe, it was left abandoned for about 60 more years. Nonetheless, a star had been born.

1596—Sebastian Vizcaino, yet another intrepid Spanish explorer, cruised in and rechristened the area San Diego—and this time the name stuck. It took yet another 150 years of comings and goings (and more than a few Spaniards in the works) before Spain charted plans for colonization.

1769—Padre Junipero Serra, the Franciscan missionary and reputed chocoholic—replete with bum leg and a borrowed mule—discovered San Diego for "real" in 1769, dedicating both the Presidio and California's first mission, San Diego de Alcala.

1821—Mexico's independence from Spain in 1821 also meant that San Diego was under Mexican rule, effecting many changes over the next couple of decades—ranchos, vaqueros, fiestas. Yippee—San Diego's fun-in-the-sun had begun!

1846—Oops, don't look now—enter the U.S. Army and the bloody Battle of San Pasqual. The result? The signing of the Treaty of Guadalupe Hildalgo made California a territory of the USA.

1867—Alonzo Horton, San Francisco merchant (and original Big Boy downtown developer) arrived in San Diego, bought a big chunk of prime real estate and relocated the city from Old Town to His Town (also known as New Town), where it remains today.

1868–1910—The San Diego Water Company was organized, acreage for Balboa Park was set aside, railroad service was initiated, fishermen flocked to the bountiful waters, agriculture seeded in Imperial Valley, a gold rush ensued in nearby Julian, the Edison electric-lighted Hotel del Coronado opened, a naval military base was established, and the Mexican revolution took place. Shops, banks and taco stands sprung up like geysers.

1910–1945—Balboa Park was developed for the 1915–16 Panama-California Exposition, with new structures added for the 1935–36 California Pacific International Exposition. World War II ruined a lot of the fun when many buildings were converted to military offices and a Navy hospital. Patients were wheeled from their sick beds for a dip in what-is-today's Lily Pond, though Sally Rand did a post-Depression fan dance on the site also—a more inspiring image. Numerous aviation "firsts" made the books, and the San Diego Zoo was created. Sailors and hookers covered the waterfront.

1948—Palomar Observatory opens.

1969—San Diego-Coronado Bay Bridge opens.

1970–1990—Arson strikes Balboa Park, destroying both Casa de Balboa and the Old Globe Theatre—both were painstakingly reconstructed. The Reuben H. Fleet Space Theater and Morley Field Sports Complex were established. Downtown, in disrepair, disuse and misuse, is saved from the wrecking ball via massive revitalization of the historic district (including construction of the Horton Grand Hotel) and the opening of Jon Jerde-designed Horton Plaza complex. A 760,000 square-foot convention center is built.

The 1990s—The first events are held at the new San Diego Convention Center and super-chic The Paladion opens across from Horton Plaza. The Gaslamp Quarter is booming with top-class hotels, indoor/outdoor cafes, retro shops, swanky restaurants, hot music clubs, theaters and galleries and a new contemporary art museum. The La Jolla Museum of Contemporary Art reopens after a two-year expansion and renovation project. The country's first year-round warm-weather Olympic training center opens in nearby Chula Vista. The America's Cup comes. And goes. The Republicans came and went. The Super Bowl is inked in for 1998.

YOU ARE HERE. NOW.

DOWNTOWN

Balboa Park offers many fascinating attractions.

Downtown is where many San Diegans flock rather than flee—much the opposite of L.A. or other big cities where you get in and out of what is usually the sleaziest, most downtrodden area as fast as possible. Okay, okay, our downtown used to be sleazy and downtrodden and, as a major metropolis, still has its moments. But all in all it's the most vibrant part of the city—drawing everyone from ravers to retirees into the action.

It wasn't always this way. Back in 1867, Alonzo Horton took one look at the landscape—water, canyons, hillsides, flatlands—and decided this was where the city center should be. No matter that another town had been settled over by the Presidio. No,

Alonzo decided that a really successful city needed to be closer to the water and proceeded to pull off a first-rate real estate coup—he bought up 960 acres along the bay (at 27-1/2 cents per) and gave them away to potential developers and homesteaders. The plan worked—and New Town was established. In came the transcontinental railroad and a depot was built practically at water's edge. Freighters began cruising in and out, the population increased sevenfold and soon the navy arrived. While San Diego thrived as a commercial and transportation mecca, businesses began to shift from the Fifth and Market pulse, toward Broadway and beyond. Residential communities moved up the coast and into the hidden recesses. World War I came and New Town went to the dogs—a new breed of brawling sailors,

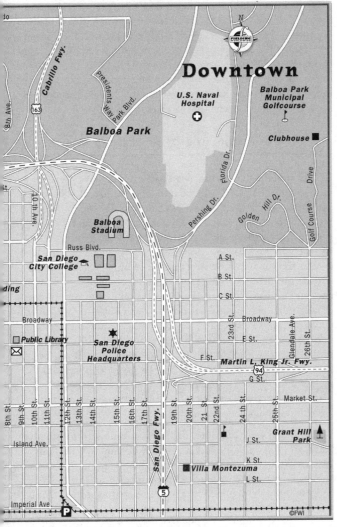

boozing gamblers and bawdy women. A rough waterfront and red-light district, known as The Stingaree. That's where you are now.

The '60s were good to San Diego. City planners had enough of the (yes, yes) sleazy and downtrodden Gaslamp Quarter—as the Stingaree came to be known—and were hot to demolish the area and start over with shiny, new buildings. Wrong. Along came a group of San Diegans who saw the Gaslamp through Alonzo Horton eyeballs and, determined to protect the city's heritage, they formed The Gaslamp Quarter Council. Today's restored Gaslamp Quarter is a 16-block National Historic District.

The '80s and '90s haven't been too bad either—the Embarcadero and Seaport Village were developed, Horton Plaza made a big splash, The Paladion bowed a refined entrance, the convention center brought big business, a new art museum made its debut—and the trolley connects them all. The Gaslamp is buzzing with the finest hotels, trendiest restaurants and gutsiest shops, as well as an onslaught of residential buildings and enterprising people—just what Alonzo had dreamed.

Downtown: Things to See and Do

Head straight for the **Gaslamp Quarter**. Take one of the tours given by the Gaslamp Quarter Foundation or just do the old up-and-down within the boundaries of Fourth Avenue to the west, Sixth Avenue to the east, Broadway to the north, and the waterfront and L Street to the south. You'll get a fairly authentic feel for the old days as you clop along the brick sidewalks, lean against the gaslamp-style street lights, or plunk your booty on a wrought iron bench. The hookers and street people you might encounter are not part of the isn't-this-cute-honeybun theme. It's the other way around—these streets are still part of their turf and you'll be able to scout out at the usual accouterments like X-rated shops and shows, tattoo parlors and sticky bars (give us a break—we're a Navy town). Concentrate if you will on the restored buildings—most constructed 1870–1930— in styles that include Frontier, Victorian, Italian and Spanish Renaissance, Romanesque, midwestern Commercial, Oriental, Modern and Contemporary.

Even if you were blind it would be impossible to miss **Horton Plaza**, the Jon Jerde-designed shopping complex. The Disneyland-on-drugs colors, shapes and shadows supersede and surpass any of the five ordinary senses. Encompassing six square blocks, and rising five stories, the plaza has become downtown's centerpiece and attraction par excellence—its cupolas, archways, gargoyles and fabulous views ranking light years ahead of absolutely zero competition. Not long ago Horton Plaza was a hangout for the seedier downtown element who bathed in the Irving Gill-built fountain out front on the Broadway side. Shopping mall developer Ernest Hahn was met with bemused derision when he went public with his nouvelle Alonzo Horton-vision of an inner-city fantasy complex. Two years later Horton Plaza opened, bringing throngs of locals and tourists to shop and dine within its fantasylike enclave; and the visitor rate shows no sign of slowing. A new crop of hotels, offices and residential buildings, built to blend with (or even shamelessly copy) the plaza, owe much of their successful draw to Jerde's go-for-broke stakes. And, yes, the fountain remains a local "gathering spot," though I haven't spotted anyone bathing in it other than a few lucky birds. Stop in

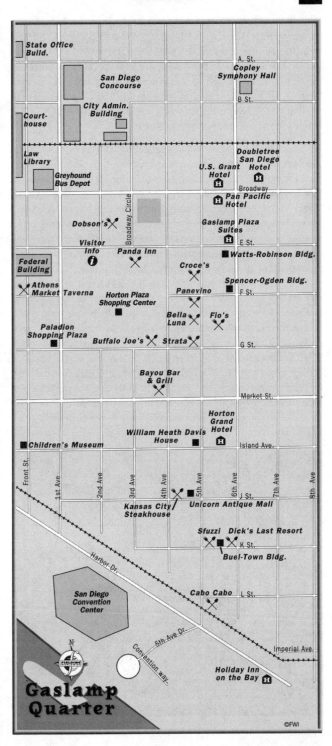

State Office Build.

San Diego Concourse

A. St.
Copley Symphony Hall

B St.

City Admin. Building

Court-house

Law Library

Doubletree San Diego Hotel

U.S. Grant Hotel 🏨

Greyhound Bus Depot

Broadway

Pan Pacific Hotel 🏨

Broadway Circle

Dobson's ✕

Gaslamp Plaza Suites 🏨

E St.

Visitor Info 🛈

Panda Inn ✕

Croce's ✕

Watts-Robinson Bldg. ■

Federal Building

Athens Market ✕

Taverna

Horton Plaza Shopping Center ■

Panevino ✕

Spencer-Ogden Bldg. ■

F St.

Bella Luna ✕

Fio's ✕

Paladion Shopping Plaza ■

Buffalo Joe's ✕

Strata ✕

G St.

Bayou Bar & Grill ✕

Market St.

Horton Grand Hotel 🏨

William Heath Davis House ■

Children's Museum ■

Island Ave.

Front St.

1st Ave

2nd Ave

3rd Ave

4th Ave

5th Ave

6th Ave

7th Ave

8th Ave

J St.

Kansas City Steakhouse ✕

Unicorn Antique Mall ■

Sfuzzi ✕

Dick's Last Resort ■

K St.

Buel-Town Bldg. ■

Harbor Dr.

Cabo Cabo ✕

L St.

San Diego Convention Center

5th Ave Dr.

Convention way

Imperial Ave.

N FIELDING WORLDWIDE

Holiday Inn on the Bay 🏨

Gaslamp Quarter

©FWI

DOWNTOWN

at the **International Visitor Information Center**, at street level on the corner of First Avenue and F Street, for walking maps, historic trails, transportation schedules and any other visitor-related requests. Glance over at **The Paladion**—New Yorkers will thrill to the site of Tiffany's and its signature statue of Atlas. As for that "perpetual clock" sold within—apparently Tiffany's doesn't realize that the Mayan calendar stops counting at 2012. (Or is Tiffany's more civilized than the Mayans?)

Wander west along Broadway, check what's on at the grandiose **Spreckels Theater**, peer into the lobby of the dazzling Wyndam Emerald Plaza), avoid who's out at the **YMCA and Greyhound Bus Terminal**, and continue to Kettner Boulevard. **One America Plaza**—a contemporary 34-story office building—is the final stop for trolleys, trains and buses which converge beneath its dramatic glass-and-steel crescent-shaped canopy. Don't flinch for a second until you've acrobated your way to safety around the cluster of tracks and flashing red warning lights. Adjacent is the two-story downtown branch of the **San Diego Museum of Contemporary Art** (opened in 1993), and the sort of hidden **Sculpture Plaza**. Both are definitely worth a browse, especially if you have a wait before the next bus or train. Even if you're not traveling by train, cross the street (careful of those tracks!) and have a look at the 1915 **Santa Fe Depot**, a Mission Revival-style terminal with dome ceiling, one of the city's more formidable landmarks until America Plaza came along and practically pillboxed its skullcap. Go west two more blocks, past the enclosed **golf course** and you'll be in the middle of *our* Broadway's longest-running play—San Diego Bay.

The Sante Fe Depot has a Mission Revival style terminal.

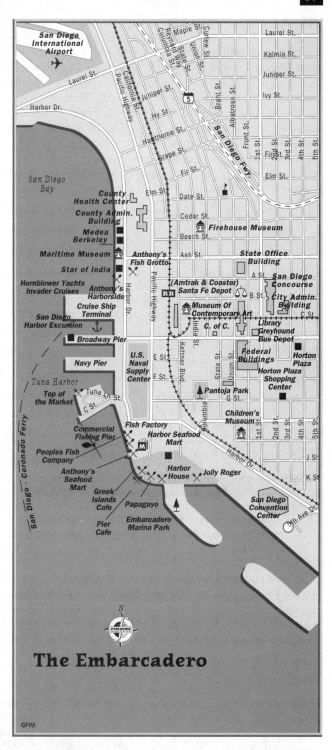

The Embarcadero

The waterfront, or **Embarcadero**, has come a way from the Alonzo-era canneries and shipyards, a strip frequented by bad boys and even badder girls. Today, walk the waterfront path along Harbor Drive and you'll see eyeball feasts of color and spectacle—houseboats cozied up to naval destroyers, tour boats shadowed by cruise ships. As in the Gaslamp Quarter, city saviors came to the rescue, turning the area into a waterfront promenade lined with restaurants, cafes, souvenir shops, a museum, new pier and convention center, and plenty of greenery. Naturally, mega-large hotel magnates jumped in at the first whiff of high room occupancy, as have coattail-riding housing and shopping-complex developers.

Still heading north, you'll come to the **B Street Pier**, San Diego's cruise ship port o' call for the big liners headed to and fro Mexico and the Panama Canal—an odd contrast to the naval carriers often sitting across the bay. The huge pastel terminal building houses an information center, gift shop and bar. Way before you get to the entrance of the **Maritime Museum**, you'll get a on-shore view of the 1863 windjammer *Star of India*, 1904 steam yacht *The Medea*, and 1898 ferry, *The Berkeley*. Enter the floating museum at the foot of Ash Street. The **County Administration Center**, on the opposite side of both Ash and Harbor, is an elegant Spanish Colonial WPA building dating from 1938—personally dedicated by Franklin D. Roosevelt. The 23-foot-high granite sculpture of a pioneer woman with a water jug over her shoulder is entitled *Guardian of Water*, completed by Donal Hord in 1939. Stroll around the back of the building to view some remarkably well-tended government gardens and inside to ogle the intricate tile work.

Author's Tip

Not even many San Diegans are aware that the County Administration Center's high-level cafeteria is open to the public. The food isn't bad, the prices are great and the view is incredible. Hours are Monday through Friday, 6:30 a.m.–3:45 p.m.

For a few blocks south of Broadway, the Embarcadero is dominated by the **Eleventh Naval District**. Look over at the **Navy Pier** and you might see a sub, destroyer or carrier looming before your eyes. Tours are usually offered on the weekends and are interesting even for dedicated landlubbers and conscientious objectors. Further along, at the **G Street Pier**, you'll run across the **U.S. Air Carrier Memorial**, a black granite obelisk, erected in 1993 to pay tribute to carriers and crews. **Tuna Harbor**, next up, is the center for San Diego's tuna-fishing fleet (one of the world's largest). From this point, keep your eyes and ears tuned for the onslaught of cyclists and joggers who favor this stretch.

Quaint Seaport Village features numerous waterfront restaurants.

Ah, **Seaport Village**! Fourteen-acres of prime waterfront estate with cobblestone paths, a wooden boardwalk and some "fake" dirt roads maneuver you into three interconnected shopping areas—done up in Spanish Mission and New England clapboard styles—filled with can't-go-home-without-it tourist shops, nosh-a-ramas and fine restaurants. Aside from Balboa Park, Seaport Village is downtown's favorite keep-the-kids-occupied attraction. Besides the mimes, clowns and performers that pop up throughout the "village," there's the exquisite **Broadway Flying Horses Carousel**—hand-carved and handpainted by I.D. Looff in 1890. So what, you say? Forget it—head to the nearby entertainment center and try your own hand at mass-produced video games.

Jutting out from Seaport Village, **Embarcadero Marine Park North** is a favorite place to fly your kite or have a picnic, while **Embarcadero Marina Park South** is the scene for the San Diego Symphony's Summer Pops concerts. Sheltered in between, at the north edge, are the Hyatt Regency and Marriott hotels where marinas berth guests' yachts as well as arrange boat rentals and fishing and diving excursions. Next door, to the south, is the architecturally correct, nautical-style **San Diego Convention Center**. Opened in 1989, the 760,000-square-foot cruise-ship-on-land with a roofless top deck has hosted a number of trade shows and is already planning future expansion. Hey, it was good enough for the Republicans. Adjacent to the Convention Center, is Fifth Street Landing where day-sailors pick up San Diego Bay Ferries and harbor excursion craft.

You'll probably want to spend forever exploring **Balboa Park's** 1400-acres of lush greenery, diverse gardens, Spanish-Moorish architecture, world-famous zoo, top-class museums and acclaimed theater spaces. There are various approaches to the park but the main gateway is at Cabrillo Bridge (also known as Laurel Street Bridge), off Sixth Avenue, north of downtown proper.

BALBOA PARK

Balboa Park covers 1200 acres just north of the central business district and contains museums, art galleries, the San Diego Zoo, theaters, an artists' colony and many

CALIFORNIA TOWER
The California Tower houses a working 100-bell carillon.

MUSEUM OF MAN

Cabrillo Bridge

El Prado

HOUSE OF PACIFIC RELATIONS

AUTOMOTIVE MUSEUM

AEROSPACE MUSEUM
Significant events in flight and space exploration are highlighted.

DOWNTOWN

sports facilities. The lush landscaping is the legacy of botanist Kate O. Sessions, who planted trees from all over the world in the park during most of her adult life.

OLD GLOBE THEATER

SAN DIEGO MUSEUM OF ART

SAN DIEGO ART INSTITUTE

ALCAZAR GARDEN

SPRECKELS ORGAN
Spreckles Organ Pavilion features concerts on Sunday afternoons and throughout the summer.

The **Museum of Man** presents exciting exhibits and events highlighting man's physical and cultural development with emphasis on the people of the Western Americas and ancient Egypt.

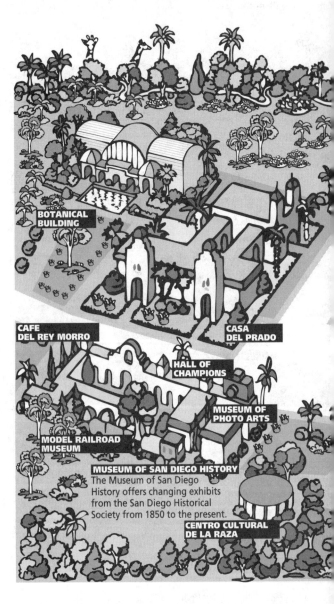

BOTANICAL BUILDING

CAFE DEL REY MORRO

CASA DEL PRADO

HALL OF CHAMPIONS

MUSEUM OF PHOTO ARTS

MODEL RAILROAD MUSEUM

MUSEUM OF SAN DIEGO HISTORY
The Museum of San Diego History offers changing exhibits from the San Diego Historical Society from 1850 to the present.

CENTRO CULTURAL DE LA RAZA

DOWNTOWN

The **Automotive Museum** features rare and exotic cars and motorcycles while the **Hall of Champions** celebrates great moments in sports history. The **Museum of Art** displays European, American and Asian collections.

SAN DIEGO ZOO

MINIATURE RAILROAD

NATURAL HISTORY MUSEUM

The Natural History Museum chronicles flora, fauna, minerology of the southwest and Baja.

SPACE THEATER AND SCIENCE CENTER

The Space Theater and Science Center present OMNIMAX® films and hands-on science exhibits.

Crossing over a canyon, the entrance leads to El Prado, the main pedestrian mall—flanked by theaters and museums—first constructed for the 1915–16 Panama-California Exposition, as were many of the buildings. Additional structures were developed, using the same Spanish theme, for the 1935-36 California Pacific International Exposition. If you're driving, be forewarned that parking in the El Prado is very limited. You'll probably end up in one of the lots closer to the zoo or Pan American Plaza. Your first stop should be the **Balboa Park Visitors Center**, in the House of Hospitality on El Prado, where you can pick up maps, brochures and discounted tickets to museums. Hang onto everything—you'll be back.

Historical Sites

San Diego

Gaslamp Quarter   ★★★★★
San Diego.
Once the center of New Town, then decayed into the notorious Stingaree, San Diego's 16-block National Historic District is currently the city's most happening place—a-bustle with chic shops, fab restaurants, rave clubs and architectural wonders. Allow plenty of time for browsing and carousing in this area bounded by Broadway to the north, L Street and the waterfront to the south, Fourth Avenue to the west, and Sixth Avenue to the east. For maps and info, stop in at the Gaslamp Quarter Association in the 1850 saltbox-come-round-the-cape William Heath Davis House *(410 Island Avenue).* Guided walking tours depart Saturdays at 11 a.m.

Villa Montezuma   ★★
1925 K Street, San Diego, East of downtown, 92102,
☎ *(619) 239-2211.*
Hours open: Noon–4:30 p.m.; Sat. and Sun.
Victoriana-lovers (and ghost hunters) should risk the not-so-great neighborhood to visit this treasure listed on the National Register of Historic Places. Built in 1887 for internationally known (back then) musician and author Jesse Shepard, the decor features sublime stained glass windows (depicting famous musicians and artists), pressed glass ceilings and superb furnishings. As for the rumored ghost—you tell me! Admission for ages 13 and under is free. General Admission: $3.

William Heath Davis House   ★★
410 Island Avenue, San Diego, at Fourth Avenue, 92101,
☎ *(619) 233-5227.*
Hours open: 1:30 p.m.–4:30 p.m.
A salt-box style New England home in the heart of San Diego? Built in 1850, this is the oldest downtown house. The Gaslamp Quarter Foundation lives on the top floor, but visitors are welcome to explore the ground level. General Admission: $1.

Museums and Exhibits

Balboa Park

Aerospace Historical Center   ★★★
2001 Pan American Plaza, Balboa Park, ☎ *(619) 234-8291.*
Hours open: 10 a.m.–4:30 p.m.

After their original home burned to the ground in 1978, both the San Diego Aerospace Museum and the International Aerospace Hall of Fame moved ship—and planes—to the 1935 Palace of Transportation. The huge curved building is crammed with flying machines that include everything from "human wings" to space capsules. Aviation buffs will want to spend all day in here. Admission for juniors 6-17, $2; children under six and military with I.D., free; seniors, $4.50. Admission is free to all on the fourth Tuesday of each month. General Admission: $6.

"Shall we join the ladies?"

Drawing by Handelsman; ©1995 The New Yorker Magazine, Inc.

Automotive Museum ★★★

2030 Pan American Plaza, Balboa Park, ☎ *(619) 231-2886.*
Hours open: 10 a.m.–4:30 p.m.

Wheels galore! Rare and wonderful cars and motorcycles. You'll thrill to the touch of a 1931 Dusenberg Model J; shake your head at a 1981 DeLorean; and nosedive to the ground when you see the very same limo Ronald Reagan was pointed toward when Hinckley's gun was pointing at him. A world-class collection! Get the facts on any vehicle in the automotive research library—and don't miss the gift shop. Admission for ages six-15, $2; seniors and military, $4; children under six, free. Admission is free to all on the fourth Tuesday of every month. General Admission: $5.

Centro Cultural de la Raza ★★

2004 Park Boulevard, Balboa Park, near the Reuben H. Fleet Space Theater, ☎ *(619) 235-6135.*
Hours open: Noon–5 p.m.
Closed: Mon., Tue.

The old water tower, appropriated by Hispanic artists in the 1970s, is really an inside-out museum. Brightly colored murals, depicting vivid—and sometimes controversial—statements, encircle the tower. Inside is a gallery with changing exhibits, a theater and cultural center—all focusing on Hispanic arts.

Hall of Champions ★★★

1649 El Prado, Balboa Park, ☎ *(619) 234-2544.*
Hours open: 10 a.m.–4:30 p.m.

Sports fans come here to relive golden moments with their favorite professional and amateur athletes through a number of heart-thumping exhibits. This is one of the few museums in the country where such a broad range of sports (more than 40) is represented. Local legends are highlighted (Florence Chadwick, Dennis Conner, Bill Walton, Archie Moore, etc.) and one exhibit spotlights disabled athletes. Admission for ages six-17, $1; seniors, military and students, $2. Admission is free to all on the second Tuesday of every month. General Admission: $3.

Marston House Museum ★★

3525 7th Avenue, Balboa Park, Northwest corner of Balboa Park, ☎ *(619) 298-3142.*
Hours open: Noon–4:30 p.m.
Closed: Mon., Tue., Wed., Thur.

The San Diego Historical Society took over management of this 1905 Irving Gill-designed home. Built for local philanthropist George Marston, the 8500-square-foot house is an outstanding example of Craftsman-style architecture. The public has only been given the chance to peek inside since 1991, oohing and aahing at the gorgeous architectural details as well as Roycroft and Stickley furniture. Authentic pieces from the Arts and Crafts movement are being added as the budget allows. A gift shop sells memorabilia. Admission for ages 13 and under is free. General Admission: $3.

The Museum of Man is one of the country's most respected anthropological museums.

Museum of Man ★★★★

1350 El Prado, Balboa Park, ☎ *(619) 239-2001.*
Hours open: 10 a.m.–4:30 p.m.

Bone up on old bones at one of the country's most notable anthropological museums. The kids will probably be most enthralled by the
party of lifesize replicas depicting homo sapiens. Cro-Magnon, Nean-
derthal and Peking Man are overshadowed by honored guest, Lucy—
a babe of 3-1/2 million-years-old (give or take a few years). Exhibitions include the original collection put together for the 1915 exposition, as well as those on the progression of North and South American
cultures. Learn more about the city's ethnic groups in the Lifestyles
and Ceremonies section, complete with high-tech gismos. You need
to make an appointment or be invited to a scheduled wedding for
entry to the pseudo Early California hacienda chapel. Admission for
ages 13–18, $2; ages six-12, $1; under six and military in uniform,
free. Free to all, third Tuesday of each month. General Admission: $4.

Museum of Photographic Arts   ★★★★★

1649 El Prado, Balboa Park, ☎ *(619) 239-5262.*
Hours open: 10 a.m.–5 p.m.
Thank God and director Arthur Ollman for bringing such a world-
class museum to a city where art (unless sports-oriented) has never
been taken very seriously. Devoted exclusively to the photographic
arts, MOPA features changing exhibitions of such artistic magnitude
that even New Yorkers fly out for the events. Both master photographers and up-and-coming will-be-knowns are on display in shows that
run from exquisite and breathtaking to controversial and disturbing.
All are memorable and thought-provoking. The gift shop stocks an
eclectic range of photography books, calendars and postcards. If
you're starving for brain food, MOPA will serve you a feast. Admission is free for children under 12, accompanied by an adult. Admission is free to all on the second Tuesday of each month. General
Admission: $3.50.

Museum of San Diego History

1649 El Prado, Balboa Park, ☎ *(619) 232-6203.*
Hours open: 10 a.m.–4:30 p.m.
Closed: Mon., Tue.
Trace the city's history from the mid-1800s to the present via the San
Diego Historical Society's archives and through a variety of national
traveling shows. The photos of the park's early days are a kick. Admis-
sion is $5 for seniors, students, and military; free for children under
five, and free for all on the second Tuesday of each month. General
Admission: $6.

Natural History Museum   ★★★★

1788 El Prado, Balboa Park, ☎ *(619) 232-3821.*
Hours open: 9:30 a.m.–4:30 p.m.
Special Hours: Open until 5 p.m. in summer,
open until 6:30 on Thursdays.

Catch up on all the flora and fauna of southern California and Baja,
check out the gems in the Hall of Mineralogy, see the ecological and
traveling exhibitions, and then head for the good stuff—dinosaur
bones and the Desert Lab (with live tarantulas and snakes). For once,
you'll get bored before the kids do. After you drag them out of the
museum, you'll have to contend with the invitation-to-climb whale
out front and the gnarly Moreton Bay fig tree out back. Never

mind—you can contemplate the earth's rotation on the 185-pound brass Foucault Pendulum, near the museum entrance. Stop at the desk to find out if nature walks or special films are scheduled. Admission for ages six–17, $3; seniors, $5. Admission is free to all the first Tuesday of each month. General Admission: $6.

San Diego Museum of Art   ★ ★ ★ ★ ★

1450 El Prado, Balboa Park, ☎ *(619) 232-7931.*
Hours open: 10 a.m.–4:30 p.m.
Closed: Mon.

The entryway alone is a work of art—coats of arms flapping above a replica 16th-century Spanish Renaissance facade, guarded by life-sized statues of long-gone painters. The museum's vast collection includes outstanding Italian Renaissance, Spanish baroque and Dutch works, as well as Southeast Asian pieces, Indian miniatures and noteworthy American, European and 20th-century paintings. Six major exhibitions are hosted annually, and lectures and other events are also on the roster. You can spend hours lingering in the gift shop or staring at the sculpture garden from the adjacent cafe. Admission for ages six-17 and students with I.D., $2; military with I.D., $4; seniors, $5. Admission is free for all on the third Tuesday of each month. General Admission: $7.

Spanish Village   ★

Village Place, west of Park Boulevard, Balboa Park, ☎ *(619) 233-9050.*
Hours open: 11 a.m.–4 p.m.

It's worth taking a stroll through this replica Spanish Renaissance village if you're already at the park or the nearby zoo. Originally built for the 1935-36 expo, and somehow appropriated by the army during WWII, the 39 cottages were eventually handed over to artisans. Watch painters, ceramists and jewelers at work, browse their galleries and scour the gift shops for more trinkets.

Timken Musseum of Art   ★ ★ ★ ★

1500 El Prado, Balboa Park, ☎ *(619) 239-5548.*
Hours open: 10 a.m.–4:30 p.m.
Special Hours: Sundays, 1:30-4:30 p.m. Closed: Mon.

The Timken is one of the best freebies in town for art lovers. The Putnam Foundation collection includes paintings by European Old Masters and 18th- and 19th-century American artists. The Russian icons are superb.

San Diego

Firehouse Museum   ★ ★

1572 Columbia Street, San Diego, at Cedar Street, 92101,
☎ *(619) 232-3473.*
Hours open: 10 a.m.–4 p.m.
Special Hours: Thurs.-Fri. 10 a.m.–2 p.m. Sat.-Sun. 10 a.m.–4 p.m.
Closed: Mon., Tue., Wed.

Who isn't awed by the romance and redness of a fire engine? Come and play "I want to be a fireman when I grow up" in San Diego's oldest firehouse. Exhibits include all your shiny fantasy trucks plus horse-and hand-drawn models, and a variety of antique memorabilia such as alarms and helmets. Firey items are on sale in the small gift shop. I know you can't resist. Admission for adults $2; ages 13–17, $1; under 12, free.

DOWNTOWN

Maritime Museum ★★★

1306 North Harbor Drive, San Diego, On the waterfront, 92101,
☎ *(619) 232-9153.*
Hours open: 9 a.m.–8 p.m.

Sharing space with historic navigational instruments and scale models
is a trio of unique vessels. Not the *Nina*, *Pinta* and *Santa Maria*, but
Star of India (1863), *Berkeley* and *Medea*. The *Star of India* (and the
star of the show) is the world's oldest iron merchant ship afloat. The
Berkeley (1898), an ornate propeller-driven ferry, was used to rescue
survivors of San Francisco's 1906 quake, while *Medea* (1904), a large
steam yacht, was used to transport British gentry. Admission for ages
13–17 and seniors, $4; ages six–12, $2; under six, free. General
Admission: $5.

The **Star of India** *at the Maritime Museum is the world's oldest
iron merchant ship.*

Museum of Contemporary Art ★★★

*1001 Kettner Boulevard, San Diego, in the America Plaza, across from the
Santa Fe Depot, 92101,* ☎ *(619) 234-1001.*
Hours open: 10 a.m.–5 p.m.
Special Hours: Open until 8 p.m. on Fri., Sun. noon-5 p.m. Closed: Mon.

Opened in 1993, this downtown branch of the La Jolla-based museum (reopened in 1996) brought a positive element to the city's gone-bust art gallery scene. The two-story museum features exhibitions from the permanent collection as well as changing shows with a decidedly contemporary bent. Visitors either walk away shaking their heads in confusion, or else stand for hours gazing at each piece (and hoping they look hip). In any case, the trolley whizzes past the front door, the train station is across the street and people who might never look at contemporary art (or any art) otherwise, will venture in while awaiting their rides. Word of warning: the one-person restroom has a disconcerting red light aimed at the toilet. Is it a smoke detector? Or, have YOU just become a piece of new art? Admission for students and seniors, $2; under 13, free. Free for all on first Tuesday of each month. General Admission: $4.

Parks and Gardens

Balboa Park

Balboa Park   ★★★★★

Sixth Avenue and Laurel Street, and Park Boulevard and Presidents Way, Balboa Park, ☎ *(619) 239-0512.*
Hours open: all day
Parks and gardens within parks and gardens within historical sites within museums within parks within gardens. San Diego's show-off 1200-acre park was developed in the early 20th century, though the land had been set aside back in 1868. You could spend many days and nights roaming the Spanish-Moorish buildings, the museums and theaters, the world famous zoo, the world's first Omnimax theatre and the world's largest outdoor organ. Unless you're attending the theater or other special event, it's best to stay out of the park after dark.

Botanical Building   ★★

El Prado, Balboa Park, ☎ *(619) 235-1100.*
Hours open: 10 a.m.–4:30 p.m.
Closed: Mon.
Part historical site, part garden, the Botanical Building shelters some 1200 tropical and flowering plants within one of the world's largest lath structures. Begonias, orchids, ferns and ivy are some of the varieties thriving beneath the iron frame of an old Santa Fe railway depot. The Lily Pond out front is a favorite hangout for lovers, lingerers and street performers.

San Diego Zoo   ★★★★★

2920 Zoo Drive, at Park Boulevard, Balboa Park, ☎ *(619) 234-3153.*
Hours open: 9 a.m.–5 p.m.

San Diego's world-famous zoo attracts hordes of visitors who come to gawk and marvel at the thousands of beasts, birds and exotic plants contained within its 100 acres. A welcome wagon of bright blue peacocks and Pepto-Bismol-pink flamingos, posted near the entrance, are just the warm-up for some really classy acts. Don't miss the walk-through aviary, koalas, new polar bear exhibit, Tiger River, Gorilla Tropics and the reptile house (with a two-headed snake named Thelma and Louise). The Children's Zoo, with baby animal nursery, is a big draw for all ages. Get a view from the top on the aerial tram, or take a guided double-decker bus tour to the major exhibits. Animal acts are staged throughout the day in the large amphitheater. Admission for ages three-11, $6, under two, free. Deluxe packages ($3 more) include the 40-minute bus tour. General Admission: $15.

The world famous San Diego Zoo spans 100 acres and thrills all ages with its thousands of beasts, birds and exotic plants.

San Diego

Japanese Friendship Garden ★★

Balboa Park, San Diego, East of the Organ Pavilion, ☎ *(619) 232-2780.*
Hours open: 10 a.m.–4 p.m.
Closed: Mon., Wed., Thur.

Do Japan in an acre. San-Kei-En (Three-Scenery Garden) is still in the development stages (you can view a model of the eventual garden) but nonetheless offers plenty of contemplative spaces. When finished, the garden will feature all sorts of Japanese eye-feast delights. Take the crooked path (designed to ward off evil spirits) straight to the Zen-like information center. Don't miss the ancient sekitei—a garden made only of sand and stone. Admission for seniors, $1; under 7, free. General Admission: $2.

Sports/Recreation

Balboa Park

Morely Field Sports Complex ★★★★★

Texas Street at Upas Street, Balboa Park, ☎ *(619) 692-4919.*

Morley Field's 300-acre canyonland complex is to sports-lovers what Sea World is to kids—the ultimate one-stop athletic center that includes swimming, tennis, archery, playgrounds galore, bocce ball, shuffleboard, a casting pool, cyclist's velodrome and—that all-time favorite, Frisbee Golf. (Yes, you heard right. It's golf played with Fris-

Fielding WORLDWIDE

SAN DIEGO

POLAR BEAR PLUNGE

SKYFARI

HORN AND HOOF MESA

EAGLES

BIRDS

BONGO CANYON

GIANT PANDAS

TREEHOUSE ALBERT'S

HIPPO BEACH

PYGMY CHIMPS

MOVING SIDEWALK

CANYON CAFE

SUN BEAR FOREST

WINGS OF AUSTRALASIA

GORILLA TROPICS

RAIN FOREST AVIARY

SCRIPPS AVIARY

BIRD AND PRIMATE MESA

ORANGUTANS

REPTILE MESA

TIGER RIVER

BUS BOARDING

WEGEFORTH BOWL

SAFARI KITCHEN

HUMMINGBIRD AVIARY

REPTILE HOUSE

FLAMINGOS

PEACOCK & RAVEN DELI

SKYFARI

SPECIAL EVENT ZONE

EXIT

ENTRANCE

CHILDREN'S ZOO

DOWNTOWN

SAN DIEGO ZOO

The world famous San Diego Zoo spans 100 acres and is home to 4000 animals representing 800 species and subspecies. For information (619) 234-3153.

HUNTE AMPHITHEATER

MOVING SIDEWALK

HORN AND HOOF MESA

LEOPARDS

CAT CANYON

KIWI TRAIL

ELEPHANT MESA

HYENAS

MEERKATS

AFRICAN KOPJE

BEAR CANYON

BATS

KANGAROOS

CAMELS

SYDNEY'S GRILL

KRAFT KOALA EXHIBIT

SYDNEY'S SHOPPE

BUS UNLOADING

PARKING

CANYON AREAS (DOWN)

MESA AREAS (UP)

bees. The rules are posted and you can play for free. There's even a pro shop.) Hours and prices vary according to sport.

San Diego

San Diego Gulls

Sports Arena, San Diego, ☎ *(619) 225-7825.*

The exhilarating Gulls, members of the International Hockey League, skate October through April in the Sports Arena. General Admission: $7–18.

San Diego Sockers

Sports Arena, San Diego, ☎ *(619) 224-4625.*

Root along with the rowdy locals over our ten-times-champs indoor soccer team, now members of the new Continental Indoor Soccer League. The season runs October through May. General Admission: $7–15.

Ticket Agencies

San Diego

Ticketmaster

San Diego, ☎ *(619) 220-8497.*

Call for outlet locations, or with credit card in hand to charge tickets for most major events.

Times Arts Tix

Broadway Circle, at Horton Plaza, San Diego, 92101,
☎ *(619) 497-5000.*
Hours open: 10 a.m.–7 p.m.

Bring cash only to purchase half-price, day-of performance and full-price advance-sale tickets for theater, music and dance performances. Half-price tickets for Sunday events can be purchased on Saturday. Discounted admissions are also available for local attractions and city tours. Call for recorded announcements.

FIELDING'S FAVORITE THINGS TO DO IN BALBOA PARK

Ride the 1910 carousel (near the zoo entrance) with its magnificently hand-carved horses, pigs, cats and frogs. Grab for the brass ring.

Have a picnic by the Lily Pond while listening to impromptu concerts by street buskers–everything from "If I had a hammer" to "Pachelbel's Canon."

Slurp a half-chocolate, half-vanilla swirled frostie cone and let it drip all the way through Spanish Village.

Raise a toast to Henry Moore at the Sculpture Garden Cafe.

Attend any performance at the Old Globe Theatre.

Play with all the gadgets and gizmos in the Science Center, then view an IMAX/Omnimax film in the Reuben H. Fleet Space Theatre, where seats are arranged so that strangers virtually lay their heads in each other's laps.

FIELDING'S FAVORITE THINGS TO DO IN BALBOA PARK

Witness a slice of oh-so-civilized Americana as players garbed in Clorox-white whites compete in lawn bowling tournaments on the Sixth Avenue edge of the park.

Sip margaritas on the patio of Cafe del Rey Moro, watch weddings in progress and lay odds on when those with eyes-only-for-each-other will be proofreading the divorce papers.

Drawing by W. Miller; ©1995 The New Yorker Magazine, Inc.

FIELDING'S FAVORITE HISTORIC DOWNTOWN BUILDINGS

San Diego County Administration Building *(1938)–An elegant 10-story Spanish Colonial edifice and WPA project–personally dedicated by FDR–with intricate tile work, handpainted murals, tranquil gardens and a piece of public art that is not entirely hated by locals.* 1600 Pacific Highway.

Villa Montezuma *(1887)–The wondrously restored Victorian home of musician-spiritualist-poet Jesse Shepard. Details are extravagant–particularly the stained-glass windows. Haunting and probably haunted.* 1925 K Street.

Nanking Cafe *(1874)–San Diego's oldest Chinese restaurant has been in operation at this site since World War II when sailors and their girls swooned at each other over chopsticks. The three-story brick building is supported by iron columns–but you might need an iron stomach to hold down the chow mein.* 467 Fifth Avenue.

Pannikin *(1909)–San Diego's (very quiet) answer to Starbucks. This former decrepit brick-and-wood furniture warehouse was, in the mid-1970s, recrafted into the main outlet for our local (and then, exclusive) coffee importer.* 675 G Street.

San Diego Post Office *(1936)–Once the main post office, now just a branch, the large, pale blue Art Moderne building provides services by day and a homeless hangout at night. Interesting alternative shops nearby.* 815 E Street.

San Diego Trust and Savings Bank *(1927)–The city's most fascinating bank building with a revolving door, marble lobby and bronze wickets at the teller cages. San Diego's first aviation beacon blinked from atop.* 530 Broadway.

Marston Building *(1881)–Current site of the oh-so-chic Fio's Cucina Italiana, this Italianate Victorian beauty once housed Marston's Department Store–one of George Marston's chain. The Prohibition Temperance Union held meetings on the site in the late 1880s–a sharp contrast to today's imbibers at Fio's bar.* 801 Fifth Avenue.

Keating Building *(1890)–A red-brick Romanesque Revival-style corner building with distinctive rounded windows–once the office setting for TV detective's "Simon and Simon," now best known as the home of the "Croce Complex."*

FIELDING'S FAVORITE HISTORIC DOWNTOWN BUILDINGS

San Diego Hardware *(1910)–50,000-plus pieces in an always-been-in-the-family business. Original elements include the tin ceiling, storefront windows and wooden floors. The upstairs has been the scene of some of downtown's most memorable "art" parties. 840 Fifth Avenue.*

Balboa Theatre *(1924)–Still sitting practically dormant at one side of Horton Plaza, the Spanish Renaissance-style theater featured vaudeville acts in the good old days. Its most striking features are the tile dome (similar to that at the Santa Fe Depot) and entryway with a mosaic scene of Balboa's discovery of the blue Pacific–and also the fact that I met Muhammed Ali there (The Champ, you know). Fourth Avenue, between Broadway and E Street.*

Downtown: For Kids

For once, a big city practically *made* for the kiddies!

They'll love the carousel, video center, toy shops and strolling performers at **Seaport Village**—but you probably won't get out of there without spending a fortune (and loading your arms) with fun food and souvenirs. They probably won't be thrilled with a historic tour of the Gaslamp Quarter—that's when you dump them at the **Children's Museum of San Diego**. They'll be entertained for hours with the exceptional variety of planned and independent activities in this huge, expansive space.

Horton Plaza might even keep small ones happy. The colors and atmosphere are so fantastic, they'll probably be slightly schizo over whether it's an amusement park or a shopping mall. Parents will even be able to sneak in some shopping—though set some bucks aside for future therapy sessions ("At first I thought it was Disneyland, then I realized mommy was trying on shoes—she tricked me, that's why I'm a serial killer").

Once those little feet hit **Balboa Park**, your only worries will be how to ever get them out of there. The zoo, alone, will occupy them all day. Then there are the hands-on exhibits and dinosaur bones at museums, the can't-take-their-hands-off displays at the Science Center, theater and puppet performances, a miniature train and another carousel.

Balboa Park

Marie Hitchcock Puppet Theatre ★★★

Palisades Building, Pan American Plaza, Balboa Park, San Diego,
☎ *(619) 685-5045.*
Closed: Mon., Tue.

Marie Hitchcock works her wizardry with imaginative hand-and-rod puppet shows. Two performances on weekdays, three on weekends. Reservations not necessary for small groups. Admission for ages two-14, $1.50; under two, free. General Admission: $2.

Model Railroad Museum   ★★★

1649 El Prado, Balboa Park, San Diego, 92101, ☎ (619) 696-0199.
Hours open: 11 a.m.–4 p.m.
Special Hours: Sat. and Sun. 11 a.m.–5 p.m. Closed: Mon.

The four large permanent model railroads are exciting to watch as they make their runs through sample California terrain. The real fun, however, is being able to play with the collection of Lionel trains and the new interactive exhibits. The kids will never let you out of the gift shop empty-handed. Admission for students, military and seniors, $2.50; under 15, free. Admission is free for all on the first Tuesday of each month. General Admission: $3.

Reuben H. Fleet Space Theater and Science Center   ★★★★★

1875 El Prado, Balboa Park, ☎ (619) 238-1233.
Hours open: 9:30 a.m.–6 p.m.
Special Hours: Wed.-Sun. 9:30 a.m.–9 p.m.

The Science Center fascinates kids of all ages with its plethora of hands-on experiments and gadetry, while the Omnimax Theater (the world's first) with 75-foot dome screen sends audiences hurling through space or on other IMAX/Omnimax chill-and-thrill adventures. The got-to-touch-everything gift shop is almost a mini-Science Center—entry is free but you're sure to walk away with arms full of space-tech items. Admission for seniors, $5; ages five-15, $3.50. Admission to the Science Center only is $2.50, adults; ages five-15, $1.25. Admission to the Science Center is free to all the first Tuesday of each month. General Admission: $6.50.

San Diego Junior Theatre   ★★

Casa del Prado, Balboa Park, San Diego, ☎ (619) 239-1311.

Founded in 1948, America's oldest children's theatre puts on live theater productions for all ages. The actors and technical crew are ages six to 18.

San Diego

Children's Museum of San Diego   ★★★★

200 West Island Avenue, San Diego, Near the Convention Center, 92101, ☎ (619) 233-8792.
Hours open: 10 a.m.–4:30 p.m.
Special Hours: Sundays noon-4:30 p.m. Closed: Mon.

This interactive museum is heaven on earth for bored children (and their exhausted parents). Throw the Nintendo out the window and toss the kids into a full spectrum of supervised activities. They'll adore the indoor/outdoor art studio, the theatre with dress-up costumes and the observation plank with spiral-slide exit. Exhibitions and celebrations are staged regularly. Parents and significant mothers should bring plenty of cash—the shop with games, crafts and toys will chew through the toughest wallet. Admission for seniors, $2; children under two is free. General Admission: $4.

FIELDING'S FAVORITE
FREE THINGS FOR KIDS

*The **beach**, of course, will keep them occupied for days– bring the pail and shovel, the flippers and inflatables.*

Flying kites at Mission Bay.

A stroll (or piggyback ride) along the Embarcadero. Small ones love watching the playful bobbing boats–just like the ones in their bathtubs.

Either inspire or scare them on a tour of one of the very serious-looking, much-too-big-for-any-bathtub, Navy ships in port.

Pack a picnic and head for Balboa Park. The kids will have a great time watching the street entertainers, climbing the huge Moreton Bay fig tree behind the Natural History Museum and just interacting with other children.

Pay a visit to the Firehouse Museum.

Tours

The Gaslamp Quarter dominates the tour action but guided jaunts also scurry visitors around the zoo, Balboa Park, Naval ships and other sites.

The Gaslamp Quarter combines historic buildings with trendy restaurants.

San Diego

59-mile Scenic Drive
San Diego.
The 59-mile scenic drive starts off from the Broadway Pier and loops around the Embarcadero, Shelter and Harbor islands, Point Loma, Mission Bay, La Jolla, Old Town and Balboa Park. If you don't make

DOWNTOWN

photo or other sightseeing stops (and if you don't get caught in rush hour traffic) the drive takes approximately three hours. Watch for the signs—blue and yellow emblazoned with a white sea gull—posted at frequent intervals.

Downtown Development

255 G Street, San Diego, Between Second and Third Avenues,
☎ *(619) 235-2222.*

Get the lowdown on downtown development by joining one of the free tours sponsored by Centre City Development Corporation (CCDC). Two-hour bus tours depart on the first and third Saturday of each month, 10 a.m.–noon; walking tours are scheduled each Saturday, 1-3 p.m.

Gaslamp Quarter

410 Island Avenue, San Diego, At William Heath Davis House,
☎ *(619) 233-4692.*

The Gaslamp Quarter Foundation sponsors this very good one and one-half hour walking tour of the historic downtown district, focusing on its architectural aspects. Self-guided tour brochures can be picked up Monday–Friday 10 a.m.–4:30 p.m. Guided tour (Sat. 11 a.m., rain or shine) cost for seniors and students, $3. General Admission: $5.

Hornblower/Invader Cruises

1066 North Harbor Drive, San Diego, Next to the cruise ship terminal,
☎ *(619) 234-8687.*

Choose from a family-oriented, narrated tour of the bay on the *Invader*, a 1905 schooner, or a more romantic dinner-and-dancing or Sunday brunch cruise aboard the *Entertainer*, a 145-foot yacht. Whale-watching jaunts are scheduled during winter months. Call ahead for reservations. Cost of harbor tours for adults, $12-17; seniors and military with I.D., $10-15; ages 3-12, $6-8.50.

Horsedrawn Carriage Tours

San Diego, ☎ *(619) 239-8080.*

Need a shot of romance? Get off the bus, jump out of the taxi and get on the phone to Cinderella Carriage Company. Horse-drawn carriages will clop one or two couples through the Gaslamp Quarter, downtown and along the waterfront. Cost for one hour is $80; 45 minutes, $60; one-half hour, $45.

Naval Ships

Broadway Pier, San Diego, Intersection of Broadway and Harbor Drive,
☎ *(619) 532-1431.*
Hours open: 1–4 p.m. Sat. and Sun.

Take a free tour on board one of the Naval ships in port. Sailor-guides are friendly and helpful.

San Diego Harbor Excursions ★★

1050 North Harbor Drive, San Diego, Near the foot of Broadway,
☎ *(619) 234-4111.*

Excursions include narrated one-and two-hour bay tours, dinner cruises and winter whalewatching. Good quality tours from an established company. Tickets are $17 and up, with discounts for seniors and children.

Walkabout International ★★★
San Diego, ☎ *(619) 231-7463.*
Especially popular with local seniors, "Downtown Sam" and other volunteers head off on Saturdays and some weekdays for a variety of downtown walking tours. Saturday excursions concentrate on historic and scenic areas while weekday treks focus on quirkier sights like pubs, thrift stores and book shops. Walkabout has been around since 1977.

Events

Events of some kind are almost always on the calendar, though Christmas and Halloween seem to grab much of the action. Concerts, parades, rodeos, ethnic events and art and music festivals keep up a steady—albeit seasonal—pace.

Balboa Park

American Indian Cultural Days ★★★
Park Boulevard and Presidents Way, Balboa Park, ☎ *(619) 281-5964.*
Native Americans from around the southwest celebrate during a May weekend filled with music and dance performances, original arts and crafts and a cornucopia of traditional foods.

Art Alive ★★
San Diego Museum of Art, Balboa Park, ☎ *(619) 232-7931.*
This four-day April event is both beautiful and kitschy—selections of art works from the museum's permanent collection are given floral interpretations. Admission for seniors, $6; under 17, $4. General Admission: $7.

Christmas on El Prado ★★★
El Prado, Balboa Park, ☎ *(619) 239-0512.*
Hours open: 5–9 p.m.
Sponsored by the park's museums, this early-December two-day event is a delightful welcome to Christmas. Activities include a Swedish Santa Lucia candlelight procession, outdoor Swedish Christmas fair, carolers, entertainment, lots of food and crafts for sale and free admission to all museums after 5 p.m.

Ethnic Food Fair ★★★
House of Pacific Relations International Cottages, Balboa Park,
☎ *(619) 239-0512.*
Each of the international cottages joins in a sort of ethnic free-for-all, featuring food, dancing and music from their respective countries.

Haunted Museum of Man ★★★★
Museum of Man, Balboa Park, ☎ *(619) 239-2001.*
Around Halloween Museum of Man is transformed ingeniously—and somewhat sadistically—into a gloriously terrifying House of Horrors. Bring someone you love or someone you hate. The kids will be talking about it for years.

DOWNTOWN

Summer Organ Festival   ★★★★
Organ Pavilion, Balboa Park, ☎ *(619) 226-0819.*
Free concerts are held Mondays at 8 p.m., late June through late August. Good place for a picnic and escape from the Monday blues.

Twilight in the Park   ★★★
Organ Pavilion, Balboa Park, ☎ *(619) 239-0512.*
Summer concerts take place Tuesdays, Wednesdays and Thursdays, 6:15-7:15 p.m, June through August. A fabulous place to unwind after a long day in the city.

El Cajon

HGH Pro-Am Golf Classic   ★★★
Singing Hills Golf and Country Club, El Cajon, ☎ *(619) 442-3445.*
This two-day September golf event features Southern California golf professionals and amateurs in a scramble format with a shotgun start.

Mother Goose Parade   ★★★★
West Main and Chambers to 2nd and Madison, El Cajon,
☎ *(619) 444-8712.*
Hey, if you love a parade with all the festive trappings, San Diego's East County can hold its own. The Mother Goose is about a half-century old, and features two hours worth of 200 floats, clowns, bands and equestrians. Held each year on the Sunday before Thanksgiving.

Imperial Beach

U.S. Open Sandcastle Competition   ★★★
Imperial Beach Pier, Imperial Beach, ☎ *(619) 424-6663.*
One of the country's largest sandcastle extravaganzas features competitions for all ages and levels of expertise. The July event features a parade and children's contest on Saturday, the main competition on Sunday. If you can't make the weekend, at least come watch the creations wash away.

Lakeside

Lakeside Western Days and Annual Rodeo   ★★★
Lakeside Rodeo Grounds, Hwy 67 and Mapleview Drive, Lakeside,
☎ *(619) 561-4331.*
Ride 'em cowboy—at least for four days each April . It's a ways out of downtown San Diego but worth the drive if you're a western enthusiast. Seven major rodeo events, lots of rib-sticking grub, entertainment and a big community celebration complete with carnival and parade should keep the chaps happy.

San Diego

America's Finest City Week   ★★★
City-wide, San Diego, ☎ *(619) 437-0369.*
This week-long celebration each August gives San Diegans the chance to preen over their city. Events include parades, a half-marathon, concerts, lots of food and drink and the heart-pounding crowning of Miss Teen USA.

Art Walk   ★★★

Downtown San Diego, ☎ *(619) 232-3101.*
This self-guided weekend festival held each April is a big, long open house for downtown galleries and local artists (many open their stu-

dios for the event). As with most festivals, food and entertainment have been kicked into the doings. Free shuttles are provided.

Lego Construction Zone ★★★

Horton Plaza, San Diego, On the Sports Deck, *(619) 232-3101.*
Compete with or marvel at other participants as they contemplate and create original LEGO constructions in the design competition.

Mainly Mozart Festival ★★★

San Diego, *(619) 558-1000.*
The works of Wolfgang Amadeus Mozart and other classical masters are featured in a 10-day festival each June. Locations of performances vary. General Admission: $15-35.

San Diego Earth Fair ★★

Balboa Park, San Diego, *(619) 496-6666.*
Hours open: 10 a.m.–5 p.m.
A one-day April festival and celebration for the Earth, such as it is. Booths, exhibits, dance and music festivals, plus related children's activities. A good place to meet green-minded friends.

San Diego Boat and Sportfishing Show ★★★

San Diego Convention Center and Marriott Hotel, San Diego,
 (619) 232-3101.
Boat and sportfishing fans come from all over the world each January for this four-day in-water extravaganza.

San Diego Comic Convention ★★★★

Convention Center, San Diego, *(619) 491-2475.*
An animated event for more than 25 years, the four-day comic convention, held in July, is well-worth a special trip. On display are all the standard oldies plus specialty, kinky and Gothic works. Slide shows, autograph signings and special guest appearances are all on the schedule.

San Diego County Sheriff's Association Rodeo ★★

Lakeside Rodeo Grounds, Hwy. 67 and Mapleview Avenue, San Diego,
 (619) 561-4331.
September's full-scale seven-event rodeo draws bucks and broncos from all over the country.

San Diego International Auto Show ★★★★

San Diego Convention Center, San Diego, ☎ *(619) 525-5000.*
Nine days in March when car lovers gather to swoon over foreign and domestic makes, futuristic concept vehicles and never-before-seen models plus all the related paraphernalia.

Street Scene ★★★★

Gaslamp Quarter, San Diego, ☎ *(619) 557-8487.*
For two unforgettable September days, the Gaslamp Quarter is transformed into a memorable music festival drawing more than 60 bands (many of them world-renowned) to perform on 10 stages. B.B. King almost always makes an appearance. Dance, eat and drink to the rhythms.

Underwater Film Festival ★★★

Civic Theatre, San Diego, San Diego Concourse, *(619) 685-3319.*
The Underwater Film Festival has been held for more than 30 years—a testimony to the popularity of its entrancing underwater marine life

films and slide shows. The September event usually lasts several days and series tickets are available.

West Coast Stickball Tournament and Car Show ★★

B Street, between Third and Eighth Avenues, San Diego,
☎ *(619) 234-0040.*

This annual July happening pits stickball teams (using broomsticks and rubber balls) against each other in the downtown city streets. The beer garden helps soften the blows.

Seaport Village

U.S. Armed Forces-Grand Military Encampment ★★

Embaracero Marina Park North, Seaport Village, Seaport Village,
☎ *(619) 271-8629.*

View 200 years of living military history, spanning the Revolutionary War to the Persian Gulf. Some of the October weekend events include costume displays, band concerts, war re-enactments and show battles.

Downtown: Music, Dance and Theater

It's not New York, San Francisco or L.A., but San Diego has an above-average performing arts scene. The landmark **Spreckels Theatre** hosts ballets, theatrical productions and many musical events, from classical to rock. The **Sports Arena**, on the way toward Point Loma, is the venue for major rock concerts, ice skating shows, the circus and such.

Alas, the San Diego Symphony is now defunct and off the scene for now, however the San Diego Opera attracts top international performers to the **Civic Theater**.

Balboa Park encompasses a number of performance spaces: **Starlight Bowl** for the Civic Light Opera and other light musicals; **Casa del Prado** for the Comic Opera; **Simon Edison Centre for the Performing Arts**, which includes the Old Globe Theatre, Cassius Carter Centre Stage and the Lowell Davies Festival Theatre. Horton Plaza's **Lyceum Theatre** stages works by the San Diego Repertory Theater, while nearby **Hahn Cosmopolitan Theater** is residence to the Gaslamp Quarter Theater. Many other contemporary and avant-garde theater pieces are performed in converted churches historic sites or run-down warehouses.

Dance

San Diego

California Ballet ★★★★

San Diego, ☎ *(619) 560-5676.*

Four works, ranging from contemporary to classical, are performed at locations throughout the county—the "Nutcracker," a San Diego toes-on favorite, is traditionally held at the Civic Theatre.

Music

Gaslamp Quarter

4th & B ★★★★

345 B Street, Gaslamp Quarter, ☎ (619) 231-4343.
Entertainment for every musical taste is on most nights of the week. Some of the more notable club bookings have included B.B. King, the Verve Jazz Fest, Suzanne Vega, and Poe. Alternative, rock, country, and comedy acts also hit the stage.

Theater

Balboa Park

Old Globe Theatre ★★★★★

Simon Edison Centre for the Performing Arts, Balboa Park,
☎ (619) 239-2255.

California's oldest professional theater stages contemporary and experimental works, as well as classics in the 581-seat Old Globe (modeled after Shakespeare's), 245-seat Cassius Carter Centre Stage and the 620-seat Lowell Davies Festival Theatre—all part of the Simon Edison Theatre for the Performing Arts. A-list actors such as Christopher Reeve (before his accident) and Jon Voight have always clamored to perform with one of the country's most prominent repertory companies, and the summer Shakespeare Festival draws fans with midsummer night's dreams.

The Old Globe Theater is a San Diego cultural landmark.

San Diego Civic Light Opera ★★★★

Starlight Bowl, Balboa Park, ☎ (619) 544-7800.
The Civic Light Opera presents a summer season of first-rate favorites.

San Diego Comic Opera ★★★

Casa del Prado Theatre, Balboa Park, ☎ (619) 231-5714.

Well-produced versions of Gilbert and Sullivan and similar works run most of the year in a homey-type theater filled mostly with season-ticket holders or friends of the cast.

Sledgehammer Theatre   ★★★

1620 Sixth Avenue, Near Balboa Park, ☎ *(619) 544-1484.*
San Diego's cutting-edge contribution to the theater scene. Avant-garde performances—often splendidly irreverent, or red-faced controversial (by San Diego standards, that is)—are performed at St. Cecelia's Church. There's at least one token naked person on stage each season and a large number of "bad" words almost all the time. A few works by New York playwright Mac Wellman have received raves. You'll look really cool here, especially if you pretend to understand everything that's going on.

Starlight Bowl   ★★★

Starlight Bowl, Balboa Park, ☎ *(619) 544-7827.*
The outdoor amphitheater is usually packed most summer evenings, mid-June through early September, for big-name musicals (staged by the San Diego Civil Light Opera Association), as well as rock bands and symphonies. Everyone tries to ignore the ever-present and ever-increasing jets roaring overhead (actors usually stop dead mid-line), and so far the audiences have not been deterred—and the planes have not been rerouted.

Gaslamp Quarter

Gaslamp Quarter Theatre   ★★★

Hahn Cosmopolitan Theatre, 444 Fourth Avenue, Gaslamp Quarter, ☎ *(619) 234-9583.*
Contemporary dramas, musicals, comedies and mysteries are staged by the long-time-in-residence theater company in the Hahn's 250-seat auditorium.

Horton Plaza

San Diego Repertory Theatre   ★★★★

Lyceum Theatre, 2 Broadway Circle, Horton Plaza, ☎ *(619) 235-8025.*
San Diego's first resident acting company operates out of two subterranean theaters—the 550-seat Lyceum Stage and the 225-seat Lyceum Space. An eclectic range of musicals, dramas and comedies—most by well-known playwrights—are produced during the fall-through-spring season. At Christmas, the Rep does a popular two-week run of "A Christmas Carol," changing the version each year—favorites were the African-American production, and the musical with ingenious "dancing food" costumes.

San Diego

East County Performing Arts Center

210 East Main Street, San Diego, ☎ *(619) 440-2277.*
Don't be put off by the somewhat-out-of-the-city location. The East County Peforming Arts Center hosts well-worth-the-drive events including nationally and internationally known symphonies, dance troupes and theatrical companies. Call for current happenings or keep your eyes peeled at the entertainment ads.

Fern Street Circus   ★★★

P. O. Box 621004, San Diego, 92162, ☎ *(619) 235-9756.*

San Diego's very own let's-ride-the-tails-of-the-Cirque-du-Soleil new-wave circus features artists from toddlers to seniors in theatrical non-performing-seal acts.

Fritz Theater ★★★

420 Third Avenue, San Diego, ☎ (619) 233-7505.
The Fritz produces a variety of provocative plays as well as expermental and "new talent" works, ranging from one-acts to full-lengthers.

Mystery Cafe ★★★

505 Kalmia Street, in Imperial House Restaurant, San Diego,
☎ (619) 544-1600.
San Diego's mystery dinner theatre has been at the same location for six years. The performances change, along with the era and scenery (the current run features a 1920s speakeasy and a bunch of gangsters and molls), but the premise stays the same—you eat a fairly standard meal, the shows goes on, and you are in it. Forget about just sitting back and watching the cute mystery unfold—no, as soon as you've swallowed your last morsel of food, you will be dished into the action—corpse, investigator, villain or—horrors—nice guy. Wanna-be actors should have a blast. Book ahead for all performances: Fridays at 8 p.m.; Saturdays at 5 p.m. and 8:30 p.m. General Admission: $35–$40.

San Diego Opera ★★★★

Civic Theatre, San Diego, 202 C Street, ☎ (619) 236-6510.
Big-shot international artists, impressed by the San Diego Opera's sterling reputation, appear in a five-opera series January through April, though special events are scheduled at other times. Performances have included "Porgy and Bess," "La Boheme" and "Rusalka." The 3000-seat auditorium features state-of-the-art stage and sound equipment as well as overhead screens that project English-language translations of original (non-English) works.

Spreckels Theatre ★★★★

121 Broadway, San Diego, ☎ (619) 235-9500.
Opened in 1912, San Diego's oldest theater, is a 1500-seat baroque queen. Its clear-as-a-bell acoustics make it one of the city's premiere venues for everything from theatrical performances to ballet, larger-than-life Mozart to small-scale rock 'n roll.

Sushi Performance and Visual Art ★★

320 Eleventh Avenue, San Diego, ☎ (619) 235-8466.
Sushi put performance art on the San Diego map and is relocating to a new location in a renovated old warehouse. Performances have included le creme de la creme of this art form (Karen Finley and Rachel Rosenthal, for example) are often solicited from the New York, San Francisco and L.A. scenes. Daring works and exhibitions are often either giggle- or thought-provoking. Not recommended for the shockable or conservative.

DOWNTOWN

Downtown: Nightlife

The Gaslamp Quarter is San Diego's center for nightlife and invites strolling any time of day.

The Gaslamp Quarter and outer fringes are San Diego's center for nightlife with pleasures for everyone from serious jazz lovers to ravers, wine-sippers and micro-brew guzzlers, grungers and cafe society. As in the days of New Town and, later, the Stingaree—Fifth and Broadway is the X that marks the nightlife pulse. It's become quite a scene within the past couple of years—vaguely reminiscent of the old Sunset Strip when sidewalks were packed with club-hopping crowds and nonstop action. For a less frenetic environment, try a club or lounge at one of the many elegant hotels nearby.

The underground dance set will find all the favorite raves: house, progressive, alternative, techno, groove, trance, ambient, hip-house, cyber industrial, Gothic darkwave, old-school flavor, hip-hop, fetish, etc. The clubs are listed in *The Reader*. (This is San Diego, remember?)

Balboa Park

Laurel Restaurant and Bar ★★★

505 Laurel Street, Balboa Park, ☎ *(619) 239-2222.*
This upscale and beyond-trendy restaurant is also an elegant club on Sunday through Wednesday nights. Live performances, from 6 p.m.–10 p.m., feature high-class sounds for the high-class clientele—ballads and showtunes, contemporary, cool jazz.

Gaslamp Quarter

Blarney Stone Pub ★★★

502 Fifth Avenue, Gaslamp Quarter, ☎ *(619) 233-8519.*
The pub is open daily for grog and cameraderie, and on Thursdays through Sundays hosts live performances of Irish folk musicians. Shows run 9 p.m.–1:30 a.m.

Buffalo Joe's ★★

500 Fifth Avenue, Gaslamp Quarter, ☎ *(619) 236-1616.*
This Gaslamp Quarter ribs-and-wings eatery presents evening entertainment ranging for big-screen sports attack to '70s retro, rock 'n' roll, jazz sounds, and dance revues. There's a late-night menu and about 20 brews on tap.

Cafe Sevilla ★★★

555 Fourth Avenue, Gaslamp Quarter, ☎ *(619) 233-5979.*
Sangria, tapas and all the hot or soft Latin you could ask for: salsa bands with dance lessons on Thursdays; flamenco dinner shows on weekends; samba shows with Brazilian buffet; flamenco guitar and live Spanish rock. Don't leave before 10:30 p.m. when the sounds turn to Latin Euro house and nuevo sonido dance.

Croce's Jazz Bar ★★★★

802 Fifth Avenue, Gaslamp Quarter, ☎ *(619) 233-4338.*
Jim Croce definitely has "got a name" in San Diego since his widow, Ingrid, used it as the headliner to promote her successful jazz club/restaurant. The rhythm-and-blues crowd might prefer Croce's Top Hat (☎ *233-4355),* the annex next door. Both clubs feature live entertainment nightly by top local musicians.

Dick's Last Resort ★★

345 Fourth Avenue, Gaslamp Quarter, ☎ *(619) 231-9100.*
The opposite of chic and trendy—beer froth and burger juice are more apt descriptions of ambience at Dick's. It's loud, boisterous and a blatant meat market. Food is served in buckets, brassieres hover over

DOWNTOWN

the bar and the staff has well-rehearsed "attitudes." The place admits to having "no class," an apt slogan. Rock bands are the usual stage hogs, though Sunday seems to be token jazz night. Dick's appeals to college students, typical tourists, sweet young things and the convention trade. The excellent beer list could make up for not much except an excuse for being there. "You can't kill a man born to hang"—so Dick decrees about himself. Catchy.

Green Circle Bar ★★

827 F Street, Gaslamp Quarter, At Ninth and F, ☎ *(619) 232-8080.*
DJ dance music runs from modern rock to techno hip hop. A haunt for dedicated clubmongers as well as the obvious uncool.

Jimmy Love's ★★★

672 Fifth Avenue, Gaslamp Quarter, ☎ *(619) 595-0123.*
At the booming corner of Fifth and G, in what used to be known as Johnny Love's (so love is love, right?), this "aviation sports bar" (you read correctly) features jazz, blues, retro '50s, and some good ole rock 'n' roll, along with a chest-pounding sports bar.

Johnny M's 801 ★★

801 Fourth Avenue, Gaslamp Quarter, ☎ *(619) 233-1131.*
Both the suits and the wet-suits descend on this cavernous disco to boogie to the blues with out-on-the-town women who often end up crying in their drinks (Thursday night is Ladies' nite—cheap drinks to drown sorrows).

La Tavola ★★★

515 Fifth Avenue, Gaslamp Quarter, ☎ *(619) 232-3352.*
Acoustic guitar strings to tug at your heart strings. Catch live flamenco performances and Spanish folk music on Fri. and Sat. nights. A fine place to end an evening.

Old Columbia Brewery and Grill ★★

1157 Columbia Street, Gaslamp Quarter, ☎ *(619) 234-2739.*
The entertainment is the beer. San Diego's first microbrewery is froth on the mug for the downtown business crowd

Patricks II ★★★★

428 F Street, Gaslamp Quarter, ☎ *(619) 233-3077.*
An Irish-style pub with New Orleans-style jazz and blues, and live entertainment nightly. A popular hot spot with occasional long lines, depending on the night and the act. Pretend your Patricks II Guiness is a Two Sisters' Hurricane (just don't take it out into the street).

Pourhouse ★★★★

528 F Street, Gaslamp Quarter, ☎ *(619) 232-7687.*
You'll meet a lifetime of new acquaintances while waiting in the very long lines backed up outside the door. This is one of the jumpingest bars in the Gaslamp Quarter, hosting local jazz, flamenco, funk and soul bands and kind-of-knowns from other cities. Dance downstairs. Sample martinis and micro-brews on the upper level.

San Diego

Casbah ★★★★

2501 Kettner Boulevard, San Diego, North of downtown,
☎ *(619) 232-4355.*

Not a club for timid mamas or wimpy dudes. It's boomin' and blastin' seven nights a week with alternative, rock and roll and acid jazz. The too-fast-to-live, too-young-to-die crowd will keep your blood moving. Stash your wallet and wear your best fake tattoo.

Grant Grill ★★★★

326 Broadway, in the U.S. Grant Hotel, San Diego, ☎ *(619) 232-3121.*
You'd be hard-pressed to find a swankier place to meet well-heeled locals or business travelers than the illustrious Grant Grill. A range of live entertainment throughout the week includes jazz, salsa and rhythm and blues. Wear your best togs and carry plenty of business cards.

Sally's ★★★★

One Market Place, San Diego, Adjacent to the Hyatt Regency and Seaport Village, ☎ *(619) 232-1234.*
Inside the Hyatt Regency, Sally's is a stylish spot for listening to weekend jazz without fighting the hordes in the Gaslamp Quarter. Look carefully and you'll recognize some of the finest local performers in the line up.

Soul Kitchen ★★★

168 East Main Street, San Diego, ☎ *(619) 579-3735.*
Closed: Mon.
A happening club for traveling teens, under 21-ers and alternative seekers. All ages are welcome—no alcohol, but lots of coffees, sodas and snacks. Still the action can get rowdy on weekends when entertainment is the loud punk, heavy metal, ska variety. Wednesday is bluegrass and open jam night, while Sunday is free poetry night. Doors open 7:30-8 p.m.

Velvet ★★★★

2812 Kettner Boulevard, San Diego, North of downtown,
☎ *(619) 692-1080.*
Full-on rock and roll club seven nights a week. Monday is open jam night. Wear ear plugs or else start clipping the ads for "Miracle Ear." Dress funky.

Waterfront ★★★★

2044 Kettner Boulevard, San Diego, North of downtown,
☎ *(619) 232-9656.*
The real thing! A genuine leftover from the old waterfront days—only now you can get a burger and hear sounds other than a street brawl or the guy next to you crying in his drink. Come Monday through Wednesday for the most "authentic ambience." Other nights feature scheduled rock and roll or country performers, usually turning on the mike at 9 p.m.

Yacht Club ★★★★

333 West Harbor Drive, San Diego, San Diego Marriott Hotel,
☎ *(619) 234-1500.*
An actual club in an actual premier hotel that actually offers a good mix of acts. Performances, 9 p.m.–1 a.m., include dance music, rock and roll, and reggae. Hint: don't wear dreadlocks and tie dye.

Author's Tip

If you want to infiltrate the local "art scene," try attending an opening exhibition at one of the galleries—usually held on Friday nights (listings are in The Reader). If you look really cool (or, better yet, if you buy something) you're apt to get an invite to a supercool after-party at a really supercool artist's loft. If not, you'll at least get a glass of free wine and a handful of goldfish-shaped cheese crackers.

Downtown: Shopping

Horton Plaza is a six block, multilevel shopping mall.

How convenient! Downtown shopping spots are interspersed amongst the tourist attractions and historical sites—or else they actually *are* the attractions and sites. **Horton Plaza**, for example. Encompassing six city blocks—bounded by Broadway, G Street, First and Fourth avenues—the multilevel plaza is a shopping mall in toon-town drag. The pied piper couldn't be more effective than architect Jon Jerde at luring followers to the dreamscape of colors, shapes and shadows. Oh yes—the shopping: 140 outlets including department stores, cinemas, theaters, restaurants, cafes, fast food (giant cinnamon rolls, hot dogs on a stick, etc.), and specialty shops offering books, music, computer software, travel accessories, fine jewelry, suggestive lingerie, safari gear, toys for everyone, and much more. Much to the dismay of local business people, the very popular farmer's market closed down after the 24-hour Ralph's supermarket opened across the street. The plaza is still undergoing a multi-million-dollar renovation which, when complete, will transform the defunct Robinson-May building into 120,000-square-feet of restaurants, entertainment and more shops. Almost everyone gets lost at least once at Horton Plaza, especially in the parking lots—one side is labeled 'fruits,' the other 'vegetables.' If you leave a car in the lot, be sure to write down the level and which fruit or veggie you're at. It also helps to find a "landmark" that will lead you back later. Merchants will validate your parking for three hours, while the cinemas will stamp you for four.

Just opposite Horton Plaza, across First Avenue, is **The Paladion**, San Diego's come-hither wink to the Rodeo Drive crowd. Opened in 1992, The Paladion's upscale shops include Tiffany, Cartier, Gucci, Gianni Versace, Salvatore Ferragamo, Alfred Dunhill and Nina Ricci. Show off your designer shopping bags over coffee and dessert at the ground-level cafe or go Italian at the rooftop restaurant. Valet parking is provided and there are no fruit or veggie names to repeat over and over to yourself between diamond- and shoe-shopping. Quelle difference!

Seaport Village, on the Embarcadero, is quite touristy and almost cloyingly quaint—still, many of the shops and galleries are really quite fascinating. Restaurants, a book shop/cafe, the wonderful Broadway Carousel and the superb setting take the edge off the 'ye-olde' cutesiness.

Antique lovers will find floors and floors of authentic old wonders at **The Olde Cracker Factory** (*448 W. Market Street*) and **Unicorn Company Arts & Antiques Mall** (*704 J Street*), both in the Gaslamp Quarter. Throughout the Gaslamp Quarter and on the periphery, independently-owned businesses bless eclectic shoppers with goodies such as original jewelry, imported Italian wear, handmade loafers, holey 501s, retro wear, custom gowns and leather harnesses.

FIELDING'S SELECT GUIDE TO FILMS THAT HAVE BEEN SHOT ENTIRELY OR PARTIALLY IN SAN DIEGO

The Flying Fleet *(1927)*. *Anita Page and Ramon Navarro.*

Hell Divers *(1931)*. *Clark Gable and Wallace Beery.*

Devil Dogs of the Air *(1935)*. *James Cagney and Pat O'Brien.*

Ramona *(1936)*. *Loretta Young and Don Ameche.*

Dive Bomber *(1941)*. *Errol Flynn and Fred MacMurray.*

Sands of Iwo Jima *(1949)*. *John Wayne.*

Hellcats of the Navy *(1956)*. *Ronald Reagan and Nancy Davis.*

The Spirit of St. Louis *(1957)*. *James Stewart*

Some Like It Hot *(1959)*. *Marilyn Monroe, Tony Curtis and Jack Lemmon.*

Attack of the Killer Tomatoes *(1976)*. *Rock Peace.*

Freaky Friday *(1976)*. *Jodie Foster.*

Airport '77 *(1977)*. *Jack Lemmon and Lee Grant.*

The Stunt Man *(1980)*. *Peter O'Toole and Barbara Hershey.*

Splash *(1984)*. *Darryl Hannah, Tom Hanks and John Candy.*

Top Gun *(1986)*. *Tom Cruise and Kelly McGillis.*

Little Nikita *(1988)*. *Sydney Poitier and River Phoenix.*

Return of the Killer Tomatoes *(1988)*. *John Astin and Steven Lundquist.*

Hunt for Red October *(1990)*. *Sean Connery and Alec Baldwin.*

Killer Tomatoes Strike Back *(1990)*. *John Astin and Rick Rockwell.*

Pretty Woman *(1990)*. *Julia Roberts and Richard Gere.*

Bugsy *(1991)*. *Warren Beatty and Annette Bening.*

The Grifters *(1991)*. *Anjelica Huston, John Cusack and Annette Bening.*

Demolition Man *(1993)*. *Wesley Snipes and Sylvester Stallone.*

Author's Tip

"Simon and Simon" has come and gone—though the reruns are on almost daily. Television series that are filmed regularly in San Diego include "Renegade" and "Silk Stalkings." The windblown hair of Lorenzo Lamas' has become an icon equivalent to the "Hollywood" sign.

DOWNTOWN

Downtown: Where to Stay

San Diego's downtown houses most of the county's finest hotels. Choose from historic digs like the **U.S. Grant**, **Gaslamp Plaza Suites** or **Horton Grand**; places fit for a king such as **The Westgate**; or one of the glitzy conventioneer and business-oriented bigname high-rises—**Hyatt Regency**, **Wyndam Emerald Plaza**, **Marriott** or **Westin Horton Plaza**. The usual chain motels are around also, as are a sprinkling of bed-and-breakfasts.

Hotels

Embarcadero

Embassy Suites Hotel   **$130–$190**   ★★★

601 Pacific Highway, Embarcadero, San Diego, 92101, Near the Convention Center, ☎ *(800) 362-2779, (619) 239-2400, FAX: (619) 239-1520.*

Single: $130–$190. Double: $130–$190.

Embassy Suites anywhere don't hold too many surprises. The trademark atrium (13 stories in this case), is filled with ozone-quenching plants, waterfalls and fountains. The spacious two room suites with galley kitchens and wet bars are real joys, no matter how cookie-moulded, and are perfect for keeping work—and associates—out of your bed. It also creates a much better impression when inviting a newfound friend up for a drink. Suites are spacious, well-decorated and the price tag includes a complimentary cooked breakfast and afternoon cocktails. The property is located just a few blocks from the Embarcadero and convention center, and is exceptionally popular—especially with the opening of its happening sports bar with wide video screen and video games. Good place to mix and mingle and get into the game. Amenities: exercise room, Jacuzzi, sauna. 337 rooms.

Credit Cards: A, DC, D, MC, V.

Holiday Inn on the Bay   **$100–$100**   ★★

1355 No. Harbor Drive, Embarcadero, San Diego, 92101, ☎ *(800) 465-4329, (619) 232-3861, FAX: (619) 232-4914.*

Single: $100. Double: $100.

The most outstanding feature of this highrise is its location—on the harbor, across from the Maritime Museum—well-suited for the vacation crowd. The property underwent badly needed renovation in 1992 but, despite the cleanup, it's still regulation Holiday Inn digs. The addition of a Ruth's Chris Steakhouse should keep the meat-lovers happy, and the hotel's popularity with overnighting flight crews should, well, keep the meat-lovers happy. Guest rooms feature the yawn-inspiring California contemporary decor, but sliding glass doors that open to balconies with knock-out views will keep a few eyes open. Amenities: Jacuzzi, balcony or patio. 605 rooms. Credit Cards: A, DC, MC, V.

Gaslamp Quarter

Horton Grand Hotel   **$80–$100**   ★★★

311 Island Avenue, Gaslamp Quarter, San Diego, 92101, ☎ *(800) 542-1886, (619) 544-1886, FAX: (619) 239-3823.*
Single: $80–$150. Double: $80–$100.

The Horton Grand, hands-down, is a sentimental favorite. It sits on the former site of San Diego's finest whorehouse and was once the home of Wyatt Earp. Need I say more? The hotel is comprised of two 1880s buildings—the Brooklyn Hotel (also known as Kahle's Saddlery Hotel) and the original Horton Grand. Threatened with demolition, the buildings were taken apart (brick by brick), warehoused and, in 1986, reopened at the present site—drawing tourists and guests to a block that might have been relegated to no-man's-land. Part Victorian, part baroque—original facades intact—these two unrelated twins are now joined at the hip by a wicker-filled atrium lobby. Rooms, with names instead of numbers, are individually decorated with period furnishings, lace curtains, gas fireplaces, WCs and pedestal sinks. The place is adored by newlyweds who want to get off to a good start and couples who are trying to save their marriages. Judging from the sounds that carry and the comments written in each bedside guestbook, the quests are successful. A small Chinese Museum pays tribute to the area's Chinatown heritage, while Ida Bailey's Restaurant pays tribute to the loveable madam whose bordello once stood here. A male ghost named Roger reportedly lingers up in Room 309—an unsatisfied former customer, perhaps? The staff all dresses in period costumes and the theme party is "on" all the time. The place is more cutesy than kitschy, and can become grating to anyone who isn't madly in love. 110 rooms. Credit Cards: A, DC, D, MC, V.

Horton Plaza

Gaslamp Plaza Suites   **$70–$180**   ★★

520 E Street, San Diego, 92101, One block from Horton Plaza, at Fifth Avenue, ☎ *(800) 443-8012, (619) 232-9500, FAX: (619) 238-9945.*
Single: $70–$180. Double: $70–$180.

Built in 1913, this imposing eleven-story gray structure was home to the city's jewelry community from the middle of World War II through the Summer of Love. Converted to a hotel in 1988, the building at least continues as a gem—gilded in Corinthian marble, brass, and mosaics—and is listed on the National Register of Historic Places. Petite or one-bedroom suites have burgundy, gray and green decor and are named for famous authors. Complimentary continental breakfast—with the morning paper—are served on the rooftop terrace where the city view will either inspire you to get-up-and-go or go back to bed. A restaurant and nightclub on the lower level are independently managed. Corner rooms have the best views. Book ahead for this one. Amenities: Jacuzzi. Credit Cards: DC, D, MC, V.

U.S. Grant Hotel   **$80–$120**   ★★★★

326 'Broadway, Horton Plaza, San Diego, 92101, ☎ *(800) 237-5029, (619) 232-3121, FAX: (619) 232-3626.*
Single: $80–$120. Double: $80–$120.

While foreign diplomats usually choose the Westgate Hotel, Americans wouldn't think of staying anywhere other than The Grant. Opened in 1910 by Ulysses S. Junior, in honor of his dad, almost every U.S. president (or wannabe president) has made it a point to stay here. JFK, FDR, Albert Einstein, and Charles Lindbergh slept here. So, also, did Bill. So can you. Listed on the National Register of Historic Places, The Grant is San Diego's grande dame. The elegant and staid formal lobby—guarded by huge marble pillars and serious furniture—makes frenetic Horton Plaza, just across the street, seem light years away. Guest rooms are spacious, soothing shelters. No surprise, decor is traditional—Queen Anne furnishings, wingback chairs, two-poster beds. Upper-level suites, fit for a president, include fireplaces to keep warm and wet bars to keep sane. Guests have access to the San Diego Athletic Club for fitness, privileges at Singing Hills Country Club for tennis and golf. Service is top-notch; the history is priceless. Amenities: exercise room. 283 rooms. Credit Cards: A, CB, DC, MC, V.

Westin Horton Plaza   **$160–$245**   ★★

910 Broadway Circle, Horton Plaza, San Diego, 92101, ☎ (800) 528-0444, (619) 239-2200, FAX: (619) 239-0509.

Single: $160–$230. Double: $175–$245.

Staying at a hotel that practically blends into whimsical Horton Plaza may feel somewhat akin to staying at Disneyland. A bright blue obelisk marks the entrance to this post-modern highrise (formerly the Doubletree Hotel) that conceals a deceptively elegant interior. Blissfully devoid of the atrium, ubiquitous amongst its peers, the marble and glass lobby offers a more fitting oasis for the movers-and-shakers and shop-till-you-droppers who pack the place at the end of a long day. The muted tones and luxurious ambience are carried through into guest rooms. Request a room with bay view. Amenities: tennis, health club, Jacuzzi, sauna, business services. 452 rooms. Credit Cards: A, DC, D, MC, V.

Wyrdham Emerald Plaza   **$140–$240**   ★★★★

400 W. Broadway, Horton Plaza, San Diego, 92101, Near the Embarcadero, ☎ (800) 626-3988, (619) 239-4500, FAX: (619) 239-3274.

Single: $140–$240. Double: $140–$240.

The former Pan Pacific's gutsy rise into the skyline, amid a group of pink hexagonal towers with jagged heights, is its greatest visual asset—inside it either pales or overwhelms. The three-story atrium with its dangling green prisms and plants brings to mind Jack and the Beanstalk, while the bland and boring guest rooms bring absolutely nothing to mind. The business services (secretaries, office space, computer terminals, etc.) and health club are first-rate, though, and clearly big draws for the primarily corporate and convention clientele. The hotel has neither a fine dining room or a nightclub (easy-listening piano entertainment in the cavernous atrium doesn't quite cut it), but there are plenty of options nearby. Request a room with bay views. Amenities: health club, exercise room, Jacuzzi, sauna, business services. 436 rooms. Credit Cards: A, DC, D, MC, V.

San Diego

San Diego Marriott Hotel & Marina   **$185–$205**   ★ ★ ★ ★

333 West Harbor Drive, San Diego, 92101, On the waterfront, ☎ *(800)*
228-9290, (619) 234-1500, FAX: (619) 234-8678.
Single: $185–$205. Double: $185–$205.

The Marriott's twin mirrored towers once loomed over the San Diego
waterfront, bouncing and reflecting all that water and sunshine. Now,
it's doing a lot of its reflecting on the Hyatt Regency next door. Still
there should be enough activity going on at the adjacent convention
center to keep everybody happy. The Marriott has a more bustling,
busy bee atmosphere—more carousing in public, more clinking of
glass. It also appeals to guests with kids in tow—the screams tend to
blend in with all the other hubbub. A separate children's pool—well
away from the adults—is another decided benefit, while the whole
family can get together and rent bicycles or boats. While most guest
rooms afford superb bay views, the older north tower has the drop
dead (and fall over) balconies. Vertigo sufferers will probably be happier in the newer (enclosed) south tower. Amenities: tennis, health
club, Jacuzzi, sauna, balcony or patio, club floor, business services.
1355 rooms. Credit Cards: A, CB, DC, D, MC, V.

Westgate Hotel   **$165–$205**   ★ ★ ★ ★

1055 Second Avenue, San Diego, 92101, Opposite Civic Center,
☎ *(800) 221-3802, (619) 238-1818, FAX: (619) 557-3604.*
Single: $165–$195. Double: $175–$205.

Never in a million years would you suspect that a palace lies within the
walls of this boring-looking, vintage-1970 highrise with airline offices
at its base. The lobby, a re-creation of an anteroom at Versailles, is
dazzling enough to make you fall to the floor and weep. Hand-cut
(and lit-up) Baccarat-crystal chandeliers, 18th-century French
antiques, Flemish and French tapestries, original works by Boucher
and Gainsborough, and a fabulous marble staircase, can make hay out
of a bad day. Accordingly, visiting foreign dignitaries wouldn't think
of staying elsewhere. High tea, accompanied by harp music, is a real
treat, as is a candlelight dinner in the formal Fontainbleau Room
upstairs. Guest rooms—all individually decorated—are opulent with
glorious antiques, Italian marble baths, 14-karat-gold fixtures. No
pool. No tennis. Who cares? A complimentary shuttle runs to the airport and downtown attractions. Or, for a complete break in mood,
guests can hop on the trolley right outside the front door and travel
from Versailles to Tijuana in less than an hour. Amenities: exercise
room. 223 rooms. Credit Cards: A, DC, D, MC, V.

Seaport Village

Hyatt Regency San Diego   **$165–$230**   ★ ★ ★ ★

One Market Place, Seaport Village, San Diego, 92101, ☎ *(800) 233-*
1234, (619) 232-1234, FAX: (619) 233-6464.
Single: $165–$230. Double: $165–$230.

Opened in late 1992, this 40-story building holds claims to fame as
the largest waterfront hotel on the West Coast. The ambience is one-
part Hyatt, one-part California—light and airy, but with a decided
"let's do business" tone. The lobby is a corporate dream, a dramatic
entrance amid Italian limestone columns and two enormous "in-
good-taste" paintings, where palm trees hover over ornate sofas, shel-

tering high-level deals from prying eyes. The adjacent bar is a perfect spot to shake hands and make a toast. Three restaurants, each named for one of the hotel owner's daughters, seem destined to sibling rivalry. A brand new 2000-square-foot kosher kitchen sits adjacent to the Manchester Ballroom, Guest rooms, decorated in a flurry of British Regency-style fabrics and furnishings, overlook the bay and feature laptop-compatible phones with voicemail. Aerobics classes and a marina with boat rentals are added leisure-time perks. The tres elegant rooftop lounge has a view to die for but—alas—the windows are tightly sealed shut. Amenities: tennis, health club, Jacuzzi, sauna, club floor, business services. 819 rooms. Credit Cards: A, CB, DC, D, MC, V.

Downtown: Where to Dine

As with the nightlife scene, downtown's trendy cucinas and trattorias are trying to out-sauce each other around and about the Fifth and Broadway corridors. You'll find plenty of watch and be-watched establishments including outdoor patios where limo-dropped diners keep their eyes raised above the riff-raff on the other side of well-guarded walls. But, in the same neighborhood, you'll also encounter an ever-expanding group of casual cafes with coffees, desserts and light meals accompanied by occasional poetry readings and live music.

The Embarcadero and Seaport Village offer top seafood and, again, the hotels have restaurants—and elbow room—to please almost everyone.

Embarcadero

Fish Market $$ ★★★★

750 North Harbor Drive, Embarcadero, ☎ (619) 232-3474.
Seafood cuisine. Specialties: Fresh mesquite-grilled fish.
Lunch: 11 a.m.–4 p.m., entrées $6–$12.
Dinner: 4-10 p.m., entrées $8–$18.
The Fish Market is a long-time favorite for fish-loving visitors and locals, and is exceptionally popular with families who can relax in the casual surroundings. Panoramic glass windows look out to the harbor and seats nearby make you feel as though you're practically on the water. An enormous array of fresh fish and seafood is hauled in off the boats daily—a blackboard announces the catches of the day. The ground level also has sushi and oyster bars and a cocktail lounge where wine is served by the glass. Top of the Market *(☎ (619) 234-4867)*, upstairs, is a clubby formal room with terrific views (binoculars loaned free), an extensive wine list and much higher prices. Sunday brunch is served in the upstairs room. Features: Sunday brunch. Reservations recommended. Credit Cards: CB, V, MC, DC, A.

Ruth's Chris Steakhouse $$$ ★★★★

1355 North Harbor Drive, Embarcadero, ☎ *(619) 233-1422.*
American cuisine. Specialties: Thick juicy steak.
Lunch: 11 a.m.–2 p.m., entrées $6–$20.
Dinner: 5-10 p.m., entrées $16–$23.

It's a bizarre name, I know, but the message is pure and simple—meat. Incredible 1-1/2-inch thick, 12-18 ounce, hand-cut babies—aged, corn-fed, the works—cooked perfectly under a special broiler that heats up to 1800 degrees, then presented on a plate—alone. Alas, you must order potatoes, veggies, anything and everything else separately—although a green sprig garnish is provided free. The steak is divine and could probably turn any veg-head into a bloody carnivore. Chicken and chops are also on the menu. The harbor view is to die for and romantics can pretend to be enthralled while discreetly mopping steak juice off their faces. Book a week ahead for weekend dinners. Jacket requested. Reservations recommended. Credit Cards: D, CB, V, MC, DC, A.

Drawing by Martin; © Cartoonists & Writers Syndicate

Gaslamp Quarter

Alize $$$ ★★★★★

777 Front Street, atop The Paladion, Gaslamp Quarter,
☎ *(619) 234-0411.*
Seafood cuisine. Specialties: Seafood, chicken, shrimp curry.
Lunch: 11 a.m.–2 p.m., entrées $10–$20.
Dinner: 5–10 p.m., prix fixe $16–$25.

Just when you thought Chino's was the big town tease with its Southwestern-meets-the-Far East flavors, along comes Alize with a tantalizing co-mingling of French and Caribbean influences. Poised at the top of The Paladion, above the Tiffany baubles and the Ferragamo shoes, this luxurious restaurant serves inventive and beautifully presented a la carte dishes for lunch and three-course prix-fixe meals for dinner. Selections might include scallops, lamb loin, chicken curry or creole-style filet mignon. Light dinners for the after-theatre crowd are served from 10 p.m. on Friday and Saturday nights. Lunch is served every day except Sunday. Features: late dining. Jacket requested. Reservations recommended. Credit Cards: V, MC, A.

Bayou Bar and Grill   **$$**   ★★★★

329 Market Street, Gaslamp Quarter, ☎ (619) 696-8747.
Cajun cuisine. Specialties: Shrimp Creole, jambalaya.
Lunch: 11:30 a.m.–3 p.m., entrées $6–$10.
Dinner: 5-10 p.m., entrées $9–$18.
A piece of the Big Easy in the old Stingaree. The New Orleans-decor dining room with lazy ceiling fans serves everyone's favorite spicy Cajun and Creole dishes—crawfish, jambalaya, soft-shell crab, seafood gumbo, red beans, etc. Finish your meal off with real Louisiana desserts like pecan pie, praline cheesecake and bread pudding. And to wash it all down with? Hurricanes, crocodile coolers and blackened voodoo beer, of course. Late dining Fri. & Sat. Sunday brunch ($12.95) is a three-course extravaganza with real beignets and bottomless champagne. Features: outside dining, Sunday brunch. Reservations recommended. Credit Cards: D, V, MC, DC, A.

Cafe Lulu   **$**   ★★★

419 F Street, Gaslamp Quarter, ☎ (619) 238-0114.
American cuisine. Specialties: Coffees.
Breakfast: 8 a.m.–2 a.m., entrées $2–$7.
This minimalist coffeehouse signalled San Diego's entrée to cafe society. Though other cafes had sprung up nearby, Lulu's automatically became the place to meet friends and business associates—the spot to look really hot while acting really cool. It's the in-place for the brie-and-baguette and filled-croissant crowd, though the chalkboard menu might offer something exceptional like quiche and soup. The coffee drinks are a strong point (drink that latte while perusing your day runner and working on your philosophy assignment and you'll fit right in). Other thirst quenchers include imported mineral waters, beer and wine by the glass, and sodas and sarsaparilla. Open until 4 a.m. on Fridays and Saturdays. Features: wine and beer only, late dining. Reservations not accepted. Credit Cards: V, MC.

Chino   **$$**   ★★★★

919 Fourth Avenue, inside E Street Alley, Gaslamp Quarter,
☎ (619) 231-9240.
Chinese cuisine. Specialties: Smoked and stir-fried shrimp, Peking quail.
Dinner: 5-10:30 p.m., entrées $11–$16.
Quel eclectic! An open "California" kitchen showcasing a unique blend of Southwestern, Thai, Hunan and Szechuan techniques—and an 18-seat sushi bar, to boot! Somehow it all works—delectably and exotically. For one-stop binge-and-purge, move over to Club E and

dance off the calories. Reservations recommended. Credit Cards: V, MC, A.

Croce's $$ ★★★

802 Fifth Avenue, at F Street, Gaslamp Quarter, ☎ *(619) 233-4355.*
American cuisine. Specialties: Fresh seafood, pastas.
Dinner: 4 p.m.–midnight, entrées $9–$20.

Along with the upstairs jazz club and the R&B club adjacent, the widow of Jim Croce plays it one more time for her man. Ingrid, listen—he's been gone since 1973, you've got the name now! The Croce memorabilia is worth seeing (once) but Ingrid's kitchen is reason to return over and over and has probably garnered more awards than her late husband's music. Fresh seafood like New Zealand orange roughy, swordfish, and stuffed salmon are can't-go-wrongs, while the Thai chicken pasta salad is as popular as a gold record. The kitchen stays open until midnight. Ingrid's Cantina & Sidewalk Cafe, part of the expanding Croce complex, features innovative Southwestern dishes and is open for daily breakfast, lunch and dinner. Features: late dining. Reservations recommended. Credit Cards: D, V, MC, DC, A.

Dakota Grill and Spirits $$ ★★★★

901 Fifth Avenue, Gaslamp Quarter, ☎ *(619) 234-5554.*
American cuisine. Specialties: Barbecued dishes, roasted garlic.
Lunch: 11:30 a.m.–2:30 p.m., entrées $6–$9.
Dinner: 5-10 p,.m., entrées $8–$16.

Be seated at street level so you can be seen, or dine upstairs and look out at the peons on Fifth Avenue. The Dakota was an instant hit from the moment it roasted its first bulb of garlic. Black-clad servers scrawl orders of mesquite-grilled, wood-fired, open-grilled and rotisseried meats, pizzas and vegetables. And garlic, ever more garlic. The Caesar salad and black bean soup are a good fill for lite weights. Or just stop in for a drink at the full bar with a selection of microbrewery beers. Lunch served Mon.-Fri., dinner until 11 p.m. on Fri. and Sat., until 9 p.m. on Sun. Features: late dining. Reservations recommended. Credit Cards: D, CB, V, MC, A.

Fio's $$ ★★★★

801 Fifth Avenue, at F Street, Gaslamp Quarter, ☎ *(619) 234-3467.*
Italian cuisine. Specialties: Gourmet pizzas, black linguine with seafood.
Lunch: 11:30 a.m.–3 p.m., entrées $6–$14.
Dinner: 5-11 p.m., entrées $8–$20.

Situated on a prime corner, Fio's is a stylish haven where local suits and clock-ticking female professionals break foccacia in front of street-side windows—pretending not to care if they're being "seen." This forerunner of what soon became a trend of trendy Italian restaurants in the Gaslamp, serves gourmet pizzas (wood-fired, of course) as well as pasta and seafood entrées. Lunch is the most hectic time when the place overflows with type-A professionals eager for a quick pizza, calzone or panini but service is efficient and meals can be eaten at the bar. Dinner only is served on weekends. Valet parking is available after 5 p.m. Reservations recommended. Credit Cards: D, V, MC, DC, A.

Grant Grill $$$ ★★★★

326 Broadway, Gaslamp Quarter, ☎ *(619) 239-6806.*
Continental cuisine. Specialties: Seafood, prime rib, mock turtle soup, salads.

Breakfast: 6:30–10:30 a.m., entrées $7.
Lunch: 11:30 a.m.–2:30 p.m., entrées $8–$12.
Dinner: 5:30-10:30 p.m., entrées $14–$26.

Back in the good old days of family values, the venerable Grant Grill was an oasis of testosterone—women allowed only on the arm of a male companion, and only if they were well-behaved. In 1967, well-behaved but liberated women forced the Grill to lift its outdated face and allow them to dine unescorted. A contemporary open rotisserie is the focal point for this still-clubby historic favorite where power lunches and seal-a-deals are as popular as the circa-1910 mock turtle soup. Seafood pastas and rack of lamb are especially good, and all main courses include an appetizer. Watch for the gleaming silver dome headed your way—your food is beneath it. Features: Sunday brunch. Jacket requested. Reservations recommended. Credit Cards: V, MC, DC, A.

Kiyo's Japanese Restaurant $ ★★★

531 F Street, Gaslamp Quarter, ☎ *(619) 238-1726.*
Japanese cuisine. Specialties: Sushi, sukiyaki.
Lunch: 11 a.m.–2 p.m., entrées $4–$8.
Dinner: 5-10 p.m., entrées $5–$10. Closed: Sun.

Kiyo, the owner, works the sushi bar and guests can request any sushi item, whether it's on the menu or not. Favorite lunchtime meals are combination plates, as well as noodle dishes and dumplings. Dinner is a bit fancier with tempura, chicken and sukiyaki on the menu. Good service, atmosphere, food and prices. A winner if you're in the mood for Japanese. Credit Cards: V, MC.

Old Columbia Brewery & Grill $$ ★★★★

1157 Columbia Street, Gaslamp Quarter, ☎ *(619) 234-2739.*
American cuisine. Specialties: Ales and beers.
Lunch: 11 a.m.–4 p.m., entrées $5–$9.
Dinner: 4-10 p.m., entrées $5–$14.

San Diego's first microbrewery is a rollicking good time. Food is fairly routine pub fare—fish and chips, burgers, grilled sausage and chili. But then, food is secondary to the real reason for a visit—tasting the variety of beers, ales and lagers made on site. The ambers are the best known, but you can try six to a dozen kinds on any night, depending on season. Port, sherry, nonalcoholic beer and wine by the glass are also available. Food is served until midnight, grog is poured until 1 a.m. on Thursdays through Saturdays. Tours are available and souvenirs are for sale. Next Door Namers at Old Columbia (☎ *(619) 230-1891)* offers fresh California-style dishes for Mon.-Fri. lunch and Mon.-Sat. dinner. What more could you want? Features: late dining. Reservations not accepted. Credit Cards: V, MC.

DOWNTOWN

Old Spaghetti Factory $ ★★★

275 Fifth Avenue, corner of K Street, Gaslamp Quarter,
☎ *(619) 233-4323.*
Italian cuisine. Specialties: Italian favorites.
Lunch: 11:30 a.m.–2 p.m., entrées $4–$8.
Dinner: 5 -10 p.m., entrées $5–$10.

This is the ultimate family restaurant—real Italian food—spaghetti and meatballs, decanters of Chianti, salad and garlic bread. No menu surprises, no one trying to wipe unfamiliar sauces onto their napkins or hide one of those strange-looking veggies specially grown at Chino's under their seat. And the kids stay blissfully occupied with the theme-park type decor. Grab a seat in the 1917 trolley car, and little Betty or Johnny might even sit still until you choke down a meatball—if not you can send them to the children's play area. The place gets packed and there are often long waits so try to get there early. Otherwise, put your name on the list, send the kids off to play and start ordering the Chianti. Open until 11 p.m. on Saturdays and Sundays. Reservations not accepted. Credit Cards: D, V, MC.

Sammy's California Woodfired Pizza $

770 Fourth Avenue, Gaslamp Quarter, ☎ *(619) 230-8888.*
Italian cuisine. Specialties: Pizza.
Lunch: 11:30 a.m.–4 p.m., entrées $6–$10.
Dinner: 4-10 p.m., entrées $6–$12.
The pizza part is Italian but the toppings are pure California. Send the sausage and pepperoni packing back to the old country—Sammy's can give you barbecued chicken, smoked gouda cheese, sun-dried tomatoes, fresh veggies and not-your-usual herbs and spices. Fresh pasta dishes, salads and calzones are also on the menu. The atmosphere is bustling, contemporary pizza parlor-gone-troppo. Dinner until 11 p.m. on Fridays and Saturdays. There are Sammy branches in Del Mar and La Jolla. Features: wine and beer only. Reservations not accepted. Credit Cards: CB, V, MC, DC.

Sfuzzi $$

340 Fifth Avenue, Gaslamp Quarter, ☎ *(619) 231-2323.*
Italian cuisine. Specialties: Italian specialties.
Lunch: 11 a.m.–2 p.m., entrées $8–$14.
Dinner: 5-10 p.m., entrées $12–$18.
It's trendy, tony, yuppie and uppity—packed with important-looking people who arrive in limos or Excaliburs or Silver Clouds. Sfuzzi—pronounced "foo-zee"—is the consumate Italian bistro, destined to make an appearance in the Lifestyles of the Rich and Famous. Those with reservations and manicured hands select from a menu with gourmet pastas and pizzas. Patrons who didn't plan well—or were too late to get a table—crowd the bar and thoughtfully peruse the wine list. Lunch is only served Monday through Saturday. Another branch is located in The Aventine, in the Golden Triangle (La Jolla) area. Features: outside dining. Reservations recommended. Credit Cards: CB, V, MC, DC, A.

Trattoria La Strada $$$

702 Fifth Avenue, Gaslamp Quarter, ☎ *(619) 239-3400.*
Italian cuisine. Specialties: Tuscan specialties.
Lunch: 11 a.m.–2:p.m., entrées $10–$16.
Dinner: 5-10 p.m., entrées $18–$28.
The young, urbane, super-hip and style-concious clientele pack the two high-ceilinged dining rooms—seemingly oblivious to the excruciating noise levels—as they chow down on Italian delights. Specialty pastas, salads and antipasto—combining imagination and tradition—are all good bets. The bar is a lively scene of those on the make and those on the go. Dinner is served until 11 p.m. on Fridays and Saturdays. Features: late dining. Jacket requested. Reservations recommended. Credit Cards: D, V, MC, DC, A.

DOWNTOWN

Horton Plaza

Panda Inn $$ ★★★★
506 Horton Plaza, San Diego, ☎ (619) 233-7800.
Chinese cuisine. Specialties: Mandarin and Szechwan dishes.
Lunch: 11 a.m.–4:30 p.m., entrées $6–$10.
Dinner: 4:30-10 p.m., entrées $8–$22.
You'd never know you were at the top of frenetic Horton Plaza once inside this sophisticated, elegant and peaceful restaurant. Three dining areas offer seating at booths or tables set with white linens and menu selections that include seasonal specialties, fresh seafood, Mandarin and Szechuan dishes and scrumptious appetizers. Request the rear dining section if you prefer a city view. Dinner is served until 11 p.m. on Fridays and Saturdays. Reservations recommended. Credit Cards: CB, V, MC, DC, A.

San Diego

Anthony's Fish Grotto $$ ★★★★
1360 North Harbor Drive, San Diego, ☎ (619) 232-5103.
Seafood cuisine. Specialties: Seafood salads, shellfish casserole.
Lunch: 11:30 a.m.–4 p.m., entrées $5–$17.
Dinner: 4-8 p.m., entrées $6–$19.
Many San Diegans would not even consider going anywhere but Anthony's for fish and seafood. The long-established, family-owned enterprise reels in diners as easily as it does fish, offering excellent quality, efficient service and reasonable prices. More than a dozen entrées and seasonal dishes are on the menu, as are scads of salads and appetizers. Meals include a choice of salads. Avoid the busy lunch hour if possible. Other Fish Grottos are located in La Jolla, La Mesa, Rancho Bernardo and Chula Vista. Reservations recommended. Credit Cards: D, CB, V, DC, A.

Anthony's Star of the Sea $$$ ★★★★★
1360 North Harbor Drive, San Diego, ☎ (619) 232-7408.
Dinner: 5:30.-10:30 p.m., entrées $17–$38.
The valet parking costs almost as much as the entrées at other restaurants. If elegance, tradition, stunning gourmet seafood and impeccable service are your thing, this venerable San Diego institution should be at the top of your dining-out list. Expect the best—a beautiful room set on pilings above the water, a vast selection of divine cuisine whisked from beneath silver domes, and professional servers and staff. The view from Anthony's is spectacular. Reservations are necessary, preferably one week in advance. Jacket and tie requested. Reservations required. Credit Cards: CB, V, MC, DC, A.

Athen's Market $$$ ★★★★
109 West F Street, San Diego, ☎ (619) 234-1955.
Mediterranean cuisine. Specialties: Appetizers, lentil soup.
Lunch: 11:30 a.m.–4 p.m., entrées $4–$9.
Dinner: 4-11 p.m., entrées $10–$22.
Cheerful, festive and located across from Horton Plaza in an 1898 building, Athens Market is the city's Greek goddess. For more than two decades, owner Mary Pappas has wowed patrons with a combination of old family recipes and personal attention, in an Aegean island setting. You know it's a good sign when the Greek community crowds in. Put together a delectable meal just from the scrumptious

DOWNTOWN

appetizers and famous lentil soup. Traditional salads and lamb, chicken and fish entrées are also excellent—and don't foreget to save room for dessert. The place is mobbed at lunch hour with local workers. Weekend evenings are like mini-Greek festivals with ethnic music and belly dancers. Features: late dining. Reservations recommended. Credit Cards: CB, V, MC, DC, A.

De Medici $$$ ★★★★

815 Fifth Avenue, San Diego, ☎ (619) 702-7228.
Lunch: 11:30 a.m.–2:30 p.m., entrées $8–$16.
Dinner: 5:30-10:30 p.m., entrées $12–$25.
Dine on regional Italian dishes in a lovely pseudo-16th-century cucina. Specialties include veal chops, lamb chops, beef tenderloin in port sauce, scampi, and delectably rich pastas. The cannoli is heavenly. Lunch is served Tuesday through Friday. Late dining Friday and Saturday. Features: late dining. Reservations recommended. Credit Cards: CB, V, MC, DC, A.

Dobson's $$$ ★★★★

956 Broadway Circle. adjacent Horton Plaza, San Diego,
☎ (619) 231-6771.
Continental cuisine. Specialties: Mussel bisque.
Lunch: 11 a.m.–2 p.m., entrées $15–$25.
Dinner: 6-11 p.m., prix fixe $18–$30. Closed: Sun.
Dobson's was one of the first non-hotel-related restaurants to make a scene downtown and continues to be a grassroots favorite. Local politicians and lawyers elbow-polish the slick bar and small two-level restaurant at lunch, while celebs and VIPs take over at night. Dobson's signature dish is a mussel bisque with puff-pastry crown. Entrées change daily and might include rack of lamb, fresh fish specialties or chicken risotto. The prix-fixe meal, served Monday through Thursday, is a real deal—soup, salad, choice of one of four entrées, dessert and wine for around $25. Lunch is served Mon.-Fri., dinner Mon.-Sat. Late dining Thurs.-Sat. Features: late dining. Reservations recommended. Credit Cards: V, MC, DC, A.

Garlix $$ ★★★

825 Fifth Avenue, San Diego, ☎ (619) 239-8600.
Dinner: 5:30-10 p.m., entrées $9–$18.
In the spirit of San Francisco's notable "The Stinking Rose," this newer establishment in the Gaslamp Quarter's restaurant corridor is devoted to an eclectic menu that reeks of...you know what. Your can have salad with your garlic, chicken with your garlic, pasta wiith your garlic, and garlic with your garlic. Either bring a date or plan on not having one for the next year. Late dining on Friday and Saturday. Features: late dining. Reservations recommended. Credit Cards: CB, V, MC, DC, A.

Hob Nob Hill $$ ★★★★

2271 First Avenue, San Diego, ☎ (619) 239-8176.
American cuisine. Specialties: Down home Americana.
Breakfast: 7–9 a.m., entrées $3–$11.
Lunch: 11 a.m.–4 p.m., entrées $6–$8.
Dinner: 4-9 p.m., entrées $6–$14.
Yearning for a back-to-the-good-old-days ride with like-mama-used-to-make eats? Hob Nob Hill, opened in 1944, is still under the same

management and ownership some 50 years later—and the decor, menu and many of the patrons have not changed a smidgen. The prices have gone from pennies to dollars, but are still bargains considering the quality and quantity of the food. The breakfasts are renowned, served all day, and include lots of omelets, pancakes, breads and cakes. Rib-sticking favorites for lunch and dinner are daily specials such as roast turkey, corned beef and braised short ribs. Sweet nostalgia! Fresh-baked goodies are available for take-out also. Hob Nob is extremely popular on Sundays. Features: own baking, wine and beer only. Reservations recommended. Credit Cards: D, V, MC, A.

Laurel $$$ ★★★★★
505 Laurel Street, San Diego, ☎ (619) 239-2222.
Lunch: 11:30 a.m.–2 p.m., entrées $8–$18.
Dinner: 5–10 p.m., entrées $12–$28.
Laurel, Laurel, Laurel...it's the whisper from every San Diego foodie's mouth—but, in this case at least, for very good reason. Master chef Douglas Organ has created a sophisiticated, French country-style ambience in which to drool and delect on stunningly prepared Mediterranean and southern French cuisine. It's elegant and yet, tres simple. Grilled lamb loin, grilled boar, roasted guinea hen, seafood soup, duck comfit, get the picture? Lunch served Monday through Friday. Boasts a full bar. Reservations required. Credit Cards: D, V, MC, DC, A.

Osteria Panevino $$ ★★★★
772 Fifth Avenue, San Diego, ☎ (619) 595-7959.
Specialties: Homemade pastas.
Lunch: 11:30 a.m.–2 p.m., entrées $9–$15.
Dinner: 5–10 p.m., entrées $10–$18.
Another Italian eatery in the Gaslamp. This one is quite a standout and wildly popular for its Northern Italian dishes in a sort of Tuscany farmhouse environment (nifty tiles and wine barrels, that sort of thing). If you can't hit the hill country this year, you'll hardly know the difference (until you walk outdoors, of course). Scrumptious homemade pastas are extremely popular, as are fish, veal and chicken dishes. The brick oven will bake you pizza to perfection, while small eaters will still be satisfied with the antipasti menu. Late dining on Friday and Saturday nights. Features: wine and beer only, late dining. Reservations recommended. Credit Cards: D, CB, V, MC, DC, A.

Planet Hollywood $ ★★
197 Horton Plaza, San Diego, ☎ (619) 702-7827.
Lunch: 11 a.m.–2 p.m., entrées $5–$12.
Dinner: 4–11 p.m., entrées $5–$12.
We have to list Planet Hollywood (don't we??) After all, Bruce, Demi, Sly, and Arnold are co-owners and they actually set foot on the premises for the opening. If you care to follow in their footsteps, bra-size, or state-of-baldness, come on down to Horton Plaza and eat fun American food (burgers, fries, pizza, salad), in an environment filled with moveie memorabilia. No reservations are taken, and you can expect a long wait at prime times but—hey, you can stock up on Planet Hollywood souvenirs at the adjacent shop. Oh well, the kids will love it. Features: late dining. Reservations not accepted. Credit Cards: V, MC, DC, A.

DOWNTOWN

Rainwater's $$$ ★★★★★

1202 Kettner Boulevard, 2nd floor, San Diego, ☎ *(619) 233-5757.*
American cuisine. Specialties: Steaks.
Lunch: 11:30 a.m.–3 p.m., entrées $7–$15.
Dinner: 5 p.m.–midnight, entrées $16–$38.

Ask anyone in town where to go for melt-in-your-mouth steaks in elegant surroundings and Rainwater's will invariably drool off their tongues. Don your Sunday best and bring a fat wallet for pay-by-the-ounce (or through-the-nose) cuts of filet, T-bone, New York or Kansas City strips or prime rib. All come with rib-sticker side dishes like potato skins, creamed corn, baked potato or onion rings. Chops and seafood are also on the menu. Rainwater's long list of awards by restaurant-and-wine writers includes its outstanding wine selections—36 domestic and imported labels poured from a unique cruvinet. Nightly prix-fixe dinners with changing menu are offered for $25-$30. Owners Laurel and Paddy Rainwater managed to turn their meaty dreams into reality. Both valet and free garage parking are available. Features: rated wine cellar, late dining. Jacket and tie requested. Reservations recommended. Credit Cards: V, MC, DC, A.

Sally's $$ ★★★★

1 Market Place, San Diego, ☎ *(619) 687-6080.*
Mediterranean cuisine.
Lunch: 11:30 a.m.–2:30 p.m., entrées $7–$16.
Dinner: 5:30-11 p.m., entrées $9–$20.

The dining room is ultra-sleek with a waterfront location. Beautifully presented Mediterranean dishes include superb fish and seafood, paella, bouillabaisse and a range of imaginative pastas. If your party has at least six people, ask to eat in the chef's kitchen where dishes will be concocted especially for your group. Live jazz performances are scheduled most weekends. Features: outside dining. Reservations recommended. Credit Cards: D, CB, V, MC, DC, A.

Seau's: The Restaurant $$ ★★

1640 Camino del Rio North, San Diego, ☎ *(619) 291-7328.*
Breakfast: 8:30 a.m.–11 a.m., entrées $4–$8.
Lunch: 11 a.m.–2 p.m., entrées $6–$12.
Dinner: 5–10 p.m., entrées $9–$16.

San Diego Charger Junior Seau's place dishes up everything an All-American could dream of—burgers, sandwiches, salads, grilled meats, fish, pastas, pizzas, and scrumptious home-baked desserts. The cigar lounge is a bonus treat. Breakfast served Saturday and Sunday. Late dining on Friday and Saturday. Features: late dining. Credit Cards: CB, V, MC, DC, A.

Seaport Village

Harbor House $$$ ★★★

831 West Harbor Drive, Seaport Village, ☎ *(619) 232-1141.*
Seafood cuisine.
Lunch: 11:30-5 p.m., entrées $6–$9.
Dinner: 5-10 p.m., entrées $14–$30.

You come here for fresh fish with a harbor view in a nautical-theme setting. The fish and seafood is adequate but unremarkable and the atmosphere is anything but intimate—unless you think a cavernous room with about 250 other diners is cozy. Still, the two-level restau-

DOWNTOWN

rant is always busy—but usually not with locals. The de rigeur sourdough bread and vegetable medley come with entrées which include
a variety of fresh fish as well as chicken, pasta and steak. Sunday
brunch is a la carte and Sunday dinners begin at 4:30 p.m. Features:
Sunday brunch. Reservations recommended. Credit Cards: D, V, MC, A.

Kansas City Barbecue   **$**   ★ ★ ★
610 West Market Street, Seaport Village, ☎ *(619) 231-9680.*
American cuisine. Specialties: Barbecued beef, chicken, pork and hot links.
Lunch: 11 a.m.–5 p.m., entrées $4–$8.
Dinner: 5 p.m.–1 a.m., entrées $5–$10.
Believe it or not, Kansas City Barbecue actually existed (and thrived)
for about a decade before Tom Cruise and Kelly McGillis warmed
their seats there in a couple of *Top Gun* scenes. No big deal—so now
a few *Top Gun* posters hang along with the rest of the memorabilia—
a lot of license plates, shutterbug photos and just plain "stuff" left
behind by patrons, famous or not. Famished locals and tourists who
hanker some "real" food, are lured to this honky-tonk either by word
of mouth or sense of smell. Succulent, slow-cooked, old-family-recipe
barbecued dishes include two side dishes—potato salad, corn on the
cob, coleslaw, beans and such. It tastes just like the Fourth of July.
Features: outside dining, late dining. Reservations not accepted. Credit
Cards: D, V, MC.

San Diego offers a variety of beaches for all interests.

FIELDING'S BEACH FINDER

San Diego County's 70 miles of sandy beaches—from Oceanside to the Mexican border—used to be (and often still are) referred to as "pristine." Not true—some places yes, some places no. There are great sunsets, terrific waves, gorgeous tanned bodies and secluded getaways; you'll also find raw sewage, surf nazis, broken glass and ugly naked people. And cops—plenty of cops (many undercover) looking for errant beach-goers to cite for violation of whatever the current ordinances might be. Glass is not allowed on any beach, dogs are banned from most areas, fires are permitted only in designated fire rings or barbecues. The alcohol ban is ever-changing—check the signs posted before you bring booze to the beach. Some beaches ban all alcohol (including the trusty six-pack), others allow you to drink only between certain hours. Drinking in the parking lots, on the boardwalks or in the bushes is always *verboten*.

Oceanside

Two miles of wide, sandy beaches; lots of marines from Camp Pendleton; one of the longest wooden piers on the west coast; good surfing around the pier and on either side of the two jetties; north edge, near San Onofre and the county line, is a hide-and-seek nude beach where the clothing-challenged leap the fence onto Camp Pendleton property where the sheriffs (as though they would want to) can't touch them.

Carlsbad

Rocky beaches due to storm erosion; best swimming at South Carlsbad State Beach (campground, also); fishing at Carlsbad State Beach.

Encinitas

Superb hideaway beaches; top surfing at Swami's and Stone Steps (long stairways at both); volleyball, full facilities, parking lot, easy access—and occasional trouble—at Moonlight Beach.

Cardiff

Reef break for surfers and lots of sand and easy access for families at Cardiff State Beach and South Cardiff State Beach; campground (always booked ahead at peak times) at San Elijo State Beach.

Solana Beach

Limited-access cliffside beaches; easy access at Pillbox, at the bottom of Lomas Santa Fe Drive, and a short walk to the secluded cliffside spots.

FIELDING'S BEACH FINDER

Del Mar

Many wide, sandy beaches (packed in summer) with easy access but difficult parking; beaches north of 15th Street are easiest to reach and across from the fairgrounds and racetrack; cliffside spots south of 15th Street are more peaceful; a grassy park and playground—and occasional wedding site—is located midway at the bottom of 15th; Torrey Pines State Beach, at the southern edge of Del Mar, has lifeguards, a parking lot, fire rings and good swimming—it's usually packed in summer.

Black's Beach

Unofficial nude beach—often not a pretty sight; treacherous cliffside access (but familiar to the search-and-rescue team and life-flight crews); excellent surfing but lots of rip currents; homosexual activity in the bushes.

La Jolla Shores

Good family beach with lifeguards year-round; mile-long flat, wide sandy beach; low-stress waves for swimming, board and body surfing, and boogie boarding; jogging on concrete boardwalk parallel to beach.

La Jolla Cove

Protected calm and clear waters; exciting tidal pools and cliff caves; 6000-acre underwater ecological reserve; perfect for swimming, snorkeling, scuba diving, family outings and rough-water swims.

Shell Beach

Small secluded cove, south of La Jolla Cove, frequented by frolicking seals.

Children's Pool

A shallow lagoon with child-size waves and no riptides (but hordes of wading toddlers and parents).

Marine Street Beach

Just off La Jolla Boulevard, a haven for the suntan and Frisbee crowd.

Windansea Beach

World-class surfing beach made famous by Tom Wolfe's book *The Pumphouse Gang*—famous today as hangout of renegade Nobel Laureate and nearly O.J. defense witness, Kary Mullis; intimidating surf nazis.

Pacific Beach

Beach and boardwalk popular with families, students and surfers; bike paths and picnic tables; lousy parking.

FIELDING'S BEACH FINDER

Mission Beach

San Diego's answer to L.A.'s Venice Beach; long beach and boardwalk crowded with the rollerblading, cycling and baby-stroller set; very crowded in summer; year-round surfing, swimming and volleyball; Belmont Park amusement complex at north (and most populated) end.

Mission Bay

4600-acre aquatic park with beaches, picnic areas, windsurfing, sailing, water-skiing, fishing, jet-skiing; skating, blading, biking and jogging paths.

Ocean Beach

Volleyball, swimming and sunbathing; Dog Beach, at the north end, allows pups to splash leash-free; surfers and street people hang out at the south end; fire rings and food vendors.

Sunset Cliffs

Secluded surf spot beneath jagged cliffs (always someone getting hurt or rescued climbing up or down); large waves, secluded sunbathing; tidal pools at south end, near Cabrillo Point; no facilities; stairs at the bottom of Bermuda and Santa Cruz avenues.

Coronado Beach

Wide stretch of sparkling white beach with the Hotel del Coronado as a backdrop; usually uncrowded; good choice for romantics; fire rings, parking and facilities.

Silver Strand State Beach

Family-oriented beach, down the Coronado isthmus; calm water with tiny silver seashells near its edge; lots of parking and facilities; campground.

Imperial Beach

The young crowd comes for surfing, swimming and partying; lifeguards during summer; parking and facilities; site of the U.S. Open Sandcastle Competition in July.

South Beach

Dogs get to roam free here, that's it.

Border Field State Beach

Just north of the Mexican border; horse riding and hiking; parking, fire rings and facilities.

Author's Tip

South Beach, Border Field State Beach and, often, Imperial Beach are frequent unhappy recipients of Tijuana's raw sewage. Do not ignore the posted signs warning of contamination. Why do you think dogs and horses are allowed free reign at these spots?

UPTOWN
SAN DIEGO

Bazaar del Mundo, now a shopper's paradise, was once Governor Pio Pico's boyhood home.

Uptown is the cultural and historical throw-everything-into-the-soup-kettle where you'll easily pick up the flavors of old Spain, traditional Italy and nouvelle California, along with some subtle aphrodisiacs and bits of moldy spice. The area is loosely grouped by locals as the commercial and residential communities that meander north of the downtown business district and

Balboa Park, up to Mission Valley and Old Town. This encompasses a continual eye-popping double-take: the most prestigious addresses in the city countered by ordinary-folk enclaves; the medical center balanced alongside the gay heart; the red-light strip juxtaposed against antique row; low-key shopping malls butting the high-action stadium.

San Diego began atop Presidio Hill in 1769, almost a century before Alonzo Horton dreamed up his New Town. It was here that the illustrious Padre Junipero Serra established California's very first mission, San Diego de Alcala—the ultimate room-with-a-view. The mission was a bust. Aside from the fact that the local Kumeyaay tribe (called "San Dieguenos" by the Spaniards) hated the entire concept of Christianity and Spanish customs (surprise, surprise), the mission site did not provide enough water and—as the population increased—the grub was pretty scarce as well. In 1774 the mission was moved to its present site, six miles east along the fertile riverbed—now full of malls, B-list hotels and ever-changing restaurant marquis. Infuriated by even more intrusion into their lands, those dastardly Kumeyaay burnt the mission to the ground and had a good old time destroying the religious objects and turning Padre Luis Jayme into dead meat. A last hurrah because, of course, in the end—they lost.

The former site, having already been proclaimed a Royal Presidio, was eventually inhabited by worn-down Native Americans, impoverished Mexicans, mixed-blood mestizos and Spanish soldiers—until 1821, year of the Mexican Revolution. Mexico's independence from Spain also meant that San Diego was now under Mexican rule, provoking a number of changes over the next couple of decades—land titles were snatched from the missions, and aristocrats with big pesos scooped up choice parcels for their ranchos. It was fiesta time.

After the revolution, pioneers began their scoot from the Presidio to the rectangular plaza below. Then came 1846 and another war—this one between Mexico and the United States. No surprise as to how that turned out. By 1848, Mexico had surrendered and the U.S. flag was flying high. Two years later, Old Town was the official center of the officially incorporated city of San Diego. In 1968, the site was proclaimed a state historic park.

Uptown: Things to See and Do

Take Fifth Avenue through **Bankers Hill** and view the exquisite Victorian homes from the late 1800s as well as some masterful Irving Gill designs. The residences are situated roughly between First and Fifth avenues. Though families with both old- and new-money are deposited within the district, a number of the homes have been converted into medical offices—giving Bankers Hill the un-gentile nickname "Pill Hill."

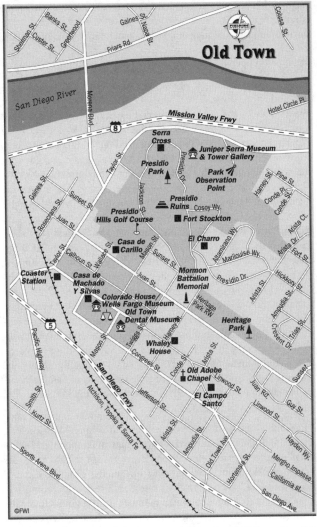

Pill Hill merges into **Hillcrest**, settled in the 1920's as San Diego's first suburb and—seventy years later—is the distinctive heart of the city's gay and lesbian scene. Cafes, restaurants, book shops, cinemas, bars and specialty shops branch out in all directions from the intersection of Fifth and University avenues. Turning east on University Avenue, you'll hit the relatively new Uptown redevelopment district. Once home to our favorite 1950s Sears Roebuck store, the recession of the 1980s signaled its sad closing. The city jumped in and bought the land for a new central library but couldn't pull it off. Subsequently developers took over and by 1989 had built everything *but* a library (as of this writing, a Quigley-designed central library is on the drawing board for *downtown* San Diego). The huge neighborhood-within-a-neighborhood encompasses various architectural themes—ranging from Mission-style to mining-town with Jerde-fantasy thrown in—and consists of condos, apartments, restaurants and shops.

Continue along University to **Park Boulevard**, riddled with retro shops, another cafe or two, the wonderful 1920s Park Theatre and, next door, The Flame—a circa 1950s, very nineties, mostly-lesbian and gay bar. Proceeding north on Park, within a short distance you'll hit **El Cajon Boulevard**. Hang a right for a gander at San Diego's "infamous" red-light district. Or keep going several more blocks to **Adams Avenue**—again, a right turn will cruise you through a stream of older suburbs such as Normal Heights and Kensington, passing along Antique Row and the Kensington Theatre—our favorite "art-film" cinema. At this point, just above **Mission Valley**, you are practically breathing into **Mission San Diego de Alcala** and **Jack Murphy Stadium** (home to San Diego's Chargers and Padres). A short ways east is **San Diego State University**, our widely reputed "party campus." Returning westward through Mission Valley and along the San Diego River, the old Kumeyaay stomping grounds—first turned into cattle fields by the Mexicans, are now completely trampled by confusing off-ramps and on-ramps, hotels and motels, a mini-convention site, singles bars and huge shopping malls. If its any comfort to the Kumeyaay in spirit, the place is always flooding unmercifully after even a minor rain. Positioned elegantly above the chaos is the Spanish Renaissance-style **University of San Diego**, an independent Catholic university well-known for its law school and weekend-wedding locale.

Perched above a wild canyon on the south side of Mission Valley (from Hillcrest, just north of Washington Avenue), is **Mission Hills**, another prestigious section dating from the early days. Its grand mansions and rolling lawns border the old Presidio and slope into Old Town. The city's finest architects—including Irving Gill—were hired to design a plethora of styles including Mission Revival, Spanish Colonial, Moorish, Italian Renaissance, Craftsman, Victorian and Oriental. The best streets are Fort Stockton Drive and Sunset Boulevard. Two of San Diego's largest hospitals sit in this area (one is the UCSD Medical Center) as does another smattering of shops and cafes. This is also the neighborhood where Betty Broderick blasted her ex and his bride. Be sure to pay a visit to **Mission Hills Nursery**, *1525 Fort Stockton Drive*, opened in 1910 by Kate Sessions, Balboa Park's first gardener.

An alternate or additional route from downtown is along **India Street**. You'll travel through **Little Italy** where, just like in the old country, the community is tightly knit and centered around the church (and pizza parlor). A short spurt of rundown dwellings, freeway overpass and dubious bars leads to **El Indio**, a legendary

half-century-or-so-old Mexican restaurant. The next block houses the India Street Art Colony which no longer has any of the
artists and Theatre it began with—just one of the first hip cafes,
an English pub and a few good ethnic restaurants. **Gelato Vero**
(the hip cafe), your one-stop cappuccino and gelato fix, marks
the intersection of India Street and Washington Avenue. Going
east, up the steep hill, leads to Hillcrest and Uptown; continuing
north on India will land you in Old Town.

Many visitors come to San Diego and never go anywhere *but*
Old Town—its full of history, bring-stuff-back-home shops, and
fiesta ambiance—and with trolley and train stops and plentiful
parking. The designated Old Town Historic Park is on 13 acres
(cars are banned) bounded by Juan, Congress, Wallace and
Twiggs streets with other historical landmarks nearby. Although
a fire destroyed many of the buildings back in 1872, eight of the
original adobes were spared and many others were either restored or reconstructed. Equal in popularity to the old sites (or
maybe more so) is the 1970s **Bazaar del Mundo**, a superbly colorful shopping feast that was formerly Governor Pio Pico's boyhood home. The **Visitor Center** is in the Robinson-Rose House,
4002 Wallace Street, on the west side of the plaza. Pick up maps
for a self-guided tour or, show up at 2 p.m. any day and join a
guided exploration of the area. Don't leave Old Town without
checking out **Heritage Park**, across Juan Street. The beautiful
Victorians—now harboring restaurants, offices and shops—were
moved from other parts of the city by preservationists just one
step ahead of the wrecking ball.

Fun for Free
Mission Valley

University of San Diego ★★★

Linda Vista Road, Alcala Park, north side of Mission Valley, 92110,
☎ *(619) 260-4681.*
Originally founded as the San Diego College for Women in 1949,
USD was designed in the Spanish Renaissance style of its namesake,
the University of Alcala de Henares in Spain. Current enrollment at
this independent Catholic university is around the 6300-mark, and
most students are attracted by the well-reputed schools of Law,
Pacific Relations and Nursing. The 180-acre campus is glorious with
get-down-and-pray views springing out from green lawns and landmark buildings. Take special note of the Founder's Chapel with its
gold-leaf details, imported Italian marble and mesmerizing stained-
glass windows.

San Diego

San Diego State University ★★★

*Interstate 8 and College Avenue, San Diego, at the eastern edge of the
city, beyond Mission Valley,* ☎ *(619) 594-5204.*
SDSU is trying hard to change its well-touted image as a major party
school—but no one believes otherwise. The campus began in 1897 as
the San Diego Normal School, became part of the state college system

in 1960, then graduated to university status in 1971. Situated on 283 acres, SDSU buildings comprise more than 4.5-million square feet. It makes for an interesting "wish-I-was-back-in-college" stroll. The art gallery usually has an interesting student or faculty exhibition on (while the engineering department might hosting a mass murder!).

Historical Sites

Old Town

Alvarado House   ★★

Mason and Calhoun streets, Old Town.
Hours open: 10 a.m.–5 p.m.
The Alvarado House is a re-do of one of Old Town's original adobes, built 1824-30. Governor Pio Pico's sister, Tomasa, once lived here. How can you pass it up?

Old Town's blacksmith and stable began operation in the 1860s.

Black Hawk Smithy & Stable   ★★

Mason and Juan Streets, Old Town.
Hours open: 10 a.m.–2 p.m.
Closed: Mon., Tue., Thur., Fri., Sun.
Just a clop away from Seeley Stables and Casa de Bandini, the stable began operation during the 1860s. Come at 2 p.m. to view the restored smithy and vintage blacksmithing techniques.

Casa de Bandini   ★★★

1660 Calhoun Street, Old Town, ☎ *(619) 297-8211.*
Hours open: 11 a.m.–9:30 p.m.
The main floor dining room, color-filled gardens and bubbling fountains are now a popular restaurant, but this 1829 Spanish hacienda was once the home of Old Town's richest man (Peruvian Juan Ban-

dini), and the community's social center. Later, in 1869, a second story was added and the hacienda became the Cosmopolitan Hotel, a traveler's rest stop.

Heritage Park ★★★★

2455 Heritage Park Row, Old Town, ☎ *(619) 565-3600.*
Hours open: 9:30 a.m.–Sunset
Saved from the wrecking ball by SOHO (Save Our Heritage Organization), these seven endangered Victorians—including a synagogue—were relocated and restored on a 7.8-acre park across from Old Town. The colorful grand dames include a bed and breakfast inn, shops and businesses.

Johnson House ★★

Mason and Calhoun streets, Old Town.
Hours open: 10 a.m.–5 p.m.
Built around 1869, the most interesting thing about this reconstructed frame dwelling is the featured archeological displays from Old Town digs.

Mexican dance troupes perform frequently at Old Town.

La Casa de Estudillo ★★★

4001 Mason Street, Old Town, ☎ *(619) 220-5426.*
Hours open: 10 a.m.–5 p.m.
Jose Maria Estudillo, commander of the Presidio, naturally ended up with the biggest and most elaborate home. Originally built in 1827, the two-story adobe has undergone restoration a couple of times and is now furnished with period furnishings and relics. Admission for ages six-17, $1. Admission includes entry to the Seeley Stables next door. General Admission: $2.

Mason Street School ★★

Mason Street and San Diego Avenue, Old Town, ☎ *(619) 297-1183.*
Hours open: 10 a.m.–5 p.m.
It's the one-room schoolhouse first built in 1865, shifted to another site, returned and restored. It will impress the kids no end to see what school COULD be like.

Mormon Battalion Visitors Center ★★★

2510 Juan Street, Old Town, ☎ *(619) 298-3317.*
Hours open: 9 a.m.–9 p.m.

UPTOWN SAN DIEGO

Mormon volunteers educate visitors on the history of the 500-troop Mormon regiment who, in 1846-47, made America's longest infantry march—a trek from Fort Leavenworth, Texas to San Diego. The tour includes a short film and informative exhibits.

Robinson-Rose House   ★★★

4002 Wallace Street, Old Town, ☎ *(619) 220-5422.*
Now home of the Visitor Center, in 1853 this two-story adobe was old San Diego's commercial heart with law and railroad offices as well as the first newspaper press. A few rooms have been gussied up with period furnishings and photo murals. Painstaking scale models depict 1870s Old Town.

San Diego Union Museum   ★★★

2626 San Diego Avenue, Old Town.
Hours open: 10 a.m.–5 p.m.
San Diego's first newspaper office was a pre-fab wood-frame house, manufactured in Maine and shipped around Cape horn in 1851. The first edition of the now defunct San Diego Union popped off the presses here in 1868. The building has been restored and furnished with period pieces.

Seeley Stables   ★★★

2648 Calhoun Street, Old Town, ☎ *(619) 220-5427.*
Hours open: 10 a.m.–5 p.m.
San Diego's stagecoach stop served the Seeley and Wright Stage Line from 1867 until the turn-of-the-century, when the railroad pretty much knocked it out of the running. A collection of horse-drawn vehicles, Western gear and Native American artifacts is on display. Admission for ages six-17, $1. Admission includes entry to La Casa de Estudillo. General Admission: $2.

Whaley House   ★★★★★

2482 San Diego Avenue, Old Town, ☎ *(619) 298-2482.*
Hours open: 10 a.m.–5 p.m.
Thomas Whaley, original owner of this 1856 two-story brick mansion, was pillar of the community and descendant of Boston Tea Party attendees. Whoopee—we're much more impressed with the four ghosts said to inhabit the house. The home, completely restored and furnished with authentic pieces, has been a theater and the County Courthouse. Check out the spinet piano—it was used in *Gone with the Wind*. Admission for seniors, $3; ages 5-18, $2; under five, free. General Admission: $4.

Old Town's six blocks contain several buildings with original or restored Spanish architecture.

San Diego

Old Town State Historic Park ★★★★★

San Diego Avenue and Twiggs Street, San Diego, Near Interstate 5 and Interstate 8 convergence, ☎ (619) 220-5422.
Hours open: 10 a.m.–5 p.m.

Presidio Hill was actually San Diego's first settlement but, about the time Mexico took rule, the land below became the new center. Designated a state historic park in 1968, Old Town's six "official" blocks are bounded by Wallace, Juan, Twiggs and Congress streets—all designated as pedestrian zones only so you can kick back on benches, tie the kids shoelaces, and stagger off the margaritas without worry. Eight original adobes remain after a devasting fire in 1872, though many other buildings were restored or rebuilt. Shops and restaurants are open into the evening. Call in at the visitor center, located in the Robinson-Rose House *(4002 Wallace Street)* for maps, brochures and to join the free walking tours at 2 p.m. daily.

Museums and Exhibits

Mission Valley

Mission San Diego de Alcala ★★★

10818 San Diego Mission Road, Mission Valley, ☎ (619) 281-8449.
Hours open: 9 a.m.–5 p.m.

Established in 1769 as the first of Padre Junipero Serra's empire of 21 missions, in 1774 the mission was moved from its original Presidio Park location to its present site in the middle of condo-mania. The museum, named for Padre Luis Jayme who was offed by the unhappy

Kumeyaays, displays early-mission relics. The simple wooden chapel still holds mass each day at 5:30 p.m. Admission to the church is free. Seniors and students, $1; under 12, 50 cents. General admission, $2. General Admission: $2.

Old Town

Junipero Serra Museum   ★★★
2727 Presidio Drive, Old Town, ☎ *(619) 297-3258.*
Hours open: 10 a.m.–4:30 p.m.
Special Hours: Sun.; noon-4:30 p.m. Closed: Mon.
Local philanthropist George Marston donated this mission-style museum to the city in 1929. It's close-to-authentic styling and site make it the perfect place to view exhibits about San Diego's Spanish colonial and Mexican eras. Don't miss a trek to the tower with its dynamite views of Mission Bay, Mission Valley and the blue Pacific. Admission for ages 12 and under is free. General Admission: $4.

Wells Fargo History Museum   ★★
Near Mason Street School, Old Town.
Hours open: 10 a.m.–5 p.m.
Now occupying the 1851 Colorado House Hotel, exhibits include a concord stagecoach and various relics, documents and artifacts.

Parks and Gardens

Old Town

Presidio Park   ★★★★
Presidio Drive, Above Old Town.
Hours open: Dawn–Dusk.
This was the original site of California's first mission, later the Royal Presidio and, until the 1820s, San Diego's only settlement. Surrounded by Mission Hills, the park shelters rolling green lawns that locals love to use for grass skiing, Frisbee games and dreaming. Inspiration Point, a somewhat uninspiring climb for those out-of-shape, offers astounding county views and is a popular site for weddings. Junipero Serra Museum is also housed on the grounds.

Sports/Recreation

Mission Valley

San Diego Jack Murphy Stadium   ★★★★★
9449 Friars Road, Mission Valley, Eastern edge of Mission Valley,
☎ *(619) 525-8282.*
The stadium, just a prayer away from Mission San Diego de Alcala, is home to both the Padres and the Chargers, and the locale for San Diego State's Aztec's home games. The Stones play here too.

San Diego

San Diego Chargers
Jack Murphy Stadium, San Diego, ☎ *(619) 280-2121.*
The Chargers kick off August through December—unless, of course, they play the Super Bowl. The Chargers Express bus will transport fans from various locations two hours before game time. Cost is $6 round trip. General Admission: $23-51.

San Diego Padres
Jack Murphy Stadium, San Diego, ☎ *(619) 283-4494.*

No matter what the status of baseball, or the team's reputation, our Padres have a devoted following. The Padres bus transports fans from several city sites two hours prior to game time. General Admission: $7-16.

San Diego State Aztecs Basketball

Peterson Gym, San Diego State University campus, ☎ *(619) 283-7378.*
San Diego is devoid of a pro basketball team so the Aztecs garner extra attention. They compete in the Western Athletic Conference and play December through March. General Admission: $7.

San Diego State Aztecs Football

Jack Murphy Stadium, San Diego, ☎ *(619) 283-7378.*
The Aztecs compete in the Western Athletic Conference (with an especially exciting showoff with Brigham Young University), and play home games at San Diego Jack Murphy Stadium—site of the post-season Plymouth Holiday Bowl.

Theme/Amusement Parks

Mission Valley

Virtual World

7510 Hazard Center Drive, Mission Valley, In the Hazard Center, Mission Valley, ☎ *(619) 294-9200.*
Hours open: 11 a.m.–11 p.m.
Choose your game and your vehicle. You can pilot a four-story-tall mechanical tank in "Battle Trek" or a hovercraft mining car in "Red Planet." Either experience accommodates up to eight people—each with an individual cockpit. The half-hour thrill includes a briefing phase, information about the planet you're going to and a mission review with printout ("take home the net destruction of your friends"). Virtual World opens at 10 a.m. on Fridays through Sundays and stays open until 1 a.m. on Fridays and Saturdays. Call ahead for reservations. General Admission: $8-10.

FIELDING'S FAVORITE THINGS TO DO IN UPTOWN

Eat pizza with extra high-fat cheese at **Filippi's***, San Diego's first pizzeria, dating from the late 1940s.*

Get all dressed up and catch the view from atop **Mister A's Restaurant** *(Lindbergh-bound jets whiz past the 12th-story windows).*

Watch any movie at all in the **Guild***,* **Park** *or* **Kensington** *cinemas.*

Butt in line at **El Indio** *for the famous salsa and chips, then steal someone's indoor or outdoor table while they're still waiting at the counter.*

Select an assortment of Karen Krasne's killer concoctions at **Extraordinary Desserts** *and devour them all at one sitting.*

Go for middle-of-the-night Chinese food and experience an amazing MSG rush at **Jimmy Wong's Golden Dragon***—former haunt of Marilyn Monroe and Mickey Rooney.*

Climb to the top of Presidio Hill and pretend it is a thousand years before Junipero Serra ever set foot there.

FIELDING'S FAVORITE HISTORIC UPTOWN BUILDINGS

2055 Sunset Boulevard (1921)

2055 Sunset Boulevard, Mission Hills.

A superb Italianate mansion with wide lay-down-and-dream lawns. It's so hard to believe the place is a private residence that signs have been posted to keep away those who are certain they've stumbled upon another Getty Museum.

Guild Theatre (1912)

3827 Fifth Avenue, Hillcrest.

Originally known as the Hillcrest Theatre, the Guild is one of the city's few holdouts from plex-o-mania. The Mission-style facade in the 1920s was the last discernible change. The balcony is horribly uncomfortable but the nostalgia factor is worth the pain.

Wednesday Club (1913)

540 Ivy Lane, Hillcrest.

A still-operating women's club designed by Hazel Waterman who worked with Irving Gill. Hazel's Mission-style structure is very similar to Gill's La Jolla Women's Club, built approximately the same time.

Quince Street Bridge (1905)

Quince Street, between Third and Fourth avenues, Hillcrest.

Spared from demise in the 1980s, the 236-foot-long wood-trestle bridge has been fixed up and reopened to joggers and strollers who high-five each other as they pass above the deep canyon.

Long-Waterman House (1889)

2408 First Avenue, Hillcrest.

This Queen Anne Victorian jumps at you with its gables, towers, dormer and bay windows and detailed porch. Built for lumberman John Long and later purchased by California Governor Robert Waterman, the residence was a turn-of-the-century social mecca.

Park Theatre (1926)

3812 Park Boulevard, Hillcrest.

San Diego's premiere example of Egyptian Revival architecture in another "art" film house. Once known as the Bush Egyptian Theatre.

FIELDING'S FAVORITE HISTORIC UPTOWN BUILDINGS

Mission San Diego de Alcala (1769)

Nearly wasted by the Kumeyaay in 1775 and restored in 1931, the austere mission chapel still holds mass every day at 5:30 p.m.

Founder's Chapel, University of San Diego (1949)

Linda Vista Road, Alcala Park.

Originally the San Diego College for Women, Founder's Chapel is housed within the school's first building. It is a masterwork of decoration with stained-glass windows, gold leaf gilding, an Italian Botticino marble altar, and a marble floor. Don't visit on the weekends unless you want to be part of a wedding.

Author's Tip

Fans of architect-great Irving Gill can get a list of his local buildings from the San Diego Historical Society at the Museum of San Diego History, Balboa Park (☎ (619) 232-6203).

Uptown: For Kids

The little darlings are probably not going to cherish antique and vintage shopping, cafe and bar hopping or the gay and lesbian scene. (Do you really want to deal with questions like "what are those two boys doing with their tongues, mommy?" More money in the psychotherapy pot.) And they could no doubt care less about art films and architecture. **Old Town**, however, should hold their interest. The atmosphere is so festive they won't even realize you've duped them into a historical tour. Stuff their faces with greasy taquitos or chips, put sombreros on their little heads and plant them in front of some mariachi musicians—they won't know what hit them. Another option is to trek or drive up **Presidio Hill**—the hillsides are just made for rolling and running off energy. And a sporting event over at **San Diego Jack Murphy Stadium** should interest at least some children—especially if they get foot-long hot dogs and sodas out of the deal.

Hillcrest

Cityfest Street Fair   ★★★

Fifth Avenue, between University Avenue and Ivy Lane, Hillcrest, Hillcrest, ☎ (619) 299-3330.

For one day in mid-August Hillcrest's main drag becomes a street fair with lots of arts and crafts booths, the usual commercial pitches, heaps of interesting food, a beer garden and a stage with live entertainment.

Mission Valley

Robert Burns Supper and Festivities ★★

Town and Country Hotel, Mission Valley, ☎ *(619) 291-7131.*
Each February Scottish patriots and Robert Burns' fans get together
for a traditional Scottish dinner to honor the esteemed poet.

Old Town

Spring Bonnet Competition ★★

Old Town Esplanade, Old Town, ☎ *(619) 291-5700.*
Spring bonnets are judged and promenaded as amateurs and pros
compete for trophies and prizes in adult and child categories.

San Diego

Dixieland Jazz Festival ★★★★

500 Hotel Circle North, San Diego, In the Town and Country Hotel,
☎ *(619) 291-7131.*
For more than fifteen years this festival has entertained Dixieland lovers with more than 30 foot-stomping, finger-banging bands from
around the U.S. and Canada.

Festival of the Bells ★★★

*Mission San Diego de Alcala, San Diego, East side of Mission Valley, near
the stadium,* ☎ *(619) 281-8449.*
The Festival of the Bells, on a weekend in mid-July, signals the founding of California's first mission with live entertainment, ethnic food
booths and children's activities.

Fiesta Cinco de Mayo Festival ★★★

Old Town, San Diego, ☎ *(619) 296-3161.*
This Mexican celebration, held every year on the Fifth of May, is a
reason to party all over the city—not to mention the other side of the
border. Old Town and Bazaar del Mundo do it well with gala festivities, historic re-enactments, lots of folkloric music and dance and
plenty of food and drink. Margaritas are de riguer for all.

Plymouth Holiday Bowl ★★★★★

Jack Murphy Stadium, San Diego, ☎ *(619) 283-5808.*
San Diego's post-season college football classic is one of the hottest
tickets in town. Now known as the Plymouth Holiday Bowl, the
game pits the Western Athletic Conference champion against a team
from the new Big 12.

Tours

Old Town does it for the guided tour scene—choose from
trolley, self-guided or park-led. San Diego State University and
University of San Diego give occasional tours, especially for in-
coming students—if interested, put on your beanie and bobby
sox and try to blend in.

Old Town

Old Town Walking Tour ★★★

4002 Wallace Street, Old Town, ☎ *(619) 220-5422.*
Show up at the Visitor Center at Robinson-Rose House any day at 2
p.m. and join a free walking tour of Old Town. Groups are led by
Park Department-trained guides, and focus—of course—is on history
and architecture.

San Diego

Old Town Trolley Tours ★★★★

San Diego, ☎ *(619) 298-8687.*
This inexpensive trackless trolley tour is a great way to get around not
just Old Town but Balboa Park, Horton Plaza, the Gaslamp Quarter,
the Embarcadero, Seaport Village and Coronado. Get on or off as
often as you like for just one fare, or don't make a move— stay on
board and be treated to a two-hour narrated spiel while doing the
complete circuit. Catch the trolley every 30 minutes, daily, 9 a.m.–
5:30 p.m. in summer; until 4 p.m. in winter. The trolley is on holiday
Thanksgiving, Christmas, and New Year's days. Fare for ages under
12 is $8. The same company is now offering three-hour trolley
tours—departing Old Town—that focus on the Navy's past, present
and future. Tours depart at 9:15 a.m. daily. Reservations are necessary. Phone (800) NAVY TOUR. (Yes, it's too many numbers but the
last one doesn't count.) General Admission: $20.

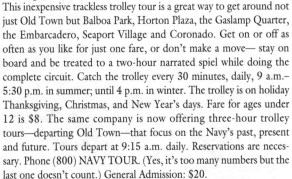

Events

Gay and civic pride, Mexican holidays and sports are on the
agenda. Occasionally one of the art-film cinemas will host a
mini-festival (check *The Reader* for listings). Often, large rock
concerts (like the Rolling Stones) are held at San Diego Jack
Murphy Stadium.

Author's Tip

*The **Learning Annex** sponsors a broad range of low-cost seminars year-
round. Participants include Deepak Chopra and other "names," as well as
ordinary folk teaching about angel awareness, import businesses and
martial arts. Pick up a copy of the current catalog in local cafes or book
shops, or plan ahead (many events are sellouts) and order from: **The
Learning Annex**, 344 Kalmia Street, San Diego 92101 (☎ (619) 544-9700).*

Uptown: Music, Dance and Theater

A couple of small theaters—both traditional and experimental—maintain spaces in Old Town and Uptown, and performances of all types are held on the university campuses. Audience-participation murder-mystery dinner theaters take place most weekends at various restaurants and seem to be the current rage—just like real murders. Old Town usually has something cooking—marimba bands, flamenco dancers, ballet folklorico, strolling guitarists.

"This one's contemporary: 'Recapturing an ecstatic vision in the young composer's mind, brought on by a carbohydrate binge.'"

Drawing by Fisher; ©1995 The New Yorker Magazine, Inc.

Theater
Old Town

Theatre in Old Town ★★★★

4040 Twiggs Street, Old Town State Historic Park, ☎ *(619) 688-2494.*
Professional theater in the heart of Old Town. Specialties are musicals—some cute and rollicking, some smarmy and bitchy. The small
space also hosts occasional college works and Old-California theme-
type vignettes. Sometimes there are some big surprises—like the summer Lily Tomlin staged her one-woman show here. The performance
schedule expands during summer months.

FIELDING'S CAN'T-LIVE-WITHOUT-AN-ART-FILM-EVEN-ONE-MORE-DAY SURVIVAL GUIDE

*San Diego is not the art-film haven of the world. Film buffs are most apt
to find mega-plex cinemas with mega-budget flicks produced solely for
double-digit IQs or single-digit age groups. But don't despair. Uptown
has several choices for the Cannes/Telluride/Tashkent set.*

Garden Cabaret
4040 Goldfinch Street, Mission Hills; ☎ *(619) 295-4221.*

Guild Theatre
3827 Fifth Avenue, Hillcrest; ☎ *(619) 295-2000.*

Hillcrest Cinemas
3965 Fifth Avenue, Hillcrest; ☎ *(619) 299-2100.*

Ken
4061 Adams Avenue, Kensington; ☎ *(619) 283-5909.*

Park Theatre
3812 Park Boulevard, Hillcrest; ☎ *(619) 294-9264.*

San Diego

Camino Theater ★★★

Linda Vista Road, Alcala Park, on University of San Diego campus,
☎ *(619) 260-4239.*
Student productions are held regularly on campus and many are quite
good. The English Department's affiliation with the Old Globe Theatre draws budding theater students from across the country.

Don Powell Theatre and Experimental Theatre ★★★

Interstate 8 and College Avenue, San Diego State University,
☎ *(619) 594-6947.*
The San Diego State University Drama Department presents an eclectic range of student productions including experimental works and
theater geared to young audiences.

Murder Mystery Dinner Theatre ★★★

*7450 Hazard Center Drive, Mission Valley, San Diego, In the Red Lion
Hotel,* ☎ *(619) 277-4800.*
THIS show claims to be the most original murder mystery dinner the-
ater, and is also interactive with dinner kicked into the act. "Scrooge's
Worst Night??", a seasonal favorite, sees Scrooge framed for murder.
Bah, humbug, bang, bang. Performances are Friday and Saturday
nights.

Open-air Amphitheater   ★★★★

San Diego State University, San Diego, Interstate 8 and College Avenue, 92182, ☎ *(619) 594-6947.*

The University amphitheater buzzes with big-name reggae, rock, and rythmn and blues. The open air inspires everyone to groove, skank and twist along with the sounds. If you're not up to the action, it's best to steer clear.

San Diego Sports Arena

3500 Sports Arena Boulevard, San Diego, 92110, ☎ *(619) 225-9813.*

The Sports Arena, in the direction of Point Loma, is San Diego's only major venue for year-round, entertainment of all kinds including family-oriented shows, big-name concerts and not-to-be-missed sports events. From Barnum and Bailey to the Violent Femmes—it all happens here. Come early (very early) on weekends to browse the huge swap meet on one side of the parking lot.

Uptown: Nightlife

It's a strange mix. Professional and semiprofessional singles hang out at bars and meat markets around Mission Valley and Hotel Circle while the gay and lesbian crowd frequent bars and meat markets around Hillcrest and Uptown. The folk, alternative and gimme-a-burger-beer-and-game-of-pool groups gather at clubs, cafes and bars along Adams Avenue and "the lesser-known streets." All the college-oriented night trappings loom as you get closer to San Diego State University. Tourists like to douse themselves with margaritas and music in Old Town.

Aren't-we-special interest groups have their own scene. Almost every cafe has free rags slanted toward earth lovers, self abusers, spirit channelers, nouveau hippies, latte addicts and the clean and sober.

Hillcrest

Bourbon Street   ★★

4612 Park Boulevard, Hillcrest, ☎ *(619) 291-0173.*

Okay, okay, it's a gay bar but it's low-key and a relaxing spot to enjoy a drink along with some good jazz and contemporary piano bar entertainment. Most performances run 9 p.m.–midnight.

Tidbits   ★★★

3838 Fifth Avenue, Hillcrest, ☎ *(619) 543-0300.*
Closed: Mon., Tue., Sun.

Kitschy, bitchy cabaret featuring full-on revues, follies, drag shows, production numbers, comedy acts and celebrity look-a-likes (Oh God, NOT Barbra again!). Showtimes are Wednesdays and Thursdays at 9:30 p.m.; Fridays and Saturdays at 9:30 and 11:30 p.m.

Mission Valley

Club Max ★★

7450 Hazard Center Drive, in the Red Lion Hotel, Mission Valley, ☎ *(619) 297-5466.*

The requisite Club Max attached to a business-oriented hotel. DJ dance music is on Thursdays through Saturdays at 9 p.m. and the karaoke mike is turned on every Wednesday at 6 p.m.

Coach House San Diego ★★★★

10475 San Diego Mission Road, Mission Valley, ☎ *(619) 563-0060.*

The diverse line-up of acts runs from Brazil Fest and comedy nights to the Electric Light Orchestra, Commander Cody and Bronski Beat. Good news for hopeful musicians—the Coach House is looking for new bands (pack your promo CD or tape in your purse or pocket). For tickets and dinner reservations, call ☎ *(619) 297-4936.*

El Tecolote ★★★

6110 Friars Road, Mission Valley, ☎ *(619) 295-2087.*

The restaurant serves the usual Mexican plates but the Cantina is the real reason to come—an extra-generous Happy Hour with lots of make-a-meal freebies, a lot of lively barmongers and non-stop sports action on the satellite television (including championship boxing matches with no cover charge).

Gourmet Lounge ★★★

500 Hotel Circle No., in the Town & Country Hotel, Mission Valley, ☎ *(619) 291-7131.*

Finally—listening and dancing the way it used to be. Hear yourself think to contemporary piano tunes and hits from the 1930s onward.

Intermezzo Lounge ★★

1433 Camino del Rio South, in the Radisson Hotel, Mission Valley, ☎ *(619) 260-0111.*

It's better than sitting alone in your hotel room. Live entertainment is in the soft and mellow category though sometimes it wends its way to risky '50s through '80s sounds. The open mike event is on Thursdays 7:30-9 p.m.

Kelly's Restaurant and Irish Pub ★★

284 Hotel Circle North, Mission Valley, ☎ *(619) 291-7131.*

Easy listening piano sounds are performed nightly from early evening through 1 a.m. Nice choice for a quiet pint and friendly conversation.

Mister O's Nightclub ★★★

1299 Camino del Rio South, Mission Valley, ☎ *(619) 299-3544.*

Live salsa bands and a DJ on Fridays, and stand-up comedy on Tuesdays beckon hot singles who need a laugh. Doors open at 9 p.m.

Pal Joeys ★★

5147 Waring Road, Mission Valley, Allied Gardens, east edge of Mission Valley, ☎ *(619) 286-7873.*

Weekend blues, jazz, rock and swing in a friendly neighborhood club. It's a bit out of the area but not too far from Jack Murphy Stadium—perfect for those who want to drown game sorrows in booze and music.

Riverfront   ★★

6608 Mission Gorge Road, Mission Valley, ☎ (619) 285-5010.
Near Jack Murphy Stadium, and behind Carls Jr., there is an honest-to-goodness interesting nightclub. Can you possibly snub your nose at on-stage acts named "Scrotum Pole?" As might be expected, the music leans to alternative. Live entertainment is on Wednesday through Saturday nights.

Normal Heights

Javabar Garden Cafe   ★★

3562 Adams Avenue, Normal Heights, ☎ (619) 281-6729.
A mellow folksy environment for mellow folksy entertainment with some Latin, blues and jazz thrown in from time to time. Feel a little Peter, Paul and Mary in your soul? Show up for the open mike session on Thursday nights.

Rosie O'Grady's   ★★★

3402 Adams Avenue, Normal Heights, ☎ (619) 284-7666.
Pubby clubby mix of live entertainment—rock and roll, down-home blues, vocals and karaoke. Performances begin at 9 p.m.

Old Town

O'Hungry's   ★★★

2457 San Diego Avenue, Old Town, ☎ (619) 298-0133.
Smack in the heart of Old Town, this place is usually packed with margarita and beer tourists. It can be a fun time and the live tunes are a mix of rock and roll, acoustic and country.

Romaine's Guadalajara   ★★

4105 Taylor Street, Old Town, ☎ (619) 295-5111.
On weekends the place pulses with live and DJ salsa dance music.

San Diego

Flame   ★★★★

3780 Park Boulevard, San Diego, Near University Avenue, Hillcrest, ☎ (619) 295-4163.
Hours open: 5 p.m.–2 a.m.
One of the favorite "alternative" clubs, leaning decidedly toward lesbians except for Tuesdays when "boys will be boys." The club also draws women who don't want to be hassled and sailor boys who love to hassle women. There are two bars (including a video bar) and a huge dance floor where couples, singles and groups groove to live bands blasting alternative, soul, progressive and country/western sounds. Prepare to be frisked or sized-up at the door. General Admission: $2-5.

Author's Tip

The 24-hour Ralph's (1030 University Avenue, Hillcrest) is a meet market within a meat market. This gigantic supermarket has grown into a bizarre social scene. Last I heard, Thursdays were the designated night for lesbian shoppers. No matter when you come, you're in for good free performance art and splendid drag shows nestled among a dazzling array of fruits and vegetables. The wee hours seem to draw the most interesting clientele.

Author's Tip

Unless you know (or don't care) what you're getting into, beware those unmarked doors in Hillcrest—the other side is most likely a "private" gay club or gym.

FIELDING'S UPTOWN CAFE SOCIETY OR, WAS THERE LIFE BEFORE STARBUCKS?

How did we ever exist? How did we ever awake? When will it all end? Cafes and portable carts have popped up *everywhere*—from the airport and train depot to practically every other door in town, though it's not quite as overwhelming as Washington State or Vancouver. Here are some suggestions for your caffeine fix or just-looking-cool stance. By the way, Hillcrest has two Starbucks within two blocks of each other—one at Fifth Avenue and Washington Avenue, another at Fifth Avenue and Robinson Avenue.

Cafe Beignet
3865 Fifth Avenue, Hillcrest.
Big Easy style; Creole espresso drinks; Zydeco music.

Chicago Coffee Co., Inc.
1080 University Avenue #H-101, Hillcrest.
Windy City style; four gourmet coffees daily; outside seating; home of "Milky Way" (espresso, hot chocolate, caramel and whipped cream).

Espresso Roma
406 University Avenue, Hillcrest.
Roma style; great lattes; hip atmosphere; upstairs, downstairs and outdoor seating.

Extraordinary Desserts
2929 Fifth Avenue, Hillcrest.
Forget the coffee, the desserts are to die for—Karen Krasne, owner and Le Cordon Bleu grad—concocts stunning edible works of art.

Quel Fromage
523 University Avenue, Hillcrest.
Hometown favorite, the first on the scene way back in 1978; superb iced cappuccino; people-watching patio; changing art exhibitions.

Twiggs Tea and Coffee Company
4590 Park Boulevard, Hillcrest.
Excellent espresso drinks; stylish decor; gallery and performance space with live entertainment.

FIELDING'S CAFE SURVIVAL GLOSSARY

Too intimidated to ask the difference between a cappuccino and a latte? A caffe mocha and a macchiato? Help has arrived. Add sugar, ground cinnamon and chocolate to taste–not too much, you'll look like a wuss.

amalfi–*single shot of espresso added to mineral water, flavored Italian syrup, cream and whipping cream.*

caffe mocha–*one-third each of espresso, frothed milk and hot chocolate.*

cappuccino–*one-third each of espresso, frothed milk and warmed milk.*

doppio–*a double hit of straight espresso.*

espresso–*the intense dark, thick extract resulting from hot water forced under pressure through one cup of tightly-packed coffee.*

espresso Americano–*a hit of espresso diluted with hot water so it looks like a "real" cup of coffee.*

latte–*one part espresso to three parts steamed milk.*

macchiato–*a hit of espresso with a dab of hot frothed milk.*

Uptown: Shopping

Mall-mania is centered in **Mission Valley**, along Friars Road, very convenient if you're staying around Hotel Circle. **Mission Valley Center**, dating back to the 1960s, marked the valley's transition from farmlands to a commercial district, and has the requisite range of malls. Nearby **Fashion Valley Center**, also a 1960s refugee, is a little classier with branches of Neiman Marcus and Nordstrom. **Hazard Center**, to the east, made its more gentrified appearance in 1990, rising upon the site of the old Hazard brickyard—department stores are absent but plenty of shops and eateries are located within the modern walls. Each of the complexes houses its very own ubiquitous cinema-plex and a recently opened AMC 20-plex. By Super Bowl time, the trolley should be ready to roll from downtown through Old Town, into Mission Valley and on to San Diego Jack Murphy Stadium.

You've probably already discovered that **Old Town** is a great spree. **Bazaar del Mundo**, in particular, is a trove of colorful shops and stalls where you can pick up ethnic clothing, books, folk art, home accessories, hand-woven textiles and other one-of-a-kinders. **Little Italy**, on India Street is the spot to grab tins of extra virgin olive oil, crusty loaves and straw-wrapped bottles of Chianti.

Drawing by S. Harris; © Cartoonists & Writers Syndicate

In **Hillcrest**, seek out Fifth Avenue, between Robinson and Washington, for books, records, punk wear, cool clothes, baubles and bangles, floral arrangements and decorator items. The **Uptown District**, as expected, is laden with more small shops. Goldfinch Street in **Mission Hills** offers additional artsy choices.

If nostalgia's your scene, pick an era—Victorian thru the '70s—and mosey over to San Diego's **Park Avenue**. A decent selection of shops will fix you up with elegant gowns, quirky duds and costume put-togethers, as well as some great bric-a-brac. **Adams Avenue** is lined with small antique and secondhand shops, moldy in appearance but ripe with bargains.

Uptown: Where to Stay

Mission Valley's **Hotel Circle**, along both sides of super-busy Interstate 8, is ringed with chain and B-list hotels, as well as big-namers like **Marriott**, **Hilton** and **Red Lion**—about 6000 rooms in all. The **Town and Country Hotel**, with its own convention center, is quite popular for smaller trade shows and seminars. Though the valley is busy and noisy, room rates are reasonable and its proximity to tourist sites makes it an attractive choice for many.

Old Town is another choice, with a few good motels and a classy B&B. Other Uptown options are primarily in the fleabag category. The sleazy motels along El Cajon Boulevard are mostly designated for guests who pay by the hour (you wouldn't want to stick around longer than that in any case).

Bed & Breakfasts

Old Town

Heritage Park Bed and Breakfast $95–$150   ★★★★

2470 Heritage Park Row, San Diego, 92110, In Heritage Park, across from Old Town, ☎ *(800) 995-2470, (619) 299-6832, FAX: (619) 299-9465.*

Single: $95–$150. Double: $95–$150.

History beds down with romance in this 1889 Queen-Anne mansion situated amongst the restored Victorians of Heritage Park. Eight rooms and one two-room suite ($225 per night) are decorated with antiques and might include four-poster or brass beds, a fainting couch and an early-American school desk. Two rooms have shared baths. Full breakfast and afternoon tea are included in the rates and in-room candlelight dinners can be arranged. The Turret Room is the most secluded and probably the sunniest guest accommodation. Rates are the same for one person or two—if you're in love with yourself, don't hesitate to come alone. 9 rooms. Credit Cards: A, MC, V.

Hotels

Mission Valley

Best Western Hanalei Hotel $100–$160   ★★★

2270 Hotel Circle North, San Diego, 92108, ☎ *(800) 882-0858, (619) 297-1101, FAX: (619) 297-6049.*

Single: $100–$120. Double: $100–$160.

The Hawaiian paradise theme in the middle of rushity-rush Mission Valley sort of works—the palms, landscaped pool, koi ponds, waterfalls and tiki torches are all properly placed. Choose from the high-rise surrounding tropical gardens, or a two-story building with poolside rooms. Since 1994 the exterior has been painted and all rooms refurbished with parrot-bright tropical prints and either new carpets or tile floors. Two restaurants, a lounge, access to adjacent golf course and free parking are more enticements. Amenities: Jacuzzi. 412 rooms. Credit Cards: A, CB, DC, D, MC, V.

Handlery Hotel and Resort $80–$150   ★★★

950 Hotel Circle North, San Diego, 92108, ☎ *(800) 676-6567, (619) 298-0511, FAX: (619) 298-9793.*

Single: $80. Double: $90–$150.

A good deal from the family-owned Handlery group. This conveniently located two-story hotel with exterior corridors offers exceptional activities and amenities at reasonable rates and is another good choice for family-toting conventioneers or active business travelers with limited expense accounts. The lobby has been recently refurbished but the guest rooms are still pretty ordinary—insignificant with the range of out-of-room experiences such as two swimming pools, water aerobics, a wading pool, spa, excercise room, paddle tennis and sports court, dining room, entertainment lounge and two coffee shops (one open 24 hours). Fees are charged for 27-hole golf course (course is closed for 1997), eight tennis courts (six lighted) and child care. Amenities: exercise room, Jacuzzi, sauna. 217 rooms. Credit Cards: A, CB, DC, D, MC, V.

Holiday Inn Hotel Circle $69–$99 ★★

595 Hotel Circle South, San Diego, 92108, ☎ (800) 433-2131, (619) 291-5720, FAX: (619) 297-7362.
Single: $69–$89. Double: $79–$99.
An exceptionally nice highrise with glistening lobby and well-appointed rooms plus enticements like a pool, spa, fitness center, video game room, restaurant, lounge and piano bar. Amenities: exercise room, Jacuzzi. 318 rooms. Credit Cards: A, CB, DC, D, MC, V.

Radisson Hotel San Diego $89–$149 ★★★

1433 Camino del Rio South, San Diego, 92108, near Jack Murphy Stadium, ☎ (800) 333-3333, (619) 260-0111, FAX: (619) 497-0813.
Single: $89–$139. Double: $99–$149.
Radisson's 14-story property is situated in the heart of Mission Valley, near Jack Murphy Stadium, shopping-mall hell, and within easy reach of major attractions and the business community. The contemporary property features large rooms with adequate furnishings, conference facilities, a restaurant, and lounge with live entertainment. A pool, Jacuzzi, and exercise room help work off the holiday or business stress. Some rooms offer private balconies, refrigerators, and private whirlpool baths. Airport and area transportation are also provided. Amenities: exercise room, Jacuzzi. 260 rooms. Credit Cards: A, CB, DC, D, MC, V.

Red Lion Hotel $89–$175 ★★★

7450 Hazard Center Drive, San Diego, 92108, ☎ (800) 547-8010, (619) 297-5466, FAX: (619) 297-5499.
Single: $89. Double: $89–$175.
The 11-story Red Lion is Mission Valley's most popular choice for business travelers who like to do their schmooze thing in the large lobby, dining room or lounge. Rooms are large, bright and restful and all have minibars. Data ports are available for those who can't live without, and luxury-level rooms feature upgraded amenities. Two pools, two lighted tennis courts, a spa, exercise room, dining room and lounge with entertainment make this a top area choice for those who need a little pleasure while tending to business. Amenities: tennis, exercise room, Jacuzzi, sauna, club floor. 300 rooms. Credit Cards: A, CB, DC, D, MC, V.

San Diego Marriott Mission Valley $109–$135 ★★★

8757 Rio San Diego Drive, San Diego, 92108, near Jack Murphy Stadium, ☎ (800) 228-9290, (619) 692-3800, FAX: (619) 296-0769.
Single: $109. Double: $109–$135.
The Kumeyaay tribe would be appalled to see this 15-story highrise sitting in the middle of the dried up San Diego riverbed. Business travelers like its proximity to nearby office complexes and tourists seem happy with the facilities, value and convenience to nearby attractions. Rooms are comfy and posh enough for the price and location, and extras include a disco, video game room, restaurant, lounge and disco. Airport transportation is provided and you can probably get dropped at one of the nearby malls, as well. Amenities: tennis, exercise room, Jacuzzi, sauna, business services. 350 rooms. Credit Cards: A, CB, DC, MC, V.

San Diego Mission Valley Hilton $109–$179   ★★★

901 Camino del Rio South, San Diego, 92108, ☎ (800) 733-2332, (619) 543-9000, FAX: (619) 296-9561.
Single: $109–$169. Double: $119–$179.

Good soundproofing helps disguise the fact that you're practically living on top of the freeway. The eight-story hotel with southwestern decor appeals to business travelers, though kids and small pets stay free. The lobby is a blessed respite from the world, but the lounge is even better. Rooms are comfortable and modern, two restaurants provide everything from snacks to steaks, golf and tennis are nearby, parking is free, and a free shuttle runs to the airport and shopping malls. Amenities: exercise room, Jacuzzi, sauna, business services. 350 rooms. Credit Cards: A, CB, DC, D, MC, V.

Town and Country Hotel $85–$150   ★★★★

500 Hotel Circle North, San Diego, 92108, ☎ (800) 772-8527, (619) 291-7131, FAX: (619) 291-3584.
Single: $85–$135. Double: $95–$150.

The kids can run wild over 32 landscaped acres—though warn them to keep out of the posies and expensive plants. The huge complex, recently renovated, has a resort feel and serves as a mini-convention center for trade shows and seminars (Deepak Chopra, among others). Nearly 1000 rooms, four restaurants, three lounges, four swimming pools and a spa are encompassed within the sprawl. Golf is adjacent, as are the shopping malls. Guests have privileges (for norminal fees) at a nearby health club and the hotel schedules many family activities. This is a great spot for conventioneers who have spouse and kids in tow. Amenities: Jacuzzi. 9554 rooms. Credit Cards: A, DC, D, MC, V.

Old Town

Best Western Hacienda Hotel Old Town $99–$119   ★★★

4041 Harney Street, San Diego, 92110, ☎ (800) 888-1991, (619) 298-4707, FAX: (619) 298-4707.
Single: $99–$109. Double: $109–$119.

The hotel's white exterior with red Spanish tile roof, open balconies and bougainvillea bowers blends well with its Old Town location. Suites spread over three levels range from super-mini (i.e. big rooms) to good-sized one bedrooms—all have high ceilings, Spanish decor, refrigerators and microwave ovens. A Mexican restaurant and cantina are on the property, and Mondays through Thursdays the manager buys guests' drinks at the hosted reception. Indoor parking and airport transportation are free, and some meeting rooms are available. Amenities: tennis, exercise room, sauna. 149 rooms. Credit Cards: A, CB, DC, D, MC, V.

Motels

Mission Valley

Days Inn Hotel Circle $55–$89   ★

543 Hotel Circle South, San Diego, 92108, ☎ (800) 345-9995, (619) 297-8800, FAX: (619) 298-6029.
Single: $55–$79. Double: $55–$89.

California's largest Days Inn offers three-stories of standardized chain-brand rooms, exceptional only for their spaciousness and mini-refrigerators. The heated pool, color TV, guest laundry and family-style coffee shop might be all you need—plus airport transportation is provided. The kids can't do a lot of damage here. Amenities: Jacuzzi. 280 rooms. Credit Cards: A, CB, DC, D, MC, V.

Old Town

Vacation Inn Old Town   **$70–$115**   ★★★

3900 Old Town Avenue, San Diego, 92110, Off Interstate 5, near Old Town, ☎ *(800) 451-9846, (619) 299-7400, FAX: (619) 299-1619.*
Single: $70–$105. Double: $70–$115.

Except for the B&B, this is Old Town's best address—Spanish colonial on the outside and surprisingly European inside. Three stories with indoor and outdoor walkways ramble over courtyards and colorful gardens. Rooms have floral fabrics and better-quality furnishings and those on the two upper floors feature balconies. Continental breakfast and afternoon refreshments are complimentary. Amenities: tennis, sauna. 125 rooms. Credit Cards: A, CB, DC, D, MC, V.

Motor Inns

Mission Valley

Best Western Seven Seas   **$49–$59**   ★★

411 Hotel Circle South, San Diego, 92108, ☎ *(800) 328-1618, (619) 291-1300, FAX: (619) 291-6933.*
Single: $49–$59. Double: $49–$59.

Another convenient-to-all but otherwise unnoteworthy motor inn. Rooms are spread over two stories, accessed via outdoor corridor, and feature ordinary appointments. Facilities for kids, however, are better than average and include not only a pool and spa but also a playground, game room and basketball court. The lounge provides other live entertainment. Kids can hang in the coffee shop. Amenities: Jacuzzi. 309 rooms. Credit Cards: A, CB, DC, D, MC, V.

Hotel Circle Inn and Suites   **$49–$89**   ★★

2201 Hotel Circle South, San Diego, 92108, ☎ *(800) 621-1345, (619) 291-2711, FAX: (619) 542-1227.*
Single: $49–$89. Double: $49–$89.

Two unexceptional levels of rooms and two-room suites surround a large pool and sundeck. The family restaurant is famous for its apple pancakes—though you don't have to stay here to try them. Amenities: Jacuzzi. 196 rooms. Credit Cards: A, DC, D, MC, V.

Old Town

Ramada Hotel Old Town   **$59–$89**   ★★

2435 Jefferson Street, San Diego, 92110, Adjacent to Interstate 5, near Old Town, ☎ *(800) 255-3544, (619) 260-8500, FAX: (619) 297-2078.*
Single: $59–$79. Double: $59–$89.

Trying hard to look like Spanish colonial hacienda, this Ramada has added fountains, courtyards and southwestern decor to the usual motor inn trappings. Popular with marauding bands of tour groups, you'd better be early to grab your share of the free breakfast and evening cocktails. If you're looking for peace in Old Town, the crowds and/or the adjacent freeway will probably drive you nuts. Amenities: Jacuzzi. 151 rooms. Credit Cards: A, CB, DC, D, MC, V.

Resort/Motel

Mission Valley

Quality Resort Mission Valley   **$59–$69**   ★★★

875 Hotel Circle South, San Diego, 92108, ☎ *(800) 221-2222, (619) 298-8281, FAX: (619) 295-5610.*
Single: $59–$69. Double: $59–$69.

A standard hotel chain that managed to pull off growing into a resort—while barely touching the prices. Smack in the heart of Hotel Circle madness, the Quality Resort has undergone major renovation and now features three pools, several spas and saunas, seven lighted tennis courts, raquetball, putting green, meeting rooms and a superb 26,000-square-foot health club. With two restaurants, a lounge, 24-hour coffeeshop, and 24-hour room service, you can hideaway here for a long time. Amenities: tennis, health club, Jacuzzi, sauna, balcony or patio. 200 rooms. Credit Cards: A, CB, DC, D, MC, V.

Uptown: Where to Dine

You'll have a lot of choices and, most likely, a hard time choosing. Uptown has nearly as many restaurants and cafes as downtown, but with a broader range of cuisine. Heavier on Thai than Italian, with California, Japanese, Chinese, Vietnamese and natural foods ranking high. Old Town, natch, is Mexican central though you'll find scads of taco joints and other fast foods on every major street. Price ranges are a stretch also—from superexpensive Mister A's to five-for-a-buck rolled tacos.

Hillcrest

Busalacchi's   **$$**   ★★★★

3683 Fifth Avenue, Hillcrest, ☎ *(619) 298-0119.*
Italian cuisine. Specialties: Veal marsala and veal piccata.
Lunch: 11:30 a.m.–2:30 p.m., entrées $7–$14.
Dinner: 5–10 p.m., entrées $8–$16.

An intimate dining room inside a century-old house that turns out authentic Sicilian specialties. Besides the veal dishes, the feast includes pastas with clams, mussels, calamari and other seafood. Dine inside the small rooms with fireplaces or on the enclosed patio. Good place to bring your sweetie. Lunch is served Mondays through Fridays. Dinner is served every day every night and until 11 p.m. on Fridays and Saturdays. Features: late dining. Reservations recommended. Credit Cards: CB, V, MC, DC, A.

California Cuisine   **$$**   ★★★★

3845 Fourth Avenue, Hillcrest, ☎ *(619) 543-0790.*
American cuisine. Specialties: Tuesday prix-fixe dinner.
Lunch: 11 a.m.–2 p.m., entrées $8–$14.
Dinner: 5–10 p.m., entrées $12–$18. Closed: Mon.

California Cusine, opened in 1983, was one of the first players in San Diego's nouvelle-and-innovative food scene. The minimalist environent—black, white and gray—is a suitable backdrop for fabulous presentations of grilled meats, wine glazes, sun-dried fruits and veggies and fresh herbs and spices. The Tuesday night, three-course prix-fixe dinner (around $15) is always a sellout. Menus change frequently, and the cellar stocks 100 wines. Service is terrific and the food is mesmerizing—keeping people happy, at least through one meal of their lives. Lunch is served only Tuesdays through Fridays. Features: outside dining, wine and beer only. Reservations recommended. Credit Cards: D, V, MC, DC, A.

Celadon $$ ★★★
3628 Fifth Avenue, Hillcrest, ☎ (619) 295-8800.
Thai cuisine. Specialties: Shrimp in coconut sauce, Bangkok summer salad.
Lunch: 11:30 a.m.–2 p.m., entrées $6–$14.
Dinner: 5–10 p.m., entrées $8–$16. Closed: Sun.
Though Celadon has been usurped by others on the Thai front, its opening in 1986 made Thai food the local rage. Pink hues and glass block, combined with plenty of ceramics and artifacts from Thailand, add dabs of serenity to the occasionally fiery meals. The seafood dishes are can't-go-wrongs, and there are plenty of choices in noodles, satays, appetizers and meats. Efficient service and delectable food in a calm atmsophere—good place to propose business or monkey business. Lunch is served Mondays through Fridays. Reservations recommended. Credit Cards: V, MC, A.

Corvette Diner $ ★★★
3946 Fifth Avenue, Hillcrest, ☎ (619) 542-1001.
American cuisine. Specialties: Burgers, meat loaf, cherry Cokes.
Lunch: 11 a.m.–4 p.m., entrées $3–$10.
Dinner: 4–11 p.m., entrées $3–$10.
The theme is '50s, the centerpiece a slick 'vette, and the cuisine is pure Americano. The juke blasts Connie Francis, Elvis and other teen idols while a bubble gum-chewing "theme" waitress takes your order. It's all a bit too cutesy and irritating but if you're cutesy and irritating or you have kids to entertain, be my guest. Bad place for a business lunch—the sound level is deafening and colleagues will not be impressed. The burgers, fries and old-fashioned soda fountain slurps are almost worth the aggravation, and the daily specials can be surprisingly creative. Be prepared for very long waits, especially on Tuesdays and Wednesdays when a magician performs in the evening. You can hang out at the full bar and down whiskey while warning the kids ad nauseum that they can't have a malt because then they'll be too full for dinner. Good luck. Features: late dining. Reservations not accepted. Credit Cards: D, V, MC, DC, A.

Crest Cafe $ ★★
425 Robinson Avenue, Hillcrest, ☎ (619) 295-2510.
American cuisine. Specialties: Onion loaves, burgers.
Breakfast: 9–11 a.m., entrées $4–$8.
Lunch: 11 a.m.–2 p.m., entrées $5–$10.
Dinner: 5–11 p.m., entrées $5–$12.
Not even my picky New Zealand friends could complain about the Crest. The decor is art deco, the service is shockingly polite, and the

burger selection is tastier than the tourist-burgers at the Corvette a few blocks away. Pastas, seafood, chicken, omelettes and gelato are also on the menu, but the piece de resistance is the famous stacked-high crunchy onion loaf—order a whole loaf (enough for four people) or a half-serve (enough for me, in a bad mood). It will keep you up all night cursing yourself for being a disgusting pig—and it will be worth every second. Features: wine and beer only, non-smoking area. Reservations not accepted. Credit Cards: D, V, MC, A.

Jimmy Carter's Cafe $ ★★

3172 Fifth Avenue, Hillcrest, ☎ (619) 295-2070.
American cuisine. Specialties: Eclectic choices.
Breakfast: 6:30 -11 a.m., entrées $3–$6.
Lunch: 11 a.m.–4 p.m., entrées $3–$6.
Dinner: 4–9 p.m., entrées $4–$9.
No, not THAT Jimmy Carter. This Jimmy Carter is a long-time local who has turned a renovated Spanish building into a 62-seater cafe. The international menu shifts gracefully (with some beer or wine) from Indian, French, and Mexican to Thai, Spanish, and Italian. Prices are good, the place is relaxed. Breakfast only is served Sundays, 8 a.m.–2 p.m. Features: Sunday brunch, wine and beer only. Reservations not accepted.

Jimmy Wong's Golden Dragon $ ★★★★

414 University Avenue, Hillcrest, ☎ (619) 296-4119.
Chinese cuisine. Specialties: MSG rushes.
Dinner: 3 p.m.–3 a.m., entrées $5–$12.
Chinese dining the way it OUGHT to be—a dark funky room, lots of red and gold, gooey white rice and MSG-laced old favorites. Jimmy's circa-1955 neon marquee—a flashing dragon spewing smoke—is a designated historical object. Hey, it was good enough for Marilyn Monroe, Mickey Rooney and a cast of other stars—though probably none would be caught dead in there now. The place is open until 3 a.m. every night, offers all the old combination plates of your Chinese dreams and is cheap. You'll love it. Features: wine and beer only, late dining. Reservations not accepted. Credit Cards: V, MC, A.

Mister A's $$$ ★★★★★

2550 Fifth Avenue, Hillcrest, ☎ (619) 239-1377.
American cuisine. Specialties: Roast tenderloin of beef, flaming baked Alaska.
Lunch: 11 a.m.–2:30 p.m., entrées $7–$13.
Dinner: 6–10:30 p.m., entrées $18–$30.
San Diego's ultimate elegant gourmet experience, serving the old money since the end of World War II. No matter how dressed up you are, the tuxedoed waiters will probably be one fashion step ahead. Be prepared for rich food and heavy sauces, and block fat percentages from your mind—one bite is enough to bring on cardiac arrest, but what a way to go. Dine on almost unheard-of delicacies like gourmet abalone, chateaubriand, tournedos of beef and the savory roast tenderloin of beef. Start off with the Caesar salad for two and finish with flaming baked Alaska or cherries jubilee. The view from this 12th-floor dining room is one of the best in town—jets whizzing past the window as you demurely sip a manhattan or martini. Lunch is served

only Mondays through Fridays. Features: rated wine cellar. Jacket and tie requested. Reservations required. <small>Credit Cards: D, CB, V, MC, DC, A.</small>

Montana's American Grill $$$ ★★★★

1421 University Avenue, Hillcrest, ☎ *(619) 297-0722.*
American cuisine. Specialties: Mixed grill, barbecued ribs.
Lunch: 11 a.m.–2 p.m., entrées $7–$14.
Dinner: 5–10:30 p.m., entrées $10–$24.

The ultimate high-tech environment for meat-lovers. The slick dining room with its sleek bar is famed for southwestern and northwestern-influenced rib slabs, grilled meats, smoked sausage, pork stews, thick steaks and chops. The food isn't cheap (or light) but, if you're on a budget (or diet), go for one of the filling soups. Good service and surroundings. Lunch is served Mondays through Fridays only, and dinner is on until 11:30 p.m. on Fridays and Saturdays. Features: wine and beer only, late dining. Reservations recommended. <small>Credit Cards: CB, V, MC, DC, A.</small>

Taste of Szechuan $$ ★★★

670 University Avenue, Hillcrest, ☎ *(619) 298-1638.*
Chinese cuisine.
Lunch: 11 a.m.–4 p.m., entrées $6–$10.
Dinner: 4 p.m.–midnight, entrées $8–$14.

Always packed with locals taking the plunge on mild or spicy Mandarin, Chinese and Szechuan favorites—lots of choices for both meat-eaters and vegetarians. The food is cheap and plentiful, but extra-good deals are the daily specials and those Chinese feasts for six, 10, and 20 people. Dinner is served until 2 a.m. on Fridays and Saturdays. Features: wine and beer only, late dining. <small>Credit Cards: V, MC.</small>

Taste of Thai $$ ★★★★

527 University Avenue, Hillcrest, ☎ *(619) 291-7525.*
Thai cuisine. Specialties: Hot, hot, hot food.
Lunch: 11:30 a.m.–3 p.m., entrées $6–$10.
Dinner: 5–11 p.m., entrées $8–$16.

This one has been a local favorite since the day it opened its doors. We come here to sweat, cry, beg for ice water—the hotter the better. Don't fear—they ask before they cook your meal. You control the heat—or be a daredevil and leave your spice life in the hands of a stranger. The food is traditional Thai done California contemporary. The spring rolls are terrific starters, and the vegetarian choices are extensive. Take-out orders are available. Features: wine and beer only. Reservations recommended. <small>Credit Cards: V, MC, A.</small>

Thai Chada $ ★★★

142 University Avenue, Hillcrest, ☎ *(619) 270-1888.*
Thai cuisine. Specialties: Chicken in peanut sauce, lemon grass yum.
Lunch: 11 a.m.–2 p.m., entrées $4–$8.
Dinner: 5–10 p.m., entrées $6–$12.

Gourmet Thai at its best. Everyone's happy with the 150-item menu listing authentic seafood, chicken and vegetarian choices. And almost everything can be prepared any way you like—wussy-spiceless to fire-breathing hot. The dining room is lovely, the appetizers scrumptious. Don't miss out on the all-you-can-eat lunch buffet ($5.95) . Lunch is served Mondays through Fridays. Features: wine and beer only. Reservations recommended. <small>Credit Cards: V, MC, A.</small>

Drawing by S. Harris; © Cartoonists & Writers Syndicate

Vegetarian Zone $$ ★★★

2949 Fifth Avenue, Hillcrest, ☎ *(619) 298-7302.*
American cuisine. Specialties: Vegetarian cuisine, iced sun tea.
Lunch: 11:30 a.m.–5 p.m., entrées $6–$10.
Dinner: 5–10 p.m., entrées $8–$11.

Even nonvegetarians don't complain about the food here ("I can't believe this is health food!"). Up and running for more than twenty years (and formerly known as Kung Food) The Vegetarian Zone keeps natural food-lovers—with that peaceful, easy feeling—coming back for garden burgers, stir-fry, tofu concoctions, omelets, soups and salads. Large portions are served in a plant-filled, New Age-y environment that attracts as many businesspeople as it does veg-heads. Breakfast is served on Saturdays and Sundays, 8:30 a.m. to 1 p.m. The deli is open daily for food to go. Features: outside dining, wine and beer only, nonsmoking area. Reservations not accepted. Credit Cards: D, V, MC.

Kensington

Barrymore $$ ★★★

4116 Adams Avenue, Kensington, ☎ *(619) 281-8021.*
Continental cuisine.
Lunch: entrées $6–$12.
Dinner: 5:30–8:30 p.m., entrées $9–$17. Closed: Mon.

It's worth the trek over to Kensington to experience the owner/chef's stylish, creative meals. Off the beaten path, in a combo residential/commercial area (across from the Ken Cinema and the public library), where you'll be treated like an honored guest by the professionally untrained but born-to-the-task owner/chef. Seafood, meat, pasta dishes and—especially—lamb or duckling, are all a smash and dinners include soup or salad. Simply fab desserts are made on the premises. No wine or beer license, so do without or bring your own. Reservations recommended. Credit Cards: D, V, MC, A.

Little Italy

Filippi's Pizza Grotto $$ ★★★★

1747 India Street, Little Italy, ☎ (619) 232-5095.
Italian cuisine. Specialties: Thick crust, high fat pizza.
Lunch: 11 a.m.–3 p.m., entrées $5–$12.
Dinner: 4–11 p.m., entrées $6–$15.
San Diego's first pizzeria, dating from the 1940s and still as popular in the 1990s. No sissy gourmet pizzas with baby this and that, just the REAL thing—thick crust, heart-stopping pepperoni, salty anchovies, olives off the branch and globs of yummy high-fat cheese. So you'll die—can you think of a better way to go? Wash it down with Chianti—it's supposed to break down the fat particles. If you're more inclined toward pasta, the spaghetti, fettuccini and ravioli are also good bets. The dining room looks the same as it always has—simple, cramped, tables covered with red-checkered cloths. Dinner is served until midnight on Fridays and Saturdays. Features: wine and beer only, late dining. Reservations not accepted. Credit Cards: V, MC, A.

Indigo Grill $$$ ★★★★

1702 India Street, Little Italy, ☎ (619) 234-5456.
Southwestern cuisine. Specialties: Spicy and creative concoctions.
Breakfast: 9-11 a.m., entrées $4–$7.
Lunch: 11-a.m.–2 p.m., entrées $6–$14.
Dinner: 5–10 p.m., entrées $9–$24.
It's southwestern-gone-mad according to locals who seem unable to distinguish "mad" from "creative." Still, the foodies run madly to chow down these magical indigenous southwestern combinations. The dining room sets a mood with Native Americana decor, desert colors, baskets, gourds and sage sticks. Your salad might be a mix of arugula, radicchio, figs and chili croutons, tossed with blackened-tomato sage vinaigrette. Or how about a quail and rabbit con carne quesadilla? Or a grilled veal chop in ancho and chipolte chili honey puree? Hot Indian bread pudding contains sun-dried cranberries and pinion nuts and is covered with vanilla and prickly-pear sauces. Get the idea? Dinner is not served on Mondays. A brunch menu is offered on Saturdays and Sundays. Features: Sunday brunch, wine and beer only. Reservations recommended. Credit Cards: D, V, MC, A.

Princess Pub and Grill $ ★★★

1665 India Street, Little Italy, ☎ (619) 702-3021.
English cuisine. Specialties: Ploughman's lunch.
Lunch: 11 a.m.– 4 p.m., entrées $5–$10.
Dinner: 4 p.m.–midnight, entrées $5–$10.
The local oh-to-be-in-merry-England pub. You don't really come here for the food—ploughman's lunch, fish and chips, bangers, steak-and-kidney pie—you come for the ATMOSPHERE and to play darts while downing one (or all) of ten English beers. Princess Di memorabilia hangs everywhere (don't confuse her photo with the dart board).

It's Anglophile kitsch, but you'll get an adequate dose of local hang-out and some respite from the Spanish heritage trail. Features: wine and beer only, late dining. Reservations not accepted. Credit Cards: D, V, MC, A.

Mission Valley

Monterey Whaling Company $$ ★★
901 Camino del Rio South, Mission Valley, ☎ *(619) 543-9000.*
Seafood cuisine.
Breakfast: 8-10 a.m., entrées $4–$7.
Lunch: 11 a.m.–2 p.m., entrées $6–$12.
Dinner: 5–11 p.m., entrées $8–$20.
Pretty much a seafood place for those who can't be bothered going elsewhere. Breakfast and lunch are fairly ordinary. Dinner is best, with fresh seasonal fish specials—most served with soup or salad. Pastas and steaks are also on the menu. Late breakfast is served on Saturdays and Sundays, replacing the lunch detail. Reservations recommended. Credit Cards: D, V, MC, DC, A.

Old Town

Berta's Latin American Restaurant $$ ★★★
3928 Twiggs Street, Old Town, ☎ *(619) 295-2343.*
Latin American cuisine. Specialties: Sauces to annihilate your insides.
Lunch: 11 a.m.–2 p.m., entrées $6–$10.
Dinner: 5-11 p.m., entrées $7–$14.
Bring the Mylanta and prepare to have your innards ripped apart. A departure from the usual tourist-cuisine and Mexican staples, Berta's cooks up regional dishes from Brazil, Argentina, Peru, et. al., while letting you soak it down with mostly Chilean wines. Almost everything on the menu is extremely spicy, and that includes the appetizers but—if you enjoy the taste and aftermath of fiery Latin cooking, or you have a shaman protecting your guts, then venga y mancha. The dining room is small and simple—the patio is nicer, especially when you start to scream. Features: outside dining. Reservations recommended. Credit Cards: V, MC, A.

Cafe Pacifica $$$ ★★★★★
2414 San Diego Avenue, Old Town, ☎ *(619) 291-6666.*
Seafood cuisine. Specialties: Hawaiian ahi, Cajun catfish.
Lunch: 11:30 a.m.–2 p.m., entrées $7–$14.
Dinner: 5:30–10 p.m., entrées $13–$25.
Interesting atmosphere—the framework of an old house, twinky-winky lights and mirroring—and luscious food. The place was already on the A-list, but an updated menu now includes more "nouvelle" preparations. Old favorites—the ahi and catfish—like old friends, have been kept on board. The specialties are the exquisitely fresh items such as Dungeness crab cakes and steamed Oregon clams as well as daily entrées of fresh fish, pasta and chops. Lunch is served only Tuesdays through Fridays. Credit Cards: V, MC, DC, A.

Casa de Bandini $$ ★★★★
Old Town State Historical Park, Old Town, ☎ *(619) 297-8211.*
Mexican cuisine. Specialties: Mex-Mex.
Lunch: 11 a.m.–4 p.m., entrées $6–$14.
Dinner: 4–9 p.m., entrées $6–$14.

Juan Bandini's stately 1929 homestead is, today, a rather raucous restaurant. The food is the usual Mexican fare of enchildas con chili verde sauce and such, but the atmosphere is enchanting—huge courtyard, colorful gardens, whitewashed walls, weekend mariachi bands and killer margaritas to douse your salsa. Ole! Features: outside dining. Reservations recommended. Credit Cards: D, CB, V, MC, DC, A.

Casa de Pico   **$$**   ★ ★ ★
Old Town State Historical Park, Old Town, ☎ *(619) 296-3267.*
Mexican cuisine. Specialties: La Especial de Juan.
Lunch: 10 a.m.–4 p.m., entrées $5–$9.
Dinner: 4–10 p.m., entrées $6–$15.
Looks like a carnival, sounds like a carnival, tastes like Tijuana. Like other Old Town restaurants, this one gets away with standard Mexican fare by providing a colorful courtyard, serenading musicians and bright colors. Absorb the atmosphere over La Especial de Juan—a well-presented but very un-especial plate with fajitas, enchiladas and chimichangas. But could you really pass up a chance to eat a meal at Governor Pio Pico's old home? Features: outside dining. Reservations not accepted. Credit Cards: CB, V, MC, DC, A.

Old Town Mexican Cafe   **$$**   ★ ★ ★ ★
2489 San Diego Avenue, Old Town, ☎ *(619) 297-4330.*
Mexican cuisine. Specialties: Big crowds.
Breakfast: 7-11 a.m., entrées $3–$6.
Lunch: 11 a.m.–4 p.m., entrées $5–$12.
Dinner: 4–11 p.m., entrées $5–$14.
Forget about going back home until you've eaten here—it's the city's most popular Mexican restaurant and on the "must" list of tourist attractions. You'll wait in line forever for the privilege of eating homemade tortillas surrounding everything Mexican. The long wait bizarrely seems proportionate with the restaurant's continual expansion. No one seems to care, particularly after downing margaritas at the bar for an hour or so. Features: own baking. Reservations not accepted. Credit Cards: D, V, MC, A.

San Diego

Yoshino's   **$$**   ★ ★ ★
1790 West Washington Street, San Diego, ☎ *(619) 295-2232.*
Japanese cuisine. Specialties: Sashimi.
Lunch: 11:30 a.m.–2 p.m., entrées $5–$10.
Dinner: 5–10 p.m., entrées $7–$16. Closed: Mon.
You'll wait in line with doctors, lawyers and local businesspeople at this in-spot for traditional Japanese goodies. The efficient staff keeps everyone moving at a bearable pace but if long waits annoy you, try coming for dinner when its slightly less crowded. The sashami is killer. Features: wine and beer only. Reservations not accepted. Credit Cards: CB, V, MC, DC, A.

CORONADO AND THE SILVER STRAND

Hotel del Coronado is the largest and oldest resort on the West Coast and has a colorful history.

It seems like an island but it isn't. Coronado ("crown," in Spanish) reached via bridge or ferry from San Diego, is actually connected to mainland California via the Silver Strand—a narrow strip of beachside highway. The Village—as the town is called by its 25,000 residents—is cozied, all safe and secure, between the North Island Naval Air Station to the north and the Naval Amphibious Base that leans south along the Silver Strand. The Naval Communication Center sits Rock-of-Gibraltar-like at the point where the peninsula connects to Imperial Beach. This security blanket appeals just fine to residents of the incorporated city—quite happy in the Old Guard enclave where generations of staid families have lived side-by-side in exclusive mansions since the city's beginnings.

Coronado has always been a snooty, sniffy, Old Money community, ever since the turn of the century when Elisha S. Babcock Jr. and Hampton L. Story (wealthy businessmen and hunting partners) decided the place would make a simply divine hunting- and fishing-resort. Between 1885 and 1888, the dynamic duo bought the peninsula, resold plots of land, mapped out the streets and water pipeline, and built and opened the illustrious Hotel del Coronado—then they went broke. It is rumored that Thomas Edison personally flipped the switch on the world's first electrically lighted hotel—though it is fact that in 1904 he lit the Del's first Christmas tree.

By 1900, John D. Spreckels—son of sugar king, Claus—gained control of the Hotel del. From the outset, the ornate 400-room resort—and soon-to-be movie set—proved irresistible to the upper crust, many who began constructing their own personal mansions along the waterfront. Spreckels, no dummy, went about turning the area into the ultimate holiday offering (for the "better" classes, of course)—he created, among other attractions, Tent City (originally known as Camp Coronado) and absolutely zero relation to any so-called tent city of present homeless days. Spreckels' Tent City, south of the Hotel del along the Silver Strand, was a posh outdoor resort with wooden-floored, striped-tent lodgings and which eventually included such niceties as an indoor swimming pool, dance pavilion, bandstand, carousel, bowling alley and floating casino. Tent City was destroyed in the late 1930's, a decade or so after Spreckels died. The Hotel, however, continued to thrive and attract slews of luminaries, politicians, royalty and other dignitaries.

The military was already firmly entrenched in the area. Though a few U.S. Marines had set up camp at North Island in 1914, it wasn't until 1917—and the American debut into World War I—that the U.S. Naval Air Station began operations in earnest (accompanied, until 1940, by some Army folks). World War II saw, among other things, the creation of the U.S. Naval Amphibious Base over on the Silver Strand. The village, to this day, remains wedged between installations. And the conservative, well-bred officers and retired military mesh well with the local peerage.

In 1969, the opening of the San Diego/Coronado Bridge created havoc with Coronado residents. What was all this traffic? Who were all these tourists? What had happened to their supreme isolation? Progress, Coronado, progress.

Some changes have been made—but not many: The Old Ferry Landing has been developed (and the old ferry has resumed operations), a couple of resort hotels are up and running and some upmarket shops and restaurants are in business.

Nonetheless, Coronado is not and never will be a flaunty, showy town (we're not counting *Some Like It Hot*). It's philosophy is simple: the rich and famous don't belong here—the wealthy and glamourous *do*.

Coronado and the Silver Strand: Things to See and Do

The 2.2-mile-long **San Diego-Coronado Bridge** rises 246 feet above San Diego Bay—hovering above subs, sailboats, yachts and freighters, and skylining both downtown San Diego and Coronado. It's a scenic-second to the Golden Gate Bridge up north but, if you're the driver, it can be a little *too* hypnotic.

The bridge was another one of those "civic debate" items—it would change the community forever; maybe, but it would be convenient and bring in money; but *new money*! Ahem. Then Governor Ronald Reagan dedicated the bridge on August 2, 1969, and the sweet trusty **Coronado ferry** ceased running that very same date at the stroke of midnight. That carriage remained a pumpkin until 1987 when it was reinstated—coinciding with the development at **Old Ferry Landing**, a sort of Seaport Village-esque complex with red domes that mimic those of the Hotel Del. Now the ferry is again used by commuting residents as well as tourists and cyclists, who take their wheels along for the ride. The bridge toll is $1 for those entering the island; the ferry costs $2 each way.

Don't miss a gander at **Le Meridien**, the understated but supremely elegant resort close by Old Ferry Landing. Streams, fish ponds, garden paths and lagoons wind in and around 16 acres of waterfront property—a breath of ooh-la-la French style that gloriously resuscitated the site of condemned-to-death Navy housing.

Either drive or catch the trackless trolley from the ferry landing for a trek down **Orange Avenue**, Coronado's main thoroughfare. About halfway across the village you'll come to **Spreckels Park**, the eight-acre town square (with bandstand) where families gather, friends gossip, concerts are performed and events are held.

Continuing along Orange Avenue, you'll pass a number of historic homes—there are 86 or so, many of them dating from the turn-of-the-century. **Star Park** on Loma Avenue is the merging point for five streets lined with historic buildings. The **Coronado Beach Historical Museum**, on Loma Avenue, can steer you along with displays and info on many of the sites, as well as old photos of the area. Another good source on the area is the **Coronado Visitors Information Center**, *1111 Orange Avenue* (☎ *619-437-8788*). Hours are Mondays through Friday, 9 a.m.-5 p.m.

At the end of Orange Avenue, you'll be face-to-face with the **Hotel del Coronado**. The glorious red-and-white Victorian— largest and oldest resort on the west coast—is pure architectural gingerbread with tall cupolas, turrets, hand-carved wooden pillars and ornate filigree. When building began in 1888, lumber and carpenters had to be brought down from San Francisco, as San Diego could provide neither the materials nor skilled labor. Construction went on round-the-clock and within just eleven months the "wonder resort" was ready for business— *and* it was equipped with state-of-the-art Edison Electric Light. The original hotel consisted of one main building with 400 rooms, but in 1963, its owners—the Hotel Del Corporation—decided it was time for a bit of "progress." *Voila!*—a seven-story tower addition with 300 too-modern rooms plus a convention center. The good news is that the corporate bigwigs also restored some of the Del's original joys such as the entryway porte-cochere and the garden gazebo. The heart-stopping, mammoth-sized **Crown Room**—famed for its 33-foot-tall arched sugar pine ceiling and zero nails (only wooden pegs)—each week puts on what is perhaps the world's ultimate Sunday brunch. The **Prince of Wales Room**—so buried in tradition it was beginning to feel like a funeral parlor—has lightened up both its decor and menu. The Hotel Del is an almost universally recognized icon—many U.S. presidents and members of royalty have been its guests; the fated meeting between the Duke of Windsor and Wallis Simpson took place here; *and*, in 1958, the Del was an on-location site for *Some Like it Hot*, starring Marilyn and Company.

Fielding's Hey! What About Electromagnetic Fields?

The following sign was posted in each guest room before the Hotel Del opened its doors to the public: "This room is equipped with the Edison Electric Light. Do not attempt to light a match. Simply turn key on the wall by the door. The use of electricity for lighting is in no way harmful to health, nor does it affect soundness of sleep."

Across the street from the Del, John D. Spreckels' old mansion—**The Glorietta Bay Inn**—is now a luxury guest house with a couple of motel-style additions. The **Coronado Yacht Club**, on Glorietta Bay, sits in Spreckels' front yard and **Coronado Golf Course** borders the waterfront and stretches around the curve, back towards the San Diego-Coronado Bridge.

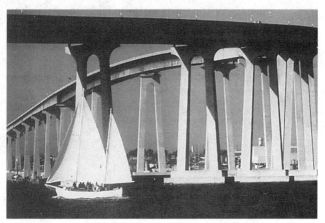

The Coronado Bridge is 2.2 miles long and 246 ft. tall.

Turning south along the **Silver Strand Highway**, you'll pass the **Naval Amphibious Base** where you might catch a glimpse of Navy SEALS practicing their tricks—those night landings on the African coast in front of CNN cameras and AP reporters call for plenty of tactical strategy. Farther down is **Silver Strand State Beach**, the new and exclusive **Loew's Coronado Bay Resort**, and the older and more exclusive **Coronado Cays**—a guarded residential community.

CORONADO TOUR

Coronado is a postcard come to life, an aquatic wonderland nestled between San Diego Bay and the Pacific Ocean.

NAVAL AIR STATION

The birthplace of U.S. military aviation offers three hour narrated tours including tales of Coronado's major contributions to American naval aviation history.

CORONADO BEACH HISTORICAL MUSEUM

This three-story Victorian House dates back to 1898 and covers the exciting history of the island. Open Weds-Sunday, 10 a.m. - 4 p.m.

BEACHES AND PARKS

The 28 miles of pristine coastline include Strand State Beach Park. The vast expanse of public beach next to Hotel Del Coronado is considered the most romantic in Southern California.

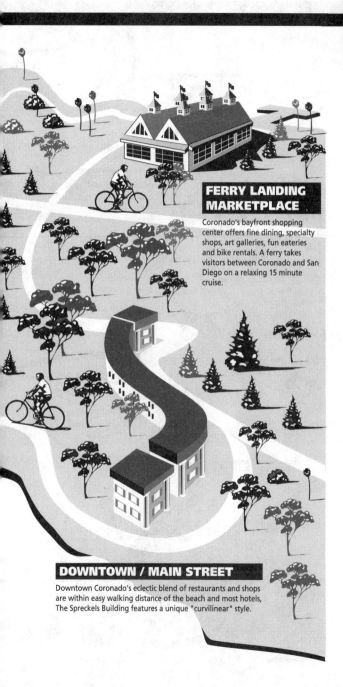

FERRY LANDING MARKETPLACE

Coronado's bayfront shopping center offers fine dining, specialty shops, art galleries, fun eateries and bike rentals. A ferry takes visitors between Coronado and San Diego on a relaxing 15 minute cruise.

DOWNTOWN / MAIN STREET

Downtown Coronado's eclectic blend of restaurants and shops are within easy walking distance of the beach and most hotels, The Spreckels Building features a unique "curvilinear" style.

OLD TIME TOURING

Enjoy a ride around The Enchanted Island in a Model T Ford. Narrated oceanfront, city and grand tours are offered.

HISTORIC MANSIONS

The Glorietta Bay Inn was once the summer mansion of multimillionare John D. Spreckels. The historic landmark is the starting point for a walking tour of many historic Coronado homes including the Duchess of Windsor cottage and the home of *Wizard of Oz* author Frank Baum.

Fielding

CORONADO BRIDGE

Praised as one of the most beautiful bridges in the United States, the sky-blue San Diego - Coronado Bridge is a two mile span built in 1969 to connect the Coronado peninsula to San Diego.

SPORTS

Coronado is a dream come true for beach lovers, bicyclists, in-line skaters, sailors, windsurfers, fishermen, golfers and tennis enthusiasts.

HOTEL DEL CORONADO

The world famous 111-year-old Victorian hotel has played host to everyone from the Duke of Windsor to Marilyn Monroe, the cast of "Baywatch" and 18 U.S. presidents. It also boasts a haunted room.

Museums and Exhibits

Coronado Beach Historical Museum   ★ ★ ★

1126 Loma Avenue, Coronado, ☎ *(619) 435-7242.*
Hours open: 10 a.m.–4 p.m.
Special Hours: Sun. noon-4 p.m. Closed: Mon., Tue.

The Coronado Historical Association restored this 1898 New England-style cottage, turning it into a museum with historical displays, original photographs and early artifacts. Ask here for info on the many other significant sites and homes nearby. Admission is free, but donations are appreciated.

Coronado's Historical Museum is a restored cottage.

Fielding's Not-to-be-Missed Coronado Historical Sites (Not Counting The Hotel Del)

Jessop House

Jessop Jewelers was San Diego's first jewelry business and Joseph Jessop was its founder. His 1901 residence is a takeoff on the family's estate in England. *822 First Street.*

Coronado Library

Can't miss it, right there at Spreckels Park. It's the Grecian temple-looking building with columns, sky-high star pines and rose gardens at the entrance. *640 Orange Avenue.*

Sacred Heart Church

A 1920 Irving Gill design, with blue mosaic tile dome and stained-glass panels of, say what? The Last Supper, Mother and the Boys. *672 B Avenue.*

Christ Episcopal Church

The Tiffany windows in this Gothic A-frame were four years in the making. *1028 Ninth Street.*

Fielding's Not-to-be-Missed Coronado Historical Sites (Not Counting The Hotel Del)

Baby Del

A mini-Hotel Del (built in the same year), moved over to Coronado from southeast San Diego by barge and given the whole Queen Anne makeover. *1410 Isabella Avenue.*

Meade House

It looks like a simple pale yellow bungalow with shutters and flower boxes but, alas, it was a primo retreat for **Wizard of Oz** author L. Frank Baum who worked on several of his **Oz** books there. Could that little dog hanging around be the reincarnation of Auntie Em? Or the evil witch? Careful what you pet! *1101 Star Park Circle.*

Fielding's Hotel Del Coronado Stun-and-Amaze-Your-Friends Trivia Trove

It's the oldest and biggest West Coast USA resort.

The hotel, in 1888, was the leader of indoor toilets in America with a staggering 75 bathrooms for its 399 guest rooms.

It is the largest all-wood building in the United States.

All those red shingles covering the roofs, towers and dormers tally approximately two million.

The ornate, castle-like project, built by crews working around-the-clock, was completed in only eleven piddly months.

The Duke of Windsor purportedly met Wallis Simpson at the Del, a meeting that would stir delicious scandal, romantic notions and upheaval to the British throne (though not nearly as scandalous as the throne's hot seat these days).

L. Frank Baum, Wizard of Oz author, developed his "Emerald City" concept at the hotel and designed the Crown Room's chandeliers besides.

President Richard Nixon used the Crown Room to host the largest state dinner outside of D.C. (for Mexican President Gustavo Diaz Ordaz).

The Crown Room's sugar pine ceiling (the largest unsupported domed ceiling in the country, except for Salt Lake City's Mormon Tabernacle) was constructed only with wooden pegs and is hand-polished with linseed oil a couple of times each year—nary a drop of paint or stain has ever touched it. The room's dimensions are 156-by-66 feet, and 33-feet tall.

An enormous weekend-long celebration marked the Hotel Del's 100th anniversary in 1988.

Coronado and the Silver Strand: For Kids

Tours of the Naval air station enlighten visitors on Coronado's contributions to naval air history.

Coronado is only so-so for kids. If you're staying at either the Hotel Del or Loew's Coronado Bay Resort, you can sign them up for a special children's program. Many children enjoy boat-watching which, on Coronado, might include anything from sailboats and yachts to freighters and destroyers.

Spreckels Park offers the usual park ambience—family picnics, high-flying kites, games-in-progress and often a band on stage. Lesser-known **Tidelands Park**, on Glorietta Boulevard near Le Meridien, is another kids-and-grown-ups retreat—22 acres with a beach, city view, play area, picnic tables and several athletic fields. Or take them clam digging down at **Silver Strand State Beach.**

Tours

The **Coronado Historical Association** sponsors walking tours of the city's historical homes and sites.

Coronado Touring   ★★★
1630 Glorietta Boulevard, Coronado, At Glorietta Bay Inn, ☎ *(619) 435-5892.*

Closed: Mon., Wed., Fri., Sun.

The Glorietta Bay Inn (John Spreckels' former home) is the starting point for one and one-half hour walking tours of Coronado historical sites, including the Hotel Del's gardens and Crown Room and a selection of if-walls-could-talk mansions (including Meade house, where L. Frank Baum whittled away on his Oz books). Tours depart Tuesdays, Thursdays and Saturdays at 11 a.m. and cost $6, adults; $3, under 12.

Coronado's landmark Hotel del Coronado is a terrific resort.

Hotel del Coronado ★★★

1500 Orange Avenue, Coronado, ☎ (619) 435-6611.

Whether you're a guest at the hotel or not, you can take a tour of the landmark resort's highlights. One-hour guided walks are offered Thursdays through Saturdays at 10 a.m. and 11 a.m. for $10 per person. A self-guided audio tour will cost you $3. Admission is free to the gallery exhibiting photos and other Del memorabilia.

Events

Something is always happening at **Spreckels Park**—a concert, contest, art show, etc. The **annual flower show**, in April, has been blooming for 75 years. **Free concerts** take place on the bandstand, Sunday evenings at 6 p.m., June through September. Coronado's **Fourth of July** and **Holiday Lights Walk** are popular seasonal celebrations.

Coronado

Coronado Flower Show Weekend ★★★★

Spreckels Park, Coronado, On Orange Avenue, ☎ (619) 437-8788.
Southern California's largest under-a-tent flower show is held annually in Spreckels Park on a blooming spring weekend. An art show, book sale and pancake breakfast are part of the festivities.

Coronado Promenade Concerts ★★★

Spreckels Park, Coronado, Orange Avenue, ☎ (619) 437-8788.
Free Sunday evening concerts take place at Spreckels Park bandstand, June to September, beginning at 6 p.m. Bring your picnic basket and blanket or lawn chairs.

Coronado Sports Fiesta ★★★

Various locations, Coronado, ☎ (619) 583-8008.
The Optimist Club of Coronado sponsors this quarter-century-old, week-long sportsathon. It's held the last week of July with events and locations spread out around the village.

Holiday Lights Walk ★★★

Old Ferry Landing, Coronado, ☎ (619) 435-8895.
Around the second week of December, choose either a two- or five-mile walking tour of Coronado's festively decorated homes. Starting and finishing point is at the Old Ferry Landing.

Independence Day Celebration ★★★★

Coronado, ☎ (619) 437-8788.
Coronado holds one of the best Fourth of July celebrations in San Diego County. The parade begins at 10 a.m., from Orange Avenue and 1st Street while 9 p.m. is the blasting hour for spectacular fireworks over Glorietta Bay.

Coronado and the Silver Strand: Music, Dance and Theater

Aside from the outdoor concerts in the park, **Coronado Playhouse** and **Lamb's Players Theatre** both offer high-quality theatrical performances.

Theater

Coronado Playhouse ★★★

1775 Strand Way, Coronado, ☎ *(619) 435-4856.*
The village venue for a variety of theatrical productions—don't expect anything too risque.

Lamb's Players Theatre ★★★

1142 Orange Avenue, Coronado, ☎ *(619) 437-0600.*
Coronado's only professional resident ensemble—formerly a touring street theater—turns out first-rate productions year-round on the Paul and Ione Harter Stage in Coronado. The old Spreckels Building, constructed as an opera house in 1917, has been turned into a modern theater and arranged so that none of its 340 seats is more than seven rows from the stage.

Coronado and the Silver Strand: Nightlife

This is a quiet town, er, village. You'll find the nightlife— such as it is—mostly in the hotel lounges and bars, though a couple of independent risk-takers offer rock and folk music. There are plenty of clubs in Imperial Beach and Chula Vista but you might want to pick up a couple of Navy SEALS to escort you.

Coronado Brewing Company ★★

170 Orange Avenue, Coronado, ☎ *(619) 437-4452.*
Sample some heady microbrews, then lean back or twist and shout to the Thursday-through-Friday live rock bands.

Island Saloon ★★

104 Orange Avenue, Coronado, Near Old Ferry Landing,
☎ *(619) 435-3456.*
Saloonatics can hear a variety of live rock and roll, reggae, or blues on Thursdays through Sundays. Performances begin at 9 p.m.

McP's Irish Pub and Grill ★★★

1107 Orange Avenue, Coronado, Near the Hotel Del, ☎ *(619) 435-5280.*

A good old neighborhood pub with Guinness, hearty burgers, corned beef and cabbage, lively patrons and nightly entertainment. Sounds range from rock and roll and blues and jazz to alternative and Celtic folk.

Mexican Village ★★

120 Orange Avenue, Coronado, Near Old Ferry Landing, ☎ *(619) 435-1822.*

Weekend rock and roll runs interference with the Mexican combination plates. Performances from 9 p.m.

Coronado and the Silver Strand: Shopping

The touristy shops at **Old Ferry Landing** offer a range of souvenirs, knick knacks, accessories and some clothing. Smart boutiques, and better shops are found mostly along **Orange Avenue.**

Coronado and the Silver Strand: Where to Stay

If you're staying in Coronado, treat yourself and bed down at least one night (in the old building) at the Hotel Del. Le Meridien and Loew's Coronado Bay Resort should both keep you happily ensconced while the Glorietta Bay Inn (in the original mansion) is a smaller scale choice in the steeped-in-history category. Face it, accommodations in Coronado are few, but at least they're *quality.*

Hotels

Coronado

Le Meridien San Diego $165–$265   ★★★★★

2000 2nd Street, Coronado, 92118, 1-1.2 blks. east of 4th Street at Glorietta Boulevard, ☎ *(800) 543-4300, (619) 435-3000, FAX: (619) 435-3032.*

Single: $165–$265. Double: $165–$265.

Okay, so the Victorian era was fine and dandy but YOU are more in the mood for something along the lines of the French Riviera. Then bienvenue a Le Meridien—a glorious low-lying waterfront hotel with lots of open spaces, beautiful gardens, a walk-in aviary and ponds and streams with golden koi, pink flamingoes and black and white swans. New England-style architecture pulls off a congenial menage a trois with California decor and Gallic flair—giving birth to airy public rooms and spacious accommodations with rattan furnishings, French-sailor colors and patterns, thick carpets, fresh flowers and balconies or patios with bay or lagoon views. Marius, the hotel's signature restaurant, is already becoming legendary, while the brasserie is less formal but still quite wonderful. The list of amenities is extensive and includes a cocktail lounge with piano entertainment, European health club and spa, yoga and aerobics classes, state-of-the-art fitness equipment, two pools plus a lap pool, six tennis courts and tennis clinic, watersports, golf course across the street, private dock, jogging and bike paths, business center, meeting rooms, bike rentals, shuttles and airport transfers. Even the locals are surprised how much they like this 1980s addition to their 1880s community. Amenities: tennis, health club, exercise room, Jacuzzi, sauna, balcony or patio, business services. 300 rooms. Credit Cards: A, CB, DC, D, MC, V.

Motels

Coronado

Glorietta Bay Inn   **$89–$275**   ★ ★ ★

1630 Glorietta Boulevard, Coronado, Across from the Hotel Del,
☎ *(800) 283-9383, (619) 435-3101, FAX: (619) 435-6182.*
Single: $89–$275. Double: $99–$275.
The main part of the inn is John D. Spreckels' 1908 home—a splendid mansion with original fixtures and touches. The lobby is all wicker and ferns, and the adjoining music salon tends to jolt your brain backwards about 10 decades. Most of the accommodations are in the newish adjacent motel-like buildings—cheerful, well-furnished (all have refrigerators) and surrounded by manicured grounds. A heated pool and free morning paper are the only amenities, though bicycles can be rented and walking tours depart from this site. Anyway, the Hotel Del is across the street and the beach, shops, restaurants and other facilities are a short stroll away. Rates here take a big jump during summer months, keeping them almost on the bottom line with Coronado's expensive resorts. 98 rooms. Credit Cards: A, CB, DC, D, MC, V.

Resorts

Coronado

Hotel del Coronado   **$169–$389**   ★ ★ ★ ★ ★

1500 Orange Avenue, Coronado, 92118, ☎ *(800) 468-3533, (619) 435-6611, FAX: (619) 522-8262.*
Single: $169–$389. Double: $169–$389.
Here lives the Queen of Superlatives. The extraordinary Hotel Del is "the most this," "the most that" and—quite simply—the MOST. If you get to splurge only once in your life and you crave a retreat to another era—one with sweeping entryways, grand public rooms, and all the trappings of an 1888 Victorian castle—make this one your address. Come for your vacation, come for your honeymoon, come because you saw a leaf fall from a philodendron in the corner. The gingerbread construction—shingled red roofs, tall turrets, cupolas, ornate filigree, intricate woodcarving, and wide verandas against a background of sweeping lawns and frothy seas—could turn Rush

Limbaugh into a simpering romantic. We see what it did to the Duke of Windsor (though he was certainly in no rush). We see what it did to Marilyn Monroe. Yes, it could happen to you—the vibes are contagious. Happily ensconced within the Del's inpenetrable walls, it is suddenly 1901—there are no gang wars, no crack on the streets, no pierced and tattooed ravers—there is no Rush Limbaugh. Life is simple, the service is elegant and you must have died and gone to heaven. For a taste of the real Del, stay in the original building even though the rooms are slightly erratic and air conditioning is via ceiling fans. (After the addition of all private baths, it turned out that some bathrooms were much larger than the sleeping quarters and vice-versa. If this worries you, inquire before booking). The newer tower rooms are more uniform (and more expensive) and have "real" air conditioning. All accommodations are fitted with lovely quality furnishings, ocean-breeze color schemes, and top-notch amenities—and they fill up quickly. Dining in the Crown Room and Prince of Wales Room are absolutely de rigeur—at least one time each—during your stay. Other on-premises treats are a terrace bistro, 24-hour Del deli, lounge with nightly dancing, bar with piano sounds, tennis, croquet, bike and boat rentals, golf at the municipal course, electronic games, babysitting and children's activities, a shopping arcade, gift shop, beauty salon, airport shuttle and limo service. Amenities: tennis, health club, exercise room, Jacuzzi, sauna, business services. 691 rooms. Credit Cards: A, CB, DC, D, MC, V.

Silver Strand

Loew's Coronado Bay Resort $195–$245   ★★★★

4000 Coronado Bay Road, Silver Strand, Coronado, 92118, South along the Silver Strand Highway, ☎ *(800) 235-6397, (619) 424-4000, FAX: (619) 424-4400.*

Single: $195–$245. Double: $195–$245.

Opened in 1991, Loew's first West Coast resort sits removed from the bustle of non-bustling Coronado, some eight miles down the Silver Strand Highway and adjacent to exclusive Coronado Cays. The fifteen-acre self-contained resort with its own private marina is perfect for water-lovers, luxury-lovers and just, plain, ordinary lovers. No one can get at you here. You can even bring the kids, then pawn them off at the Commodore Kids Club—a year-round program of planned activities for ages four-12 (they'll think you're doing THEM a favor). The four-story building is entered via a posh lobby with two dramatic staircases. Rooms are elegantly furnished and feature pale colors, floral prints and balconies with exquisite views of the ocean, bay or marina. Eat in the formal room or the casual indoor/outdoor cafe, plus there's a poolside grill, lounge with nightly entertainment, and gourmet deli. Other facilities include a fitness center, five lighted tennis courts and pro shop, beauty salon, meeting space and boat, bike, windsurfer and jet-ski rentals. Amenities: tennis, health club, Jacuzzi, sauna, business services. 438 rooms. Credit Cards: A, CB, DC, D, MC, V.

Coronado and the Silver Strand: Where to Dine

Author's Tip

*Take a cafe break at **Kaffeen's** (1201 First Street), right by the Ferry Landing pier, with great San Diego skyline-views. Iced coffee and espresso drinks are made with coffee ice cubes, and mochas are crowned with chocolate whipped cream. Live music plays on Thursday evenings.*

Unlike other cities, hotel dining in Coronado is the biggest treat—not the last resort. Examples: Le Meridien's Marius and L'Escale; the Hotel del's Crown Room and Prince of Wales. You'll find cafes and pubs around town and the Old Ferry Landing, and I have a few non-hotel bites to share.

Coronado

Brigantine $$$ ★★★
1333 Orange Avenue, Coronado, 92118, ☎ (619) 435-4166.
Seafood cuisine.
Lunch: 11:30 a.m.–2:30 p.m., entrées $7–$11.
Dinner: 5–10:30 p.m., entrées $11–$20.
Like the Chart House, the Brigantine is part of a chain and is too popular to ignore. The Coronado branch features the requisite nautical-style, darkened bar where ice cubes clink above the tony, boaty schmooze and a wood paneled dining room that offers fresh seafood, salads and steak. Picks from the oyster bar are half-price during happy hour, Mondays through Fridays, 3-6 p.m. Dinner is served until 11:30 p.m. on Fridays and Saturdays. Credit Cards: D, CB, V, MC, A.

Chart House $$$ ★★★★
1701 Strand Way, Coronado, 92118, ☎ (619) 435-0155.
American cuisine. Specialties: Steaks, seafood, prime rib.
Dinner: 5–10:30 p.m., entrées $21–$30.
Except for the menu, this Chart House is anything but just one of a chain. Set inside the Hotel Del's old boathouse—with matching cupola—the interior is a knockout with numerous antique tables, an 1880 mahogany, teak and stained glass bar and about 20 Tiffany lamps. In summer the outdoor deck might lure you outside and the views, any time of year, are dyamite—Glorietta Bay, the San Diego-Coronado Bridge, the Coronado Yacht Club. You'll scarcely notice the run-of-the-mill food—typical Chart House steaks, prime rib and seafood adorned with absolutely no surprises. You've come for the atmosphere and antiques—so be happy. Features: outside dining. Reservations required. Credit Cards: D, CB, V, MC, DC, A.

Chez Loma $$$ ★★★★
1132 Loma Avenue, Coronado, ☎ (619) 435-0661.

Continental cuisine. Specialties: The duck.
Dinner: 5:30-10 p.m., entrées $15–$24.

Romantic notions, creative cuisine and an antique-furnished 1889 historical home combine forces at one of Coronado's most treasured dinner houses—keeping candles lit and tables-for-two filled in both the inside dining room and the enclosed terrace. The baby-bottom tender duck has been a staple since the restaurant opened in 1975. Other entrées change with the chef's inspiration and include seafood, chicken and veal dishes—all served with soup or salad, rice or potatoes and fresh veggies. A superior assortment of California vintages and microbrewery beers help those culinary marvels slither down your throat. Save room for espresso and dessert. Features: wine and beer only. Reservations required. Credit Cards: D, V, MC, A.

Crown Room $$$ ★★★★★

1500 Orange Avenue, Coronado, ☎ (619) 435-6611.
Continental cuisine. Specialties: History, workmanship and Sunday Brunch.
Breakfast: 7-11 a.m., entrées $12.
Lunch: 11:30 a.m.–3 p.m., entrées $12–$20.
Dinner: 5–9:30 p.m., entrées $20–$28.

The California/French cuisine—particularly the seafood choices—are excellent but you really come to the Crown Room to woo, wow and chow. This original 1888 restaurant has hosted dignitaries and royalties who, in turn, have hosted remarkable dinners and receptions in this room. There is not one single nail holding that 33-foot-tall sugar pine dome ceiling in place—only hand-fitted wooden pegs. The Duke of Windsor and Wallis Simpson, remember? Marilyn Monroe, remember? The Sunday brunch ($25) is famous—but packed. The long tables are crammed with an almost coma-inducing array of hot entrées, salads, desserts, pastries, omelettes—you name it. Look up, while you're standing in line—those crown chandeliers were designed by L. Frank Baum, *Wizard of Oz* creator. The Sunday dinner buffet ($35) is equally as sumptuous and features dancing to a live band that cranks out real alternative hits—tangos, rumbas, mambos and sambas. Features: Sunday brunch. Jacket requested. Reservations required. Credit Cards: D, CB, V, MC, DC, A.

Marius $$$ ★★★★★

2000 2nd Street, Coronado, ☎ (619) 435-3000.
French cuisine. Specialties: French Provencale.
Dinner: 6–10 p.m., prix fixe $39–$70. Closed: Mon., Sun.

Dinner at Marius—the hands-down, most-acclaimed gourmet dining room in the San Diego area—is a reason to live. You can order off the menu ($26-30 for main courses), but the three- or five-course prix-fixe dinners are the best choice. The cost is bumped up for the inclusion of paired European and California wines—worth every single centime. The snobbish restaurant has recently put forth an effort to be a little more California friendly (though jacket and tie are still required) by trying to draw the riffraff that earn less than six figures per year. The cuisine is pure French Provencale, perfectly prepared and presented. The dining room is a tour de force of intimacy with soft lighting, gourmet-friendly paintings, bone china, crystal, sterling silver and fresh flowers. Ignore any uppity attitudes and make this restaurant experience a personal celebration—it'll impress the pants off any date. Features: rated wine cellar. Jacket and tie requested. Credit Cards: D, CB, V, MC, DC, A.

Miguel's Cocina $ ★★★

1339 Orange Avenue, Coronado, ☎ (619) 437-4237.
Mexican cuisine. Specialties: Mexican specialties.
Lunch: 11 a.m.–2 p.m., entrées $4–$8.
Dinner: 5–10 p.m., entrées $6–$12.
The atmosphere is festive—lots of color, costumed staff, a courtyard patio with palm fronds, Mexican background music. It's popular with the locals and chances are good you'll spend some time waiting for a table especially on weekends. Food is the usual Mexican fare with an "old family recipe" slant. Features: outside dining, Sunday brunch. Reservations not accepted. Credit Cards: CB, V, MC, DC, A.

Peohe's $$$ ★★★

1201 First Street, Coronado, 92118, ☎ (619) 437-4474.
Seafood cuisine. Specialties: Fresh mahimahi and ahi.
Lunch: 11:30 a.m.–2:30 p.m., entrées $10–$21.
Dinner: 5:30–9:30 p.m., entrées $21–$30.
At first glance you might feel as though you've entered a theme park—the bright Polynesian decor is anything but subtle with waterfalls, arched bridges, tropical plantings, palms and orchids, streams trickling around custom dining tables and a staff gussied up in island garb. You'll get into the swing once you taste the fresh fish or seafood dishes (at least a couple of catches are flown over from Hawaii every day) like mahi mahi, ahi, crunchy shrimp and tuna salad. You'll never go away disappointed with the view—it's one of the best in Coronado and a special hit with the Sunday brunch crowd. Lunch is served Mondays through Saturdays. Dinner is served until 10:30 p.m. on Fridays and Saturdays. Features: outside dining, Sunday brunch, late dining. Reservations recommended. Credit Cards: D, V, MC, DC, A.

Primavera $$$ ★★★★

932 Orange Avenue, Coronado, ☎ (619) 435-0454.
Italian cuisine. Specialties: Northern Italian specialties.
Lunch: 11 a.m.–2:30 p.m., entrées $7–$12.
Dinner: 5-10:30 p.m., entrées $14–$22.
It's a local fave for northern Italian specialties—magnifico appetizers, Caesar salad, scampi, seafood, veal and lamb. And pasta, of course. The long, split-level dining room is suitably elegant and the bar is indisputably fashionable. Tiramisu addicts should loosen their belts for dessert. Lunch Mon.-Fri. Reservations recommended. Credit Cards: D, CB, V, MC, A.

Prince of Wales Room $$$ ★★★★

1500 Orange Avenue, Coronado, ☎ (619) 435-6611.
Continental cuisine. Specialties: Eclectic.
Dinner: 5–10 p.m., entrées $20–$30.
Hallelujah! The Prince of Wales has finally lightened up. Yes, we loved that old, dark, traditional room but it had become rather stale—despite the great food and service. Come on, this is an ocean resort, not the middle of New York City. So the Prince (much like a certain namesake) has been gutted, reborn and doing a bit of image improvement. It's working, at least for this Prince of Wales. The dining room

is still small and intimate, but ocean-view windows are in place, as are revamped seating arrangements, tableware, tile, carpets, and wall coverings. The menu has tossed away its too-heavy-for-the-climate overcoat, as well. American regional cuisine includes the usual choices of seafood, game, beef, poultry and pasta—all stylishly prepared and presented. Desserts are imaginative, the wine list is well-chosen and the service is excellent. Jacket requested. Reservations required. Credit Cards: D, CB, V, MC, DC, A.

Silver Strand

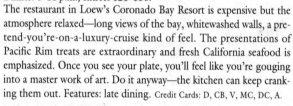

Azzura Point   **$$$**   ★★★★

4000 Coronado Bay Road, Silver Strand, ☎ *(619) 424-4000.*
Continental cuisine. Specialties: Pacifc Rim flavors.
Dinner: 6–11 p.m., entrées $21–$30.

The restaurant in Loew's Coronado Bay Resort is expensive but the atmosphere relaxed—long views of the bay, whitewashed walls, a pretend-you're-on-a-luxury-cruise kind of feel. The presentations of Pacific Rim treats are extraordinary and fresh California seafood is emphasized. Once you see your plate, you'll feel like you're gouging into a master work of art. Do it anyway—the kitchen can keep cranking them out. Features: late dining. Credit Cards: D, CB, V, MC, DC, A.

POINT LOMA, HARBOR ISLAND AND SHELTER ISLAND

Point Loma is a popular spot for whalewatching.

Point Loma's brain-zapping natural beauty is almost as dazzling as it was in 1542 when Portuguese explorer Juan Rodriguez Cabrillo landed—thereby "discovering" San Diego (which he named San Miguel). Unfortunately the gray whales don't feel the same way—they used to bear their babies nearby until greedy whalers practically forced them into extinction. The droves of human blubber, however, that come out to the point is anything *but* extinct—Cabrillo National Monument is the most-visited National Park site in America.

About three centuries after Cabrillo dropped anchor at what is now Ballast Point (formerly known as Fort Guijarros), the U.S. dropped anchor on the public by turning most of the point into a submarine base. In 1913, Woodrow Wilson dedicated a measly allotment to the memorial but more land was added later. In

1959, a more generous Dwight Eisenhower shifted acreage from the Navy to the National Park Service, which still oversees the tourist mecca today.

The point's rugged cliffs, dramatic coastline, snarling pine and juniper trees and stately old-money residences are a jolting contrast to the rest of the community—a conglomeration of military installations, cheesy motels and gag-in-the-bag fast food joints. Yet the old guard of military officers, city leaders and caught-the-big-one Portuguese descendants are unaffected—hanging tight between their tall hedges and private marinas.

Curving eastward, back toward downtown, a couple of short detours will land you on Shelter Island and—across from the airport—Harbor Island. Both are remarkable for being completely *unnatural* features. Shelter Island—San Diego's marina and yacht central—is the circa-1950 product of dredged soil from bay- deepening escapades. It's ditto for Harbor Island, a circa-1969, jump-the-gun-project created for, yes *again*—the Republicans—though the 1972 convention never happened (at least not in San Diego). Besides—neither are islands at all but narrow drive-to peninsulas now covered with grassy lawns, big palms, picnic benches, several fancy hotels and lots of tourists.

Point Loma, Harbor Island and Shelter Island: Things to See and Do

---

FIELDING'S KINKIEST GROUP BOAT EXCURSION

There are almost as many dead people as live tourists hanging around Cabrillo National Monument. The waters beyond are a favorite scattering place for cremated remains. Scheduled boats take "groups" out to sea, say a prayer (we think), and then ash them away into the wild blue yonder. Relatives and friends watch from the cliffs (if you see a gathering of black-clad hanky clutchers, chances are they're not just taking in the view).

Begin at the very point—**Cabrillo National Monument**, near the end of **Cabrillo Memorial Drive**. This 144-acre tribute to Our Founder, Juan Rodriguez Cabrillo, is probably the **best view** in San Diego County. Poised above rugged 400-foot cliffs, your senses can do a grand sweep of San Diego Harbor, Coronado and the North Island Naval Air Station, and Mexico. (Think what it must look like from atop the sandstone **Cabrillo statue**.)

The **Visitor Center** features the usual info plus exhibits relating to the city's military presence, a scale model of Cabrillo's ship *San Salvador*, whale-watching and tide-pooling displays and charts, nautical memorabilia and a wonderful gift shop. The park operates a shuttle service to various viewpoints for those who have difficulty walking or who are dragging around small kids.

If you're in town between mid-December and mid-March, go up to the sheltered **Whale Overlook**, where you'll probably be able to catch a glimpse of 15,000-or-so **gray whales** as they migrate from the Bering Sea to Baja. They keep a fair distance away—first, because of the dreaded whalers and now because of the dreaded whale-watchers getting-ever-closer on excursion boats.

Nuclear-powered subs have taken over Cabrillo's old parking spot at **Ballast Point**—it's off-limits to the public, anyway. The three-mile **Bayside Trail** will wind you around the Diegueno Indians' old hunting and stomping grounds—more great scenery. Keep to the marked paths and you won't need to worry about being snagged by a poisonous plant or cracking through an eroding bluff.

The original 1855 **Point Loma Lighthouse** is a glitzied-up white Cape Cod-style house with its oil lamp encased in brass and iron. It's open to visitors, though no longer in use—that cliff-top beacon was too high for fog-enshrouded navigators to pinpoint (correct—America's southernmost Pacific coast lighthouse was used sans foghorn for almost *forty* years!). The "new" improved version, built in 1891 at sea-level, is still used by the U.S. Coast Guard and sits all the way at the end of Cabrillo Memorial Drive.

On the western side of the monument, follow the dirt trail down to the bottom of the cliffs (you can also drive down to the coast guard station). Watch your tootsies on the slippery rocks while exploring the **tidepools** with 100-or-so species of marine life—octopuses, starfish, anemones and such. (Don't even *think* about snatching any creatures for your cute home aquarium—thankfully all tidepool life is protected by law.)

Backtracking north, you will again pass through the Navy presence of **Fort Rosecrans Military Reservation**. Those 40,000 white headstones, lined up formation-style on either side of Cabrillo Drive, mark the bones of residents at **Fort Rosecrans National Cemetery**.

Turn west at Catalina Boulevard to get a closer look at **Point Loma Nazarene College**, a cliff-top private Christian college that, at the turn of the century, was **Madame Katherine Tingley's Theosophical Institute** (the building with the purple domes—part of the Madame's original "Lomaland"—is a give away). The Lomaland community, in operation 1897-1942, undoubtedly shocked the hell out of the staid neighbors with its ahead-of-celebrity-channels Egyptian gates, Greek theater, Raja Yoga Academy, Temple of Peace, blue- and purple-domed buildings, octagonal homes, grow-your-own gardens and divine spiritual pathways. The enterprise began a steady fizzle in the 1930s, eventually going through a series of wheel-and-deal ownerships, the hideous destruction process and, voilá—Point Loma Nazarene College. Madame Tingley—who was no fan of Christianity—is said to haunt the campus. And she must be *pissed*!

Sunset Cliffs Park, across the street from the college, is a favorite with local shutterbugs and sunset-viewers. Salt-spray, jagged cliffs—the whole drama unfolds through Japanese lenses every night. The beaches along Sunset Cliffs, between Hill Street and Point Loma Avenue (at the Ocean Beach border), are popular with surfers and snoozers. Keep in mind that erosion has made these delicate sandstone bluffs very dangerous to climb and that posted signs should be taken seriously. The lifeguards and rescue teams are beginning to look really bored when they have to haul out another ignorant carcass.

Catalina Boulevard becomes Chatsworth Boulevard at Point Loma Avenue. Take Canon Street to Scott Street, almost at the water's edge. Wander along the waterfront and check out the colorful fishing boats, charter outfits, and the **San Diego Yacht Club**—long lost home of the Americas Cup. Turn onto Shelter Island Drive to **Shelter Island**—San Diego's boat-building center—where you can price your custom model and save up for it by eating a picnic lunch (or, throw a line off the public pier, and catch your own). South of the pier, **Tunaman's Memorial** is a bronze sculpture honoring the tuna industry's founding fathers. Another bronze—**The Yokohama Friendship Bell**, at the southern tip of the island—was presented in 1960 as a gift from our sister city.

Follow Scott Street onto Harbor Drive, through the **Fleet Anti-Sub Warfare School**, the **U.S. Naval Training Center**, the **U.S. Marine Corps Recruit Depot**, and **Lindbergh Field**. The grassy strip on your right is **Spanish Landing**—your look-at-the-big-planes-and-pretty-sailboats resting spot—with more to come as you turn onto North Harbor Drive and the hotels, gardens, jogging paths and picnic sites of **Harbor Island**. That beacon shining on the west end, facing Point Loma, is coming off **Tom Ham's Lighthouse**—the place you will probably stop for a drink.

Beaches

San Diego

Sunset Cliffs Park   ★★★★★

San Diego, Hills Street to Sunset Cliffs Boulevard.

The south end of the park, across the street from Point Loma Nazarene College, is a large grassy park, but most people seem more drawn to the crumbling sandstone cliffs stretching north, hovering precariously above the well-known surf beach below. It's a treacherous climb down and broken bodies, being hauled away by lifeguards and rescue teams, are forever being paraded on the evening news. Shutterbugs and sunset gazers should keep well away from cliffs' edge while they click and point.

Historical Sites

San Diego

Cabrillo National Monument   ★★★★★

South end of Cabrillo Memorial Drive, San Diego, ☎ *(619) 557-5450.*

Hours open: 9 a.m.–5:15 p.m.

A memorial to Portuguese explorer Juan Rodriguez Cabrillo who in 1542 became the first known European to set his eyes on San Diego. It's easy to see why this is supposedly the most-visited national monument in the country. Rugged 400-foot-high cliffs, 144-acres of knock-your-socks-off scenery, and spectacular bosom-clutching views keep a hold on locals, tourists and cremated dead people (who are taken by boat to be scattered at sea). A favorite attraction is the Whale Overlook, a sheltered observatory where the California grays can be spotted on their migration south between mid-December and mid-March. Whale exhibits and a taped narration assist hopeful watchers. The Bayside Trail, a three-mile dirt path, follows the footsteps of the Diegueno Indians (who discovered San Diego long before Cabrillo!). Don some sturdy shoes, pick up a map at the Visitor Center and keep an eye out for the poisonous plants and crumbling bluffs. At low tide (check with the ranger station) you can explore the Tidepools on the western side, filled with hundreds of sea creatures and plants. The original 1855 Cape Cod-style Point Loma Lighthouse has been restored, is now open to the public and also offers recorded info. The bookshop and gift store offer a good range of souvenirs and studies, and the observation deck behind the gift shop features military and aircraft displays. Admission is $4 per vehicle or $2 per person coming some other way. The Bayside Trail, tidepools and lighthouse close earlier than the rest of the grounds, though hours are extended in summer months. General Admission: $4 per vehicle.

Fort Rosecrans National Cemetery ★★★

Cabrillo Memorial Drive, San Diego, North of Cabrillo National Monument, ☎ *(619) 553-2084.*

Hours open: 8 a.m.–5:15 p.m.

More than 40,000 snowy white headstones, lined up in perfect formation, cover the bones of generations of local military troops who never came marching home from the war. The huge obelisk is a memorial to those killed in the 1905 boiler explosion aboard the *USS Bennington*. The bittersweet view across the harbor is quite magnificent. The cemetery opens at 9 a.m. on Sundays.

Tunaman's Memorial ★

San Diego, South of the fishing pier, on the west side of Shelter Island.

Yes, it's Tunaman! Not just one, but three big bronze anglers cast off and commemorate the founders of the world's largest tuna industry. Fishers and Portuguese descendants might be interested in the list of Portuguese families and founders.

Shelter Island

Yokahama Friendship Bell ★

Shelter Island, Southern tip of Shelter Island.

If you're already on Shelter Island and you've seen the Tunaman's Memorial, you may as well check out the big bell. Presented in 1960 by our sister city, the two-five ton bronze Friendship Bell symbolizes undying friendship. Oops, which way did that nuclear sub go?

Sports/Recreation

Shelter Island

San Diego Yacht Club ★★

1011 Anchorage Lane, Shelter Island, Off Shelter Island Drive,
☎ *(619) 222-1103.*

The boathouse-looking, snooty club with a membership that includes some of the world's most famous sailors—including the occasionally inhospitable Dennis Connor and his namesake team. The club was at the center of America's Cup activities after the Perth coup but, alas, the cup has moved to Auckland.

Universities

San Diego

Point Loma Nazarene College ★★★

3900 Lomaland Drive, San Diego, West at Catalina Boulevard,
☎ *(619) 221-2200.*
Special Hours: When school is in session.

This private Christian college was the former home of ahead-of-the-New Age Madame Katherine Tingley and her Theosophical Institute. The original homestead—known as Lomaland—was a daring school of philosophy and culture, in operation 1897-1942. The utopian "commune" was startling for its time—especially in this staid neighborhood—made more so by the construction of octagonal homes, blue-and purple-domed structures, a raja yoga academy, vegetable gardens and a Greek theater. The building with the purple domes, in the middle of campus, is one of the few original buildings that still remain.

Drawing by Miller; ©1995 The New Yorker Magazine, Inc.

FIELDING'S FAVORITE THINGS AT CABRILLO NATIONAL MONUMENT

Wondering if the Cabrillo statue looks anything like Cabrillo, who left no portraits in existence.

Shopping for souvenirs at the gift shop.

Screaming, "There's one!" at the Whale Overlook in the middle of July.

FIELDING'S FAVORITE THINGS AT CABRILLO NATIONAL MONUMENT

Trying to identify poisonous plants along the Bayside Trail from the sketches on the park map.

Wondering if any dead people's ashes have floated into the tidepools.

FIELDING'S STARTER KIT FOR POTENTIAL YACHTIES AND RUNAWAYS

Buy your dream or sign onto someone else's as cook or crew—then take off for the South Pacific or Mexican Riviera like you always promised yourself.

Bay Club Marina
> *2131 Shelter Island Drive;* ☎ *(619) 222-0314.*

Best Western Shelter Island Marina Inn
> *2051 Shelter Island Drive;* ☎ *(619) 222-0561.*

Cabrillo Isle Marina
> *1450 Harbor Island Drive;* ☎ *(619) 297-6222.*

Driscoll's Wharf
> *4918 North Harbor Drive;* ☎ *(619) 222-4930.*

Gold Coast Anchorage
> *2353 Shelter Island Drive;* ☎ *(619) 225-0588.*

Half Moon Marina
> *2323 Shelter Island Drive;* ☎ *(619) 224-3401.*

Harbor Island West Marina
> *2040 Harbor Island Drive;* ☎ *(619) 291- 6440.*

Kona Kai Marina
> *1551 Shelter Island Drive;* ☎ *(619) 222-1191.*

Marina Cortez
> *1880 Harbor Island Drive;* ☎ *(619) 291-5985.*

Marriott Marina
> *333 West Harbor Drive;* ☎ *(619) 230-8955.*

Shelter Cove Marina
> *2240 Shelter Island Drive;* ☎ *(619) 224-2471.*

Shelter Island Yachtways
> *2330 Shelter Island Drive;* ☎ *(619) 222- 0455.*

Sheraton Marina
> *1380 Harbor Island Drive;* ☎ *(619) 692-2249.*

Sun Harbor Marina
> *5104 North Harbor Island Drive;* ☎ *(619) 222-1167.*

Sunroad Resort Marina
> *955 Harbor Island Drive;* ☎ *(619) 574-0736.*

Point Loma, Harbor Island and Shelter Island: For Kids

The tykes will love almost everything and—best—it's free or cheap. You know they'll adore the **whale-watching** and **tidepool-exploring**. The cliffs and wide views might scare them—but that could be fun for *you*. The colorful boats, big fish and *really* big planes should fascinate the little pants off them—and a real live skipper, sailor or fisherman will probably go over well. I wouldn't push the real live fish on them for lunch— better to stick with the picnic idea. They can run wild and unwittingly take part in the family photo opportunities at **Shelter Island** and **Harbor Island**, or even **Spanish Landing**. Bring balls.

Author's Tip

When whale-watching with your kids and confronted with "Is that one, daddy?" just say yes, no matter what. Otherwise you'll never be able to concentrate on really spotting a whale.

Tours

Tours are limited to **whale-watching** excursions (see "Downtown" chapter), or fishing and diving charters. Monthly **birdwatching** walks depart from Cabrillo National Monument.

Point Loma

Birdwatching   ★ ★ ★

Cabrillo National Monument, Point Loma, End of Cabrillo Monument Drive, ☎ *(619) 557-5450.*

Birdwatchers should hitch on to one of the monthly, volunteer-led walks to seek out our feathered friends. Tours depart from the Cabrillo National Monument Visitor Center.

Shelter Island is the hub of San Diego's sailing activities.

FIELDING'S HANDY GUIDE TO WHALE-WATCHING EXPEDITIONS

It's a big event *and* big business for the tourist industry. Each year, between mid-December and mid-March, more than 15,000 gray whales trek 5000 miles from the Bering Strait to breeding grounds off Baja California. And visitors go nuts to catch a glimpse. For those who'd rather watch with their feet planted on earth, Cabrillo National Monument has a sheltered observatory as well as exhibits and an explanatory audio tape. Or, for a closer study...

Classic Sailing Adventures
☎ *(619) 224-0800.*
Two 6-passenger trips daily, beginning mid-December; four hours long; $45 per person.

Fisherman's Landing
☎ *(619) 221-8500.*
Two trips daily, beginning late-December; biologist-narrated; $15 with discounts for seniors, juniors and military.

H&M Landing
☎ *(619) 222-1144.*
Two trips daily, beginning mid-December; three- or five-hours long; $17 with discounts for seniors, juniors and military.

Hornblower/Invader Cruises
☎ *(619) 234-8687.*
Two trips daily, beginning mid-December; narration and video documentary; three-and-a-half hours long; $17 with discounts for seniors, juniors and military.

FIELDING'S HANDY GUIDE TO WHALE-WATCHING EXPEDITIONS

Point Loma Sportfishing
☎ *(619) 223-1627.*
Daily trips beginning late-December; two trips on weekends; $15 with discounts for juniors.

San Diego Harbor Excursion
☎ *(619) 234-4111.*
Two trips daily, beginning late-December; fully narrated; three hours long; $17 with discounts for seniors, juniors and military.

Events

Back to **whale watching**! In late January, the Cabrillo National Monument hosts an annual **Whale Watch Weekend**.

In May, the **San Diego Wooden Boat Festival** takes place on Shelter Island. Come June, the **San Diego International Triathlon** is launched at Spanish Landing, across from the airport. August lures runners to **America's Finest City Half Marathon**, beginning from Cabrillo National Monument.

If interested, you can attend weekly **graduation ceremonies** at the U.S. Marine Corps Recruit Depot. Also, the **Sports Arena** is in this area—site of most super-big indoor sports events, music concerts and the circus.

Lindbergh Field

San Diego Triathlon ★★★
Spanish Landing, Harbor Island, Across from Lindbergh Field,
☎ *(619) 232-3101.*
Starting off from Spanish Landing, this very active event consists of a 1000-meter swim, 30-km bicycle ride and a 10-km run.

San Diego

America's Finest City Half Marathon ★★★
Cabrillo National Monument, San Diego, End of Cabrillo Monument Drive, ☎ *(619) 232-3101.*
Runners start from Cabrillo National Monument, follow San Diego Bay, jag through downtown streets and end up at Balboa Park.

America's Schooner Cup ★★★
Harbor Island, San Diego, ☎ *(619) 223-3138.*
Late March/early April schooner races start off at Harbor Island, slide past Shelter Island to the tip of Point Loma.

San Diego Harbor Parade of Lights ★★★★
Shelter Island, San Diego.

Spectators are dazzled for two weekends each December when the San Diego Parade of Lights makes its annual pilgrimage from the southwest tip of Shelter Island, past Harbor Island, through San Diego Harbor, ending at Seaport Village.

San Diego Wooden Boat Festival   ★★
Shelter Island, San Diego, ☎ (619) 574-8020.
Approximately 100 boats participate in this festival that allows public inspection on both land and water, as well as nautical exhibits, crafts, food and music.

Whale Watch Weekend   ★★★★
Cabrillo National Monument, San Diego, End of Cabrillo Monument Drive, ☎ (619) 557-5450.
January's Whale Watch Weekend is an ideal way to break into the "sport." You watch from a perfect lookout—the glassed-in observatory at Cabrillo National Monument—and learn all from whale exhibits, a taped educational narration, informative lectures and a children's program. Rangers are on hand to answer questions and point you in the right direction. General Admission: $4 per vehicle.

Point Loma, Harbor Island and Shelter Island: Music, Dance and Theater

Occasional student and repertory performances at **Point Loma Nazarene College** are the only backup for the big acts over at the Sports Arena. **Humphrey's Half Moon Inn**, on Shelter Island, hosts a summer series of outdoor "Concerts by the Bay" featuring headliners such as Boz Scaggs, Ringo Starr, James Brown, Jerry Lee Lewis, George Benson, and Bill Cosby. So *there!*

Theater
Point Loma

Salomon Theatre
3900 Lomaland Drive, Point Loma, Point Loma Nazarene College, ☎ (619) 221-2433.
Catch occasional college theatrical performances at the campus with the phenomenal view.

Point Loma, Harbor Island and Shelter Island: Nightlife

POINT LOMA, HARBOR ISLAND AND
SHELTER ISLAND

The classy hotels and restaurants on Shelter and Harbor islands have lounges and bars with the usual range of vocalists, jazz duos and piano hits plus occasional big-name entertainers and club acts.

Over by the Navy and Marine bases, it's a dismal selection of grim bars, topless joints and strip clubs. The restaurant/bars around the Sports Arena are in the desperate singles, young-marrieds-on-the-make, it's-happy-hour! category.

Harbor Island

Tom Ham's Lighthouse   ★ ★ ★

2150 Harbor Island Drive, Harbor Island, *(619) 291-9110.*
The food is unexceptional but the view, at the west point of Harbor Island, makes it worth a stop. The lighthouse—with beacon flashing every few seconds from a replica of the original Point Loma Lighthouse—is Coast Guard-approved. Soft jazz piano accompanies the sunset but, unless you're a glutton for punishment, skip the after dark karaoke.

Lindbergh Field

Sheraton Harbor Island   ★ ★

1380 Harbor Island Drive, Near Lindbergh Field, *(619) 291-2900.*
Both towers feature varied entertainment.

San Diego

Humphrey's Concerts by the Bay   ★ ★ ★ ★ ★

2241 Shelter Island Drive, San Diego, At Humphrey's Half Moon Inn, ☎ *(619) 523-1010.*
Humphrey's increasingly popular series of outdoor summer concerts draws big name diverse entertainers like Ringo Starr, Bill Cosby, Boz Scaggs, Buddy Guy, Dana Carvey and Pat Methany Group. Many of the shows are fast sellouts so buy your tickets way ahead at Humphrey's or through TicketMaster. During the winter jazz is on the schedule and the music moves indoors.

Point Loma, Harbor Island and Shelter Island: Shopping

You mean *besides* the gift shop at **Cabrillo National Monument**? How about boats, nautical gear and seashells?

Order your **custom yacht** or other vessel at one of the Shelter Island boatyards: **Driscoll Custom Boats**, **Koehler Kraft Company**, **Nielsen Beaumont Marine, Inc.**, **Shelter Island Boatyard** or **Shelter Island Yachtways, Ltd**.

FIELDING'S FAVORITE SEAFARER'S SHOPS

Hook, Line & Sinker
   1224 Scott Street, Shelter Island; ☎ *(619) 224-1336.*
   Rods and reels for any size fish, plus creative bait that could also make good earrings.

Seabreeze Nautical Books and Charts
   1254 Scott Street, Shelter Island; ☎ *(619) 223-8989.*
   Heaps of nautical gadgets and bric-a-brac, as well as books and art.

West Marine
   1250 Rosecrans; ☎ *(619) 225-8844.*
   Everything a sailor could dream of—fittings, trinkets, captain's caps and other gear.

Point Loma, Harbor Island and Shelter Island: Where to Stay

Harbor Island practically sits in the airport's lap—choose from a two-tower **Sheraton** or a **Travelodge**. Shelter Island, closer to Point Loma, has a lineup of several tropical-resort suspects—**The Bay Club Hotel and Marina**, **Best Western Shelter Island Marina Inn**, **Humphrey's Half Moon Inn**, **Kona Kai Continental Plaza Resort and Marina**. Both non-island islands offer grassy strips of parkland and gorgeous scenery.

The pickings aren't so good in Point Loma—the **Best Western Posada Inn** is decent and there are a couple of okay motor inns near the Sports Arena. Other choices are either so-so or down-right iffy. The chains and small independents have a presence almost equal to that of the Navy.

POINT LOMA, HARBOR ISLAND AND SHELTER ISLAND

Hostels

Lindbergh Field

Travelodge Hotel-Harbor Island   **$79–$89**   ★★★

1960 Harbor Island Drive, Lindbergh Field, 92101, ☎ (800) 255-3050, (619) 291-6700, FAX: (619) 293-0689.
Single: $79–$89. Double: $79–$89.

There's nothing flash or trendy about this older place but it's ideal for those seeking a good near-the-water neighborhood, restful earth-tone rooms with great views, and reasonable rates (harbor views run $15-25 higher). At nine stories tall, it sits below the Sheraton but isn't dwarfed by it. Bonuses are a small heated pool, exercise room, sauna, whirlpool, business center, dining room, lounge with entertainment and airport transportation. Amenities: exercise room, Jacuzzi, sauna, business services. 208 rooms. Credit Cards: A, CB, DC, D, MC, V.

Hotels

Lindbergh Field

Sheraton on Harbor Island   **$180–$220**   ★★★★

1380 Harbor Island Drive, Lindbergh Field, 92101, ☎ (800) 325-3535, (619) 291-2900, FAX: (619) 296-5297.
Single: $180–$200. Double: $200–$220.

Until a few years ago the Sheratons on Harbor Island were two side-by-side neighbors—Sheraton Grande (now the West Tower) and Sheraton Harbor Island East (now the East Tower). It's a lot simpler now that both towers have been combined into one hotel with a shuttle service running back and forth between the towers and low-rise buildings. Business travelers opt for the fancier West Tower with extra-spacious rooms, writing tables and sitting areas. The completely renovated East Tower, with extensive sports facilities and cheery rooms, is geared more toward on-a-holiday guests. Almost every room in both towers overlooks either the bay or yacht harbor. Luxury levels offer upgraded perks. Guests have access to three restaurants, lounges with live entertainment, 24-hour room service, business center, three heated pools, two wading pools, sauna, spas, playground, health club with aerobics classes, jogging paths, boat and bike rentals and airport transportation. Amenities: tennis, health club, Jacuzzi, sauna, club floor, business services. 1050 rooms. Credit Cards: A, CB, DC, D, MC, V.

Shelter Island

Bay Club Hotel & Marina   **$110–$150**   ★★★★

2131 Shelter Island Drive, Shelter Island, 92106, ☎ (800) 672-0800, (619) 224-8888, FAX: (619) 255-1604.
Single: $110–$140. Double: $110–$150.

This two-story, low-rise—shingled instead of thatched—is not as overwhelmingly "tropical-ized" as its neighbors, though it does give in to rattan furnishings and island-print tapestries. It's a good choice for visitors who want location without too many theme-type trappings. The rooms, reached by interior corridors, are light and breezy with refrigerators and outside terraces overlooking either the bay or marina. Buffet breakfast and airport transportation are included in the rates and the property has its own restaurants, lounge with entertainment, gift and liquor shop. Amenities: exercise room, Jacuzzi, balcony or patio. 105 rooms. Credit Cards: A, CB, DC, D, MC, V.

San Diego Yacht and Breakfast   **$130–$245**   ★★★

Sunroad Resort Marina, 955 Harbor Island Drive, San Diego, 92101, Harbor Island, ☎ *(800) 922-4836, (619) 297-9484, FAX: (619) 295-9182.*
Single: $130–$245. Double: $130–$245.

Hankering for something different than the usual high-rise hotel or low-life motel? Bed and breakfast without all the irritating strangers sharing your wake-up coffee? This outfit will bunk you down on a 41-foot luxury yacht or a 40-foot dockside villa. All amenities are provided including, TVs, stereos, VCRs, phones, refrigerators, microwaves, and breakfast vouchers for the marina resort deli. Other resort facilities availablee to guests are a heated pool and spa. Discounts to a selection of the area's better restaurants are also included. Water views at your doorstep. Amenities: Jacuzzi. Credit Cards: A, MC, V.

Inns

Shelter Island

Best Western Shelter Island Marina Inn **$89–$99**   ★★★

2051 Shelter Island Drive, Shelter Island, 92106, ☎ *(800) 922-2336, (619) 222-0561, FAX: (619) 222-9760.*
Single: $89–$99. Double: $89–$99.

A cozy, water's edge inn with attached marina for guests who arrive by boat (extra charge for the slip). Standard rooms are well-furnished but on the teensy side—okay if you're just using it to bed down, otherwise spring for one of the suites with kitchenettes. Rooms and suites have harbor or marina views. Hang out in the sky-lighted lobby, restaurant and lounge, or around the large pool with sundeck and spa. Free parking is available. Amenities: Jacuzzi, balcony or patio. 97 rooms. Credit Cards: A, CB, DC, D, MC, V.

Motels

Point Loma

Best Western Posada Inn   **$72–$102**   ★★

5005 North Harbor Drive, Point Loma, 92106, two blocks south of Rosecrans Street, ☎ *(800) 231-3811, (619) 224-3254, FAX: (619) 224-2186.*
Single: $72–$82. Double: $78–$102.

Most of the rooms at this six-story inn, adjacent to Point Loma, afford terrific harbor views with lower prices than the "island" resorts. The rooms are cozy and well-furnished, and a restaurant, lounge, small pool, spa and exercise room are on the premises. You're within walking distance of Point Loma shops and seafood set-ups. Covering parking and transporation to the airport or Santa Fe depot are free. Amenities: exercise room, Jacuzzi, balcony or patio. 111 rooms. Credit Cards: A, CB, DC, D, MC, V.

Lexington Hotel and Suites   **$79–$119**   ★★

3888 Greenwood Street, Point Loma, 92110, Adjacent to I-5 and I-8, Sports Arena area, ☎ (800) 944-8668, (619) 299-6633, FAX: (619) 291-8333.

Single: $79–$119. Double: $79–$119.

Close to the Sports Arena and two major freeways, this three story motel is a cut above the other outlying shlock, offering both rooms and suites, a pool and spa, complimentary Continental breakfast, gift shop, meeting rooms, and free airport transportation. Amenities: Jacuzzi. 198 rooms. Credit Cards: A, CB, DC, D, MC, V.

Resorts

Shelter Island

Humphrey's Half Moon Inn   **$99–$169**   ★★★

2303 Shelter Island Drive, Shelter Island, 92106, ☎ (800) 345-9995, (619) 224-3411, FAX: (619) 224-3478.

Single: $99–$149. Double: $99–$169.

It's your Hawaii/San Diego combo deal—a sprawl of tropicality with lush landscaping, fanning palms, waterfalls, tiki torches and poolside bars for that emergency pina colada. Rooms are appropriately rat-taned and nauticalized and some have marina or harbor views. This is home of Humphrey's summer series of Concerts by the Bay, but great jazz is featured year-round. Sweetening the deal are the waterfront seafood restaurant, large pool and spa, bicycle rentals, private marina and lawn games including croquet and putting green. Hot tip for music lovers: come in the summer and shell out the extra bucks for one of the suites with concert-frontage balconies. Amenities: Jacuzzi. 182 rooms. Credit Cards: A, CB, DC, D, MC, V.

Kona Kai Continental Plaza
Resort and Marina   **$130–$500**   ★★★★

1551 Shelter Island Drive, Shelter Island, 92106, ☎ (800) 566-2524, (619) 222-1191, FAX: (619) 221-5953.

Single: $130–$500. Double: $145–$500.

Sparkling clean and thoroughly renovated, thee Kona Kai Continental Plaza Resort and Marina (and mouthful) has finally reopened for business. The old Kona Kai—all thatched and paradise-found—was a celebrity hideaway from the 1950s through '70s. Despite a bit of room-sprucing in 1994, the part hotel/part member's club, dated and deteriorating, couldn't keep up with Jones's-gone-troppo competition. Under new ownership, the Kona Kai has a new name, and finally, some new life. Guest rooms are light and bright, furnished with quality bleached woods and cheery fabrics, and most have views of the gardens or 511-slip marina. A waterfront restaurant and lounge are open, as are the two swimming pools, spa, two tennis courts, banquet facilities, and an upgraded health club. A complimentary shuttle does the airport run. Amenities: tennis, health club, Jacuzzi, sauna. Credit Cards: A, CB, DC, D, MC, V.

Point Loma, Harbor Island and Shelter Island: Where to Dine

Do not leave Point Loma without experiencing **Point Loma Seafood**, the freshest catch in town. It's both a fish market and takeout place, serving the most sublime right-off-the-boat seafood—perpetually jammed with savvy locals and smart visitors.

Other Point Loma restaurants are of the cafe variety, with a couple of better places thrown in.

On Harbor Island, you'll want to try **Tom Ham's Lighthouse** and **The Boathouse**. On Shelter Island, **The Chart House** and **Red Sails Inn** are sure bets. The hotels and resorts all have at least one good dining room (especially **Humphrey's**).

Harbor Island

Boathouse   **$$$**   ★★★
2040 Harbor Island Drive, Harbor Island, ☎ *(619) 291-8011.*
Seafood cuisine. Specialties: Grilled swordfish.
Lunch: 11 a.m.–2 p.m., entrées $6–$14.
Dinner: 5–10 p.m., entrées $8–$28.
One of Harbor Island's better choices was also one of its first—in biz for more than two decades. Happy, cheery, breezy environment for your grilled seafood and stead. The lunchtime salads are worthy of a visit. Dinner only is served on Saturdays. Reservations recommended.
Credit Cards: D, CB, V, MC, DC, A.

Charley Brown's   **$$$**   ★★★★
880 Harbor Island Drive, Harbor Island, ☎ *(619) 291-1870.*
American cuisine. Specialties: Steak and seafood.
Dinner: 5–10 p.m., entrées $14–$28.
Great choice for San Diego visitors who want to pretend they're really cruising on the Mississippi River. Unimaginative steak, seafood and prime rib are served aboard this ain't-goin'-nowhere, purpose-built paddlewheeler (the former *Reuben E. Lee*). Two levels of dining and drinking areas offer lovely bay- and city-views. Warning to landlubbers: even though this boat isn't moving you might feel as though it is. Features: Sunday brunch. Reservations recommended. Credit Cards: D, CB, V, MC, DC, A.

Tom Ham's Lighthouse   **$$$**   ★★★★
2150 Harbor Island Drive, Harbor Island, ☎ *(619) 291-9110.*
American cuisine. Specialties: Flashing beacon.
Lunch: 11 a.m.–3 p.m., entrées $7–$12.
Dinner: 5–10 p.m., entrées $10–$32.
If you're seeking a terrific meal, this is not the place to come—steak, seafood, the requisite pasta dishes are all on the menu, but the view is the star attraction. The Coast Guard-approved lighthouse juts out

into the water, its beach flashing every few seconds (a nightmare for migraine sufferers). There's Sunday brunch and a children's menu but, best is the Happy Hour (Mondays through Fridays, 4-7 p.m.) when you can catch the view and some nibbles for the price of a few drinks. Features: Sunday brunch. Reservations recommended. Credit Cards: D, CB, V, MC, DC, A.

Point Loma

Fairouz Cafe & Gallery $$ ★★★

3166 Midway Drive, Point Loma, ☎ *(619) 225-0308.*
Mediterranean cuisine. Specialties: Lamb dishes , vegetarian buffets.
Lunch: 11 a.m.–5 p.m., entrées $6–$10.
Dinner: 5–10 p.m., entrées $7–$12.

The owner is also an artist and his works are on exhibit (and for sale) in the gallery. The family-run restaurant serves serves luscious Greek and Lebanese specialties including lamb dishes and vegetarian choices. You'll be more stuffed than the grape leaves after diving into one of the combination plates or all-you-can-eat buffets (vegetarian dishes only until 5 p.m.). Terrific atmosphere and value. Credit Cards: V, MC, A.

Pizza Nova $ ★★★

5120 North Harbor Drive, Point Loma, ☎ *(619) 226-0268.*
Italian cuisine. Specialties: Gourmet pizza.
Lunch: 11 a.m.–10 p.m., entrées $5–$12.
Dinner: 11 a.m.–10 p.m., entrées $5–$12.

Is it possible? A waterfront restaurant that serves something other than seafood? Yes, yes! Get your nouvelle-California, wood-fired pizzas and calzones plus a view to boot. All the standard gourmet ingredients are used such as ricotta, Thai chicken, gorgonzola, et al. Pizza Nova has been successful enough to open branches in La Jolla and Hillcrest. Features: wine and beer only. Credit Cards: D, V, MC, A.

Point Loma Seafoods $ ★★★★

2805 Emerson Street, Point Loma, ☎ *(619) 223-1109.*
Seafood cuisine. Specialties: Ceviche, crab sandwiches, seafood cocktails.
Breakfast: 9 a.m.– 6:30 p.m., entrées $4–$8.
Lunch: 9 a.m.–6:30 p.m., entrées $4–$8.
Dinner: 9 a.m.–6:30 p.m., entrées $4–$8.

The catch is so fresh it practically jumps off your tongue as you savor the ceviche, seafood sandwiches on sourdough, fish and chips, shrimp cocktails and other tasties. Chase your meal with fresh lemonade and chocolate chip cookies. The joint is always packed with locals and tourists, making it hard to grab a seat in the small dining area. Get your order to go and relish it while sitting by the shore. The retail market sells a remarkable assortment of fresh-from-the-sea catches as well as smoked varieties. Reservations not accepted.

Red Sails Inn $$ ★★★★

2614 Shelter Island Drive, Point Loma, ☎ *(619) 223-3030.*
Seafood cuisine. Specialties: Shrimp, Alaskan king crab legs.
Breakfast: 7-11 a.m., entrées $2–$8.
Lunch: 11:30-4 p.m., entrées $4–$8.
Dinner: 4–11 p.m., entrées $7–$20.

Save this one for your "authentic waterfront seafood" experience—in case you're running dry. In operation since 1935, the Red Sails will provide you with the view, location, nautical decor, indoor- and out-door-dining, and rowdy sailors hanging at the bar—and, oh yes, the fish. Meals are basic—the charbroiled numbers, chowders, shrimp and chips, an oyster bar—and the service is no-nonsense. Features: outside dining, late dining. Credit Cards: D, V, MC, A.

Venetian $$ ★★★

3663 Voltaire Street, Point Loma, ☎ *(619) 223-8197.*
Italian cuisine. Specialties: Venetian pizza.
Lunch: 11 a.m.–4 p.m., entrées $6–$14.
Dinner: 4–9 p.m., entrées $7–$16.
Family-owned and operated since 1965, The Venetian turns out crispy-crusted, spicy-sauced Venetian pizza and other regional special-ities (shrimp, calamari, cannelloni, etc.). The food is consistently good, the portions are huge and the prices won't break you. Dinner is served until 10 p.m. on Fridays and Saturdays. Credit Cards: D, V, MC, A.

Yakitori II $$ ★★★

3740 Sports Arena Boulevard, Point Loma, ☎ *(619) 223-2641.*
Japanese cuisine. Specialties: Sushi and yakitori.
Lunch: 11 a.m.–2 p.m., entrées $5–$10.
Dinner: 5–10 p.m., entrées $6–$14.
An old favorite with local sushi-ites and restaurant reviewers. It's out of the main business drag, but close to the Sports Arena and close enough to just about every place else. Come for the sushi and yakitori. Reservations recommended. Credit Cards: D, V, MC, A.

Shelter Island

Humphrey's $$$ ★★★★

2241 Shelter Island Drive, Shelter Island, ☎ *(619) 224-3577.*
Seafood cuisine. Specialties: New England Clambake.
Breakfast: 6:30 -11 a.m., entrées $4–$6.
Lunch: 11 a.m.–2 p.m., entrées $5–$10.
Dinner: 5:30–10 p.m., entrées $14–$27.
You can get a steak or pasta dish, but fresh seafood is the draw—that and, of course, the bay view and great jazz in the cocktail lounge (Sundays through Wednesdays, it's the piano bar on other nights). The New England Clambake hits you with a whole Maine lobster, clams and mussels, corn and potatoes. The seafood selections are extensive—a long fishing line of catches, accompanied by the names of the boats where they took their last gasp. The Sunday champagne brunch ($20) will make you lazy, hazy and maybe even romantic for the entire day. Dinner is served until 11 p.m. on Fridays and Satur-days. Features: outside dining, Sunday brunch, late dining. Reserva-tions recommended. Credit Cards: D, CB, V, MC, DC, A.

MISSION BAY
AND BEACHES

Sea World's marine zoological park spans 150 acres.

Mission Bay and Sea World, need I say more?

Cabrillo took one look at Mission Bay back in 1542 and promptly christened it Baja Falso (False Bay). Sure, it might be *facing* the ocean, but la-di-da—the place was full of swamplands and certainly no port for any decent man's boat. A series of channels and dikes were eventually constructed in an attempt to force the San Diego River to behave itself and empty into the sea. And then came the '60s—the *1960s*—and they were certainly good to Mission Bay.

City planners—with the help of taxpayers and the Army Corps of Engineers—dredged the place and turned it into a 4600-acre aquatic park with 17 miles of ocean frontage, 27 miles of bayfront beaches, 90 acres of developed parklands, 7000 parking spots and 2500 boat slips. And admission is *free!* Not bad. Development is strictly enforced—only one-fourth of the land is leased out to a lucky scattering of resort hotels, boatyards, sport-fishing outfits and the big fish at Sea World.

Bridges link Mission Bay with Ocean Beach, nestled alongside Point Loma, and Mission and Pacific beaches—communities where the '60s either never ever left or else have returned with a vengeance.

Mission Bay and Beaches: Things to See and Do

Mission Bay Park can easily take up your entire visit. Even if you hadn't planned on stopping, once you do you'll be there forever. *What* business meeting? *What* hot date? *What* children to support? Strip down to a bathing suit or shorts, kick off your shoes and have some *real* fun knocking around the park with its staggering number of coves and bays. Bring or rent a bike, snorkel and mask, flippers and water-skis, rollerblades or kayaks. Definitely bring a kite. Crash one of the ever-present birthday parties, family reunions or company picnics. Jump into a game of Frisbee. Do nothing except lie on the grass and stare at the sky.

The **Visitor Information Center**, on East Mission Bay Drive at the Interstate 5 exit, will send you off with maps and info on everything from where to rent sports equipment to which locksmith can help you get back into your car. If you're seeking a running mate or group to join, this is the mustering place. The five-mile-long path, paralleling Interstate 5 is the premiere jogging, biking and kite-flying area. **Mission Bay Golf Course** is up at the north end, while man-made **Fiesta Island** is down south, accessed off East Mission Bay Drive. Water- and jet-skiers and unleashed dogs favor the 465-acre island and, as of late, so do some troublemakers. (A party-goer was shot to death in the Summer of '95. I'm sure it will comfort you to know that a cop pulled the trigger. We *will* keep Mission Bay safe!)

Our beloved **Sea World** is reached via Sea World Drive, at the very south edge of Mission Bay, where it borders the San Diego River and encompasses 100 lush and fish-filled acres.

Ingraham Street bisects Mission bay west of Sea World. Turning right will lead you to **Vacation Isle** with a family-oriented village and the powerboat-lover's **Ski Beach**. Keep going north to **Crown Point Shores**, one of the best action-watching and get-together sites.

Instead of taking Ingraham Street, you can choose **West Mission Bay Drive** which will wind to more beaches and coves (**Bonita Cove** is a good one for volleyball), past the sternwheeler *Bahia Belle*—taking off for sunset cruises regularly since the '60s. You'll skirt around private homes that have the bay as their backyard all the way to **Belmont Park**—a renovated amusement park with an easy-to-spot screamer's roller coaster.

Quivira Basin, off Mission Bay Drive on Quivira Road, curves around the huge marina and sportfishing enterprise. At **Marina Village** you'll find small shops and bay-view restaurants, and at **Mission Bay Park Headquarters** you can pick up more maps and info—though you'll probably be a pro if you've made it this far.

Adjacent to Belmont Park, **Mission Bay Boardwalk** is San Diego's equivalent of L.A.'s Venice Beach—a steady onslaught of barely-clothed whirling dervishes flying past on anything outfitted with wheels. Prepare yourself for all that goes with it—massive crowds (summers and weekends are the worst), scant parking, fabulous people-watching, lots of tattooed drunks, pretty strung-out beach bunnies and some rather ugly, strung-out no-lifes. The area is patrolled constantly by bike-riding cops in sand-colored shorts who try valiantly to ignore the beach bunnies and concentrate on the "bad" element. Cruising in the area has reached such epidemic proportions that it has actually been banned—cops are supposedly eyeballing vehicles and if they think anyone has driven up and down the street more than they should to find a parking place (which would be *hours*), they'll issue citations. FYI—the nastiest part of the beach is at the bottom of Ventura Place, the best is up toward Pacific Beach.

At **Pacific Beach** the boardwalk becomes sidewalk, but you'll still have to dodge the dervishes. Escape from the havoc with a stroll along the 1920's **Crystal Pier**—at the foot of Garnet Avenue—lined with dicey motels and real (dicey) fishermen. Then, if you're up to it, plunge eastward, along Garnet Avenue—the center for The Pierced And Tattooed And Pseudo Hippies. Aside from the requisite "parlors," you'll find accouterments such as retro shops, used 501 outlets, recycled clothing enterprises and a smattering of good cafes. Interspersed is a peculiar mix of rave clubs, single's bars and favorite grocery stores.

Back at Sea World Drive, you have the option of turning on to Sunset Cliffs Boulevard which will take you across a short bridge to **Ocean Beach**—*real* hippies, *real* natural foods shops, *real* tie-dyed t-shirts. And *really* good surf. **Newport Avenue**, off Sunset Cliffs Boulevard, is the top shopping strip with all the good '60s and '70s shops, a wonderful antique mall, a bunch of cafes, one of San Diego's best surf shops and the old **Strand Theater**. The **Ocean Beach Pier**, at the foot of Niagara Avenue, is one of the most interesting walks in the city (especially if you like local "color"), and the beach beginning south of the pier is a top spot for board- and body-surfers. North of the pier, the beach caters to more surfers, swimmers (watch signs for safe areas), volleyball players, a contingency of shady characters and—at the north end—packs of wild dogs, happily roaming leashless at **Dog Beach**.

Sports/Recreation
Mission Beach

Mission Bay Park   ★ ★ ★ ★ ★

Mission Bay, Mission Beach, Interstate 5, exit at East Mission Bay Drive,
☎ *(619) 276-8200.*
Hours open: Dawn–Dark

San Diego's 4600-acre aquatic park, just north of Old Town and
downtown, is the city's sports paradise. The former marshes and
swamplands have been transformed into a massive playground—50/
50 water/land—with 17 miles of ocean frontage, 27 miles of bayfront
beaches, 90 acres of developed parklands, a myriad of coves, bays and
channels and thousands of parking places and boat slips. On-the-go
activities include sailing, swimming, waterskiing, windsurfing, golf,
jogging, power walking, cycling, rollerskating, softball and almost
every other land or bay possibility. Make your first stop the Visitor
Information Center *(☎ (619) 276-8200)*, at the East Mission Bay
Drive exit, off Interstate 5. The free guide is full of useful info such as
where to rent boats, bikes and sports equipment and a map designat-
ing which sports are permitted where. The center is open Mondays
through Saturdays 9 a.m.–5 p.m., and Sundays 9:30 a.m.–4:30 a.m.
Hours are extended in summer months. You can also pick up maps
and guides at Mission Bay Park Headquarters *(☎ (619) 221-8900)*
in Quivira Basin, at the western edge of the park. Hours are Mondays
through Fridays 8 a.m.–5 p.m.

*Belmont Park's Giant Dipper wooden rollercoaster is illuminated
with 1600 lights at night.*

Theme/Amusement Parks

Mission Beach

Belmont Park ★★★★★

3126 Mission Boulevard, Mission Beach, ☎ (619) 488-0668.
Hours open: 10 a.m.–9 p.m.

We almost lost Belmont Park. The 1920s amusement center, complete with big dipper and hand-carved carousel, is not quite the beauty it was during its World War II heydey but at least the best chunks have been salvaged. The glorious old park evaporated into ruin by the '70s, was closed down, and eventually fell into the clutches of a seamy, homeless element. After neighborhood protest and some heated clashes between preservationists and developers, it was decided that the roller coaster, The Plunge and Looff Liberty Carousel would be renovated—the compromise, however, was that the 18-acre park would also encompass a shopping and dining complex (better than condos!). The shops and restaurants of "new" Belmont Park appear less than successful, but visitors still adore the oldies. The wooden Giant Dipper (still prompting laughter and screams) is outfitted with 1600 sparkly, twinkly lights that, at night, outline its nostalgic silhouette. The 175-foot-long Plunge, one of the world's largest indoor saltwater swimming pools, is in a dazzling done-up palace with two-story-high murals. Prices of rides vary as do hours. Admission to The Plunge is $2.50, adults; seniors and under 17, $2. Hours are extended in summer months.

Sea World ★★★★★

Sea World Drive, Mission Beach, Off Interstate 5, at Mission Bay Park,
☎ (619) 226-3901.
Hours open: 10 a.m.–5 p.m.

Come only if you don't mind spending lots of bucks and you're not completely reviled by the sight of performing whales, dolphins, seals and other creatures. Children, of course, will be oblivious to both the cost and the acts. The more the merrier, right? Sea World's marine zoological park, spread across 150 acres of tropical landscaping, houses famous exhibits such as Penguin Encounter, Shark Encounter, Wings of the World, and Shamu—the kissing killer whale. Visitors interact with Alaskan sea otters and bottlenose dophins at Rocky Point Preserve and can play touchy-feely with local marine life at the California Tide Pool. The enclosed playground at Cap'n Kids' World will rid the small ones of any excess energy on work-it-off trampolines, climbing towers, swinging bridges and other creative equipment. Check the view from the 265-foot glass Sky Tower or the six-minute sky tram. Admission for both is separate. Food and souvenir outlets are looming wherever you look and none are wallet-friendly. Guided tours and summer-evening entertainment are offered. Hours are extended during summer and holidays. If you plan to spend a lot of time here, inquire at your hotel for discount passes or package deals that include admission. Admission for adults, $30.95; ages three-11, $22.95. Parking is $5 for vehicles, $7 for RVs and $2 for motorcycles. Not cheap, is it? General Admission: $30.95.

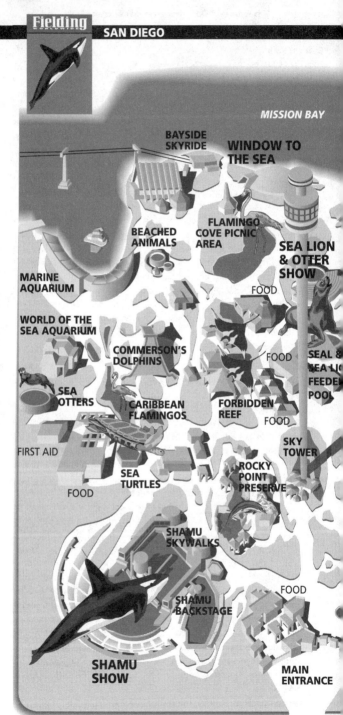

SEA WORLD

Spread across 150 acres, Sea World is a tropical playland where adults and children can observe and interact with whales, dolphins, penguins, sea otters, turtles and other marine creatures. The park also offers shows, rides and backstage tours.

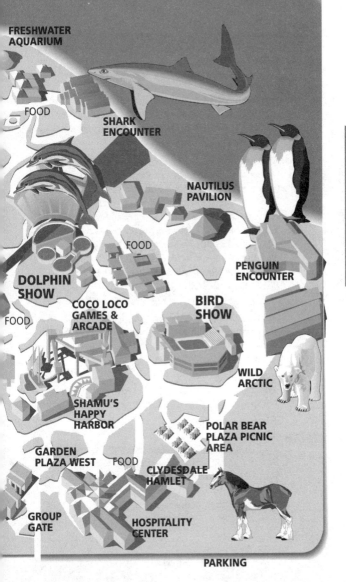

FRESHWATER AQUARIUM

FOOD

SHARK ENCOUNTER

NAUTILUS PAVILION

PENGUIN ENCOUNTER

FOOD

DOLPHIN SHOW

COCO LOCO GAMES & ARCADE

BIRD SHOW

FOOD

WILD ARCTIC

SHAMU'S HAPPY HARBOR

POLAR BEAR PLAZA PICNIC AREA

GARDEN PLAZA WEST

FOOD

CLYDESDALE HAMLET

GROUP GATE

HOSPITALITY CENTER

PARKING

Tours

Mission Beach

Bahia Belle   ★★★

998 West Mission Bay Drive, Mission Beach, Bahia Hotel dock, Mission Bay Park, ☎ *(619) 488-0551.*

The sternwheeler takes guests on sunset cocktail/dancing cruises from the Bahia Hotel over to the Catamaran Hotel—both under same ownership. Under 21's must be accompanied by someone over 21. Cruises depart Wedensdays through Sundays, 7:30 p.m., July through August; Fridays and Saturdays, 7:30 p.m., January through June and September through November. Fare is $5; ages under 12, $3.

FIELDING'S TOTAL EQUIPS

Mission Bay Sport Center

On the Mission Beach edge of Mission Bay Park; ☎ *(619) 488-1004.*

Serious watersport buffs should make the effort to drive or sail to this semi-isolated shop at Santa Clara Point. You can take lessons and rent equipment, then try it out at nearby Sail Bay cove.

South Coast Surf Shop

One of San Diego's finest surf shops has three beach locations for surfboards, boogie boards, snowboards, skateboards, wetsuits, footwear and beachwear. Consignment and rental service is available, as is free advice. **South Coast Surf Shop**, *5023 Newport Avenue, Ocean Beach* (☎ *(619) 223-7017)*; **South Coast Longboards**, *5037 Newport Avenue, Ocean Beach* (☎ *(619) 223- 8808)*; **South Coast Windansea Surf Shop**, *740 Felspar, Pacific Beach* (☎ *(619) 483-7660)*.

Hamel's Action Sports Center

704 Ventura Place, Mission Beach; ☎ *(619) 488-5050.*

Long-established company specializing in sales and rentals of bikes, rollerblades, rollerskates, boogie boards. Lots of action in and around the shop.

Seaforth Boat Rentals

1617 Quivira Road, Mission Bay Park; ☎ *(619) 223-1681.*

Rent rowboats, sailboats and water-ski boats by the hour or day.

Pilar's Beachwear

3745 Mission Boulevard, Mission Beach; ☎ *(619) 488-3056.*

One-stop shopping for women's beach togs. Sizes range from 6-26, and feature mix-and-match sizes, separates and maternity, baby and preteen selections. Styles run from string show-alls to camouflage gear.

Author's Tip

In some circles Ocean Beach has the dubious reputation as a home base for derelicts. Don't take the grimaces and warnings too seriously. It's true that the community harbors its share of losers (what town doesn't?), but it's also a tightly-woven neighborhood that shelters civic pride and individuality—besides some choice surf spots and view sites. The noise from overhead jets is probably the worst drawback.

FIELDING'S FAVORITE°HIDEOUTS

A stroll or bike ride along Bayside Walk, a concrete path stretching from Santa Clara Point in Mission Beach, around Bahia Point, to the southern tip of the park. Residents of the bayfront homes are often outside barbecuing thick wienies and saucy meat— if you don't look too hungry you might get invited to lunch.

A walk along the half-mile Ocean Beach Pier, usually inhabited by a variety of seagulls, fishermen, outcasts, local residents and— nudging danger around the pilings below—brazen surfers. The view is exceptional.

Browse (and then buy!) self-published endeavors of local Ocean Beach poets and writers, at Paras Newstand, 4861 Newport Avenue.

Rummage through past times and strangers' memories at Ocean Beach Antique Mall, 4878 Newport Avenue.

Stray over to Kate Sessions Park at the outer—and upper—limits of Pacific Beach for a serious view from Soledad Mountain.

Mission Bay and Beaches: For Kids

Are you serious? Drop them off at the entrance to Mission Bay Park, hand them some spending money and come back for them when they're 18. Throwing in a kite would be a nice touch. Actually you could almost get away with this during summer months when kids, ages six-15, can sign up for **youth camp** at the Mission Bay Sports Center. Week-long sessions focus on watersports and safety—if your kids like to soak, they'll have a blast.

Sea World, of course, is a kid's dream but be prepared to shell out some bucks. Along with hefty admission, they'll want food, drinks and *lots* of souvenirs. Isn't it worth it to see their wonderful little expressions as they ogle trained seals, dolphins and penguins? In case they start looking too angelic, you can scare them over at the shark exhibit. The tidepool is a fun, hands-on encounter with delicate marine life.

Kids of all ages will enjoy **Belmont Park**. It costs, but not nearly as much as Sea World. Older kids will love the **Giant Dipper**, a restored 1920's historical landmark outlined at night by more than a thousand twinkling lights; younger ages might be happier on the antique carousel. Every swimmer seems to adore **The Plunge**, an incredible indoor freshwater pool (measuring 175-feet-long)—also renovated and dating from the '20s. Be forewarned: the kids will spot lots of cotton candy, junk food and trinkets for sale.

If you're low on cash or want to avoid the hassle, the kids will probably be just as happy eating a picnic lunch and playing for free anywhere in Mission Bay Park. Especially if you bring that kite.

Events

Three big events are held annually at Mission Bay Park. For two days in April, the **San Diego Crew Classic** tests the skills of rowing teams from throughout the United States and Canada. Crown Point Shores is the starting point of the competition.

Fiesta Island is the setting for the somewhat disgusting, usually raunchy, over-the-top **Over-the-Line Tournament**—a local variation of softball. Thousands of players and spectators try to outgross each other for two weekends each July. Best not to bring the kids to this one.

Grab your earplugs before you head off to the **San Diego Bayfair and Unlimited Hydroplane Championship**. One weekend each September, powerboats take off from Ski Beach on Vacation Isle.

Watch the cool fireworks from inside or outside Sea World each **Fourth of July** and get there *early*.

Ocean Beach has been putting on a **Kite Festival** for almost 50 years. The March festivities include kite building and decorating, followed by a parade to the beach to fly the creations. In October, Ocean Beach is also the site of the **Sandcastle Event and Family Fun Carnival**.

Both Ocean Beach and Pacific Beach put on annual **Christmas Parades**.

Mission Beach

Penguin Ski Day Fest   ★★★

De Anza Cove, Mission Beach, Mission Bay Park, ☎ *(619) 276-0830.*
You too can earn a Penguin patch by hitting the water at De Anza Cove and water-skiing sans wetsuit on New Year's Day. Or else, just bundle up and watch from the shores as would-be penguins shrivel up and turn blue.

San Diego Crew Classic

Crown Point Shores, Mission Beach, Mission Bay Park, ☎ *(619) 488-0700.*

Going strong for more than two decades, April's rowing competitions pits teams from throughout the United States and Canada.

Unlimited Hydroplane Championship

Ski Beach, on Vacation Isle, Mission Beach, Mission Bay Park, ☎ *(619) 268-1250.*

The noise is deafening, the action is exciting. The powerboat races are launched mid-September at Ski Beach in Mission Bay Park.

World Championship Over-the-Line Tournament

Fiesta Island, Mission Beach, Mission Bay Park, ☎ *(619) 688-0817.*

San Diego's local take on softball has been playing the world championship tournament for more than 40 years. It sounds wholesome but, believe me, it isn't. Thousands of rowdy, drunken, anything-goes players and spectators descend on Fiesta Island for two weekends each July. The raunchy X-rated team names seem to inspire them all.

Ocean Beach

Ocean Beach Kite Festival

4726 Santa Monica Avenue, Ocean Beach, ☎ *(619) 224-0189.*

All age groups participate in kite building, decorating and flying contests. The kites are made and judged at the Ocean Beach Recreation Center before parading to the beach to take flight. The March festival has been held for almost a half-century.

Ocean Beach Sandcastle Event

Ocean Beach Pier, Ocean Beach, End of Newport Avenue, ☎ *(619) 222-2683.*

Sandcastle building plus a family fun carnival with exhibitor booths, entertainment and lots of food. Held in October.

Rugby Tournament of Champions

Robb Field, Ocean Beach, ☎ *(619) 543-9114.*

Mid-February's Old Mission Beach Athletic Club's Rugby Tournament of Champions features national, collegiate and club teams. Games begin at 7 a.m.

Pacific Beach

Pacific Beach Block Party

Garnet Avenue, Pacific Beach, ☎ *(619) 483-6666.*

The annual block party at the beach is a mid-May happening with live entertainment, arts and crafts, food booths and a children's activity area.

Mission Bay and Beaches: Nightlife

There's always something doing on the beaches and boardwalk at night though the action is quite possibly unsavory. The fancy hotels at Mission Bay Park always have something cookin' in their bars and lounges—gentle vocal and piano sounds, hot jazz progressions and occasional well-known celebs.

Numerous bars and clubs are scattered around Ocean, Mission and Pacific beaches—some for respectable singles, others for weekend ravers and still others for beached troublemakers. Some of the coffeehouses feature live evening entertainment.

Bay Park (on the east side of Interstate 5) and Clairemont (east of Bay Park), though somewhat out of the way, offer several lively clubs and bars.

Mission Beach

'Canes Bar and Grill ★★

3105 Ocean Front, Mission Beach, ☎ (619) 488-1780.
A younger and rowdier crowd parties here for live rock and alternative bands. Sundays feature two satellites and 22 tellies for the sports groupies. Free parking is a real plus.

Cannibal Bar ★★★★

3999 Mission Boulevard, Mission Beach, in the Catamaran Hotel, ☎ (619) 488-1081.
The Catamaran Hotel's long-time-operating tropical nightclub with Wednesday-through-Sunday funk, rock and blues entertainment. Performances begin at 9 p.m.

Ocean Beach

G Lounge ★★

2228 Bacon Street, Ocean Beach, ☎ (619) 222-8131.
You'll find something going on here every night of the week. Live music acts include everything from alternative, rock, and disco to progressive house funk (are you still with me?). Non-music types can hang at the billiards tables and guzzle beer or sip cocktails.

Winston's Beach Club ★★★★★

1921 Bacon Street, Ocean Beach, ☎ (619) 222-6822.
Bands are scheduled nightly in this converted bowling alley, dedicated mostly to '60s life and all that went with it (and in Ocean Beach never went away). Put on your best tie-dye, baby and shake to live rock, reggae, blues, alternative and deadhead.

Pacific Beach

Blind Melons ★★★

710 Garnet Avenue, Pacific Beach, ☎ (619) 483-7844.

Live blues, blues, blues, more blues, rock and reggae at a cry-in-your-drink blue, hot club. Performances begin at 9 p.m.

Daily Planet

1200 Garnet Avenue, Pacific Beach, ☎ (619) 272-6066.
One of the singles arenas infiltrating Rave Street in a hard-to-miss green, purple and bright yellow corner building. Black clothing and nose rings unnecessary for the down-to-earth crowd and rather prissy-ish dance music, and light rock sounds, though some alternative bands have been added. Locals tend to take over the place for televised sporting events. Live performances begin at 9 p.m.

Emerald City

945 Garnet Avenue, Pacific Beach, ☎ (619) 483-9920.
Dance the night away with ravers, sailors, singles and couples. Music is mostly alternative with a smattering of house, hip hop, '70s funk and industrial. The college students descend on Friday's when an official I.D. gets them half-price entry. Saturday features $2 sex drinks, whatever they may be. Excellent sound and light.

Fibber McGee Irish Bar and Restaurant

1466 Garnet Avenue, Pacific Beach, ☎ (619) 272-8540.
Relatively relaxing club/bar/pub/restaurant with rock music Thursdays through Saturdays, Irish folk on Sundays, and blues (plus open-mike opportunities) on Tuesdays and Wednesdays. Or ignore the music and play pool or darts.

Improv

832 Garnet Avenue, Pacific Beach, ☎ (619) 483-4520.
Closed: Mon., Tue., Wed.
Lots of yucks from both national and local funny people in an East Coast-like, art deco-style club.

Javanican

4338 Cass Street, Pacific Beach, ☎ (619) 483-8035.
Everyone's favorite coffeehouse entertainment—acoustic guitar, blues harmonica, original vocals. Tuesdays is open-mike night and *you* could be on stage. Kick-back atmosphere and caffeine highs, slightly off the main drag. Performances run 8-10 p.m.

Moose McGillycuddy's ★

1165 Garnet Avenue, Pacific Beach, ☎ (619) 274-2323.
The names get cuter and cuter. Moose's appeals to older collegiates and young urban unprofessionals. Dance music nightly plus acoustic rock and light tunes.

Tiki House

1152 Garnet Avenue, Pacific Beach, ☎ (619) 273-9734.
Impressive local blues line up on Thursdays and Fridays. Other nights feature rock and roll, alternative and rockabilly acts.

Zanzibar Coffee Bar and Gallery ★★

976 Garnet Avenue, Pacific Beach, ☎ (619) 272-4762.
Acoustic rock, pop, blues and jazz on Thursdays through Saturdays at one of the rave scene's favorite coffeehouses.

San Diego

Barefoot Bar and Grill

1404 West Vacation Road, San Diego, In the San Diego Princess Resort,
☎ *(619) 274-4630.*

The fancy San Diego Princess Resort has a happening club Thursdays
through Sundays. Enjoy your blues, reggae, rock and roll in a high-
life venue.

Brick by Brick

1130 Buenos Avenue, San Diego, East side of Interstate 5, ☎ *(619) 275-
5483.*

On the site of the old Spirit Club, San Diego's first alternative club
where black was hip before it became a uniform. Local and out-of-
town bands stage alternative, rock and grunge concerts Thursdays
through Sundays. Pool, video games, cocktails, Sam Adams on tap
and $1.50 fluorescent 16-oz. pints help set the mood.

Cargo Bar

*1775 East Mission Bay Drive, San Diego, In the San Diego Hilton Beach
and Tennis Resort,* ☎ *(619) 276-4010.*

The Hilton's local watering hole features a dynamite bay view, nautical theme decor and a variety of entertainment stretching from salsa to
fashion parades.

Tio Leo's

5302 Napa Street, San Diego, East of Interstate 5, ☎ *(619) 542-1462.*
Tio Leo's and Brick by Brick are on the same side of the freeway and
that's the only resemblance. The music menu changes nightly but
everything is on the soft-and-easy non-edge—light rock, rockabilly,
swing, blues, contemporary sounds and cabarets. Dance lessons are
sometimes offered.

FIELDING'S FOR-REAL BEACH BAR

Hang out at a real, true, authentic, fair dinkum beach bar. **The Pennant**
*is the place to down a few brews, rah-rah at televised sports, and carouse
on the upper-level outdoor deck with cops, teachers, butchers and
wanted-poster boys. 2893 Mission Boulevard, Mission Beach (☎ (619) 188-
1671).*

Mission Bay and Beaches: Shopping

You won't get away from **Sea World** or **Belmont Park** without
loading up on souvenirs.

Buy **sporting equipment** at shops in Mission Bay Park and Pacific
Beach, and surfers should head for the best **surf shop** in Ocean
Beach. All the beach areas are loaded with t-shirt and bikini

shops. Ocean Beach is the town for real **hippie gear** (lava lamps, smoking accessories), as well as some good antiques. Pacific Beach is your one-stop shopping center for **retro wear**, **pierced jewels and studs**, **custom tattoos**, **well-holed Levi's**, **alternative records**, and **used clothing**.

Mission Bay and Beaches: Where to Stay

If you're looking for peace, Mission Bay's nonstop frenzied play haven is probably not your best neighborhood.

Visitors can choose from one of the classy, activity-oriented hotels and resorts lucky enough to have a lease on **Mission Bay Park**. Most of them are perfect for families with kids. There are a couple of okay places on the beaches—otherwise it's noisy, no-frills motels.

Motels
Mission Beach

Ocean Park Inn   **$85–$145**   ★ ★

710 Grand Avenue, Mission Beach, 92109, Pacific Beach area, ☎ *(800) 231-7735, (619) 483-5858, FAX: (619) 274-0823.*
Single: $85–$145. Double: $85–$145.
A beachfront inn, rising three stories above the sand, located near plenty of action. Contemporary rooms have balconies or patios with ocean views. Aside from the pool and spa, perks include complimentary continental breakfast, free underground parking, valet service and safe deposit boxes. Amenities: Jacuzzi, balcony or patio. 73 rooms.
Credit Cards: A, CB, DC, D, MC, V.

Pacific Shores Inn   **$58–$95**   ★ ★ ★

4802 Mission Boulevard, Mission Beach, 92109, Pacific Beach area,
☎ *(800) 367-6467, (619) 483-6300, FAX: (619) 483-9276.*
Single: $58–$90. Double: $58–$95.
A decent motel choice one-half block from the beach—ideal for seniors and anyone trying to dash the madding crowd. The two-story inn has clean, comfy rooms (some kitchens), a small heated pool and accepts small pets (sparing you the revenge of puppy or kitty left behind). 56 rooms. Credit Cards: A, CB, DC, D, MC, V.

Pacific Terrace Inn   **$135–$215**   ★ ★

610 Diamond Street, Mission Beach, 92109, Pacific Beach area, ☎ *(800) 344-3370, (619) 581-3500, FAX: (619) 274-3341.*
Single: $135–$205. Double: $135–$215.
A contemporary, three-story apartmentlike hotel with the beach at its front door. Large, stylish rooms have minibars, refrigerators, mostly oceanview patios or balconies, quality European amenities and terry robes. Underground parking is free. Amenities: Jacuzzi, balcony or patio. 73 rooms. Credit Cards: A, CB, DC, D, MC, V.

Resorts

Mission Beach

Bahia Resort Hotel   **$125–$325**   ★★★★

988 West Mission Bay Drive, Mission Beach, 92109, In Mission Bay Park,
☎ *(800) 288-0770, (619) 488-0551, FAX: (619) 490-3328.*
Single: $125–$325. Double: $125–$325.

A decibel's throw from Belmont Park's roller coaster and rowdy Mission Beach, the family-friendly Bahia nonetheless rests peacefully on a 14-acre inner-Mission Bay peninsula. Rooms, in one- and five-story buildings, curve around the bay, creating an inner sanctum for gardens, tennis courts, pool and spas. No one will be shocked to find that accommodations are decked out in tropical furnishings and motifs. A restaurant, lounge, water sports, bike and rollerblade rentals are on hand. Guests are also privy to facilities at the sister Catamaran Hotel, and have sailing rights between the two resorts on the Bahia Belle sternwheeler. Amenities: tennis, exercise room, Jacuzzi, sauna, balcony or patio. 325 rooms. Credit Cards: A, CB, DC, D, MC, V.

Catamaran Resort Hotel   **$140–$325**   ★★★★

3999 Mission Bay Boulevard, Mission Beach, 92109, Pacific Beach edge of Mission Bay Park, ☎ *(800) 288-0770, (619) 488-1081, FAX: (619) 488-1619.*
Single: $140–$325. Double: $140–$325.

Six two-story buildings and a 13-story high-rise echo the tropics with island landscaping, palms and ferns, tiki torches and waterfalls, babbling brooks and koi ponds, and a chic atrium lobby. The rooms are okay (fab views from upper levels of the high-rise) but the facilities are better. Besides the restaurant, popular Cannibal Bar and piano lounge, the range consists of the pool/spa/exercise room, beach, rental boats and bicycles, and bay cruises aboard the Bahia Belle, Amenities: exercise room, Jacuzzi. 312 rooms. Credit Cards: A, CB, DC, D, MC, V.

Dana Inn & Marina   **$70–$130**   ★★★

1710 West Mission Bay Drive, Mission Beach, 92109, On Mission Bay Park, ☎ *(800) 345-9995, (619) 222-6440, FAX: (619) 222-5916.*
Single: $70–$130. Double: $80–$130.

You can walk to Sea World from this low-lying inconspicuous property on Mission Bay—the perfect choice if hotsy-totsy resorts make you cringe. The rooms are good enough, though not fancy, and the facilities are more than adequate for most visitors—casual family-style coffee shop, pool, spa, tennis, shuffleboard, ping-pong, a marina with boat rentals, and free parking, airport transportation and shuttle to Sea World. Bring the kids and don't stress out if they track sand or drip water. Amenities: tennis, Jacuzzi, sauna. 196 rooms. Credit Cards: A, CB, D, MC, V.

Hyatt Islandia   **$115–$190**   ★★★

1441 Quivira Road, Mission Beach, 92109, Off W. Mission Bay Drive, in Mission Bay Park, ☎ *(800) 233-1234, (619) 224-1234, FAX: (619) 224-0348.*
Single: $115–$190. Double: $115–$190.

The 16-story tower looms a little too much for the genteel bay location, but the newer lanai rooms are less offensive to the eye. Obviously it's the high-rise that offers the killer views; the lanai digs butt up against the marina—convenient if you parked a boat at one of the slips, otherwise a bit cramped. This is a prime spot for boaties who love to drop anchor alongside their seafaring brethren. Aside from restaurants (one offers a super Sunday brunch), lounge, pool and spa, guests can sign up for charter fishing or rent boats, diving gear and bikes. Airport transportation and shuttle to area attractions are free. Amenities: exercise room, Jacuzzi, sauna, club floor. 422 rooms. Credit Cards: A, CB, DC, D, MC, V.

San Diego Hilton Beach & Tennis Resort $135–$235   ★ ★ ★ ★ ★

1775 East Mission Bay Drive, Mission Beach, 92109, One-half mile north of Sea World Drive exist off I-5, ☎ (800) 445-8667, (619) 276-4010, FAX: (619) 275-7991.
Single: $135–$235. Double: $155–$235.
The resort's multi-million-dollar inside/outside renovation, inaugurated in 1993, has completely changed its old (and we mean really old) stale Polynesian ambience. Visitors who stayed here in the "old days," will be wide-eyed by the new Mediterranean styling with terra cotta clay tile roofs, white stucco walls, tile patios and walkways, and Roman columns and posts. Accommodations in low bungalows or the 127-room tower are now fitted with light wood furnishings, Italian-marble bathrooms, new plumbing, two phones with voice mail, video system, minibars, refrigerators, private balconies and patios. Other re-dos include an enormous ballroom, meeting and convention facility and a dining complex with fine dining, an indoor/outdoor cafe and bars. The pool and tennis club have also been overhauled and you'll have plenty of room to do your strokes in the over-Olympic-sized pool. The recreation options at this 18-acre waterfront palace are extensive (and cost extra): boating, water-skiing, scuba diving, windsurfing, canoeing, paddleboating, cycling. Jogging is free and so are your feet. The Kids Club Program is heaven for families—complimentary child care with lots of planned activities for children over age five. Amenities: tennis, health club, exercise room, Jacuzzi, sauna, business services. 357 rooms. Credit Cards: A, CB, DC, D, MC, V.

San Diego Princess Resort $130–$195   ★ ★ ★ ★ ★

1404 West Vacation Road, Mission Beach, 92109, Mission Bay Park, on Vacation Isle, ☎ (800) 344-2626, (619) 274-4630, FAX: (619) 581-5929.
Single: $130–$195. Double: $135–$195.
Covering 44 acres on Vacation Isle, this is the consumate resort complex and perhaps the only real competion for the San Diego Hilton on the other side of the bay. Summer months its packed with wealthy families doing their let's-all-go-somewhere-together vacation and, at any time, you might run into movie crews who just love the location and landscaping. Is it the South Seas? Mexico? Gilligan's Island? Rooms are in deliciously private bungalows or motel units hidden amid the palms and flowers. Renovations have added contemporary styling with cheerful carpets, bedspreads, windows treatments, sofas and redesigned closets, vanities and counters. The main pool—one of five—now features a swim-up bar. The long list of activities includes restaurants, tennis courts, 18-hole putting course, shuffleboard, volleyball, jogging path, bike- and boat-rentals, a marina and health club. Sea World-faring families might save a small bundle by booking the

hotel's special package deals. Amenities: tennis, health club, exercise room, Jacuzzi, sauna, balcony or patio, business services. 462 rooms. Credit Cards: A, CB, DC, D, MC, V.

Mission Bay and Beaches: Where to Dine

Dining options in Mission Bay Park are at the resort hotels or Quivira Basin. No one goes hungry at Sea World or Belmont Park or, in fact, at the beaches. You'll find takeout joints, cafes and trendy-foodie delights along the main drags and offroads of Mission, Pacific and Ocean beaches. Straying east of Interstate 5, you'll come across many more choices—some extraordinary, but most fairly ordinary.

Mission Beach

Baci's   **$$$**   ★★★★

1955 Morena Boulevard, Mission Beach, ☎ *(619) 275-2094.*
Italian cuisine. Specialties: Homemade pasta.
Lunch: 11:30 a.m.–2:30 p.m., entrées $8–$15.
Dinner: 5:30-10:30 p.m., entrées $21–$30. Closed: Sun.
An unexpected joy stashed away on a boring street parallel to Interstate 5 and Mission Bay Park. The atmosphere is sophisticated Italy and the cucina is mamma-mia perfect—melt-in-your-mouth homemade pastas, veal, seafood, chicken—traditionally prepared. Arrive early and sip martinis in the stylish lounge—you'll feel like you've slid into another era (not the '60s, for a change!). Jacket requested. Reservations recommended. Credit Cards: D, CB, V, MC, DC, A.

Saska's Steak & Seafood   **$$**   ★★★

3768 Mission Boulevard, Mission Beach, ☎ *(619) 488-7311.*
American cuisine. Specialties: Prime beef "Saska" steak.
Breakfast: til 2 a.m. entrées $5–$9.
Lunch: 11:30 a.m.–5 p.m., entrées $4–$12.
Dinner: 5:30 p.m.–2 a.m., entrées $6–$20.
Saska's is an old-timer, survivor of many Mission Beach sagas and episodes, and pretty much a straight steak-and-seafood number (the "Saska" steak—a 10-ounce top sirloin—has been a top menu item for close to a half-century). Local architect Tom Grondona—known for his playful, quirky designs—updated the building with an upstairs cafe, neon and cut-outs. The patio is popular on summer evenings and sunny days. Most notable are the rib-sticking, middle-of-the-night breakfasts with egg dishes and Mexican specialties—either eye-openers or killers, depending on what your plans are for the rest of the night. Breakfast is served until 3 a.m. on Fridays and Saturdays. Features: outside dining, Sunday brunch, late dining. Credit Cards: V, MC, DC, A.

Montgomery Field

94th Aero Squadron $$$ ★ ★ ★ ★

8885 Balboa Avenue, Montgomery Field, ☎ *(619) 560-6771.*
American cuisine. Specialties: Prime rib, filet mignon.
Lunch: 11 a.m.–4 p.m., entrées $7–$15.
Dinner: 4:30-10 p.m., entrées $10–$28.
The dining room is the recreation of a French farmhouse, circa WW I, where you can pretend to be a member of the 94th Aero Squadron (Eddie Rickenbacker, etc.) while chowing down on prime rib, filet mignon, chicken or any of about 20 main courses. The view, overlooking Montgomery Field, is aero-kitsch and packs flightseers in for weekday Happy Hour and Sunday Brunch ($14.95). Lunch is served Mondays through Fridays. Features: Sunday brunch. Reservations recommended. Credit Cards: D, CB, V, MC, DC, A.

Ocean Beach

Belgian Lion $$$ ★ ★ ★ ★ ★

2265 Bacon Street, Ocean Beach, ☎ *(619) 223-2700.*
American cuisine. Specialties: Cassoulet.
Dinner: 5:30-10 p.m., entrées $20–$35. Closed: Mon., Tue., Wed., Sun.
Save the Belgian Lion for your special end-of-the-week dinner. The family-run dining room is renowned for its Belgian/French delicacies ranging from feathery-light salmon to an intense cassoulet, The atmosphere is that of a delightful European "weekend in the country," where you are the supreme invited guest. The staff lays on the Old-World charm and the wine list will make you weep. Features: non-smoking area. Jacket requested. Reservations required. Credit Cards: V, MC, A.

Bungalow $ ★ ★ ★ ★

4996 West Point Loma Boulevard, Ocean Beach, ☎ *(619) 224-2884.*
American cuisine. Specialties: Magic.
Two intimate dining rooms, alit with candles and fireplace flickers, flatter diners as they swoon—if not over each other— then most certainly over the magical concoctions that metamorphose from the kitchen. The gourmet treats might consist of game, poultry, red meat or fish—all imaginatively and creatively prepared and served with sublime sauces. Save this one for a special occasion or else end an ordinary day on a very high note. Jacket requested. Reservations recommended. Credit Cards: D, CB, V, MC, DC, A.

Cecil's Cafe and Fish Market $ ★ ★ ★

5083 Santa Monica Avenuce, Ocean Beach, ☎ *(619) 222-0501.*
American cuisine. Specialties: Gourmet pizzas, fish tacos.
Breakfast: 7-11 a.m., entrées $3–$7.
Lunch: 11 a.m.–2 p.m., entrées $4–$9.
Dinner: 5-9 p.m., entrées $6–$12.
Cecil's lives downstairs from big brother Quiig's and is a more casual, laidback choice—with the same smash views but lower prices and more down-to-earth food. Expect eggs and pancakes for breakfast; gourmet pizzas, fish tacos, salads and grilled sandwiches for lunch and dinner. Lunch is served Mondays through Saturdays, breakfast and dinner are on daily. Credit Cards: V, MC, A.

Quiig's Bar & Grill $$ ★ ★ ★ ★

5083 Santa Monica Avenue, Ocean Beach, ☎ *(619) 222-1101.*

MISSION BAY AND BEACHES

American cuisine. Specialties: Fresh fish and salads.
Lunch: 11:30 a.m.–2:30 p.m., entrées $6–$14.
Dinner: 5:30-10:30 p.m., entrées $7–$18.

When Quiigs opened in 1985, it seemed doomed by the curses of locals who didn't want such a trendy establishment in their gone-'60s enclave. The owners (locals themselves) managed to "do the right thing" by pushing ambience to the max while keeping prices low. The ocean-view and burgers-amongst-friends atmosphere paid off and now Quiigs *is* trendy—and much higher-priced. Try the fresh fish and creative salads along with your ocean view. Lunch is served only Mondays through Fridays. Features: Sunday brunch. Reservations recommended. Credit Cards: D, V, MC, A.

Pacific Beach

Chateau Orleans $$ ★★★★

926 Turquoise Street, Pacific Beach, ☎ *(619) 488-6744.*
Cajun cuisine. Specialties: Spicy dishes.
Dinner: 6-10 p.m., entrées $10–$20. Closed: Sun.

A New Orleans-esque dinner house with hot, spicy Cajun faves—chicken, fish, pasta plus blackened prime rib, Loosy-anna sausage, filled pastries, crawfish etoufee and popover bread. Dinners are huge and include salads, a stuffed pastry and popovers. But, alas, it's Turquoise Street—not Bourbon Street—outside. Features: wine and beer only. Reservations recommended. Credit Cards: CB, V, MC, DC, A.

Karinya Thai Cuisine $$ ★★★

4475 Mission Boulevard, Pacific Beach, ☎ *(619) 270-5050.*
Thai cuisine. Specialties: Appetizers, pad Thai noodles.
Lunch: 11:30 a.m.–2:30 p.m., entrées $6–$10.
Dinner: 5:30-10 p.m., entrées $8–$16.

Order your Thai dishes mild, medium or hot ("medium" is hot, and "hot" is killer). The appetizers could fill up most people happily, plus save the ordeal of picking entrées from the extensive menu. Noodle dishes are choice can't-go-wrongs, as are the scallops in three sauces and chicken in red curry. Kick back Thai-style on floor pillows at squat tables, or opt for the old table-and-chair routine. Lunch is served Tuesdays through Fridays. Credit Cards: V, MC.

Lamont Street Grill $$ ★★★

4445 Lamont Street, Pacific Beach, ☎ *(619) 270-3060.*
American cuisine. Specialties: California cuisine.
Dinner: 5-10 p.m., entrées $11–$16.

A Pacific Beach bungalow-turned-restaurant. Lamont Street Grill was pretty much the talk of the town when it opened—but that was in the pre-foodie days when there was little competition for chi-chi-isms. The food, service and atmosphere continue to be consistent and good. Steaks, seafoods, salads and pastas are staples, prepared with nouvelle California freshness and spice. Reservations recommended. Credit Cards: D, V, MC, A.

Palenque $$ ★★★

1653 Garnet Avenue, Pacific Beach, ☎ *(619) 272-7816.*
Mediterranean cuisine. Specialties: Chicken with mole.
Lunch: 11 a.m.–2 p.m., entrées $5–$10.
Dinner: 5-10 p.m., entrées $7–$14.

A family-run restaurant offering a good selection of Mexican regional specialties. The proprietors—heralding from Acapulco—fill patrons' plates with thank-God-it's-not-another-combination-plate, south-of-the-border surprises. One old family recipe—camarones en chippotle—is a delectable dish of large shrimp in a chili/tequila cream sauce. The dining room is decorated with the requisite pinatas and such, but features comfortable seating. Or you can eat on the outside patio. This is a welcome treat for anyone who thinks Mexican cusine is all tacos and refried beans. Lunch is served Tuesdays through Sundays. Features: wine and beer only. Reservations recommended. Credit Cards: V, MC, A.

Sushi Ota   **$$**   ★★★
4529 Mission Bay Drive, Pacific Beach, ☎ *(619) 270-5670.*
Japanese cuisine. Specialties: Sushi bar and appetizers.
Lunch: 11 a.m-2 p.m., entrées $4–$20.
Dinner: 5-10 p.m., entrées $4–$20.

Tucked away in a strip mall, just north of Mission Bay Park, locals flock here for the scrumptious sushi bar and extensive appetizer menu—as well as for traditional Japanese choices. You can make an exquisite meal from more than 30 appetizers including seafood, tempura, stuffed dumplings and broiled salmon. You can get off cheap with a few items, or clean out your wallet on a crazed sushi-and-starters binge. Plan on the binge. Reservations not accepted. Credit Cards: V, MC, A.

FIELDING'S FAVORITE PICNIC BASKETS

A visit to the bay or beaches cries for a picnic lunch or dinner. Shop where the locals go for the best goodies to pack.

OB People's Natural Foods
4765 Voltaire Street, Ocean Beach; ☎ *(619) 224-1387.*
A real authentic '60s co-op with organic fruit, veggies, juices, as well as bins filled with nuts, cheeses, dried fruits and bulk treats.

Boney's Market Place
1260 Garnet Avenue, Pacific Beach; ☎ *(619) 270-8200.*
More organic pickings, plus grocery items, bulk bins and juices.

Trader Joe's
1211 Garnet Avenue, Pacific Beach; ☎ *(619) 272-7235.*
The local favorite for discounted gourmet cheeses, chips, pretzels, chocolates, bagels, smoked salmon, pates, mineral waters, juices, wine, beer and myriad other selections. Branches of Trader Joe's are also located in La Jolla, Encinitas and Oceanside.

"Just ignore them. They're summer people."

Drawing by Crawford; ©1995 The New Yorker Magazine, Inc.

LA JOLLA AND THE GOLDEN TRIANGLE

Torrey Pines golf course offers spectacular ocean views.

The Native Americans used to call the place "La Hoya," meaning "the cave" (no doubt for the cliffside caves they once frequented). The Spaniards rechristened it "La Jolla," same pronunciation, but now defined as "the jewel." The 30,000 mostly rich and prominent residents refer to their ritzy enclave simply as "the village"—though, unlike Coronado-ites who use the same designation for *their* town—*this* village is really part of the City of San Diego (and just 12 miles from downtown), albeit with its own ZIP code. Whoop-de-doo. Beverly Hills 90210 meet La Jolla 92037.

The village is fairly well defined as the commercial area around Prospect Drive (the 92037 equivalent of Rodeo Drive) and Girard Avenue—a collusion of toniness and trendiness—that spills shamelessly over the cliffs and into the azure waters and shoreline grottos that once belonged to the La Hoyans—now overrun with parading tourists, diehard surfers and fancy-schmancy La

Jollans. The remainder of the La Jolla area stretches south to Pacific Beach, north to the Torrey Pines State Reserve and Del Mar, and east to Interstate 5.

You can't miss the name "Scripps" in your face at almost every turn. Ellen Browning Scripps, the community's benefactor—monied via her newspaper business—began buying Prospect Street real estate in 1896, moving into her own cottage a year later. Ellen, along with brother E.W. and half-sister Virginia, instilled civic pride in La Jolla, bestowing upon it world-renowned Scripps Institute of Oceanography, the Children's Pool, a big chunk of Torrey Pines Park, and the beginnings of most of the local Irving Gill buildings. Scripps Park, along La Jolla Cove, is named for Ellen alone, while many other structures—Scripps Pier, Scripps Hospital, Scripps Clinic and Research Foundation, etc.—are named for the whole clan, all big-money donors.

Though wealth is the common thread running throughout La Jolla, the word "common" is the giveaway. Unlike Coronado-town, *old* money is not the main criteria for acceptance—*any* money will do. La Jolla harbors a goodly share of scientists (the late Jonas Salk), beloved authors (the late Dr. Seuss), physicians, attorneys and such—it also attracts (and puts up with) an element of celebrity riff raff, scam artists and let's-play-rich-until-we-go-bankrupt folks. Besides, the whole town is *not* well-to-do. The homes right along the beaches or high up in the palm-shaded, terraced hills are appropriately expensive and exclusive. The rest of 92037 is a blend of well-kept but otherwise "normal" residences with the usual non-exciting boxy rooms, stucco walls and we're-so-scared security systems. The village and its environs even harbor a number of unexciting apartment and condo complexes, as well as—horrors!—a scattering of humble cottages resided in by steady blue-collar workers or split-the-rent-three-ways roommates. And, odd though it may seem, La Jolla is actually a college town—the University of California at San Diego sits just off Interstate 5, at the top of the hill.

The Golden Triangle is the inland area formed by the intersection of Interstates 5 and 805 with Highway 52. Virtually barren until the late 1970s, it is now filled with business parks, first-rate hotels, some of La Jolla's best restaurants, a major shopping mall, the couldn't-miss-it-if-you-tried Church of Jesus Christ of Latter-day Saints and a veritable sea of look-alike condos.

Fielding's Best La Jolla Views

Pannikin's Brockton Villa Restaurant, at La Jolla Cove (1235 Coast Boulevard).

George's at the Cove—from the dining room if you're a big spender, otherwise from the less expensive cafe or terrace (1250 Prospect Street).

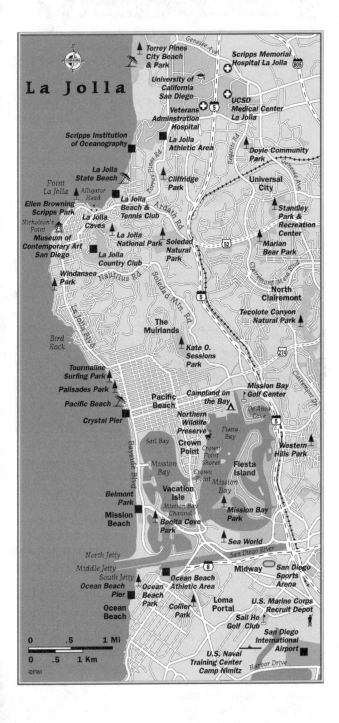

La Jolla

- Torrey Pines City Beach & Park
- Scripps Memorial Hospital La Jolla
- University of California San Diego
- UCSD Medical Center La Jolla
- Veterans Adminstration Hospital
- Scripps Institution of Oceanography
- La Jolla Athletic Area
- Doyle Community Park
- La Jolla State Beach
- Cliffridge Park
- Universal City
- Point La Jolla
- Alligator Head
- La Jolla Beach & Tennis Club
- Ardath Rd
- Standley Park & Recreation Center
- Ellen Browning Scripps Park
- La Jolla Caves
- La Jolla National Park
- Soledad Natural Park
- Marian Bear Park
- Nicholson's Point
- Museum of Contemporary Art San Diego
- La Jolla Country Club
- Regents Rd
- North Clairemont
- Windansea Park
- Nautilus Rd
- Soledad Mtn Rd
- Tecolote Canyon Natural Park
- Bird Rock
- The Muirlands
- Kate O. Sessions Park
- La Jolla Blvd
- Tourmaline Surfing Park
- Palisades Park
- Pacific Beach
- Crystal Pier
- Pacific Beach
- Campland on the Bay
- Mission Bay Golf Center
- Northern Wildlife Preserve
- De Anza Cove
- Western Hills Park
- Bayside Blvd
- Sail Bay
- Crown Point
- Crown Point Shores
- Fiesta Bay
- Fiesta Island
- Mission Bay
- Crown Point
- Mission Bay
- Belmont Park
- Vacation Isle
- Mission Bay Channel
- Mission Bay Park
- Mission Beach
- Bonita Cove Park
- Sea World
- San Diego River
- North Jetty
- Middle Jetty
- South Jetty
- Ocean Beach Pier
- Ocean Beach Park
- Ocean Beach Athletic Area
- Midway
- San Diego Sports Arena
- Ocean Beach
- Collier Park
- Loma Portal
- U.S. Marine Corps Recruit Depot
- Sail Ho Golf Club
- San Diego International Airport
- U.S. Naval Training Center Camp Nimitz
- Harbor Drive

0   .5   1 Mi
0   .5   1 Km

©FWI

Fielding's Best La Jolla Views

Top O' the Cove, a romantic (and costly) cliffside restaurant (1216 Prospect Street).

The clifftops at Torrey Pines State Reserve (end of North Torrey Pines Road).

The balcony off the ladies' room at La Valencia Hotel (1132 Prospect Street).

From 800-foot-tall Mount Soledad (you can't miss the huge cross—if it's still there after the religious-equality battles—on Soledad Drive).

Perched on the head of Angel Moroni, the 10-foot-tall gold-leaf icon atop the Church of Jesus Christ of Latter-day Saints.

La Jolla and the Golden Triangle: Things to See and Do

A couple enjoys the beauty of a La Jolla beach.

There are a few different approaches. You can go the slow, beachy way along Mission Boulevard, through Mission and Pacific beaches, where the road becomes La Jolla Boulevard—and the **Bird Rock** section of town. Either stay on the boulevard—not very special except for several excellent restaurants—or cruise along the streets closer to the west for a gaggle at the beach and one of the nicer residential neighborhoods. **Windansea Beach**, at the end of Nautilus Street, is one of the more famous surfing beaches—made more so by Tom Wolfe's *The Pump House Gang*. Take your chances if you want to surf here—Windansea and adjacent beaches are *not* tourist-friendly. Taking Nautilus east will lead you up to **Mount Soledad**, La Jolla's highest point, where you can ooh and aah the view from the cross at the top. (The cross, of course, is another much ballyhooed problem—traditionalists want it to stay, religious-freedomists say it should either go or else be joined by a Star of David, statue of Buddha and bust of Krishna. The Mormons don't care—they've *got* their big Moroni on the other side of the freeway.)

In **the village**, explore the entire length of **Prospect Street**, checking the art galleries, Euro-style boutiques, jewelry shops, chic restaurants, and the pink 1920s **La Valencia Hotel**, a longtime favorite escape for celebrities. A drink in the hotel's **Whaling Bar** is a must for lost-era hounds. The **San Diego Museum of Contemporary Art**, also on Prospect, reopened in early 1996 after a complete renovation and expansion by architect Robert Venturi (the pre-renovated building was in the remodeled, Irving Gill-designed, Ellen Browning Scripps home).

Turning off Prospect Avenue onto **Coast Boulevard**, you should definitely sneak into **La Jolla Cave and Shell Shop** both for shell-shopping and a trip down the long, dark stairs to **Sunny Jim Cave**. Slightly farther, is the Nirvana-esque **La Jolla Cove** and **Ellen Browning Scripps Park**. Divers and snorkelers explore at the protected underwater preserve at the north end, bodysurfers take over **Boomers Beach** slightly southward. The palm-lined walkways and cool green grass at the park, above the raggedy sandstone cliffs, are popular with hand-in-hand strollers, sunset-gazers, photographers, Frisbee players and the usual dreamers. Magical **tidepools** appear in the rock pockets when the tide creeps in (be careful, though, not to get trapped). At the south end of the park, the shallow **Children's Pool** is a delight with the little ones.

Explore the rest of the village—Girard Avenue with more boutiques, cafes, specialty stores, and **The Athenaeum** music-and-art library, and the adjacent **La Jolla Library**. On the streets between Girard Avenue and Prospect Avenue, you'll find a mix of shops, residences, Gill designs and other notable architecture. **La Jolla Town Council,** *1055 Wall Street* ☎ *(619-454-1444)*, can help with visitor info.

North of the cove, as you leave the village, swing north onto La Jolla Shores Drive. Along this stretch you'll hit the **La Jolla Beach and Tennis Club,** the exquisite surfing- and swimming beaches at **La Jolla Shores, the Scripps Institute of Oceanography and Scripps Pier.** La Jolla Shores Drive curves and climbs a short distance (with an extraordinary view), through a residential neighborhood, ending at North Torrey Pines Road and one entrance to the **University of California at San Diego** (UCSD). Campus touring should include visits to the **Central Library** (if only to marvel at how the spaceshiplike building could actually be standing upright), the **Price Center**—the student heart with cafe, cinema, travel center and bookstore—and **The Stuart Collection,** an outdoor art gallery with somewhat controversial works by internationally known artists.

Back on North Torrey Pines Road, you'll see signs pointing to the **Salk Institute for Biological Studies**—another architectural tour de force, and the Torrey Pines Glider Port. At the foot of the steep cliffs, lies **Torrey Pines City Park Beach (or Black's Beach),** the unofficial nude haven where many a limb has been broken by panting idiots who would die for a close peak at some bare flesh.

At the top of the road, you have three choices. Go straight, over Interstate 5, to **The Aventine,** an enormous and architecturally controversial complex which contains the **Hyatt Regency,** some of La Jolla's finest restaurants, offices and a health club. Towering at the south, you will not miss the ten-spired Gothicstyle **Church of Jesus Christ of Latter-day Saints** and the angel Moroni sucking up freeway fumes. East along Genesee Avenue, **University Towne Centre** is a prime shopping target with—besides department and chain stores—an ice skating rink, cineplex food hall and various restaurants.

If you turn right, you're back on the UCSD campus—the road will curve around the library and Price Center, eventually bringing you out the other side at the Veteran's Hospital and **La Jolla Village** mega-malls. You can also reach this area from downtown by taking the La Jolla Village exit from Interstate 5—or from the village, by making a straight shoot up Torrey Pines Road. The junction of Torrey Pines Road and La Jolla Village Drive spills into the lap of **La Jolla Playhouse,** on the UCSD campus, and the new, expanded **Stephen Birch Aquarium-Museum** (with more than 30 huge aquariums and not *one* performing fish!).

A left onto North Torrey Pines Road will scoot you past the **Scripps Clinic and Research Foundation** (our Mayo Clinic—good for Mother Teresa, bad for Jonas Salk), as well as other medical- and scientific-research facilities, a couple of expensive resort hotels, **Torrey Pines Municipal Golf Course and Torrey Pines State Reserve**.

Historical Sites

La Jolla

Church of Jesus Christ of Latter-day Saints   ★

> *Nobel Drive, La Jolla, Along east side of Interstate 5.*
> Unless you're willing to undergo conversion and full-body baptism, forget about getting inside the Mormon Temple. The jaw-dropping, next-to-the-freeway site of this Gothic bizarrity—with its 10 steel spires and 10-foot gold-leafed angel Moroni statue—is closed to the public. There *was* a sort of "let's get it over with" public viewing before the temple officially opened—ticketholders had to don paper slippers before being allowed to walk into the grand edifice. But, know what? After the doors closed to the lookie-loo sightseers (Thank Moroni), the brand new carpet was ripped up, tossed out, and replaced with brand newer carpet—untouched-by-non-Mormon-feet.

Museums and Exhibits

La Jolla

Mingei Museum of World Folk Art   ★★★★

> *House of Charm in Balboa Park, La Jolla, Across from Nordstrom's,*
> ☎ *(619) 453-5300.*

Hours open: 10 a.m.–4 p.m.
Closed: Mon.

The Mingei (Japanese for "art of the people"—loosely defined) is a must-see for ethnic art-lovers. Now in its new Balboa Park home, the museum's permanent collections and changing exhibitions include arts and crafts from all over the world that encompass costumes, textiles, pottery, sculpture, jewelry and toys. The gift shop sells an interesting selection of ethnic pieces where you can pick up everyday baubles and bangles, note cards, one-of-a-kind wearable art or high-end ceramics. Admission for children is $2. General Admission: $5.

San Diego Museum of Contemporary Art ★★★★

700 Prospect Street, La Jolla, In the village, 92037, ☎ *(619) 454-3541.*
Special Hours: Tues.-Sat. 10 a.m.–5 p.m.; Sun., noon–5 p.m. Closed: Mon.

MOCA, in its new expanded version, Reopened in 1996 and still rates plenty of stars. Ellen Browning Scripps' Irving Gill designed-estate was incorporated in the original museum—revamped twice by architect Robert Mosher. In 1992, Robert Venturi was given the task of expanding and renovating La Jolla's cultural focal point. Hovering above the cove, the new building garners even more views than before and visitors are hard-pressed to decide what they'd rather be studying—the blue horizon or the permanent and changing exhibitions of post-1950s art. As before, the museum offers a full program of concerts, film festivals and lecture series, plus a sculpture garden and larger book- and gift-shop. Contemporary art aficionados can still opt for the scaled-down downtown branch, across from Santa Fe Depot. Open Wed. until 8 p.m. Free to all on first Tues. of the month. Adults, $4; seniors, students, military, $2; under 12, free.

Stuart Collection ★★★★

UCSD, La Jolla, ☎ *(619) 534-2117.*

Some of the hottest and most controversial sculptors and artists have their commissioned works spread throughout the UCSD campus. Niki de Saint Phalle's 14-foot smash-of-color Sun God stands near Mandeville Auditorium; Terry Allen's Trees belt C&W sounds and soft poetry, startling and teasing strollers near the library and Student Health Center; Seven Vices, a neon piece by Bruce Nauman, flashes seven sets of vices and virtues nightly atop a lab building (lighted seven-foot-tall duos like "temperance and gluttony" rival the Mount Soledad cross and the Mormon temple's angel Moroni for heavenward gazing). All the works are worthy of a few good over-coffee debates. Pick up walking maps and guides to the 12-piece collection at the information center in the Price Center or at the information kiosk on Gilman Drive.

Parks and Gardens

La Jolla

Torrey Pines State Reserve ★★★★

Torrey Pines Park Road, La Jolla, At the bottom of Torrey Pines Road,
☎ *(619) 755-2063.*
Hours open: 9 a.m.–Sunset

This 1750-acre reserve, established in 1921, is one of only two sanctuaries for the Torrey Pine *(Pinus torreyana)*, America's rarest pine tree—a twisted quirk of nature, dating back centuries. Hikers (especially New Agers communing with nature) and cyclists love to wind along the paths—lingering until they've bonded with the sunset, a tantalizing sight from atop the 300-foot-high cliffs. Pick up trail maps and other info at the 1922-built park headquarters (another gift from Ellen Browning Scripps). Leave your car at the beach lot or up the hill near the park office. General Admission: $4, parking.

Theme/Amusement Parks

La Jolla

Stephen Birch Aquarium-Museum ★★★★★

2300 Expedition Way, La Jolla, South of La Jolla Village Drive, ☎ *(619) 534-3474.*
Hours open: 9 a.m.–5 p.m.

Operated by the Scripps Institution of Oceanography (part of UCSD), this "improved" version of the aquarium opened in late 1992. We actually liked the old one better—it was homier, had natural tidepools and was *free*. Nostalgia aside, the newer aquarium is really quite extraordinary and not to be overlooked, especially if you have children in tow. The museum section offers educational and interactive exhibits on an astounding variety of sea-oriented phenomena and products, but the knockout attractions are really the 30-plus tanks filled with California- and Mexico-based neon- and crayon-colored saltwater fish. Other must-sees include a 70,000-gallon simulated kelp forest tank, 12-minute simulated sub ride, an artificial tidepool and fantastic book/gift shop. Admission for seniors, $5.50; ages 13-18, $4.50; ages three-12, $3.50. Parking costs $3. General Admission: $6.50.

The Stephen Birch Aquarium museum features tanks full of colorful marine life.

Universities

La Jolla

Central Library ★★★

UCSD Campus, La Jolla, ☎ *(619) 534-3339.*
Hours open: 9 a.m.–11 p.m.

How does this spaceship-like building stand on its own two-story pedestal? Who cares! The campus icon is a mecca for research and reference materials. You can browse the books for free, but a library membership allowing withdrawals comes at nominal charge. The library opens at 9 a.m. on Saturdays and at 1 p.m. on Sundays.

University of California at San Diego ★★★★

North Torrey Pines Road, La Jolla, between Genesee Avenue and La Jolla Village Drive, ☎ (619) 534-2230.

A much more serious university than get-down-and-party San Diego State, across town. Founded in 1960 as part of the University of California system—and set on 1200 densely wooded, scenery-a-second, prime La Jolla acres—UCSD ranks high as a top research facility, with such notable aquisitions as Scripps Institute of Oceanography (founded in 1903), San Diego Supercomputer Center and the School of Medicine. This campus of the University of California system is also distinctive for its five colleges—Revelle, Muir, Third College, Warren, and Fifth College—each with its own educational philosophy, requirements and traditions (Muir College is the most popular). More than 90 percent of the 17,000-plus enrollment are California residents and about one-third of all undergraduates live on campus. Faculty members include Nobel Prize winners, members of the National Academy of Sciences and Guggenheim Fellowship recipients. Don't miss visits to Scripps Insitiute of Oceanocraphy, the Central Library or The Stuart Collection, as well as performances and cinema at the Price Center and Mandeville Auditorium. Pick up campus info and schedules at the Price Center.

Views

La Jolla

Mount Soledad ★★★

Soledad Road, La Jolla, High above the village, west of I-5.

Super views from 800-foot-high Mount Soledad, a long-time pilgrimage for locals and tourists who come to gush over the cityscape below. Various crosses have stood nearby since 1913 (including one emblazoned by the KKK) but a freedom-of-religion controversy may, at some point, either force that cross to fall or give it a supper table of company—a Star of David, Buddha Belly, Ankh and any other religious symbol that some group or individual might want to see displayed.

FIELDING'S FAVORITE LA JOLLA AND THE GOLDEN TRIANGLE ARCHITECTURE

United Methodist Church

6063 La Jolla Boulevard.

It certainly *does* look like a church, but at one time these buildings housed a trolley depot, Mexican restaurant and bar that catered to celebrities like Raymond Chandler.

San Diego Museum of Contemporary Art

700 Prospect Street.

The former estate of Ellen Browning Scripps, originally designed by Irving Gill and later updated by Robert Mosher, and, more recently, by Robert Venturi.

La Jolla Woman's Club

715 Silverado Street.

Funded by Ellen Browning Scripps, this elegant 1914 structure is one of the finest examples of Irving Gill's work.

La Valencia

1132 Prospect Street.

Our favorite pink stucco art deco hotel, La Jolla's equivalent to Hollywood's Garden of Allah—except the GOA was demolished years ago.

Top O' the Cove

1216 Prospect Street.

A charming turn-of-the-century bungalow that turned again, mid-1950s, into a swanky restaurant.

Casa de Mañana

849 Coast Boulevard.

It may be a retirement home now, but during the good old days—when the casa was a palatial Spanish Colonial resort—stars like Ginger Rogers and Rita Hayworth used to kick up the rug.

Salk Institute

10010 North Torrey Pines Road.

Don't miss a peak at Louis Kahn's architectural marvel where the world's top scientific geniuses ponder retro viruses and bio-futurism.

UCSD Central Library

How does this spaceshiplike edifice stand on its own two-stories? Look beyond the newer addition—that is actually built around the trademark pedestal.

FIELDING'S FAVORITE LA JOLLA AND THE GOLDEN TRIANGLE ARCHITECTURE

Aventine

3777 La Jolla Village Drive.
Michael Graves' controversial humongathon on the Golden Triangle side of Interstate 5. Within are the Hyatt Regency, offices, restaurants and a health club.

Church of Jesus Christ of Latter-day Saints

"What *is* that thing?" you scream, as your car practically grazes the ten-spired Gothic temple alongside Interstate 5. That 10-foot-tall gold-leaf figure is none other than angel Moroni—one-time angelic confidante to church founder, Joseph Smith. Unless you're a bonafide Mormon (yes, they *do* know), you won't get inside.

La Jolla and the Golden Triangle: For Kids

Even in ritzy La Jolla there's a bit of free entertainment for the kids. You can't go wrong at the **Children's Pool,** a sheltered, calm-water bay where toddlers splash and older tots snorkel. If you don't want to get them wet, stay up top at **Scripps Park** and play catch or Frisbee—let them watch the surfers and divers, inspiration for their beach-bum dreams. **La Jolla Cave and Shell Shop** will keep them occupied, but you'll probably leave toting a collection of shells and fossils. **The White Rabbit** (*7755 Girard Avenue*), a children's bookstore, is so enchanting it might even prompt the kids to beg for a storybook instead of a Nintendo game.

La Jolla Recreation Center, at the junction of Prospect Street and La Jolla Boulevard, is where the local kids go for playground action and planned summer activities.

The **Stephen Birch Aquarium-Museum is** good for days' worth of entertainment and is cheap compared to Sea World. The whole family can gurgle away at the thirty-plus gigantic tanks aswim with color-spectrum saltwater fish. Anyone over the age of three qualifies for the 12-minute pseudo-sub ride, while the tidepool will keep the under-three's hooked.

The shopping malls at **La Jolla Village** and **University Towne Center** are unsurprisingly filled with movie-plexes and video arcades, and **University Towne Center** has an indoor ice skating rink with skate rentals and an upstairs food court.

Tours

Guided **walking tours** of La Jolla village and historical sites are offered almost every weekend. The scientifically and architecturally-inclined should sign up for one of the freebie tours of the prestigious **Salk Institute.** Art- and sculpture-lovers won't want to miss a self-guided walking tour of **The Stuart Collection,** an outdoor gallery spread out upon the UCSD campus.

La Jolla

La Jolla Cave and Shell Shop ★★★★

1325 Coast Boulevard, Near La Jolla Cove, 92037, ☎ *(619) 454-6080. Hours open: 10 a.m.–5 p.m.*

Depending on your interests, physical condition, claustrophobia tolerance and tolerable companions, you may have to divide this attraction between the cave and the shell shop. The shell shop is a safe bet for everyone—a trove of ocean-echo shells, crystals, fossils and other touchy-feelies. To visit Sunny Jim Cave, however, you must enter through the shell shop and navigate 133 dark and narrow stairs or else make a quarter-mile swim from the cove. Admission is charged for cave access (from the shell shop) and stairwell climbs. Sunday hours are 11 a.m.–5 p.m.

La Jolla Tours ★★

910 Prospect Street, La Jolla, At the Colonial Inn, ☎ *(619) 453-8219.*

Walking tours lasting one and one-half-two hours will brief you on historic buildings, scenic sites and Sunny Jim Cave. Tours depart from the Colonial Inn, Thursdays through Saturdays at 10 a.m. (tours do not operate on Thanksgiving Day, Christmas Day or New Year's Day. Antique and art gallery tours are also offered. There's a four-person minimum for each tour. Reservations are necessary. General Admission: $9.

Salk Institute of Biological Studies ★★★

10010 North Torrey Pines Road, La Jolla, Near Torrey Pines Glider Port, ☎ *(619) 453-4100.*

The Salk Institute rates as one of the world's largest independent biological research centers. Visitors get a close-up view of Louis Kahn's wondrously designed building where resident geniuses and international scientists put their gargantuan brains together to solve some of the world's most perplexing biological quandries. Guided tours depart Mondays through Fridays (except holidays), on the hour, 10 a.m-noon.

Events

La Jolla's annual **Easter Hat Parade** has been hopping for more than a decade. Later in April, the **La Jolla Half Marathon** finishes over at the cove. June ushers in the **La Jolla Festival of the Arts and Food Faire,** an event that draws established artists and chefs, and, in late August, Wall Street is shut down and the area is mobbed for the annual **Off the Wall Street Dance.**

Around the second week of September, the cove gets packed with participants in the **La Jolla Rough Water Swim,** the largest competition in the United States.

What did I forget? Oh, yes—**The Buick Invitational of California** is held at Torrey Pines Golf Course for one week each February, flooding the area with celebs, politicos and golf groupies.

Golden Triangle

NAS Miramar Air Show ★★★★★

Miramar Naval Air Station, east of the Golden Triangle, ☎ *(619) 537-6289.*
For more than 40 years, the Miramar Naval Air Station has hosted its August air show featuring all kinds of aviation displays and performances—including a stellar appearance by the gravity-defying Blue Angels. Admission and parking are free but the place gets filled up early. If you're willing to shell out some cash, you can reserve special seating in advance.

La Jolla

Buick Invitational of California ★★★★★

Torrey Pines Golf Course, La Jolla, On North Torrey Pines Road, ☎ *(619) 281-4653.*
The Buick Invitational of California—an annual PGA Tour men's golf tournament held since 1952—draws more than 100,000 spectators to Torrey Pines Golf Course each February. Pro-Am Day is an ace event with local and national celebrities participating and attending.

La Jolla Easter Hat Parade ★★★

Prospect Street and Girard Avenue, La Jolla, In the village, ☎ *(619) 454-2600.*
Easter bonnets are paraded through the streets, beginning at Prospect Street and Girard Avenue. Cheer the award winners—vying for prizes from local merchants—at Colonial Inn, following the parade.

La Jolla Festival of the Arts and Food Faire ★★★★

9490 Genesee Avenue, La Jolla, La Jolla Country Day School, ☎ *(619) 456-1268.*
This June-weekend event, held on the La Jolla Country Day School campus, features top-notch cuisine and award-winning artists from throughout the country.

La Jolla Half Marathon   ★★★

Del Mar Fairgrounds/La Jolla Cove, La Jolla, ☎ *(619) 454-1262.*

In April, La Jolla's Half Marathon actually begins up the coast at the Del Mar Fairgrounds, finishing its circuit at La Jolla Cove. Not-so-serious or non-runners can take part in the five-mile walk or fun run.

La Jolla Rough Water Swim   ★★★★★

La Jolla Cove, La Jolla, ☎ *(619) 456-2100.*

On the first Sunday after Labor Day, swimmers jump in the cove to take part in the La Jolla Rough Water Swim. Dating from 1913, this is the largest rough water swimming competition in the United States and includes masters men's and women's swims, an amateur swim and a junior swim. You can watch the big splash for free.

Off the Wall Street Dance   ★★★★

On Wall Street, La Jolla, In the village, ☎ *(619) 534-1503.*

For one evening in late August, La Jolla's Wall Street is shut down to traffic and turned into one of the hottest party spots in the county—with live bands, entertainment, food booth, games and all the accompanying esprit.

La Jolla and the Golden Triangle:
Music, Dance and Theater

La Jolla Playhouse, San Diego's Tony-award winning professional theater—housed on the UCSD campus—actually began in 1947 as a summer stock theater, founded by actors Gregory Peck, Mel Ferrer and Dorothy McGuire. The theater building, with two stages, offers an exciting and eclectic mix during its mostly summer season—Holly Hunter, Sigourney Weaver and other notable actors have performed there. **La Jolla Stage Company** presents popular, noncontroversial hits throughout the year in Parker Auditorium at La Jolla High School.

The existence of a major university means lots of imaginative, creative, up-and-coming music, dance and theatrical performances almost all-year-round.

Churches in and around the village often host live chamber music and classical ensembles on weekends—frequently with free or very reasonable admission.

The opening of the new, improved **San Diego Museum of Contemporary Art** has brought with it a full calendar jammed with acclaimed orchestras, soloists, jazz musicians, dance troupes and film fests.

Theater

La Jolla

La Jolla Playhouse ★★★★★

*La Jolla Village Drive and Torrey Pines Road, La Jolla, On UCSD campus,
92037, ☎ (619) 550-1010.*

La Jolla Playhouse began life in 1947, closed in 1964 and lay dormant
until 1983 when it returned with a vengeance—earning, one decade
later, a Tony Award for best regional theater. The playhouse consists
of two spaces—the 492-seat Mandell Weiss Theatre and the 400-seat
Mandell Weiss Forum—and stages a terrific assortment of musicals,
dramas and contemporary works that cast actors such as Holly
Hunter, John Goodman and Linda Hunt. Audiences are occasionally
privy to big-time Tony winners before they hit Broadway (*Big River*,
A Walk in the Woods, and The Who's *Tommy*, for example). As in
1947, summer is the playhouse's main season and there are usually
matinee performances. Tickets range $20-$40, and season-holders—
natch—get first dibs. Don't despair—half-price tix and cheapie "no-
show" seat-warmer replacements are not unheard of.

La Jolla Stage Company ★★★★

*750 Nautilus Street, La Jolla, Parker Auditorium, La Jolla High School,
92037, ☎ (619) 459-7773.*

La Jolla High School's Parker Auditorium is the venue for year-round
fluffed and frou-frou-ed "safe" productions of popular comedies and
Broadway hits. Even the kids might want to sit through some of the
highly costumed song-and-dance numbers.

UCSD Theatre ★★★★

UCSD campus, La Jolla, ☎ (619) 534-4574.

Catch first-rate student theater-department productions—ranging
from classical interpretations to avant-avant-avant-garde works. A
variety of stages are utilized—including La Jolla Playhouse during its
off-months. Ticket prices vary from free or dirt cheap to moderate.

La Jolla and the Golden Triangle: Nightlife

Author's Tip

*Intelligent-movie lovers might want to check the marquis at the 1950s
Cove Theatre (7730 Girard Avenue). Newly released foreign films are
usually on the bill.*

Restaurants and clubs along Prospect Avenue often feature live
music in the evenings and, once again—hotel lounges and bars
are top prospects for nightlife. Singles happy-hour, hangouts
and meat markets proliferate around La Jolla Village and the

Golden Triangle areas (they pour in after work—or go home and change and *pretend* they've looked that way all day).

La Jolla

Avanti Restaurant ★★★★

875 Prospect Street, La Jolla, In the village, ☎ *(619) 454-4288.*

When it first opened, Avanti was the sophisticated yuppie haven of La Jolla. It slacked off when some of clientele shifted neighborhoods (or went bankrupt), but is still one of the nicer places to hang for drinks and music. Most nights you can enjoy jazz, rhythm and blues, salsa, Latin or Brazilian sounds. Wear chic togs.

Comedy Store ★★★★

916 Pearl Street, La Jolla, In the village, ☎ *(619) 454-9176.*

A yuck-a-minute at the sister club to West Hollywood's Comedy Store. Giggle, guffaw and belly laugh at some of the best local and national comedians. You could be watching the next Jay Leno or Gabe Kaplan. Ha ha. Performances are Tuesdays through Thursdays at 8 p.m., Fridays and Saturdays at 8 p.m. and 10:30 p.m.

El Torito ★★

8910 Villa La Jolla Drive, La Jolla, Near La Jolla Village Square, ☎ *(619) 453-4115.*

A meat market all the way. The bar is always packed with slobbering beer guzzlers and exploding cleavage. Prepare to be pinched and grabbed all the way to your table—if you're easily offended, wipe this place off your list. If you're into the scene—and young, hard, tanned bodies—come and party. The Mexican food is plentiful, the margaritas icy and Saturday nights line up some) live entertainment.

Grille at La Jolla ★★★

1250 Prospect Street, La Jolla, In the village, ☎ *(619) 459-8631.*

Live piano or jazz duos most nights in a just-trendy-enough atmosphere. Or get into the act yourself—Mondays and Tuesdays are open-mike nights for vocals, guitar, piano and flute.

Hard Rock Cafe ★★★

909 Prospect Street, La Jolla, In the Village, ☎ *(619) 454-5101.*

A branch of The Hard Rock Cafe right in the middle of staid La Jolla? Chalk it up to the town's feeble attempt at "coolness." By my standards (and I am cooler than blue ice), the Hard Rock hasn't been cool forever—but then I'm already down on Planet Hollywood and the Fashion Cafe. Anyway, weekend rockers can do the dance-and-party number amid lots of memorabilia from really cool times. Early closings though—11 p.m. on weeknights, midnight on weekends. Tell you something?

Il Forno Bistro and Bar ★★

909 Prospect Street, La Jolla, In the village, ☎ *(619) 459-5010.*

No competition for the Hard Rock Cafe, next door. Il Forno offers a cool-down with piano variety or flamenco entertainment, Wednesdays through Saturdays.

Marine Room ★★★

2000 Spindrift Drive, La Jolla, at the Spindrift Cocktail Lounge, ☎ *(619) 459-7222.*

The cocktail lounge of this oh-so-chic restaurant is a great place to spring for drinks and, on Thursdays through Saturdays, listen to contemporary sounds.

Milligan's Bar and Grill ★★

5786 La Jolla Boulevard, La Jolla, Near Bird Rock, ☎ *(619) 459-7311.*
An "out-of-the-village" option for live sounds—piano, jazz quartets and the like play every night but Mondays, usually 7–11 p.m.

Robusto ★★★

5660 La Jolla Boulevard, La Jolla, ☎ *(619) 459-1972.*
Situated in La Jolla's Bird Rock district, this intimate club hosts live jazz and blues performances on Friday, Saturday, Monday, and Wednesday. Show time is 8:30 p.m.

Sports City Cafe & Brewery ★★★★

8657 Villa La Jolla Drive, La Jolla, ☎ *(619) 450-3463.*
Upstairs from the AMC theater complex in La Jolla Village Square (on the west side of I-5), in true La Jolla style, you can have it all—microbrews, sports action, and terrific live entertainment by top local blues, jazz and rock musicians.

Taxxi ★★

1025 Prospect Avenue, La Jolla, In the village, ☎ *(619) 551-5230.*
Yes, yes, yes—something besides easy listening or Hard Rock soft rock in the village proper. How about funk, DJ dance music or acid jazz. It's happening Wednesdays through Saturdays.

Top o' the Cove ★★★

1216 Prospect Street, La Jolla, In the village, ☎ *(619) 454-7779.*
Top o' the Cove is top o' the list if you feel like dressing up for views and romance. Thursdays through Saturdays, you get music to boot— mellow tunes and pop classic, maybe with some soft vocals tossed in ("...a sigh is just a sigh...").

La Jolla and the Golden Triangle: Shopping

If you have deep pockets and a fat wallet, by all means do your shopping on Prospect and Girard avenues (park the chauffeur and limo over at La Valencia). You'll find the whole range of Rodeo Drive-isms, high-end European fashion, plus "pretty" art and prized antiques. Be sure to take in **Coast Walk,** along the ocean-side of Prospect Avenue, with several levels of trendy shops and eateries. Bookhounds—that rare breed—will have a ball at **John Cole's Book Shop** *(780 Prospect Street)* and **Warwick's** *(7812 Girard Street).* **D.G. Wills** *(7461 Girard Avenue)* stocks an extraordinary collection of used books on practically every subject.

La Jolla Village, parallel to Interstate 5, and **University Towne Center** (UTC), east of Interstate 5 on Genesee Avenue, are the mall-o-manias. La Jolla Village is the most chaotic but also has the most stuff (electronics, cheap imports, 24-hour pharmacies, discount linens, supermarkets, etc.), while UTC features a Nordstrom's and other department stores—along with specialty shops and schlock chain branches (though the calmer environment renders them a tad less offensive).

La Jolla and the Golden Triangle: Where to Stay

During the 1930s and '40s **La Valencia** was *the* La Jolla address for visiting glamour girls and dashing actors. Nowadays it attracts both an older, more distinguished clientele as well as hit-the-sack honeymooners. Other top village choices are **The Empress Hotel, Colonial Inn, Best Western Inn by the Sea, Prospect Park Inn,** and **The Bed & Breakfast Inn at La Jolla**.

If you want to sit square on the beach, **Sea Lodge** is your home away from home—particularly good for families. Up the hill, near Interstate 5, two suite-hotels will appeal to those who want a little elbow room. The **Hyatt Regency** in The Aventine is a first-class choice with loads of facilities and some of the best restaurants in town. **La Jolla Marriott** is half-a-mile away.

Golfers, Scripps Clinic visitors and Torrey Pines bluffs buffs should get a thrill out of either **Sheraton Grande Torrey Pines** or the **Lodge at Torrey Pines**, low-key resorts that straddle nature and science on North Torrey Pines Road.

Bed & Breakfasts

La Jolla

Bed & Breakfast Inn at La Jolla   **$85–$225**   ★ ★ ★ ★

7753 Draper Avenue, La Jolla, 92037, In the village, ☎ *(619) 456-2066. Single: $85–$225. Double: $85–$225.*

Wouldn't you know that the only B&B in La Jolla would be in a renovated 1913 Irving Gill house? In true B&B tradition, all 16 rooms are individually decorated—canopy beds, four posters, wicker or rattan, Laura Ashley prints, etc. And, of course, there are terry robes, decanters of sherry, bowls of fresh fruit, afternoon wine and cheese. Guests are free to wander about the sitting room, sun deck and gardens (planned by Kate Sessions). Five rooms are situated in a newer wing so—if that's important to you—inquire before booking. Rates include Continental breakfast. 16 rooms. Credit Cards: MC, V.

Hotels
Golden Triangle

Embassy Suites $128–$188 ★★★

4550 La Jolla Village Drive, Golden Triangle, 92122, East of I-5,
☎ *(619) 453-0400, FAX: (619) 453-4226.*
Single: $128–$188. Double: $128–$188.
Embassy Suites' signature plant-filled, water-flowing atrium with restaurant and deli is the centerpiece of this 12-story all-suite operation.
One- and two-bedroom "apartments" are comfortably furnished,
have refrigerators and microwaves, and separate living rooms. Guests
have use of a pool, spa, sauna, exercise room, restaurant and deli and
evening beverages are complimentary. Amenities: exercise room,
Jacuzzi, sauna. 335 rooms. Credit Cards: A, CB, DC, D, MC, V.

La Jolla Marriott $198–$198 ★★★★

4240 La Jolla Village Drive, Golden Triangle, 92037, ☎ *(800) 228-
9290, (619) 587-1414, FAX: (619) 546-8518.*
Single: $198. Double: $198.
A 15-story glitz parade for visiting execs and business parade, smack
in the heart of the Golden Triangle. Public areas are large and luxurious, with contemporary artwork and oversized sofas—perfect for seal-
a-deals and hush-hush negotiations. Restaurants, bars, and lounges
with entertainment keep guests fed and amused and the large fitness
center includes 29 state-of-the-art exercise machines. Rooms are
cheerful, with contemporary furnishings and decor, and deluxe amenities. Facilities are the usual executive-pleasing options of two pools,
spa, saunas, exercise room, conference facilities and meeting rooms.
Amenities: exercise room, Jacuzzi, sauna, business services. 360
rooms. Credit Cards: A, CB, DC, D, MC, V.

La Jolla

Colonial Inn $120–$220 ★★★

910 Prospect Street, La Jolla, 92037, ☎ *(800) 832-5525, (619) 454-
2181, FAX: (619) 454-5679.*
Single: $120–$220. Double: $120–$220.
Renovations enhanced—rather than trashed—this 1913 building, La
Jolla's oldest hotel and just a Frisbee toss from La Valencia. If you
want lots of resorty facilities, this probably isn't the place to stay but
it's a hard one to beat for great turn-of-the-century atmosphere.
Rooms and public areas are formally furnished, halls are lit with
sconces, ceiling fans provide most of the cool air. As with La Valencia,
you can choose a village- or ocean-view room. Putnam's, the hotel's
restaurant, is a favorite hang for local execs. Civilized tea is served in
the lobby each afternoon and piano entertainment is provided for
your easy-listening evenings. Staff and service is wonderfully accom-
modating—sort of in the style of a mini-Ritz-Carlton. Rates include
complimentary Continental breakfast. 75 rooms. Credit Cards: A, CB,
DC, D, MC, V.

Hyatt Regency La Jolla $125–$190 ★★★★★

*3777 La Jolla Village Drive, La Jolla, 92037, The Aventine, east of Inter-
state-5,* ☎ *(800) 233-1234, (619) 552-1234, FAX: (619) 552-6066.*
Single: $125–$165. Double: $125–$190.
The 16-story postmodern-plus-plus Michael Graves design is the primary focus of The Aventine complex, Graves's controversial tour de

force at the edge of Interstate 5. Rivaling only the nearby Mormon church for on-the-road shock value, the hotel has nonetheless been a big hit. It couldn't get more conveniently located—right at the side of the freeway, close enough to the village, beach, golf course, UCSD and corporate offices. And The Aventine encompasses not only its own office building but a dining complex with several deservedly ballyhooed upscale restaurants. Ecelectic design elements ranging from towers and colonades to Roman sculptures and Italian marble floors embellish the high-powered lobby and public areas. Guest rooms are beautifully decorated with cherry wood furnishings and quality carpets and soft goods. The amenities are first class and geared toward everything befitting its push-for-success business clientele—four restaurants, lounge with entertainment, pool and spa, two lighted tennis courts, a business center, conference rooms, health club and 32,000-square-foot sporting club. And, in case you've got kids in tow, Camp Hyatt for Kids will keep them busy with planned activities. Amenities: tennis, health club, exercise room, Jacuzzi, sauna, club floor, business services. 400 rooms. Credit Cards: A, CB, DC, D, MC, V.

La Valencia $165–$370   ★★★★★

1132 Prospect Avenue, La Jolla, 92037, In the village, ☎ *(800) 451-0772, (619) 454-0771, FAX: (619) 456-3921.*
Single: $165–$370. Double: $165–$370.

La Jolla's 1920s landmark hotel, located on the Prospect Avenue main drag and right above the cove, is a pink stucco art deco joy reminiscent of kinder, gentler times—like the 1930s and '40s when dashing gents and glamorous movie queens (Charlie Chaplin, Mary Pickford, Greta Garbo, etc.) used to sashay along the corridors. Now it attracts mostly honeymooners, execs and dignified others, and very un-thirtysomething couples like Tom Cruise and Nicole Kidman. The property is a stunning "life-is-perfect" blend of pinkishness, Mediterranean styling, romantic cubbyholes, cove-view windows and perfectly tended grounds. Six of the hotel's eight floors sit below lobby level. Village-view rooms are naturally cheapest, but the extra money is well-worth a waterfront location (especially if you want to get that marriage off to a *really* good start). The Sky Room restaurant offers French cuisine, high prices, *the* view, and a corner on the market for "popping the question." Cafe La Rue and Tropical Patio—for seafood and Continental dining—adjoins the not-to-be-missed Whaling Bar. Toss in live piano music in the lobby lounge (nightly except Sundays), Sunday brunch, the garden pool and spa, sauna, exercise room, shuffleboard, meeting rooms and access to tennis. Complimentary airport transportation is provided. Amenities: exercise room, Jacuzzi, sauna. 100 rooms. Credit Cards: A, CB, DC, D, MC, V.

Lodge at Torrey Pines $85–$155   ★★★

11480 North Torrey Pines Road, La Jolla, 92037, Near Torrey Pines Golf Course, ☎ *(800) 777-1700, (619) 453-4420, FAX: (619) 453-0691.*
Single: $85–$155. Double: $85–$155.

Until the Sheraton Grande came along in 1989, The Lodge at Torrey Pines—in the Torrey Pines Golf Course backyard—was *the* golfer's haven. It's still a favorite with the loud-colors, big plaids and pom pom-capped set—and the views are the same as the posh Sheraton next door. If you feel more comfortable clinking the cubes in a hi-ball than balancing a glass of Chardonnay, this is a best bet. Rooms have been redone with dark woods and Oriental prints—a grotesque clash with guests' fashion statement. Amenities are comparatively simple but perfect for the clientele—restaurant, lounges, coffeeshop, pool, meeting rooms, exercise room, putting green and—of course—the adjacent golf course (for a fee). Amenities: exercise room. 71 rooms. Credit Cards: A, CB, DC, D, MC, V.

Sheraton Grande Torrey Pines $175–$260 ★★★★★

10950 North Torrey Pines Road, La Jolla, 92037, Near Torrey Pines Golf Course, ☎ *(800) 325-3535, (619) 558-1500, FAX: (619) 450-4584. Single: $175–$260. Double: $175–$260.*

Wipe out that image of a high-rise hotel in some large metropolis. this Sheraton is a low-lying blink off North Torrey Pines Road, its four stories practically merging into the oceanfront bluffs as well as adjacent Torrey Pines Golf Course. The elegant interior is all marble, granite and rich polished woods, while the guest rooms are extra-large with contemporary decor and knock-out-view balconies (a toss-up between the sea and the 18th-hole). Service and facilities cater mostly to guests who take those things for granted in their lives—a fine dining restaurant, lounge with entertainment, pool, spa, saunas, health club, putting green, three lighted tennis courts, business center, conference facilities, meeting rooms, butler service, limo rides, 24-hour concierge and even bicycle rental. Amenities: tennis, health club, exercise room, Jacuzzi, sauna, balcony or patio, business services. 400 rooms. Credit Cards: A, CB, DC, D, MC, V.

Motels

La Jolla

Best Western Inn by the Sea $95–$150 ★★

7830 Fay Avenue, La Jolla, 92037, In the village, ☎ *(800) 462-9732, (619) 459-4461, FAX: (619) 455-2578. Single: $95–$140. Double: $105–$150.*

Five-stories high and five blocks from the beach. Modern rooms—most with private balconies—have village or water views. Only a coffeeshop is on the premises but there are plenty of good restaurants and cafes within walking distance. A pool, spa, exercise room and meeting facilities are available to guests, and parking is free. Amenities: exercise room, Jacuzzi, balcony or patio. 132 rooms. Credit Cards: A, CB, DC, D, MC, V.

Prospect Park Inn $85–$150 ★★

1110 Prospect Street, La Jolla, 92037, In the village, ☎ *(800) 433-1609, (619) 454-0133, FAX: (619) 454-2056. Single: $85–$95. Double: $130–$150.*

Yes, there *is* a small, charming European pension-type inn right here in La Jolla. The only public room is a living room/lounge but the entire village—with restaurants, clubs, cafes and shops—is outside the doorstep. Choose from a variety of well-furnished accommodations—some have kitchens, separate sitting rooms or balconies with wide-angle ocean views. Complimentary Continental breakfast and free parking are included in the tab. This is a favorite choice for European visitors. Amenities: balcony or patio. 23 rooms. Credit Cards: A, DC, D, MC, V.

Residence Inn by Marriott   **$95–$189**   ★★

8901 Gilman Drive, La Jolla, 92037, La Jolla Village Square, ☎ (619) 587-1770, FAX: (619) 552-0387.

Single: $95–$105. Double: $95–$189.

Up near Interstate 5, UCSD and the Golden Triangle, the Residence Inn offers lots of space in lieu of gushy service. One- and two-bedroom suites feature exterior corridor access, living rooms, some fireplaces and kitchens with microwaves. Guests are treated to complimentary evening beverages Mondays through Fridays, plus have use of two pools, meeting rooms and airport shuttle. Amenities: Jacuzzi. 287 rooms. Credit Cards: A, CB, DC, D, MC, V.

Resorts

La Jolla

Sea Lodge   **$109–$379**   ★★★★

8110 Camino del Oro, La Jolla, 92037, At La Jolla Shores, ☎ (800) 237-5211, (619) 459-8271, FAX: (619) 456-9346.

Single: $109–$379. Double: $109–$379.

A red-roofed Spanish-style resort, sitting three stories low along the best part of La Jolla Shores beach. The entire property exudes a "yippee-we're-on-vacation-at-the-beach" mentality and is a top choice for families. Rooms are spacious, with rattan furnishings, refrigerators and balconies looking out to lush gardens or the blue Pacific. Besides beach activities, the motor inn offers a restaurant, lounge, pool, spa, sauna, fitness center, tennis and a pitch-and-putt golf course. Book early for summer holidays. Amenities: tennis, health club, exercise room, Jacuzzi, sauna, balcony or patio. 128 rooms. Credit Cards: A, CB, DC, D, MC, V.

La Jolla and the Golden Triangle: Where to Eat

FIELDING'S FAVORITE PEOPLE-WATCHING SPOT

*The **Pannikin**, La Jolla's very first coffeehouse, sits at the edge of the village, a few skips from the corner of Girard Avenue and Pearl Street. The two-level outdoor patio is a perfect place to drink strong brews and keep up on the local scene—a constant parade of fashion statements, gold-chain wearers, surf bums, and—God help us—ridiculously cliched morons either feigning to read real literature or else scribbling journal notes for a forthcoming novel (gag me with an iced mocha).*

Dining choices stretch as long as your intestines—from silver service gourmet with commanding views of the sea, to cheesey little take-out joints stuck in some claustrophobic mall.

The Marine Room and **Top O' the Cove** are venerable old favorites, with **George's at the Cove** catching up fast. Prospect Avenue is, of course, lined with a range of spots including Mexican patios, seafood houses, international restaurants, ice cream parlors, a mini-McDonald's and even a **Hard Rock Cafe.** More restaurants—including **Cindy Black's,** one of the best in town—are situated along La Jolla Boulevard, near the Bird Rock end of town.

The Golden Triangle, particularly at The Aventine, is the location of some of the trendiest and tastiest in-spots—**Cafe Japengo** and **Sweetlips,** for instance. Surrounding the malls and business areas are the usual TGIF-type places, with dreary menus, cutesy servers and on-the-make patrons.

Golden Triangle

Hops! Bistro & Brewery   **$**   ★★★

4353 La Jolla Village Drive, Golden Triangle, ☎ *(619) 587-6677.*
American cuisine. Specialties: Hand-crafted brews.
Lunch: 11 a.m.–2 p.m., entrées $5–$10.
Dinner: 5-10 p.m., entrées $5–$10.
A trendy microbrewery with at least six handcrafted brews on tap at all times, along with lots of real American grub, pizzas, pastas, salads, snacks and nibbles (nothing is over $10). The singles set and after-workers crowd this place throughout the week, though Hops! is open on weekends also. Happy hour runs from 4-6 p.m. and 10 p.m. until closing. Credit Cards: D, V, MC, DC, A.

La Jolla

Alfonso's   **$$**   ★★★

1251 Prospect Street, La Jolla, ☎ *(619) 454-2232.*
Mexican cuisine. Specialties: Nachos, carne asada burritos.
Lunch: 11 a.m.–11 p.m., entrées $4–$15.
Dinner: 11 a.m.–11 p.m., entrées $4–$15.
A funky cantina and Mexican restaurant right in the heart of La Jolla village. Alfonso's has been around forever—almost as long as the generation's-old secret family recipes. Carne asada Alfonso is specialty of the house, and new (or old) dishes come and go. As with almost every Mexican restaurant, the usual combination plates are available for non-risk takers. Atmosphere is festive and best on the outside patio (the indoor cantina is a little too dark). Good food, memorable margaritas. Dinner is served until midnight on Fridays and Saturdays. Features: outside dining, late dining. Credit Cards: D, V, MC, A.

Cafe Japengo   **$$$**   ★★★★

8960 University Center Lane, La Jolla, ☎ *(619) 450-3355.*
Asian cuisine. Specialties: Pacific Rim concoctions, sushi.
Lunch: 11 a.m.–2 p.m., entrées $12–$20.
Dinner: 5-11 p.m., entrées $16–$28.
Cafe Japengo, in The Aventine complex, is one of *the* places to be seen. Power lunchers and trendy diners hide away in the stylish dining room—all bamboo, marble, and black iron—pretending they seek privacy and anonymity. Don't believe it—they (and *you*) are being

watched by all. Feast upon Pacific Rim delicacies—the flavors of Hawaii, California, Japan, China, Thailand—divinely presented. The creative appetizers are enticing enough to make into a meal. The sushi bar stays open until midnight on Fridays and Saturdays. Features: late dining. Jacket requested. Reservations recommended. Credit Cards: CB, V, MC, DC, A.

Cindy Black's $$$ ★★★★★

5721 La Jolla Boulevard, La Jolla, ☎ (619) 456-6299.
French cuisine. Specialties: creative French.
Dinner: 5:30-10 p.m., entrées $21–$30.
Chef/artiste Cindy Black whips up country French cuisine with a Southwestern kick for devoted fans awaiting in the country French dining room. Meals are costly but worth every cent. Those with limited budgets and adventurous palates can experience a "mini-Cindy" at one of the three-course prix-fixe dinners ($15 and up) on Sundays and Mondays. Lunch is served Fridays only, 11:30 a.m.–2 p.m. Sunday dinner hours are 5-8 p.m. Jacket requested. Reservations required. Credit Cards: D, V, MC, DC, A.

Daily's Fit & Fresh $ ★★

8915 Towne Centre Drive, La Jolla, ☎ (619) 453-1112.
American cuisine. Specialties: Three-bean-and-corn chili.
Lunch: 11 a.m.–2 p.m., entrées $3–$6.
Dinner: 4-7 p.m., entrées $3–$6.
Finally—a grab-a-quick-bite health food choice with flavorful, low-fat meals. The cardiac surgeon-founder has seen to it that every single thing on the menu is under 10 grams of fat, with low sodium and low calories. In case you think this translates to bland and boring—wrong! Try the three-bean-and-corn chili or grilled chicken pockets. You'll be back for more. Reservations not accepted.

French Gourmet $$ ★★★

711 Pearl Street, La Jolla, ☎ (619) 454-6736.
French cuisine. Specialties: quiches, pates, pastries.
Breakfast: 9-11 a.m., entrées $4–$8.
Lunch: 11 a.m.–3 p.m., entrées $6–$12.
Dinner: 5-10 p.m., entrées $7–$16.
Satisfy your French cravings without draining your wallet. The French Gourmet is another long-time local favorite—a mini-priced bistro with the atmosphere, taste, and style to match any counterpart in France. The pastries are to die for—cause for celebration, as well as running a neck-in-neck tie with Haagen-Daz for the broken-hearted. Fresh fish dishes, quiches, pates, omelettes, and other bistro fare are similarly divine. Features: own baking, non-smoking area. Credit Cards: V, MC.

George's at the Cove $$$ ★★★★★

1250 Prospect Street, La Jolla, ☎ (619) 454-4244.
Seafood cuisine. Specialties: Fresh seafood, seafood pastas.
Lunch: 11:30 a.m.–2:30 p.m., entrées $8–$16.
Dinner: 5-10 p.m., entrées $16–$26.
George's can do no wrong—patrons are wowed by over-the-cove views, luscious food and a choice of price ranges. You'll pay top dollar for divine seafood specialties in the elegant jacket-and-tie main dining room. But you can get off cheaper—and dress more casually—in the

indoor/outdoor Cafe and Ocean Terrace (a different menu, but still great). Fresh seafood is the winning ticket—especially the pasta dishes. Desserts are killer. Dinner is served until 11 p.m. on Fridays and Saturdays. Features: outside dining, Sunday brunch, non-smoking area, late dining. Jacket and tie requested. Reservations recommended. Credit Cards: D, V, MC, DC, A.

Harry's   **$**   ★★★

7545 Girard Avenue, La Jolla, ☎ *(619) 454-7381.*
American cuisine. Specialties: Pancakes, omelets.
Breakfast: 6 a.m.–3 p.m., entrées $4–$9.
La Jollans have been doing breakfast at Harry's for decades. This is where Ward and June would've taken Wally and The Beave; where Lucy and Ethel might've met up with Ricky and Fred; where *you* can go with a friend, lover or alone to savor such lost-era delights as corned beef hash, oatmeal with raisins, 15 kinds of omelets, banana pancakes, hash browns, bacon, sausage and eggs. Each table gets its own pot of fresh-brewed coffee. Closing time on Sundays is 2 p.m. Features: outside dining, own baking, Sunday brunch, wine and beer only, rated wine cellar, non-smoking area, late dining, private dining rooms. Reservations not accepted. Credit Cards: V, MC, A.

Kiva Grill   **$$**   ★★★

8970 University Center Lane, La Jolla, ☎ *(619) 558-8600.*
Southwestern cuisine. Specialties: Lamb fajitas, grilled mahimahi.
Lunch: 11:30 a.m.–4 p.m., entrées $6–$12.
Dinner: 5-10 p.m., entrées $10–$19.
Pueblo atmosphere, Southwestern decor and cuisine, the requisite scene for singles doing their Santa Fe-ish number. Daily specials are worth a try, as are the mesquite-broiled meats and blue-corn crusted salmon with lobster filling. Happy hour—Mondays through Fridays, 4-7 p.m.--is a particularly festive event for the pick-up and pick-me-up crowd. Lunch is served Mondays through Saturdays, and dinner until 11 p.m. on Fridays and Saturdays. Features: Sunday brunch, late dining. Reservations recommended. Credit Cards: D, V, MC, DC, A.

Manhattan   **$$$**   ★★★

7766 Fay Avenue, La Jolla, ☎ *(619) 554-1444.*
· *Italian cuisine. Specialties: pastas, veal dishes.*
Lunch: Noon-2 p.m., entrées $7–$15.
Dinner: 5-10 p.m., entrées $12–$22.
La Jolla on the outside, Manhattan on the inside. The slightly off-the-beaten-path Empress Hotel is the hiding place for this New Yorkish, Italian restaurant befitting a Cuomo. Gangster-dark rooms with sink-down-and-high leather booths are the perfect setting for delicious pastas, scampi, veal and lamb dishes. And they do a mean Caesar salad. Service is very professional. Lunch is served Mondays through Fridays. Reservations recommended. Credit Cards: CB, V, MC, DC, A.

Marine Room   **$$$**   ★★★★

2000 Spindrift Drive, La Jolla, ☎ *(619) 459-7222.*
Continental cuisine. Specialties: Fresh seafood, beef dishes.
Lunch: 11:30 a.m.–2:30 p.m., entrées $7–$16.
Dinner: 6-10 p.m., entrées $16–$30.
More people come to this 1941 restaurant for the wave-crashing La Jolla Shores view than for the only semi-exceptional cuisine. Occa-

sionally those waves crash a bit too hard, shattering the wall-o'-windows plate glass—especially during Southern California's rare but powerful storms. Owned and operated by La Jolla Beach & Tennis Club (from where it's joined at the hip), the Marine Room exudes all that beachy-bally sophistication—carried through to its menu with traditional favorites (beef and game). The fresh seafood dishes are more creative and the wine list is exemplary. Live entertainment and romantic dinner/dancing are offered in the cocktail lounge on weekends. Dress to impress—whomever. Lunch is served Mondays through Saturdays. Features: Sunday brunch. Jacket requested. Reservations required. Credit Cards: D, CB, V, MC, DC, A.

Marrakesh $$$ ★★★

634 Pearl Street, La Jolla, ☎ *(619) 454-2500.*
American cuisine. Specialties: Hand washing ceremony, bastilla, lamb, feasts.
Dinner: 5-10 p.m., entrées $15–$25.
Prepare for the exotic—possibly erotic—sitting on the floor, washing of the hands, partaking of the morsels. You'll get the full Moroccan-style treatment. Multi-course feasts are this Sahara-esque dining spot's trademark and might include (besides the wash-water), lamb dishes, marinated veggies, soups, bastilla, roast chicken, prawns, filled pastry pockets, baklava, refreshing tea or gut-searing coffee. Come with a full wallet and an empty stomach. Dinner is served until 11 p.m. on Fridays and Saturdays, and belly dancers jingle in your face most weekends and some weekdays. Reservations recommended. Credit Cards: D, CB, V, MC, DC, A.

Pannikin Brockton Villa $ ★★★

1235 Coast Boulevard, La Jolla, ☎ *(619) 454-7393.*
American cuisine. Specialties: French toast, bagels, pastries.
Breakfast: 8-11 a.m., entrées $4–$9.
Lunch: 11 a.m.–2 p.m., entrées $4–$9.
The Pannikin Coffeehouse gang has done it again by taking over an old cove-front beachhouse and turning it into a refreshingly informal breakfast- and lunch-house with light supper served Thurs.-Sun. Expect waits, crowds, fighting over tables—especially on summer weekends—to savor Pannikin-blend coffees along with hint-of-orange French toast, lox and bagels, rich oatmeal, sugary pastries, and fresh sandwiches. Suppers include dishes such as crab cakes and teuila chicken farfalle. Beer and wine served. Reservations not accepted. Credit Cards: V, MC, A.

Putnam's $$$ ★★★

910 Prospect Street, La Jolla, ☎ *(619) 454-2181.*
Continental cuisine.
Breakfast: 7-10 a.m., entrées $9.
Lunch: 11 a.m.–2 p.m., entrées $9–$18.
Dinner: 5-10 p.m., entrées $14–$26.
Do lunch with the La Jollans in this clubby, wood-paneled bistro housed inside the Colonial Inn. Cuisine runs the range from fresh seafood and aged beef to creative pastas and Southwestern flavors. The locals have been sipping and supping here for years. Breakfast and lunch are served daily. Features: Sunday brunch, late dining. Reservations recommended. Credit Cards: CB, V, MC, DC, A.

Royal Thai Cuisine   **$$**   ★★

737 Pearl Street, La Jolla, ☎ (619) 551-8424.
Thai cuisine. Specialties: Shrimp dishes.
Lunch: 11 a.m.–3 p.m., entrées $6–$13.
Dinner: 5-10 p.m., entrées $6–$13.

One of several Royal Thai establishments in San Diego and Orange counties, the food is consistently well-prepared, contains no brain-damaging MSG, and has plenty of mind-clearing spices. The shrimp dishes are some of their best menu items—chili hot or minty cool. Delivery (at nominal charge) is available. Special deals are the Saturday and Sunday brunches, as well as the nightly prix-fixe dinners ($15.95). Dinner is served until 11 p.m. on Fridays and Saturdays. Features: Sunday brunch, wine and beer only. Credit Cards: D, V, MC, A.

SamSon's Deli-Restaurant   **$**   ★★★

8861 Villa La Jolla Drive, La Jolla, ☎ (619) 455-1461.
American cuisine. Specialties: Deli delights.
Breakfast: 7 a.m.–11 p.m., entrées $4–$8.
Lunch: 11-4 p.m., entrées $4–$10.
Dinner: 4-11 p.m., entrées $5–$12.

A real New York-style Jewish deli that opens early and stays open late—with an adjoining bakery/deli for take-home treats. The menu is lengthy and filled with traditional dishes—white fish, omelets, bagels and lox, corned beef sandwiches, kosher bologna, pastrami, beet borscht, knockwurst, and such. Don't miss the matzo ball soup—the balls are *enormous* and the broth will cure almost any ill. Two dining rooms are decorated with movie biz schlock—the perfect ambience for your kosher pickle heartburn. SamSon's stays open until midnight on Fridays and Saturdays, but closes at 10 p.m. on Sundays. Features: wine and beer only, late dining. Reservations not accepted. Credit Cards: CB, V, MC, DC, A.

Spot   **$$**   ★★

1005 Prospect Street, La Jolla, ☎ (619) 459-0800.
American cuisine. Specialties: Pizza and ribs.
Lunch: 11 a.m.–4 p.m., entrées $4–$15.
Dinner: 4 p.m.–1 a.m., prix fixe $5–$18.

La Jolla's oldie-but-goodie still draws the locals for Chicago-style pizza, ribs, steaks, burgers and *lots* of drinks. The low-key, casual atmosphere is something of a shock after shopping Prospect Avenue, but you can't beat the down-to-earth food at nearly-bargain prices. Almost everything can be ordered to-go—handy for impromptu picnics at closeby La Jolla cove. Features: late dining. Reservations not accepted. Credit Cards: D, CB, V, MC, DC, A.

Top O'The Cove   **$$$**   ★★★★★

1216 Prospect Street, La Jolla, ☎ (619) 454-7779.
Continental cuisine. Specialties: Romance, baby.
Lunch: 11:30 a.m.–3 p.m., entrées $9–$16.
Dinner: 5:30-10:30 p.m., entrées $25–$32.

Number six, number six, number six—that's your table for romance (or if you're about to die). This cliffside bungalow—once a private home—has, for decades, been touted as the "most romantic restaurant in San Diego" (some say it's the most romantic in the country) and table number six is the supreme magical setting for question-popping couples. You might have a hard time grabbing it though—The

Table is usually booked weeks ahead and has supposedly been snatched for every New year's Eve through the year 2000. But, hey, it's not the only table in the house! Aside from glorious end-of-the-world views, this cozy cottage features fig trees, crackling fires, a gazebo and patio, and a sophisticated upstairs bar. Meals are straight-forward classical choices—filet mignon, chops, veal, duck, lamb and seafood dishes. The award-winning wine list offers about 1000 selections. Lunch is served Mondays through Saturdays. Features: Sunday brunch, rated wine cellar. Jacket and tie requested. Reservations recommended. Credit Cards: CB, V, MC, DC, A.

Trattoria Acqua $$ ★★★

1298 Prospect Street, La Jolla, ☎ *(619) 454-0709.*
Mediterranean cuisine. Specialties: Pastas, pizzas.
Lunch: 11 a.m.–2 p.m., entrées $7–$14.
Dinner: 5-10 p.m., entrées $12–$18.

It's been getting great reviews from the local critics (whatever they know)—the Mediterranean/California style dining room is airy and eye-appealing, the pastas and pizzas are imaginative, and it has a super view of La Jolla shores. Dining is in the lovely restaurant or out on the terrace or in a gazebo. Cuisine is basically Italian, with dabs of Span-ish, Turkish and Moroccan tossed into the pot. Lunch is served Mon-days through Fridays, dinner is served until 11 p.m. on Fridays and Saturdays. Features: outside dining, Sunday brunch, late dining. Reservations recommended. Credit Cards: V, MC, A.

NORTH COUNTY

Humans are enclosed in trams while the animals roam free at San Diego's Wild Animal Park.

All of the beach and near-beach towns stretching between Del Mar (just north of Torrey Pines State Reserve) and Oceanside (the San Diego/Orange county line) are shoved together under a North County banner—though some take the stretch far beyond coastal limits and toss *inland* cities and communities into the deal. Locals don't seem to mind as long as those not-of-the-sea parts are clearly defined as inland North County.

Coastal areas—Del Mar, Solana Beach, Cardiff-by-the-Sea, Encinitas, Leucadia, Carlsbad, Oceanside—blend together geographically (connected by an old highway that undergoes a series of name changes), but are quite distinct in atmosphere, activity and median income.

Del Mar—once referred to as "the poor man's La Jolla"— has in past years become so trendy and exclusive that for many it's a primary destination. Not that this is some big surprise. Hollywood stars and the horsey set have been descending upon the posh oceanfront enclave since the 1930s when Bing Crosby, Pat O'Brien, Gary Cooper and other laying-odds cohorts organized

221

the Del Mar Thoroughbred Club—bringing top jockeys and high-strung ponies to "where the turf meets the surf." Bing, Desi Arnaz and Jimmy Durante were just a few of the big betters. (The track-front street is even named after Jimmy—though there's no mention of Mrs. Calabash, wherever she is.) Aside from the track, Del Mar is also notable for its chic plaza with shops, restaurants and ambience so fashionable that wealthy La Jollans bus in (via limo, of course) on the weekends. Permanent residents are mainly doctors, lawyers, university professors and other professionals—drawn by the wide beaches, tucked-into-the-hillside homes and independent stronghold (*no* city incorporation, and *yes*—every tiny improvement requires nitpicking scrutiny and approval by citizen's committees).

East of Del Mar (but never say *inland*) are super-exclusive **Fairbanks Ranch** (Douglas Fairbanks Jr.'s old property) and **Rancho Santa Fe**. Both are sprawling with money, celebrities, and super-luxurious estates. Rancho Santa Fe, known simply as "Rancho" or "The Ranch," is the more established of the two—dating from the 1920s, many of its Spanish Colonial Revival buildings were designed by architect Lillian Rice. Both areas offer "if you have to ask, you can't afford it" shops and restaurants, particularly Rancho which also harbors a prominent inn, resort and renowned golf course that no one's invited to.

Continuing north along the coast are—in order—**Solana Beach**, **Cardiff-by-the-Sea**, **Encinitas**, **Leucadia**, **Carlsbad** and **Oceanside**. The first four are laid-back, true California beach towns comprised of surfers and beach bums, old timers and New Agers—with an ample smattering of students, hippies, renegades and non-urban unprofessionals—drawn to the salty air, SoCal lifestyle and unpretentiousness. Skateboarders, cyclists and joggers take up as much room on the highway as do vehicles (most of them carrying surfboards)—mostly everyone stopping en-route for a low-fat latte or fresh-squeezed juice, along with a neighborly chat. Railroad tracks run parallel to the road and interspersed amongst and between are cafes, beach bars, upmarket restaurants, health food supermarkets, head shops, florists, flea markets, antique malls, retro specialists, bikini and surf shops, adventure outfitters, crystal and rock purveyors, holistic health centers, yoga and karate schools and design centers.

Even though Cardiff, Encinitas and Leucadia have actually been incorporated into the City of Encinitas, locals still refer to them by their homegrown names. For decades, each of the communities singularly enjoyed simple beach culture but "progress" and demand turned the east side of the freeway (all the way from Del Mar to Oceanside) into a plethora of planned communities and all that goes with—shopping centers on every corner, suburban inauspiciousness, and honky-honk traffic jams. **Solana Beach** is separated from Cardiff by **San Elijo Lagoon**, a migrating-bird

North San Diego County

haven that developers are just aching to plunk a hotel atop (so far, residents and environmentalists have successfully kept the lagoonies at bay). Cardiff is pretty much a blink of coastline, waterfront restaurants, a campground, some shops and hillside homes. The golden domes of Self-Realization Fellowship, a religious community founded in 1937 by Indian guru Paramahansa Yogananda, signal the beginning of old Encinitas town (alternately called "flower capital of the world" and "poinsettia capital of the world." The ocean is now mostly obscured beneath high cliffs and established neighborhoods until you reach the end of Leucadia. Along the way, you'll pass by inoffensive shopping plazas, community businesses and quintessential back-to-the-'60s beachiness. Behold those barefoot and stoned skateboarders wearing dreads and tie-dye, as they miraculously balance surfboards in one hand, smoothie glasses in the other.

Unlike the other coastal towns **Carlsbad** used to be known mainly for its **La Costa Hotel and Spa** connection on the other side of Interstate 5. La Costa is still there, but the city—not to be *completely* overshadowed by its southern neighbors—decided to glitzy up *its* village, resulting in a splendid cluster of small businesses, antique shops, restaurants and cafes. When the in-the-works 35-acre **LEGO Family Park** opens in 1999, Carlsbad's popularity will show a far more dramatic increase—bringing in a projected 1.8 million plastic brickbuilders.

Oceanside, up the road on the other side of **Buena Vista Lagoon,** is practically synonymous with **Camp Pendleton**, the Marine Corp's largest amphibious training base. Founded in 1942, just after Pearl Harbor was attacked, the base encompasses 125,000 acres on both sides of Interstate-5. The rest of Oceanside is a sprawl of GI-related businesses, fast-food joints and nondescript shopping centers, as well as beaches, a harbor and fishing pier. Mission San Luis Rey, the largest of California's missions, is just east of the interstate. Unfortunately, Oceanside has a growing—and increasingly severe—gang problem and is probably best avoided by lookie-loos.

Inland North County is a straight shoot from downtown via Interstate 5. Beyond Miramar Naval Air Station, you'll pass clone housing developments, bedroom communities like Poway and Rancho Penasquitos and Mediterranean-esque Rancho Bernardo with its prestigious inn. From the coast you can take State Highway 78, north of Carlsbad, through Vista and San Marcos, coming out at Escondido.

Harboring a population of 100,000, **Escondido** is not **even** in the rural realm anymore. The city's incredible world-class arts center attests to that by luring some of the country's finest performers—a strange feat for such an out-of-the-way and nontrendy community. Nearby are the **Wild Animal Park**, and **San Pasqual** *(site of the battlefield)*.

The Lawrence Welk resort complex in Escondido is popular with golf and tennis enthusiasts.

The rest of the inland area is a weave of hills and dales, orchards and groves (especially avocado), country clubs and Indian reservations. **Welk Resort Center** and super-luxe **The Golden Door** (pampering spa to the pampered stars and other rich rejuvenation-seekers) are both along the way and **Palomar Mountain** isn't too far off.

The quaintish community of **Fallbrook**, reared up against Camp Pendleton's backside, is a mixed bag of fruit growers, marine recruits, quiet families, white supremacists, itinerant farmworkers and antique dealers.

North County: Things to See and Do

The **Del Mar Plaza**, of course *(corner of Camino del Mar and 15th Street)*. You aren't *anyone* unless you at least raise a glass at one of its restaurants or watering holes. Designed by Jon Jerde (one and the same who dollied Horton Plaza, downtown), the multilevel, oceanview piazza sports many of Jerde's trademark whimsies—though Del Mar's version is très chic to match the visitors. Wander around the ritzy shops and restaurants, then cross the street and explore **L'Auberge**, the equally glam resort hotel, before walking a short block to **Seagrove Park** and the beach. Don't miss **the track**—even it it's off-season, you can still check out the satellite-betting facility. **Fairbanks Ranch** and **Rancho Santa Fe** (watch the signs, heading east from Del Mar on Via de la Valle) are worthwhile treks for the monied crowd—or those who get off sniffing it on others (dress accordingly or you won't even get close enough for your nostrils to flare). Continuing east along the **Del Dios Highway**, around **Lake Hodges**, will give you a scenic approach into **Escondido**.

The ethereal gardens at **Self-Realization Fellowship**, on the old highway in Encinitas, are open to the public—just don't show up in beach attire. At Encinitas Boulevard, turn east to **Quail Botanical Gardens** and **Paul Ecke Poinsettias**.

Explore the beach communities at your leisure—the way locals do—stopping here and there to pick up a fine antique, an article of recycled clothing, surf accessories, or five-taquitos-for-a- dollar. La Costa Avenue, at the north side of Leucadia, is the road that will take you to **La Costa Resort and Spa**—not much fun now that the mafia's moved elsewhere.

In the town of Carlsbad, **Alt Karlsbad Haus** features memorabilia from the days when Carlsbad was thought to have similar water to that of Karlsbad spa, its German namesake. (Ha! Tell that to residents around nearby **Batiquitos Lagoon** who have been holding their polluted noses for *years*.) **Buena Vista Lagoon**, separating Carlsbad from Oceanside, is another story. Its 200-acre ecological preserve attracts many species of birds and plant life, and you can find out all about them at the **Audubon Society Nature Center**.

The **Oceanside Harbor and pier** are the center of North County's watersports. If you have proper i.d. and wish to tour **Camp Pendleton**, show up at the main gate on Vandegrift Boulevard for a visitor pass and self-guided directions. No self-respecting surfer would pass up a peek at **The California Surf Museum**, on Pacific Street, and the history, architecture and religion crowd will want to visit **Mission San Luis Rey**, east of Interstate 5 on Mission Avenue. A number of other historical buildings are lurking around the downtown area— including Irving Gill and Julia Morgan designs.

Inland explorations might lead you to **Rancho Bernardo**, with its hillside rows of white stucco homes and red-tiled roofs—plus parklands, golf courses, the renowned inn and some better shops and restaurants.

At **Escondido**, the go-sees include **The San Diego Wild Animal Park**, **San Pasqual Battlefield State Historic Park**, **California Center for the Arts**, and a couple of **wineries**.

Fallbrook is worth a pit stop, especially for avocado fiends and antique hounds. Another of California's missions— **Mission San Antonio de Pala**—sits on the Pala Indian Reservation. If you have a little extra time, spend a day up at **Mount Palomar** and the **Mount Palomar Observatory**.

FIELDING'S TEN HIGHEST SAN DIEGO COUNTY MOUNTAIN PEAKS

Hot Springs Mountain (San Ysidro Mountains)	**6533 feet**
Cuyamaca Peak (Cuyamaca Mountains)	**6512 feet**
Cuyapaipe Mountain (Laguna Mountains)	**6378 feet**
Monument Peak (Laguna Mountains)	**6272 feet**
Wooded Hill (Laguna Mountains)	**6223 feet**
Combs Peak (Bucksnort Mountain)	**6193 feet**
San Ysidro Peak (San Ysidro Mountains)	**6147 feet**
High Point (Palomar Mountain)	**6140 feet**
Rabbit Peak (Santa Rosa Mountains)	**6045 feet**
North Peak (Cuyamaca Mountains)	**5993 feet**

Historical Sites

Escondido

San Pasqual Battlefield State Historic Park ★★★

> *On SR 78, Escondido, Eight miles east of Escondido,* ☎ *(619) 220-5430.*
> *Hours open: 10 a.m.–5 p.m.*
> *Closed: Mon., Tue., Wed., Thur.*
> Kick around the 50-acre park that commemorates the Battle of San Pasqual—an 1848 Mexican-American squabble between General Kearny and General Pico and their various troops. Stop at the visitor center for a pamphlet to guide you along the half-mile nature trail (it isn't all blood and guts). You'll catch a good view of the valley. The park is closed on Thanksgiving, Christmas and New Year's days.

Oceanside

Audubon Society Nature Center ★★★

> *2202 South Hill Street, Oceanside, at Buena Vista Lagoon,* ☎ *(619) 439-2473.*
> *Hours open: 10 a.m.–4 p.m.*
> *Closed: Mon.*

NORTH COUNTY

The Nature Center, adjacent to Buena Vista Lagoon, educates visitors to the 200-acre ecological preserve—home to nearly 200 species of resident- or visiting birds, 50 species of plant life and a variety of animals. A short walking trail, kid's nature games, a native-plant garden and gift shop are part of the package. The Center also offers field trips, monthly lectures, special children's programs and monthly bird counts. Opening time on Sundays is 1 p.m.

Mission San Luis Rey de Francia ★★★

4050 Mission Avenue, Oceanside, east of Interstate 5,
☎ *(619) 757-3651.*
Hours open: 10 a.m.–4:30 p.m.
Special Hours: Mon.-Sat. 10 a.m.–4:30 p.m. Sun. 11:30 a.m.–4:30 p.m.
Founded in 1798 by Father Lasuen (and named for King Louis IX of France), Mission San Luis Rey is the largest of California's 21 missions. It's worth a visit just to ogle the wooden interior of the church and the original Native American decorations—as well as the grave markers in the cemetery dating back to 1798. The museum contains some interesting artifacts and exhibits from Native American, Spanish Mission, Mexican Secularization and American Military periods. The grounds are a great place for a picnic and a snack shop can help you out if you've forgotten your basket. Admission for ages 7-12 is $1. Sunday opening time is 11:30 a.m., and the mission is closed on Thanksgiving, Christmas and New Year's days. General Admission: $3.

San Diego

Mission San Antonio de Pala ★★★

On Pala Mission Road, San Diego, Pala Indian Reservation,
☎ *(619) 742-3317.*
Hours open: 10 a.m.–3 p.m.
Closed: Mon.
This 1816 mission was originally built as a branch of Mission San Luis Rey. It's been restored and is still in use by the Native Americans. You can visit the mission for free, but it costs $2 to check out the museum and mineral room.

Museums and Exhibits

Carlsbad

Alt Karlsbad Haus ★

2802A Carlsbad Boulevard, Carlsbad, ☎ *(619) 729-6912.*
Hours open: 10 a.m.–5 p.m.
Find out why Carlsbad is named for Karlsbad (if you care). Bascially, entrepreneur John Frazier decided a big selling point for his coastal land (Carlsbad) was the fact that the wasser was very similar to that at the German Karlsbad spa. Voila! The mini-museum also features a gift shop. Opening time on Sundays is at noon.

Mount Palomar

Palomar Observatory ★★★★★

Route 76 east from Interstate 5, follow signs, Mount Palomar, ☎ *(619) 742-2119.*
Hours open: 9 a.m.–4 p.m.
You can't miss it—the observatory's largest dome (there are four) measures 135-feet high and 137-feet in diameter—big enough for

that humongous 200-inch Hale telescope with a light range of about one billion light years. Don't get excited—ordinary Joes aren't allowed to look through it, just at it. The museum will educate you about research past and present through displays and videos (the photos of some of the discoveries are particularly interesting). The museum stays open until 4:30 p.m.; the observatory is closed December 24-25. Free admission.

Oceanside

California Surf Museum ★★★

308 North Pacific Street, Oceanside, ☎ *(619) 721-6876.*
Hours open: 10 a.m.–4 p.m.
Closed: Tue., Wed.
This small museum, currently situated across from the Oceanside Pier, is looking for another site so check the address before you make a special trip over. Even non-surfers will enjoy waxing up on the sport's history, culture and heroes. What was a woodie? What is "hang ten?" How many Beach Boys are there? Admission is free but donations are gladly accepted.

Parks and Gardens

Encinitas

Quail Botanical Gardens ★★★

230 Quail Gardens Drive, East of Interstate 5, in Encinitas,
☎ *(619) 436-3036.*
Hours open: 8 a.m.–5 p.m.
Thousands of rare plants, as well as a bird refuge and waterfall are hidden away on some 30 acres of peaceful retreat. Get out your watercolors or psycho-babble journal and spend a day here chilling out. Admission for ages 5-12, $1.50; admission is free to all on the first Tuesday of each month. General Admission: $3.

Self-Realization Fellowship ★★★★

215 West K Street, Encinitas, ☎ *(619) 436-7220.*
Hours open: 10 a.m.–5 p.m.
Closed: Mon.
Self-Realization Fellowship—a religious organization founded by Paramahansa Yogananda in the early 1900s— welcomes all to its ethereal, clifftop meditation gardens with tropical plantings, mesmerizing fish ponds and hypnotic views. Basic rules apply: no smoking, eating or drinking, bathing attire, cameras. A respectful attitude is respectfully requested. Gardens open at noon on Sundays.

Theme/Amusement Parks

Escondido

San Diego Wild Animal Park ★★★★★

15500 San Pasqual Valley Road, Escondido, ☎ *(619) 747-8702.*
Hours open: 9 a.m.–4 p.m.
The humans are enclosed and the animals roam free. (How can you tell?) About 3000 animals—zebras, elephants, rhinos, tigers, giraffes, and the like— wander semi-happily around more than 2000 acres while visitors view them from lookout points on a 1.5-mile walking trail or via a 50-minute monorail ride. Regions of Africa and Asia and an Australian rainforest have been re-created and the botanical pre-

NORTH COUNTY

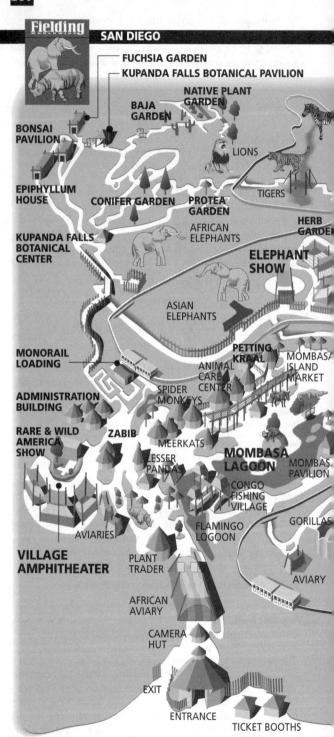

SAN DIEGO

FUCHSIA GARDEN
KUPANDA FALLS BOTANICAL PAVILION

NATIVE PLANT GARDEN

BAJA GARDEN

BONSAI PAVILION

LIONS

EPIPHYLLUM HOUSE

TIGERS

CONIFER GARDEN

PROTEA GARDEN

AFRICAN ELEPHANTS

HERB GARDEN

KUPANDA FALLS BOTANICAL CENTER

ELEPHANT SHOW

ASIAN ELEPHANTS

MONORAIL LOADING

PETTING KRAAL

MOMBASA ISLAND MARKET

ANIMAL CARE CENTER

ADMINISTRATION BUILDING

SPIDER MONKEYS

RARE & WILD AMERICA SHOW

ZABIB

MEERKATS

MOMBASA LAGOON

MOMBASA PAVILION

LESSER PANDAS

CONGO FISHING VILLAGE

GORILLAS

AVIARIES

FLAMINGO LOGOON

VILLAGE AMPHITHEATER

PLANT TRADER

AFRICAN AVIARY

AVIARY

CAMERA HUT

EXIT

ENTRANCE

TICKET BOOTHS

WILD ANIMAL PARK

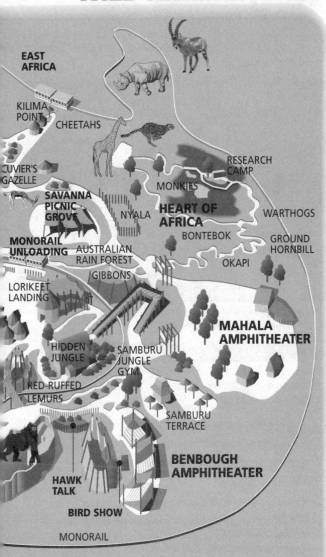

EAST
AFRICA

KILIMA
POINT

CHEETAHS

CUVIER'S
GAZELLE

RESEARCH
CAMP

MONKIES

**SAVANNA
PICNIC
GROVE**

NYALA

**HEART OF
AFRICA**

WARTHOGS

BONTEBOK

**MONORAIL
UNLOADING**

AUSTRALIAN
RAIN FOREST

GROUND
HORNBILL

OKAPI

GIBBONS

LORIKEET
LANDING

**MAHALA
AMPHITHEATER**

HIDDEN
JUNGLE

SAMBURU
JUNGLE
GYM

RED-RUFFED
LEMURS

SAMBURU
TERRACE

**BENBOUGH
AMPHITHEATER**

**HAWK
TALK**

BIRD SHOW

MONORAIL

Spread over 2200 acres, the San Diego Wild
Animal Park is a sanctuary for 1600 birds (285
species), 1600 mammals (121 species) and 41
endangered species. The wildlife roam free while
people observe from trams and walkways.

serve also shelters more than two million plants. Hippo Beach is a newer attraction where zoo-goers get a close-up view—through tempered glass—of Africa's most dangerous mammals as they travel through water at about 15 miles per hour (SURE the glass is strong enough!). Nairobi Village is the scene for daily animal and bird shows—if you must. The park stays open until 6 p.m. mid-June to Labor Day. Admission for ages over 55, $15.95; ages three-11, $11.95. Admission includes monorail ride, all exhibits and animal shows. Parking is another $3. General Admission: $18.95.

Mombasa Lagoon lilypads lead little adventurers to another section of San Diego Wild Animal Park.

FIELDING'S WHAT'S IN A NAME?

The main road binding coastal communities from Del Mar to Oceanside changes names as it changes towns.

North Torrey Pines Road becomes Camino del Mar in Del Mar;

Camino del Mar becomes Old Highway 101 in Solana Beach;

Old Highway 101 becomes First Street in Encinitas;

First Street becomes Old Highway 101 in Leucadia;

Old Highway 101 becomes Carlsbad Boulevard in Carlsbad;

Carlsbad Boulevard becomes Hill Street in Oceanside.

If in doubt or lost, most locals will know what you're talking about if you ask directions to "Old Highway 101." Just keep in mind that businesses and restaurants use the "official" designations for their addresses.

"It's a guy thing."

Drawing by D. Reilly; ©1995 The New Yorker Magazine, Inc.

North County: For Kids

Again we have those delightful **beaches**, the county's ubiquitous free entertainment for everyone. **South Cardiff State Beach**, and **Swami's**, just south of the Self-Realization Fellowship grounds, offer excellent tidepool exploration opportunities (you need to navigate a lot of stairs to get down to Swami's, while the South Cardiff spot has easy access).

For **park activities**, try Del Mar's ocean-edge **Seagrove Park, Solana Beach's San Dieguito Park**, and **Escondido's Felicita Park** plus you're bound to come across plenty of other local playgrounds and runaround areas. In Carlsbad, the **Children's Museum** provides a really cool hands-on learning center.

The San Diego Wild Animal Park will delight most kids— unless they're animal haters, in which case take them over to **San Pasqual Battlefield** site where they can relive (vicariously, we hope) the bloody 1846 shootout in which Kit Carson took part.

Up at **Palomar Mountain,** a visit to **Palomar Observatory** and a peek at the stars through a high-powered telescope should render the little ones silent and reverent for the rest of their isn't-life-such-a-miracle? existence. No? Well, screw it—take them to the malls and video parlors.

Carlsbad

Carlsbad Children's Museum   ★★★★

> *300 Carlsbad Village Drive, Carlsbad,* ☎ *(619) 720-0737.*
> *Hours open: Noon–5 p.m.*
> *Closed: Mon.*
>
> It's a hands-on family learning center focusing on science, history, the arts and environmental awareness. Kids won't even realize it's a learning experience when they're let loose in the marketplace, creative corner, mirror magic and castle play sections. Admission is free for children under two. The museum opens at 10:00 a.m. on Friday and Saturday, 11:30 a.m. on Sunday. General Admission: $3.50.

Tours

North County tours are limited to the self-guided variety at **Camp Pendleton Marine Base**, **Oceanside historical buildings**, **San Pasqual Battlefield State Historic Park**, and **Palomar Observatory**.

Oceanside

Camp Pendleton   ★★

> *Vandegrift Boulevard, Oceanside,* ☎ *(619) 725-5566.*
> Pull out proper I.D. (driver's license, vehicle registration and proof of auto insurance) at Camp Pendleton's main gate and you'll be issued a visitor pass and self-guiding tour brochure. Some of the sites to see on this 125,000-acre Marine Corps base are the Amphibian Vehicle Museum, Bunkhouse Museum and 19th-century adobe ranch house. Tours are allowed daily, dawn to dusk.

Downtown Oceanside History Walk   ★★

> *P.O. Box 125, Oceanside, 92049,* ☎ *(619) 722-4786.*
> Oceanside isn't just Marines, surfers and gangs. The Oceanside Historical Society produces a pamphlet that will guide you from the Civic Center complex to 20 historic resource buildings (including Irving gill and Julia Morgan designs). The walking tour is about two miles long.

Events

There are some goodies. In January, the **Mercedes Championships**—six days of golf heaven—are held at La Costa Resort and Country Club. Later in the month, Carlsbad is the starting point for the **San Diego Marathon.**

Mid-March heralds the **Oceanside Whale Festival** and, at the end of April, the **Fallbrook Avocado Festival** pays tribute to its green friends.

Championship riders gallop to the **Del Mar National Horse Show,** for two weeks of early-May competition. The **Ramona Rodeo,** held about a week later, is one of America's top rodeos. Back on the coast, Solana Beach celebrates the onslaught of summer with its May weekend **Fiesta del Sol.**

June events include the **Camp Pendleton Rodeo and Carnival** and the not-to-be-missed **Del Mar Fair**—an old-fashioned county fair with rides, exhibits and top-name performers. **Fourth of July** at the fairgrounds features not only trippy fireworks, but launching of the **Hot Air Balloon Classic.** Following the fair comes the Del Mar Thoroughbred Club **racing season**, running through mid-September.

It's back to La Costa Resort and Spa for the August **Toshiba Tennis Classic**. In mid-August, the **World Body Surfing Championships** attracts big-time, fin-only competitors to Oceanside Pier and Beach.

Cardiff's Greek Orthodox Church puts on a traditional **Greek festival** sometime in September.

October is a busy month: a **Surf Festival** in Solana Beach; **Tour de North County** bike race from Inland North County; a three-weekend **Renaissance Fantasy Faire** near Fallbrook; and the **Century Club Golf Matches** at Fairbanks Ranch.

In December, you can combine Christmas festivities with something *really* uplifting—the **Reenactment of the Battle of San Pasqual**, out at the Historic Park near Escondido.

Cardiff-by-the-Sea

Greek Festival   ★ ★ ★

> *3459 Manchester Avenue, Cardiff-by-the-Sea,* ☎ *(619) 942-0920.*
> Join the September fun at Saints Constantine and Helen Greek
> Orthodox Church with traditional Greek entertainment, dancing,
> food, pastries, crafts and games for the kids.

Carlsbad

Mercedes Championships   ★★★★★

La Costa Resort and Spa, Carlsbad, ☎ (800) 918-4653.

This big-time traditional golf event (formerly known as Tournament of Champions), each January, brings the best of the best to La Costa Resort and Country Club for practice rounds, a Pro-Am and the Tournament.

San Diego Marathon   ★★★★★

Plaza Camino Real, Carlsbad, ☎ (619) 792-2900.

In late January, San Diego's only marathon takes off from Plaza Camino Real (a shopping mall) in Carlsbad, covering an interesting course which includes 14 miles of scenic coast line. Lesser zealots can participate in a half-marathon or five-km run/walk.

Toshiba Tennis Classic   ★★★★★

La Costa Resort and Spa, Carlsbad, ☎ (619) 436-3551.

Top pros compete in this early-August women's tennis tournament at the prestigious La Costa Resort and Spa.

Del Mar

Del Mar Fair   ★★★★★

Del Mar Fairgrounds, Del Mar, ☎ (619) 755-1161.

The place to be from mid-June through the Fourth of July. Del Mar residents try to clear out of town to make way for the onslaught of visitors to San Diego's annual county fair. The hooplah includes a midway, carnival rides, games, exhibits, arts and crafts, animals and flowers and *heaps* of food concessions. Nightly concerts—free with admission—draw the biggest names from pop to punkdom. The fair culminates with a spectacular fireworks display. Gates are open from 9 a.m. until 10 p.m., until midnight on Fri. and Sat.

Del Mar National Horse Show   ★★★

Del Mar Fairgrounds, Del Mar, at the racetrack, ☎ (619) 755-1161.

The two-week national event, held in early May, showcases Olympic-caliber and national championship riders, horse and rider teams and draft horse competition.

Del Mar Thoroughbred Racing   ★★★★★

Del Mar Racetrack, Del Mar, ☎ (619) 755-1141.
Closed: Tue.

The Beautiful People and the not-so-lovely-losers flock into town from late July through mid-September, when the Del Mar Thoroughbred Club presents exciting thoroughbred action—nine races a day, six days per week. Post time is 2 p.m., except the first five Fridays when it's bumped up to 4 p.m. No races are held on Tuesdays. General admission is $3, clubhouse admission is $6.

Hot Air Balloon Classic   ★★★★

Del Mar Racetrack Grandstand, Del Mar, ☎ (619) 481-6800.

This Fourth of July event is part of the festivities at the Del Mar Fair. The San Diego Balloon Association literally launches its hot air classic from the fairgrounds—sending colorful balloons soaring into the early-evening sky.

Escondido

Re-enactment of the Battle of San Pasqual ★★

San Pasqual Battlefield State Historic Park, Escondido,
☎ *(619) 489-0076.*
Before you get carried away with Christmas, relive the 1846 Battle of
San Pasqual (Mexican-American War). The early-December action
includes the battle re-enactment and military encampment, as well as
food and other entertainment.

Fairbanks Ranch

Century Club Golf Matches ★★★★

Fairbanks Ranch Country Club golf course, Fairbanks Ranch,
☎ *(619) 281-4653.*
The Century Club Golf Matches, in October, have been going on for
more than a quarter century. San Diego area pros and amateurs join
in the competition.

Fallbrook

Fallbrook Avocado Festival ★★★

On Main Street, Fallbrook, ☎ *(619) 728-5845.*
Pay homage to our succulent-tasting, creamy green friends at Fallbrook—the place where most of them are born. The April fest takes
place on Main Street and features the usual carnival-type arts and
crafts and fun and games.

Renaissance Fantasy Faire ★★★

Hwy. 15 No., exit Hwy. 76 E. and follow signs, Fallbrook,
☎ *(619) 743-0985.*
Three October weekends of Ye Olde England come to life with the
re-creation of a 15th-century marketplace along with the requisite
"pleasure faire" entertainment (artists, magicians, minstrels, crafts,
food and grog). Dig out your old hippie gear—no one will know the
difference.

Oceanside

Camp Pendleton Rodeo and Carnival ★★

Camp Pendleton, Oceanside, ☎ *(619) 725-6195.*
Although this June deal is basically for enlisted personnel and their
dependents (with six standard rodeo events as well as women's barrel
racing), civilians are welcome to take part in non-rough stock events.

Oceanside Whale Festival ★★★

Harbor Beach, Oceanside, ☎ *(619) 722-2133.*
Oceanside honors the California gray whales' migration in mid-
March with a flurry of activities including whale-watching trips, life-
size sand sculptures, arts and crafts, food concessions and family
entertainment. Show up anytime between 9 a.m. and dusk.

World Body Surfing Championships ★★★★

Oceanside Pier and Beach, Oceanside, ☎ *(619) 966-4535.*
Watch—or participate in—the annual championships. Daring international and U.S. bodysurfers take to the ocean waves equipped with
only a pair of swim fins. Ages 12 and up can join in the three-day
August event.

NORTH COUNTY

Ramona

Ramona Rodeo ★★★

Fifth and Aqua, Ramona, ☎ *(619) 789-1311.*

Ramona hosts one of the country's top 50 rodeos for three days in late May. Western dances and specialty acts kick up plenty of heels.

Solana Beach

Fiesta del Sol ★★★

Fletcher Cove, Solana Beach, ☎ *(619) 755-4775.*

Lots of fun in the sun at Solana Beach on a weekend in late May. The kick-off-to-summer celebration consists of a surfing contest, live bands, beach games, children's activities and arts and crafts. Stop by 10 a.m. to dusk.

Surf Festival ★★

Fletcher Cove, Solana Beach, ☎ *(619) 755-4775.*

The October surf festival features two days of contests, food and entertainment in surf's-up Solana Beach.

Vista

Tour de North County ★★

Rancho Buena Vista High School, Vista, ☎ *(619) 450-6510.*

It's *not* the Tour de France, but it *is* fun and easy as you like. Choose your own bike tour (five to 75 miles) through North County—and enjoy the scenery. Fun, not speed, is the primary focus of this annual October race.

Author's Tip

Along some North County beaches, ordinarily on the evening of an equinox, you might encounter filmy ethereal creatures–bearing candles and burning incense–dancing and splashing in the sea foam, intoning indecipherable sounds. Don't worry–it's just a coven of witches.

North County: Music, Dance and Theater

You'll find some hot stuff happening. **California Center for the Arts**, in Escondido, offers dynamite musical concerts and dance and theatrical performances by an impressive entourage of international well-knowns. **Welk Resort Theatre**, out at Mr. Bubble's place, puts on an appealing range of high-budget entertainment.

Theatrical productions are regularly staged at a variety of theater spaces in Solana Beach, Poway, Escondido and Fallbrook. Two community colleges—Mira Costa in Oceanside and Palomar in San Marcos—offer a variety of quality student endeavors.

Theatre

Escondido

California Center for the Arts ★★★★★

340 North Escondido Boulevard, Escondido, ☎ *(619) 738-4100.*
This world-class showcase for the arts draws an astounding array of internationally acclaimed performers for musical, theatrical, dance and variety performances. Fresh talent, provocative works, something for everyone. The 12-acre center also features a museum and conference center. Where does Escondido get its arts budget???

Lawrence Welk Theatre ★★★

8860 Lawrence Welk Drive, Escondido, ☎ *(619) 749-3448.*
Professional musicals, comedies and variety shows are presented in Mr. Bubbles' 330-seat dinner theater. The buffet-style dinner precedes the show.

Patio Playhouse Community Theatre ★★

1511-23 East Valley Parkway, Escondido, ☎ *(619) 746-6669.*
Closed: Mon.
Community productions of dramas, musicals and comedies—usually suitable for the whole family.

Fallbrook

Fallbrook Players ★★

231 North Main Street, Fallbrook, ☎ *(619) 728-0998.*
More community presentations, staged in the Mission Theatre. Could be a good topper after a day of avocado and antique shopping.

Oceanside

MiraCosta Theatre ★★

One Barnard Drive, at MiraCosta College, Oceanside, ☎ *(619) 757-2121.*
Student productions—mostly written, directed and staged by the theater department—include traditional works and children's classics, as well as off-the-wall experimental pieces.

Poway

Poway Center for the Performing Arts ★★★

15498 Espola Road, Poway, ☎ *(619) 748-0505.*
Closed: Mon.
A wide range of performances—from Oscar Wilde's erudite satire, to music and dance festivals, to delightful children's theatre. A pleasant surprise in this rural-istic community.

San Marcos

Palomar College Performing Arts Department ★★★

1140 West Mission Road, Palomar College, San Marcos, ☎ *(619) 744-1150.*
Excellent theatrical, dance and musical presentations by the community college's theatre department, symphony orchestra and dance department (for which Palomar is especially well-known).

Solana Beach

North Coast Repertory Theatre ★★★

987D Lomas Santa Fe Drive, Solana Beach, ☎ *(619) 481-1055.*

The North Coast Rep is almost always worthy of special notice. Dramas, classics, comedies, musicals are performed with professional aplomb. Overlook the fact that the theater is tucked away in a shopping center (it's an inoffensive shopping center).

Author's Tip

*If you're in the mood for a flick, forego the multiplexes east of Interstate 5 for **La Paloma,** on First Street, in Encinitas. The neighborhood theatre, dating from the 1920s, shows cheap first-run films (with an occasional artier piece thrown in) and also stages musical concerts and local theater performances. In the '60s and '70s the cinema was outfitted with mattresses and back rests and "smoking" was ignored. Those times have changed (regular seating and no-smoking ordinances, in effect) but, still, La Paloma retains a lot of charm.*

North County: Nightlife

The Belly Up Tavern, a cavernous converted Quonset hut in Solana Beach, takes North County honors for top nightlife venue— the only one to attract a full roundup of international talents (Leon Russell, Leon Redbone, Warren Zevon, etc.), as well as the hottest up-and-comings (such as Candye Kane & the Swingin' Armadillos). After that, its the usual brand of beachy restaurant and bar, jazz, rock and mellow sounds echoing up and down the coast. Oceanside and inland areas tend to be rowdy and redneck.

Fielding's Favorite North County See-and-Be-Seen Scene:

*For the trendy, tony, coiffed and pedicured: the upper-level oceanview deck at the **Del Mar Plaza**, corner of 15th Street and Camino del Mar, Del Mar.*

*For the bicycle pants, half-assed ravers, and "someday I'm going to be a writer" crowd: **Pannikin Coffee & Tea**, 510 North Highway 101, Encinitas (Leucadia).*

*For the "God, I'm so spiritual" and never-were hippies: **Casady's Whole Foods Supermarket**, 745 First Street, Encinitas.*

For the "HEY! I'm a Marine" chest-pounders: any of the bleak bars or X-rated clubs on Hill Street or Oceanside Avenue, in Oceanside.

Cardiff-by-the-Sea

Ki's Coffee on Top ★★★

2591 South Highway 101, Cardiff-by-the-Sea, ☎ *(619) 436-5236.*
Located on the coast highway, Ki's healthy-food restaurant offers an
upper-level coffee bar with super ocean views and simpatico jazz or
acoustic sounds most nights of the week.

Carlsbad

Alley ★★

421 Grand Avenue, Carlsbad, ☎ *(619) 434-1173.*
North County visitors might want to swing by this smaller club for a
sampling of local blues and rock acts. Something's on every night of
the week, with jam sessions scheduled at 4 p.m. on Sundays.

Arthouse Coffee and Gallery ★★

2931 Roosevelt Street, Carlsbad, ☎ *(619) 730-0270.*
An eclectic mix of coffee beans, art and evening entertainment—usually blues and acoustic "apropos coffeehouse" performers. Poetry
readings are on the roster most Sunday evenings, and Tuesday is
open-mike night.

Coyote Bar and Grill ★★

300 Carlsbad Village Drive, Carlsbad, ☎ *(619) 729-4695.*
A happening, trendyish singles' spot in Carlsbad. Wednesdays, Thursdays and Fridays are usually rock and roll nights, with blues on Saturdays and jazz on Sundays. Tuesdays is—gag—karaoke night.
Performances run from 6-10 p.m.—perfect for the get-to-bed-early
crowd.

Neiman's Bar and Grille ★★★

2978 Carlsbad Boulevard, Carlsbad, ☎ *(619) 729-4131.*
Housed inside the historic "twin inns" building, Neiman's yuppified
restaurant keeps the TGIF crowd happy with Friday and Saturday
night blues and rock numbers. Performances are 7-11 p.m.

Rookies Sports Bar and Grill ★★

2216 El Camino Real, Carlsbad, ☎ *(619) 757-1123.*
Satellite sports, food and tunes on the La Costa side of Carlsbad bring
in the lookin'-for-action singles and wannabe-singles. Wednesday
through Saturday nights feature rock and roll or some exceptionally
good local blues bands. Performances run 8:30 p.m. to 12:30 a.m.

Sand Bar ★★★★

3878 Carlsbad Boulevard, Carlsbad, ☎ *(619) 729-3170.*
The Sand Bar, at Tamarack Beach in Carlsbad—an old North County
favorite—has taken on a bit of a new twist to keep up with the times.
Still a down-home slouchy beach bar, the entertainment schedule has
pushed it into a slightly higher league with live blues, reggae and rock
acts every night of the week. Tops for casual atmosphere, brews and
down-to-sea-level meals.

Encinitas

First Street Bar ★

636 First Street, Encinitas, ☎ *(619) 944-0233.*
A step up from barfly, this simple local pub (filled with simple locals)
offers a hodge-podge of blues, country, reggae or rock on Wednesdays, Fridays and Saturdays. Performances begin at 9 p.m.

Sharky's ★

485 First Street, Encinitas, ☎ (619) 436-7397.

Reggae and rock with the take-what-you-can-get set at this local—occasionally raucous—hangout. Don't be surprised if the name has changed again by the time you read this.

Author's Tip

From Rancho Santa Fe, catch the Del Dios Highway toward Escondido. Turn off at Lake Hodges and wind your way down to **Hernandez' Hideaway** *(19320 Lake Drive, ☎ (619) 746-1444). Family-owned for more than two decades, this is a perfect get-away-from-the-madding-crowd place for authentic Mexican cuisine and superb margaritas.*

Poway

Big Stone Lodge ★★

12237 Old Pomerado Road, Poway, ☎ (619) 748-1135.

Put on your best armadillo boots and tightest jeans for weekend country-and-western dancing in this former Pony Express station. Even if you're not a C&W fan, the friendly cowboys and cowgirls will no doubt seduce you into the swing.

Solana Beach

Belly Up Tavern ★★★★★

143 South Cedros Avenue, Solana Beach, ☎ (619) 481-9022.

North County's way cool nightclub. This cavernous converted Quonset hut showcases big-namers like Leon Russell, Leon Redbone, Todd Rundgren and Warren Zevon, as well as top local acts. The hot concerts require tickets but you can catch cool blues, swingin' country, and other warm-ups and matinee numbers for free. The cafe opens at 11 a.m. daily (noon on Sundays) for burgers and munchies. Most of the ticket-required performances begin 8:30-9 p.m.

AUTHOR'S AWARDS FOR FAVORITE ONE-NIGHT STANDS

San Diego men are not all yuppies, surfers or golfers. My top honors for most fun dates in the County are (may I have the envelope, please):

1. The guy who borrowed an unlocked tank from the unlocked National Guard lot and joyrode around his neighborhood—mowing down anything he damn well felt like, popping up at times to wave at friends (whose possessions he avoided). He had a good old time up until the very second the cops shot him dead.

2. The dude who jumped onto Del Mar racetrack—race in progress—and galloped with the ponies, causing the horsey crowd to unilaterally whinney and snort. At last report, he had been trotted over to County Mental Health.

3. The 300-lb. Samoan who breezed through North County early one evening, robbing at gunpoint a variety of victims along the main coastal highway. The sheriffs set up road blocks and sent out the helicopters but they were unable to spot the heavy-set, dark-skinned criminal-wearing a blue Hawaiian print shirt and driving a bright red convertible (top down) through the snowy-white community. Still large, he is still at large.

North County: Shopping

The too-exclusive-to-be-on-earth **Del Mar Plaza** will start you off (and, depending on your budget and how much you max out your cards, possibly finish you off). You'll find top-of-the-line specialty shops (one with all-white clothing, another with all-black clothing—sigh, can you even believe how imaginative and tony it all is?), custom jewelry, gift items, art galleries, a good book shop and just all that be-seen-ness. Even the supermarket looks more like a culinary art gallery than—for Del Martians—the corner "pick up a quart of milk and a roll of toilet paper" shop.

Flower Hill, on the other side of the racetrack and Interstate 5, was—pre-plaza—*the* trend-modum. It still has some niceties, but really most locals only stumble by for the cinemas (still an old-fashioned *four* in one plex) and some eateries. Shops in **Rancho Santa Fe** are *so* exclusive that no one even *thinks* about who might be watching them—everyone's dressed to the hilt *anyway* and no one even bothers to check price tags (they point and a 'sales associate' whisks it away to be wrapped).

Beach-town shopping can be a lot of fun. Along the highway and off-streets between Del Mar and Oceanside, you'll find everything from used paperbacks and imported rolling papers to healing crystals and surfboard fin protectors. New age shops, t-shirt outlets and health food stores blend in with historical landmarks, mortuaries, mom-and-pop shops, elegant eateries and scuzzy liquor stores.

Cedros Street, running parallel on the east side of the old highway in Solana Beach, is known as a dynamic design center (in a California coastal sort of way). Belly Up Tavern, also on this street, is now flanked by some really interesting home furnishing shops. The **antique mall** is crammed with treasures—but not too many bargains. **State Street**, in Carlsbad, is another antique-lovers haunt, as is the inland village of **Fallbrook**.

Mall freaks will find happiness at Escondido's **North County Fair**, (the county's largest mall) and Carlsbad's **Plaza Camino Real**. Almost the entire stretch of El Camino Real, from Del Mar to Oceanside, is basically one very long strip mall. Just two decades ago, it was an isolated road lined with flower fields and gentle countryisms—broken only by La Costa Resort and Spa and Palomar Airport. It's all for you, consumers.

FIELDING'S SELECT GUIDE TO NORTH COUNTY SHOPPING

Lou's Records

454 North Highway 101, Encinitas, ☎ *(619) 753-1382.*
The favorite shop for new and used CD's, cassette's and
LPs. Great collection of imports, local and independent
labels.

J.B. Victoria

930 First Street, Encinitas, ☎ *(619) 633-1326.*
Specializing in angels in many forms plus candles, incense,
books, gift items, jewelry, ethereal clothing, New Age
music.

Jimbo's Naturally

*12853 El Camino Real, San Diego, east of Del Mar and Inter-
state 5,* ☎ *(619) 793-7755.*
A huge, glitzy health food supermarket with separate deli
and bakery section. Also a large range of vitamins, teas,
nutritional supplements, essential oils and natural reme-
dies.

Harley's House of Harleys

1555 East Hill Street, Oceanside, ☎ *(619) 433-2060.*
Pick up your new or used dream machine, or fix up the
one sitting in your garage. The "designer store" features t-
shirts, leathers and Harleyism gifts.

V G Donuts & Bakery

106 Aberdeen Drive, Cardiff-by-the-Sea, ☎ *(619) 753-2400.*
Easily San Diego County's best donut shop, been around
for years.

Sunset

897 First Street, #101, Encinitas, ☎ *(619) 753-6655.*
New and used surfboards, body boards, ding repairs, wet
suits and accessories.

Hansen's

1105 First Street, Encinitas, ☎ *(619) 753-6595.*
Huge sporting goods shop with new and used surfboards,
body boards, skates, skis, snowboards, beach gear and
sportswear.

Chino's

6123 Calzada del Bosque, Rancho Santa Fe,
☎ *(619) 756-3184.*
The world's most wonderful vegetable shop, where you'll
see the finest chefs picking baby veggies, perfect greens,
and specialty herbs.

North County: Where to Stay

The best addresses in North County include: **L'Auberge Del Mar Resort and Spa** and **Del Mar Hilton**, in Del Mar; **Rancho Valencia** and **The Inn at Rancho Santa Fe**, in Rancho; **La Costa Resort and Spa** and **Carlsbad Inn Resort**, in Carlsbad; and **Rancho Bernardo Inn** and **Welk Resort Center**, in Inland North County.

You'll also find a trickling of Doubletree and Best Western types and a scattering of bed and breakfast inns. Independently owned motels and motor inns, both along the coast and inland, can be anything from "personal and charming" to 1950ish Bates'-style.

Winter or off-season rates at even some of the best resorts can be quite reasonable. Not so along the coast during summer or when the ponies are running in Del Mar—every decent room (and even those barely decent) gets snatched up months ahead and at highly inflated rates. Even the **campgrounds** at San Elijo and Carlsbad beaches are often reserved a year ahead. In the worse scenario, you'll just be stuck at a low-end out-of-town scroungy motel in a bed that your mother would *never* approve of.

Bed & Breakfasts

Carlsbad

Pelican Cove Inn	**$85–$175**	★★★

320 Walnut Avenue, Carlsbad, 92008, Two blocks east of Carlsbad Boulevard, ☎ *(619) 434-5995.*
Single: $85–$175. Double: $85–$175.

The Cape Cod-style inn is set in a quiet residential neighborhood, close to the beach and Carlsbad village. Eight luxurious rooms—all with private baths and entrances, fresh flowers and fruit, down comforters and gas fireplaces—cater to the romance-minded (whether alone or a deux). Guests can loll about the gazebo, sundeck or garden, or stroll a short ways to the beach (and loll about THERE). The inn will send you off with beach chairs, towels and picnic baskets. Leave your work at home! 8 rooms. Credit Cards: A, MC, V.

Del Mar

Rock Haus	**$90–$150**	★★★

410 15th Street, Del Mar, 92014, Above Del Mar Plaza, ☎ *(619) 481-3764.*
Single: $90–$150. Double: $90–$150.

The Rock Haus used to be kind of isolated up the hill from Camino del Mar—then The Plaza moved into its front yard. It's a brilliant place for romancers and quiet types—with all that early Del Mar charm creaking throughout the 10 guest rooms. Most rooms have ocean views, one has a fireplace, four have private baths, and six share "the facilities." B&Bers eat breakfast in the enclosed ocean (and plaza) view terrace. A two-night minimum stay is required on weekends and some holidays. 10 rooms. Credit Cards: A, MC, V.

Hotels

Del Mar

Del Mar Hilton   **$75–$140**   ★★★

15575 Jimmy Durante Boulevard, Del Mar, 92014, Across from the race-track, ☎ *(800) 445-8667, (619) 792-5200, FAX: (619) 792-0353. Single: $75–$125. Double: $90–$140.*

This low-lying resorty Hilton sits right across from the Del Mar race-track and fairgrounds—making it a super-convenient choice for the pony players and fair-goers. It certainly doesn't have the elegance of L'Auberge but it's a good option for those who shun gushy pampering—plus the prices are lower. Rooms are cheerful, well-decorated and some have balconies or patios. The dining room, restaurant and lounge (with entertainment) are all popular with local Del Martians. Amenities: Jacuzzi, sauna, balcony or patio, business services. 245 rooms. Credit Cards: A, DC, D, MC, V.

Doubletree Club Hotel Del Mar   **$75–$125**   ★★

11915 El Camino Real, Del Mar, 92130, East of Interstate 5 and Del Mar, ☎ *(800) 222-8733, (619) 481-5900, FAX: (619) 481-0990. Single: $75. Double: $75–$125.*

The five-story Doubletree sits east of Del Mar village but right in the hub of many business and commercial enterprises in that area. The hotel is kid-friendly and under-18's can stay for free in their parents' room. The whole place is comfy and well-tended. Amenities are adequate for the price range—a pool, wading pool, spa, exercise room, restaurant and lounge. Area transportation is provided—a big bonus for anyone who has experienced fairgrounds and racetrack gridlock. Amenities: exercise room, Jacuzzi, family plan, business services. 225 rooms. Credit Cards: A, CB, DC, D, MC, V.

Motels

Del Mar

Stratford Inn   **$75–$150**   ★★

710 Camino del Mar, Del Mar, 92014, In the village, ☎ *(800) 446-7229, (619) 755-1501, FAX: (619) 755-4704. Single: $75–$150. Double: $75–$150.*

Stratford Inn used to be the only decent place to stay in Del Mar—not so since the arrival of L'Auberge and the Hilton. Still, it's only a few blocks from the beach and the main fashion parade, and offers large rooms—some with ocean views, patios or balconies and 18 units with kitchens. Two pools and a spa are it for the amenities, but everything else is close at hand. Amenities: Jacuzzi, balcony or patio. 98 rooms. Credit Cards: A, CB, DC, D, MC, V.

Encinitas

Radisson Inn Encinitas   **$79–$105**   ★★

85 Encinitas Boulevard, Encinitas, 92024, East of Old Highway 101 (First Street), ☎ *(800) 333-3333, (619) 942-7455, FAX: (619) 632-9481.*

Single: $79–$99. Double: $85–$105.

The low-rising Radisson sits near Moonlight Beach in Encinitas, east of the Old Highway on a somewhat congested street (but so convenient to shopping and the freeway). The rooms are surprisingly well furnished and some have ocean views and kitchen facilities. Guests have use of a pool and spa and continental breakfast is complimentary. Ciao Luna, on the property, offers simple and reasonably priced Italian-American meals. Amenities: Jacuzzi. 91 rooms. Credit Cards: A, DC, D, MC, V.

Solano Beach

Ramada Inn **$75–$107** ★★

717 South Highway 101, Solano Beach, 92075, ☎ *(800) 232-2407, (619) 792-8200, FAX: (619) 792-2370.*
Single: $75–$99. Double: $75–$107.

Along the main drag in Solana Beach, this Ramada is close to the beach and the Del Mar racetrack and fairgrounds. It's a reliable choice for standard rooms (all with balconies or patios, some with kitchens), and sits next door to that SoCal staple, the California Pizza Kitchen. Daily Continental breakfast is complimentary. Amenities: exercise room, Jacuzzi. 115 rooms. Credit Cards: A, CB, DC, D, MC, V.

Resorts
Carlsbad

Carlsbad Inn Beach Resort **$140–$198** ★★★

3075 Carlsbad Boulevard, Del Mar, 92008, Across from the beach, ☎ *(800) 235-3939, (619) 434-7020, FAX: (619) 729-4853.*
Single: $140–$198. Double: $140–$198.

Pretend the Really Big One has hit and Germany is sitting on the Pacific Ocean. This Old World-style sprawl with gabled roofs and deutscher decor is a popular beach resort (access across the street) with large rooms (all with VCRs, some with kitchens and fireplaces), a pool, sauna, spa, exercise room, playground and bicycle loans. Carlsbad village restaurants and bars are a short walk away. Amenities: exercise room, Jacuzzi, sauna. 62 rooms. Credit Cards: A, CB, DC, D, MC, V.

La Costa Hotel and Spa **$225–$420** ★★★★

2100 Costa del Mar Road, Del Mar, 92009, East of Interstate 5, at La Costa Avenue exit, ☎ *(800) 854-5000, (619) 438-9111, FAX: (619) 438-3758.*
Single: $225–$420. Double: $225–$420.

La Costa is still a prime hideaway for celebs and politcos but, since the Mafia (reputedly) cleared out some years ago, it's lost a lot of pizzazz. Along with Rancho Bernardo, it's a hard one to beat for golf and tennis getaways—plus it boasts that famous get-pampered spa. The contemporary resort is made up of low, unpretentious buildings with stylish contemporary rooms and lots of neutral (i.e. bland) color schemes. The facilities are world-class—36 holes of golf, 21 tennis courts, health club and complete beauty spa, pools, saunas, shops, four restaurants, lounges with entertainment, movie theater, business center, children's program and plenty of privacy. Amenities: tennis, health club, exercise room, Jacuzzi, sauna, business services. 480 rooms. Credit Cards: A, CB, DC, D, MC, V.

Del Mar

L'Auberge Del Mar Resort and Spa $165–$315   ★★★★

1540 Camino del Mar, Del Mar, 92014, In the village, ☎ *(800) 553-1336, (619) 259-1515, FAX: (619) 755-4940.*
Single: $165–$315. Double: $165–$315.

The three-story L'Auberge—just like its turn-of-the-century predecessor, the Hotel Del Mar—is the place to stay. Just like the Plaza, across the street, it is the place to be seen. Certainly the most elegant hotel/resort along the North County coast, L'Auberge offers lavish elegance—the snazzy lobby, divine restaurant, bar, cafe, health club and beauty spa. Its all dark woods and herbal wraps, landscaped gardens and yoga lessons, crackling fires and Deepak Chopra, snobbishness and ayurvedic awakening. You will impress everyone you know in the whole wide world if you send them a letter on the hotel's lovely stationary. Rooms are beigey and light. Many have ocean views, balconies and gas fireplaces. How can you resist? Amenities: tennis, health club, exercise room, Jacuzzi, sauna, balcony or patio. 123 rooms. Credit Cards: A, CB, DC, D, MC, V.

Escondido

Welk Resort Center $110   ★★★★

8860 Lawrence Welk Drive, 92026, Nine miles north of Escondido on Interstate 15, ☎ *(800) 932-9355, (619) 749-3000, FAX: (619) 749-6182.*
Single: $110. Double: $110.

The late Mr. Bubbles' tribute to himself. This self-contained resort complex—set in a valley surrounded by rolling hills—is in its own little world, fairly remote from everything except the Interstate that passes by. Facilities are first rate and include three golf courses, tennis, pools, spas, a shopping complex, an award-winning musical theater, restaurant and lounge, deli and pizzeria, yogurt and ice cream shop and loads of activities. Rooms have a southwestern feel with light woods and splashes of turquoise—not that anyone spends much time in them. It's just all very bubbly. Amenities: tennis, Jacuzzi, sauna, business services. 132 rooms. Credit Cards: A, CB, DC, D, MC, V.

Rancho Bernardo

Rancho Bernardo Inn $115–$255   ★★★★★

17550 Bernardo Oaks Drive, Rancho Bernardo, 92128, Off Interstate 15 at Rancho Bernardo Road, ☎ *(800) 542-6096, (619) 487-1611, FAX: (619) 673-0311.*
Single: $115–$255. Double: $115–$255.

Set in the pseudo-Mediterranean inland community of Rancho Bernardo, this inn is nothing short of heaven for golfers and tennis racketeers. It's complete indulgence with five golf courses, the Vic Braden Tennis College, state-of-the-art health spa, pools, spas, meeting rooms and a children's camp during summer and holidays. Wait, there's more—dining rooms, lounges, entertainment, afternoon tea plus one of the county's finest French restaurants (El Bizcocho). Rooms are country-clubish with so-happy-to-be-here decor, and some have balconies or patios. Airport transportation and bicycle rentals are also available. Amenities: tennis, health club, Jacuzzi, sauna, business services. 287 rooms. Credit Cards: A, CB, DC, D, MC, V.

Rancho Santa Fe

Rancho Valencia Resort $335–$470   ★★★★★

5921 Valencia Circle, Rancho Santa Fe, 92067, ☎ *(800) 548-3664,*
(619) 756-1123, FAX: (619) 756-0165.
Single: $335–$470. Double: $335–$470.

Tucked away in the rolling hills of Rancho Santa Fe, this sister hotel
to La Jolla's prized La Valencia is probably one of the most romantic,
luxurious—and expensive—hideaways in the country. The early California style property has no rooms—only casitas—private hideout
suites with red-tile-roofs, plenty of room, plush decor, fireplaces and
terraces. Tennis is one of the resorts major come-hithers—18 courts
with a resident pro. Other lovelies include a championship croquet
lawn (is that class or what?), pool, saunas, spas, an exercise room, dining room, lounge and round-the-clock room service. Amenities: tennis, exercise room, Jacuzzi, sauna, balcony or patio, business services.
43 rooms. Credit Cards: A, CB, D, MC, V.

North County: Where to Dine

The Del Mar Plaza, has been the flavor of every month since it
opened a few years back. **Il Fornaio**, **Epazote**, and **Pacifica**—inside
the plaza—are all outstanding. **Cilantro's** (relative to Epazote)
continues to get raves. **Bully's**, on Camino del Mar, is the local
meat fix and what used to be the **real** Del Mar.

Your dress-up and sky's-the-limit pick *has to be* **Mille Fleurs,** in
Rancho Santa Fe. French, romantic, stunning food and service—
always at the top of every list of "bests." **El Bizcocho**, at the Rancho Bernardo Inn, ranks way up there as well.

The coast is bustling with hot eateries these days—fish houses,
designer pizzas, nouvelle cuisine, ham and eggs, vegetarian
gourmet, brunches and buffets, cafes and takeaways—and a
burrito around every corner. You won't go hungry—unless you
go broke.

Carlsbad

Fish House Vera Cruz $$ ★★★

417 Carlsbad Village Drive, Carlsbad, ☎ *(619) 434-6777.*
Seafood cuisine. Specialties: Simple and delectable fresh fish.
Lunch: 11 a.m.–2:30 p.m., entrées $7–$15.
Dinner: 5-10 p.m., entrées $10–$20. Closed: Sun.
Hurray—a family-style place that serves no-frills seafood meals. It's
not cheap but you'll get excellent value for your money—super-fresh
seafood, friendly service and a relaxed environment. The menu
changes daily according to what just popped off the boat. The oyster
bar provides the usual treats. Another location (the original) is in San

Marcos *(360 Via Vera Cruz)*. Reservations not accepted. Credit Cards: D, V, MC, A.

Neiman's $ ★★★

2978 Carlsbad Boulevard, Carlsbad, ☎ *(619) 729-4131.*
American cuisine. Specialties: Regular, normal food.
Lunch: 11:30 a.m.–2 p.m., entrées $4–$10.
Dinner: 5-11 p.m., entrées $4–$10.

These turn-of-the-century twin inns used to be a favorite fried chicken place. Neiman's took over in the 1980s, leaving the original building intact (though polished up) and making the meals more California-friendly—seafood, pasta, salads, sandwiches, etc. Choose from either (or both) of the hip-joined twins. The casual cafe—housed in the popular bar—serves daily lunch and dinner. The pricier circular dining room is open for dinner only (5-9 p.m. Mondays through Thursdays, until 10 p.m. on Fridays and Saturdays). Sunday brunch is available in both rooms. Features: Sunday brunch, late dining. Reservations recommended. Credit Cards: A.

Tip Top Meats $ ★★★

6118 Passeo del Norte, Carlsbad, ☎ *(619) 438-2620.*
American cuisine. Specialties: Cheap prices, big meals.
Breakfast: 7-11 a.m., entrées $2–$5.
Lunch: 11 a.m.–4 p.m., entrées $3–$6.
Dinner: 4-8 p.m., entrées $3–$6.

Getting ready to scream at the sight of one more Pacific Rim, Southwestern, or bowl-of-pasta meal? Can't stand being around one more yuppie or having your hair and clothes scrutinized? Broke? Tip Top is one of those institution-type places—regular, normal people in clean clothes eating down-home cooking and chatting with one another. Breakfast is amazing—for about $3 you get eggs, toast and as much bacon or sausage as you can wolf. Or how about a $5 steak or prime rib—with all the trimmings—dinner? No booze, but the coffee pot is bottomless. Reservations required. Credit Cards: V, MC.

Del Mar

Bully's North $$$ ★★★

1404 Camino del Mar, Del Mar, ☎ *(619) 755-1660.*
American cuisine. Specialties: Red meat, prime rib.
Lunch: 10 a.m.–4 p.m., entrées $5–$10.
Dinner: 4:30 p.m.–midnight, entrées $6–$25.

In the days before the Plaza, Bully's was Del Mar's local hangout supreme. It's still primo for carnivores—the prime rib, various cuts of steaks, Bully's burgers, juicy (and greasy) beef bones are artery-cloggers supreme. Non-meating wimps can choose omelets, chicken or seafood. Meals come with soup or salad, potatoes or rice (or cottage cheese and sliced tomatoes for those who really think that will make a difference in their weight). The bar is lively, filled with sports-loving patrons, and is still packed during racetrack season. The bar stays open until 1:30 a.m. Other Bully's locations are in La Jolla and Mission Valley, but this is the special one. Features: outside dining, late dining. Reservations not accepted. Credit Cards: CB, V, MC, DC, A.

Cilantro's $$$ ★★★

3702 Via de la Valle, Del Mar, ☎ *(619) 259-8777.*
Southwestern cuisine. Specialties: shark fajitas, tapas.

Lunch: 11 a.m.–2 p.m., entrées $7–$14.
Dinner: 5-10 p.m., entrées $14–$22.

Creative southwestern cuisine in the usual Santa Fe-ish/Tao-ish sub-
dued and sun-splashed environment (usually filled with high-powered
young pros). Cilantro's offers gourmet meals that combine chicken,
seafood and beef with southwestern spices and chili sauce. If you
don't want to spend the bucks for a whole meal, munch on the
tapas—they're almost as good, plus the tapas bar stays open later. Features: outside dining, Sunday brunch. Reservations recommended.
Credit Cards: V, MC, A.

Epazote $$$ ★★★

1555 Camino del Mar, Del Mar, ☎ (619) 259-9966.
Southwestern cuisine. Specialties: Pacific Rim cuisine, tapas.
Lunch: 11 a.m.–2 p.m., entrées $7–$16.
Dinner: 5-10 p.m., entrées $12–$26.

Cilantro's sister restaurant is a little more Mex than Southwestern,
and tosses in Pacific Rim dishes as well. As with other Del Mar Plaza
restaurants, Epazote draws the well-heeled trendies or wanna-be's
who've robbed the piggy bank. Stick to the tapas and you won't have
to break the bank. Otherwise, try some of the creative tacos, fresh fish
specials, and spit-roasted meats. Margaritas are super and the ocean-
view terrace is the place to show-off your best silk tie or designer scarf.
It gets noisy and crowded when the work day ends. Dinner is served
until 11 p.m. on Fridays and Saturdays. Features: outside dining, Sunday brunch. Reservations recommended. Credit Cards: V, MC, A.

Il Fornaio $$$ ★★★★

1555 Camino del Mar, Del Mar, ☎ (619) 755-8876.
Italian cuisine. Specialties: Angel hair pasta, stuffed focaccia.
Lunch: 11:30 a.m.–11 p.m., entrées $10–$22.
Dinner: 11:30 a.m.–11 p.m., entrées $10–$22.

Il Fornaio (original location in San Francisco) was the first restaurant
to cause a culinary commotion in placid little Del Mar. It brought
class, focaccia, lower-echelon mafia wanna-bes, and La Jollans who
swore they would never lift a fork in the slums of Del Mar. Since the
day it opened, the classic Italian eatery has been packed with the well-
heeled slurping on pastas and crunching at focaccias. The outdoor
oceanview piazza is the place to be seated. Expect long waits—join
the regulars out front who sip Chardonnay and look beautiful until
their number comes up. The same menu is offered for both lunch and
dinner. Sunday hours are 10 a.m.–10 p.m. Pick up breads and cookies
at the bakery on premises. Features: outside dining, own baking, Sunday brunch, non-smoking area, late dining. Reservations recommended. Credit Cards: V, MC, DC, A.

Jake's Del Mar $$ ★★★

1660 Coast Boulevard, Del Mar, ☎ (619) 755-2002.
American cuisine. Specialties: Seafood, steaks, mud pie.
Lunch: 11 a.m.–2 p.m., entrées $7–$12.
Dinner: 5-10 p.m., entrées $10–$18.

The food is unremarkable but the oceanfront location—one that's
not on the main highway—makes it worth a visit. The menu is pretty
standard—chicken, seafood, steak, pastas, salads. You can sit on the
enclosed patio and just have drinks and appetizers but it will probably

end up costing as much as a whole meal. It's another wait-around-for-a-table favorite, but you won't get bored zoning out on the crashing wave view. Lunch is served Tuesdays through Saturdays. Features: Sunday brunch. Reservations recommended. Credit Cards: V, MC, A.

Johnny Rocket's   **$**   ★★
1555 Camino del Mar, Del Mar, ☎ *(619) 755-1954.*
American cuisine. Specialties: Burgers and malts.
Lunch: 11 a.m.–10 p.m., entrées $4–$9.
Dinner: 11 a.m.–10 p.m., entrées $4–$9.
Finally, a place to take the kids—and in Del Mar Plaza, yet! Children and '50s freaks gravitate to the nostalgic burger and malt parlor (part of a nationwide chain). Other menu choices include tuna melts, grilled cheese sandwiches, cherry Cokes, apple pie, and—of course—knockout fries. Sit at the counter or in booths—both have nickel-a-tune jukeboxes to play. A few tables have been moved outdoors for those who think passersby enjoy the sight of chins dripping with burger juice. Features: outside dining. Reservations not accepted. Credit Cards: V, MC.

Pacifica Del Mar   **$$$**   ★★★

1555 Camino del Mar, Del Mar, ☎ *(619) 792-0476.*
Seafood cuisine. Specialties: Fresh fish.
Lunch: 11 a.m.–2 p.m., entrées $8–$15.
Dinner: 5-10 p.m., entrées $12–$26.
The ocean view and outdoor terrace-setting are top-notch, as are the fresh seafood dishes. Pacifica Del Mar caters to the California nouveau palate with Pacific Rim, Cajun and Southwestern flavors and touches that put a kick into the salads, soups and entrées. Good choice for sunset dining. Dinner is served until 11 p.m. on Fridays and Saturdays. Features: outside dining, Sunday brunch, late dining. Reservations recommended. Credit Cards: CB, V, MC, DC, A.

Pamplemousse Grill   **$$$**   ★★★★

514 Via de la Valle, Del Mar, ☎ *(619) 792-0090.*
Specialties: Wild mushroom-filled ravioli.
Dinner: 5 p.m.–10 p.m., entrées $16–$30. Closed: Mon.
Located across from the Del Mar Fairgrounds and Racetrack, Pamplemousse has been making restaurant critics swoon over its grilled items, wild mushroom-filled ravioli, extraordinary flavor combinations, and picture-pretty provencal decor. Go for the smoked muscovy duck. A full bar is also offered. Reservations recommended. Credit Cards: V, MC, A.

Spices Thai Cafe   **$$**   ★★★★

3810 Valley Center Drive, Suite 903, Del Mar, ☎ *(619) 259-0891.*
Lunch: 11 a.m.–2 p.m., entrées $7–$12.
Dinner: 5 p.m.–10 p.m., entrées $7–$18.
Tucked away in a boring shopping center between Del Mar and the Golden Triangle, east of Interstate 5, Spices nonetheless quickly became one of the secret word-of-mouth places to locals. Eventually the word spread to San Diegans, now to everyone. Every dish is beautifully prepared and a treat to eat (custom-spiced dishes range from prissy bleeding-ulcer mild to gut-of-steel fiery). The noodle dishes, tofu in coconut curry, and roasted duck are all pleasers. Genteel environment, but occasionally rude and brusque staff (ah, the price of

fame). Features: wine and beer only. Reservations recommended.
Credit Cards: V, MC, A.

Encinitas

Kim's Restaurant $ ★★

745 First Street, Encinitas, ☎ (619) 942-4816.
Asian cuisine. Specialties: Steamed fish, vegetarian dishes.
Lunch: 11 a.m.–2 p.m., entrées $3–$8.
Dinner: 5-9 p.m., entrées $5–$12.

Excellent Vietnamese cuisine in a relaxing dining room with friendly
service. The menu goes on forever and includes spring rolls, roasted
Cornish hens, steamed fish and a zillion chicken, beef, seafood and
noodle dishes. Vegetarians will be happy with the tofu and mock
chicken specialties. Features: wine and beer only. Credit Cards: V, MC, A.

Potato Shack Cafe $ ★★★

120 West I Street, Encinitas, ☎ (619) 436-1282.
American cuisine. Specialties: Potatoes, potatoes, and more potatoes.
Breakfast: 7 a.m.–2 p.m., entrées $4–$8.

Breakfast and lunch offer the same menu—potatoes. Order them
fried, boiled, baked, hashed, smothered, and topped. You can also get
plate-sized pancakes, sausages, omelets and other breakfast favorites.
Locals adore this place—it's exceptionally crowded on weekends,
when it stays open until 3 p.m. Another branch has opened in Del
Mar *(2282 Carmel Valley Road)*, but it's the Encinitas location that
has the true beach-town ambience. Features: outside dining. Reservations not accepted. Credit Cards: V, MC.

Vigilucci's $$ ★★★

505 First Street, Encinitas, ☎ (619) 942-7332.
Italian cuisine. Specialties: pastas, gnocchi in white sauce.
Lunch: 11 a.m.–2 p.m., entrées $7–$12.
Dinner: 5-10 p.m., entrées $9–$18.

Terrific Italian trattoria on an Encinitas corner with authentic atmo-
sphere, waiters and menu. The pastas are exceptional, especially the
gnocchi, tagliatelle alla Bolognese (with ground veal, duck and
chicken). Lunch is served Mondays through Saturdays. Reservations
recommended. Credit Cards: D, V, MC, DC, A.

When in Rome $$$ ★★★★

1108 First Street, Encinitas, ☎ (619) 944-1771.
Italian cuisine. Specialties: pasta dishes, polenta with homemade sausage.
Lunch: 11:30 a.m.–2:30 p.m., entrées $8–$15.
Dinner: 5:30-9:30 p.m., entrées $11–$22. Closed: Mon.

Formerly in Leucadia, When in Rome took over the premises of the
old Portofino Restaurant. The dining room is stunning, with three
separate areas and the same lovely atmosphere for which the Portofino
was famed. The country Italian cuisine is magnifico—artistic presentations and creative concoctions of pasta dishes, fresh seafood and imaginative appetizers. Many of the veggies are homegrown by the owners
and all of the baked goods are prepared on site. Dinner is served until
10 p.m. on Saturdays, and until 9:30 p.m. on Sundays. Features: own
baking. Reservations recommended. Credit Cards: V, MC, A.

Escondido

Billiard Gallery Sports Grill   **$**   ★

717 North Escondido Boulevard, Escondido, ☎ *(619) 743-7665.*
American cuisine. Specialties: Monster burgers.
Lunch: 11 a.m.–2 a.m., entrées $3–$6.
Dinner: 11 a.m.–2 a.m., entrées $3–$6.

You can play pool, watch sports on TV, suck down a Monster burger
and bring the kids with you (until 10 p.m.). It's cheap, fun, real life.
The cuisine includes pizza, salsa and chips, fries, chicken sandwiches,
buffalo wings, zucchini sticks, chili and such. The Monster burger is
the specialty of the house—two quarter-pound steakburgers smothered with onions, lettuce, tomatoes, cheese and bacon. This is no
place for wimps. (Thank you, God.) Features: late dining. Reservations not accepted.

Rancho Bernardo

El Bizcocho   **$$$**   ★★★★★

17550 Bernardo Oaks Drive, Rancho Bernardo, ☎ *(619) 487-1611.*
French cuisine. Specialties: Roast duck, rack of lamb, seafood.
Dinner: 6-10 p.m., entrées $30–$45.

Prepare for a memorable evening at one of the best French restaurants
in San Diego County. Everything is a la carte in this luxury-laden din-
ing room overlooking the golf course. Continental specialties are
painstakingly created from the freshest ingredients available. Every-
thing is superb, but the roast duck, fresh seafood and rack of lamb are
standouts. The wine list is equally divine. For a total gourmet pig-out,
do the all-you-can-eat Sunday brunch—it might kill you, but you'll
die happy. Dinner is served until 10:30 p.m. on Fridays and Satur-
days. Features: Sunday brunch, rated wine cellar. Jacket and tie
requested. Reservations required. Credit Cards: D, CB, V, MC, DC, A.

Rancho Santa Fe

Mille Fleurs   **$$$**   ★★★★★

6009 Paseo Delicias, Rancho Santa Fe, ☎ *(619) 756-3085.*
French cuisine. Specialties: Fresh seafood.
Lunch: 11:30 a.m.–2:30 p.m., entrées $18–$30.
Dinner: 6-10 p.m., entrées $34–$50.

It's expensive, but a lot cheaper than a trip to France—which is where
you'll be transported at least for one meal of your life. Mille Fleurs
perpetually wins honor upon honor for its ambience, elegant country
Frenchisms, wine list, romantic setting and, yes—the cuisine. The a la
carte menu changes daily and always features died-and-gone-to-
heaven selections of appetizers, soups and entrées. The veggies come
from famous Chino's, down the road, and you might spot the chef
picking through the fresh crops on his way to the kitchen. Owner Ber-
trand Hug makes the rounds to welcome all guests. Lunch is served
only Mondays through Fridays. Jacket requested. Reservations
required. Credit Cards: V, MC, DC, A.

Solano Beach

Nobu Japanese Restaurant   **$$**   ★★★

315 South Highway 101, Solano Beach, ☎ *(619) 755-0113.*
Japanese cuisine. Specialties: Sushi , appetizers.
Lunch: 11 a.m.–2 p.m., entrées $5–$14.
Dinner: 5-10 p.m., entrées $10–$20.

Choose from a vast assortment of sushi items or gorgeous appetizers, as well as multi-course feasts, a la carte entrées, and teppan table-cooked seafood, steak and veggies. For crowds and noise, eat at the sushi bar—otherwise try for one of the more intimate dining rooms. Prepare for long waits, especially on weekends. Dinner is served until 11 p.m. on Fridays and Saturdays. Reservations recommended. Credit Cards: V, MC, A.

Solano Beach

Fidel's $$ ★ ★ ★

607 Valley Avenue, Solano Beach, ☎ *(619) 755-5292.*
Mexican cuisine. Specialties: Mex-Mex.
Lunch: 11-2 p.m., entrées $3–$8.
Dinner: 5-10 p.m., entrées $5–$14.

Festive atmosphere and all your favorite Mexican dishes in a colorful and sprawling building. A trip across the border without worrying about car insurance and problemos. North County residents have been bringing their kids, parents and out-of-town guests here for YEARS. Even the area is enticing—Eden Gardens, a hidden-away Mexican enclave in Solana Beach that's very close to the racetrack and fairgrounds. Visitors from Duluth may even be appropriately scared. Be seated on the outdoor patio or in one of the many dining areas—lighting ranges from "is my lipstick smudged?" to "who are you,any-way?" There's another location in Carlsbad (**Fidel's Norte**, *3003 Carlsbad Boulevard,* ☎ *(619) 729-0903*). Features: outside dining. Credit Cards: V, MC.

FIELDING'S FAVORITE POWER LUNCH

On the oceanfront patio at Il Fornaio, Epazote, or Pacifica in the Del Mar Plaza.

FIELDING'S FAVORITE FLOWER POWER LUNCH

The counter/cafe inside Casady's Whole Foods Market, on the Encinitas main drag.

SOUTH OF THE BORDER

Ensenada is a scenic 65 mile drive south of San Diego.

Mexico is simply a different country, but it seems like another world. The segue from happy-and-healthy San Diego to the impoverished, chaotic squalor of Tijuana is usually a big shockaroo—even for San Diegans. Hard to imagine what Baja California was like before European settlement when many culture-rich Indian tribes inhabited the area. These days it seems the region's only hunters and gatherers are the hawkers and tourists. Still, for many visitors, a trip to San Diego would not be complete without a journey across the border—if for no other reason than to impress the folks back in Kansas ("Really, you went to Mexico! Is it as dangerous as they say?"). Yes and no.

257

Baja California is not all Tijuana (TJ, to us). It's a 1000-mile long desert, mountain, sand and sea peninsula—beginning at the border and ending down at Cabo San Lucas (another tourist trap—albeit prettier and less congested). That's another story however (and another book). For San Diegans—and their visitors— the customary Mexican odyssey consists of the Tijuana/ Rosarito Beach/Ensenada itinerary—though Ensenada is pushing it for a one-day visit, it *is* possible to squeeze it in (the distance between Tijuana and Rosarito is about 15 miles, Rosarito to Ensenada adds another 50 miles). All three cities are decidedly tourist oriented yet are distinctively different.

Even if you've been to Mexico before, the sudden change from First World U.S. to Nether World TJ is the equivalent of hitting a brick wall at 500 miles per hour. Mexico's fourth largest city (population about two million), sitting at the world's busiest international border, just 18 miles from comparatively *empty* downtown San Diego is an electric-chair jolt of sounds, sights, smells, flavors, auto body shops and tile warehouses, cheap dentists and over-the-counter drugs, sophisticated restaurants and hot discos, lousy roads and to-die-for souvenirs. Tourists—suburban families, retired seniors, groups of sailors, cliques of college students and singles descend on TJ looking for some action.

Action, of course, is what gave TJ it's reputation as a "hotbed of sin, " mostly stemming from Prohibition days when Americans crossed the border for all that illegal fun—drinking, gambling and pleasures of the flesh (or—for some—fur). No red-blooded Southern California child growing up in the '50s or '60s made the age of 14 without hearing dire stories about Spanish fly, gearshifts, back alley abortions, *very* friendly donkeys and German shepherds and a notorious club known as *The Blue Fox*. These tales, however, only made the place *more* enticing. Alas, Avenida Revolución—whore central—was cleaned up in the '70s and '80s—and is now the main drag for tourist shops and restaurants. (After the '70s, the drugs and sex were mostly in California, anyway.) The brothels and sex shows (*and* the Spanish fly) are still around—as almost any sailor will assure you—but they're just not as *obvious*.

Rosarito Beach (Playas de Rosarito), 15 miles away, *used* to be an isolated seaside community—a romantic getaway in the 1920s when the Rosarito Beach Hotel was its only hotel. And it remained that way until around 1980 when many American retirees and lifestyle-changers decided to set up camp—building (and long-term leasing) condos, timeshares, weekend retreats and dream homes. Restaurants, bars and shops followed along. And there you have it—an Americanized resort with about 40,000 people.

Ensenada, another 50 miles south, has also undergone growth and change since the 1980s. Set against Bahia de Todos Santos

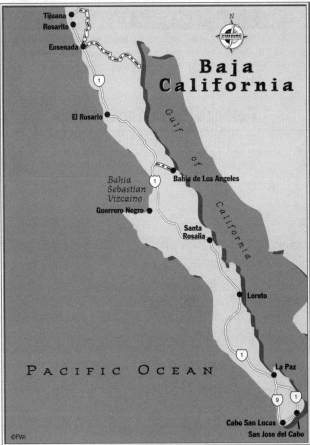

(All Saints' Bay—so christened by Juan Rodgriguez Cabrillo in 1542), Ensenada is a major seaport with fishing fleet and processing plant—a pit stop for luxury liners, and a super-popular weekend getaway choice for Southern Californians who come to swim, party, surf, laze on the beaches outside of town, eat and drink. The city's population is around 230,000 but swells considerably with the tourist assault. The developers, of course, have blasted the place with an explosion of hotels, timeshares, restaurants, bars and strip malls. During weekdays and the off-season, Ensenada retains a semblance of its old character.

For more information on Baja read *Fielding's Baja* by Jack and Patty Williams, $18.95, at bookstores and available by calling ☎ *1-800-FW-2-GUIDE.*

Author's Tip

Hot off the telephone wire: I just heard that **San Diego Motor Imports**
(☎ (619) 470-2006) *will rent vehicles to border-crossers and the company
rents Hummers! About $200 per day—and I doubt if that includes unlim-
ited mileage.*

Fielding's Mexico Survival Guide

The Rosarito Beach Hotel has been a favorite since 1926.

Yes, you can be relaxed and have a good time—just not *completely* relaxed or *too* good. Take some precautions, use common
sense and have some respect for your host country. After all,
you're in *their* home turf now. *Remember that!*

Unsticking the Red Tape

If you're a U.S. or Canadian citizen, entering Mexico via road,
all you need is proof of citizenship—but it has to be either an
original birth certificate (no photocopies!) *and* photo identifica-
tion, *or* a valid passport. If you're traveling south of Ensenada or
planning to stay longer than 72 hours, you'll need a **tourist card.**
These are free and can be issued at any Mexican consultate office
or government tourism office, or inside the border at the information booth. Then the card needs to be certified by a Mexican
immigration or customs officer—do it at the border crossing or
at the Ensenada Immigration office (*Boulevard Azueta, near
Boulevard Lazaro Cardenas*).

Naturalized U.S. citizens must present a Certificate of Citizenship (issued by the INS), a Certificate of Naturalization or a valid
passport.

Visitors from other countries—make *certain* you have a multi-
ple-entry visa *before* you cross into Mexico!

The Big Crossover

It's not so daunting. Going over, you're usually just flagged through by Mexican officials. Coming back is a bit different. You'll be asked a few questions: Where are you from? Where did you go? How long was your visit? What did you buy? Even if you only went down for margaritas and sombreros, you will somehow instantly feel like kingpin in a Colombian drug cartel. Be polite and forthcoming with your answers and you should cruise right through. Otherwise, you might get pulled over to the "secondary inspection" for more grueling questions and a search.

U.S. residents are allowed to bring home up to $400 in goods, duty free, as long as your purchases are for personal use (ahem, not for resale—yes, we *know* you could make a killing off the glassware, alone, but…alas). If you've got the family with you, each member is allowed the exemption (which can be pooled). Over 21's can also bring back one liter of alcohol, 200 cigarettes, and 100 non-Cuban cigars (interesting how there are so many hot-ticket Cuban cigars around, no?). Perfumes, agricultural products and medications are also limited—inquire with customs at the border.

Border Crossings are located at **San Ysidro** (open 24 hours) or about six miles east at **Otay Mesa** (open 6 a.m.–10 p.m.). San Ysidro, on weekends and holidays, is a madhouse crush—no matter if you're walking or driving. The border at **Tecate,** much farther east, is open 6 a.m.-midnight.

How to Get There

Driving can be your easiest breeze, or your worst nightmare. It depends on your tolerance level, if you can cope with the rough and rutted roads, unfamiliar signs and heavy traffic. If you *do* drive, you should *definitely* purchase Mexican **auto insurance**— which is issued through a Mexican-licensed company (you'll see booths and offices as you near the border). Your U.S. policy will not cut if you're involved in an accident on "the other side." In Mexico, you are considered guilty until proven innocent (no matter what you have or haven't done) and, without acceptable insurance, the smallest fender bender can land you in the Tijuana pokey—a lovely thought, correctamundo? Invest the $6-8 bucks per day. Also, *don't* drive at night if at all possible—it can be deadly.

If you're only making a brief trek over to TJ, consider taking the **trolley** to the border and walking across. Or you can drive, park in one of the attended parking lots on the U.S. side ($5-8 per day) and make the walk. Taxis are waiting to take you into town (about $5).

If driving, and continuing to Rosarito Beach and Ensenada, you have a choice between two roads. Ensenada Cuota, Mexico Route 1, is the toll road that runs from the TJ border crossing to

Rosarito Beach and Ensenada. Three toll booths along the way will collect about $3 each off you. The old Ensenada Highway, **Ensenada Libre,** is the free road. It's slower but a lot more interesting. In both Rosarito and Ensenada, ditch your car as soon as possible and walk everywhere. When looking for an address, note that many sites are located via their kilometer point from the beginning of the highway (i.e. Km 33)—usually markers are posted. Don't want to hassle with *any* of it? Sign up for a guided bus tour. Both **Gray Line** (☎ *(619) 491-0011)* and **Five Star Tours** (☎ *(619) 232-5049)* will take you from downtown San Diego to downtown TJ, and Gray Line offers extended tours as well. The **Tijuana/Baja Information Office** (☎ *(800) 522-1516,* AZ, CA, NV, *(800) 225-2786,* elsewhere in U.S., *(619) 298-4105)* can also assist with tours and reservations.

Help!

Phones: from the U.S., dial *011-52,* the area code and number. Area codes are *66* (TJ), *661* (Rosarito Beach), *617* (Ensenada).

U.S. Consulate: Tapachula 96, Colonia Hipodromo, Tijuana (☎ *66-81-7400).*

The Attorney General for the Protection of Tourists Hotline: (☎ *55-88-0555).*

Chamber of Commerce: Avenida Revolución and Calle 1 (☎ *66-88-1685).*

Tourism Offices: Avenida Revolutión between Calles 3 and 4 (☎ *66-83-1405),* also just inside the San Ysidro border crossing (☎ *66-83-1405);* Boulevard Avenida Juarez and Calle Acacias, Rosarito Beach; Quinta Plaza, Rosarito Beach (☎ *661-2-0396);* Blvd. Costero 1477 (☎ *617-23022)* or Blvd. Costero, at entrance to town (☎ *617-23078),* in Ensenada).

Fielding's Dios Mío!
What Does That Sign Mean???

Mexico uses pictorial road and traffic signs (not that you can always see them in time). Basically they're self-explanatory— just in case, here's a handy list of translations for you (though it will be too late by the time you check the book). Especially keep an eye out for the "three-person-family-running-across-the- road" sign. These are posted on the U.S. side of the border and warn drivers that entire groups of aliens might appear in front of them at any second.

Road Signs	
Spanish	**English**
Alto	**Stop**
Escuela	**School**

Road Signs

Spanish	English
Puente Angosto	Narrow Bridge
Ganado	Cattle
Cruce. F.C.	Railroad Crossing
Ceda El Paso	Yield Right of Way
Curva Peligrosa	Dangerous Curve
Camino Sinuoso	Winding Road
Hombres Trabajando	Men Working
Vado	Dip
Zona de Derrumbes	Slide Area
Circulación	One Way
Doble Circulación	Two Way
Solo Izq.	Left Turn Only
Conserve Su Durecha	Keep to the Right
No Rebase	No Passing
No Voltear en U	No U Turn
Prohibido Estacionarse	No Parking
Desviación	Detour
No Hay Paso	Road Closed
Despacio	Slow
Prohibido Estacionarse	No Parking

Fielding's Other Places in Baja

Tecate: If you want to stick near the border and stay away from the tourists (and all the hype that goes with), Tecate is a perfect choice. It's a typical Mexican community (population 50,000) where ordinary life goes on within sight of the almighty U.S. This small border town (with practically zilch border hassles) offers delightful insight into Mexican culture. Hang out at the plaza or visit the famous brewery. That's it. Get there from the U.S. via State Highway 94, or from Tijuana on Mexico Highway 2 or Toll Highway 2D ($4, one way).

San Felipe: On the Gulf of California side of Baja, the little fishing village of San Felipe (population 15,000) ranks as a favorite winter resort—wide beaches, adequate tourist facilities, enough souvenirs to keep everyone happy. Unfortunately, for some visitors, it can become a nightmare—particularly on holidays when it attracts party-round-the-clock rowdies with off-roaders and motorcycles. From the U.S. take State Route 111 from Calexico, cross the border at Mexicali and continue on Mexico Highway 5 to San Felipe. From Ensenada, cut over on Mexico Highway 3. 124 miles from Mexicali, 153 miles from Ensenada.

San Quintin: South of Ensenada, along Highway 1, San Quintin (population 22,000) is one of the major stopping points for travelers doing the entire peninsula—two commercial centers with places to stay and stuff to buy. Bahia de San Quintin, however, is a favorite for surf fishing, clam digging, boating and some heavy duty off-roading. 119 miles from Ensenada.

Author's Tip

Be extremely cautious about buying (i.e. long-term leasing) real estate in Mexico. Though many foreigners do pull off seemingly kosher deals south of the border, rip-offs—and huge monetary losses—are all too common. The laws are different in Mexico (made up as they go) and the bank trusts are often meaningless. Also, the U.S. Consulate does not intervene. If you get ripped off, you will need to hire a Mexican lawyer and then you will probably get ripped off again (and again).

Author's Tip

Many alternative health clinics have sprung up in the Tijuana/Rosarito area. They usually offer in-patient treatment for the catastrophically ill, using nontraditional (and non-FDA and AMA approved) therapies and drugs. Some of these clinics are reputable and trustworthy, but—as with land deals—others are unscrupulous. If you or a loved one is headed toward this path, ask the doctor or clinic for references and take the time to contact former patients or their family members.

South of the Border: Things to See and Do

In **Tijuana,** you'll probably go straight to **Avenida Revolución** and stay there. It'll suck you in with its local color, colorful locals, restaurants and shops. On Calle 2, bisecting Avenida Revolución, **Mexitlan** is a full block's worth of detailed archeological models as well as shops, restaurants and cafes. On Calle 1, near Avenida Revolución, **Museo de Cera** (Wax Museum) features wax renditions of favorite Mexicans and Spaniards as well as some kinky others like Michael Jackson and Mahatma Gandhi (there's an odd couple for you).

At Avenida Revolución and Calle 7, **El Palacio Fronton** is the headquarters for **jai alai** action. If you're into the bullfights, you'll want to hit the rings at **El Toreo de Tijuana,** a couple of miles east of downtown, or **Plaza Monumental,** six miles west. **Hipodromo de Agua Caliente,** a few miles east of city center, has long been a scene for racing. Alas, horse racing has been discontinued but you can still see (and bet on) the flying greyhounds.

La Bufadora Blowhole near Ensenada is a natural wonder.

Nearby are two bastions to Tijuana's wealthy denizens **Parroquía Espiritu Santo**, where they pray, and the **Grand Hotel,** where they play.

Slightly more refined types should explore the getting-swankier-by-the-dia **Zona del Rio** area, along Avenida Paseo de los Heroes—between Boulevard Agua Caliente and the border. Visit the **Cultural Center** with its museum, OMNIMAX theater, planetarium, and performing arts center. Then walk over to **Plaza Rio Tijuana,** a huge shopping complex with department stores, restaurants and myriad shops.

See what's going on at **Playas Tijuana,** the oceanfront neighborhood (basically, the rich part of town), that will probably harbor another shopping center or two by the time these words see print.

There's not much to see or do in **Rosarito Beach**—that's why many people come here. Hang out at the long, sandy beach or join the joggers and horse riders who favor this stretch. Surf's up spots include **Popotla, Calafia,** and **Costa Baja,** along the old highway. Hang out at the still-gorgeous **Rosarito Beach Hotel** and drink beer or margaritas or go over to the Festival Plaza for a wilder scene. Take a stroll down **Boulevard Benito Juarez, the main drag. Puerto Nuevo,** a fishing community famous for its lobster restaurants (about 30 of them) is about 13 miles south of town along the old highway.

In **Ensenada,** the tourist area is centered along **Avenida Lopez Mateos,** a block east of the waterfront. After you've finished with the hotels, shops, restaurants and bars, and the state tourist office, wander over to Boulevard Costero and Avenida Riviera for a peek at **Riviera del Pacifico,** the 1920s mansion where The Beautiful People swarmed to gamble and party. Boulevard Costero follows the waterfront at **Ensenada Harbor** where you can check out the **Plaza Cívica, Sportfishing Pier,** and the indoor/outdoor **Fish Market**— filled with counters of local seafood. If you have a car and feel like driving, go up into the **Chapultepec Hills** to **El Mirador,** for an exquisite view of the whole Bahia de Todos Santos. One other go-see sight is **La Bufadora,** a blowhole in the Punta Banda cliffs that spurts water some 75 feet into the air. Get there via Highway 1, then turn west onto Highway 23 at Maneadero, following it to the tip—about 16 miles from Ensenada. It's a slow—somewhat arduous and dangerous drive to get there but, hey, isn't a blowhole worth it?

Historical Sites

Tijuana

Tijuana Cultural Center   ★★★★

Paseo de los Heroes and Avenida Independencia, In Zona Rio, Tijuana, ☎ *(66) 84-1111.*

Hours open: 9 a.m.–8:30 p.m.

Centro Cultural Tijuana, an ultramodern building (designed by Pedro Ramirez Vasquez, architect of Mexico City's fabled Museum of Anthropology), is the city's center for art and culture. The museum houses both a permanent collection and changing exhibits of mainly contemporary Mexican artists. The OMNIMAX theater shows pop-out-at-you films (including a Mexican tour), and the 1000-seat concert hall presents world-class symphony, opera and dance performances. The center also houses a really good book shop with both English and Spanish titles, and a restaurant. Museum admission for children is 50 cents. OMNIMAX admission (including museum entry) is $4.50, adults; $2.50, ages two and over. General Admission: $1.

Museums and Exhibits

Tijuana

Mexitlan   ★★★★

Calle 2 and Avenida Ocampo, Tijuana, ☎ *(66) 38-4101.*

Hours open: Noon–8 p.m.
Closed: Mon.

Another structure by Mexican whiz-kid architect Pedro Rammirez Vasquez. Taking up an entire city block, Mexitlan features an outdoor display of about 150 scale models—full of detailing—depicting the country's most wondrous buildings, archeological sites, plazas, stadiums, churches, villages and other monuments, and covers four centuries of history. Naturally, there are shops, restaurants and cafes. Admission for ages under 12 is free, and parking is free also. General Admission: $3.25.

Museo de Cera

8281 Calle 1, at Calle Madero, Tijuana, ☎ (66) 88-2478.
Hours open: 10 a.m.–8 p.m.

The Wax Museum, opened in 1993, depicts 60 Mexican and foreign notables in life-size wax versions. See Emilio Zapata, Mahatma Gandhi, Laurel and Hardy, Mikhail Gorbachev, Whoopi Goldberg, Marilyn Monroe, Michael Jackson and Freddy from *Nightmare on Elm Street*. Is that a bizarre group or what??? General admissionis $1; ages under six, free. General Admission: $1.

Tijuana

Charreadas

Tijuana, ☎ (66) 81-3401.

Several charro (rodeo) grounds around Tijuana host Sunday afternoon events from May through September. Admission is usually free.

El Toreo de Tijuana

Boulevard Agua Caliente, Tijuana, ☎ (66) 85-2210.

If bullfights are your thing—and you don't mind paying the price, you can watch the work of top international matadors on Sundays at 4:30 p.m., May through September (no fights in June). Plaza de Toros Monumental, six miles east of town in the Playas Tijuana area, offers bullfights in July and August (also on Sundays at 4:30 p.m.). In San Deigo ☎ (619) 232-5049. General Admission: $7–35.

Hipodromo de Agua Caliente

Boulevard Agua Caliente, Tijuana, ☎ (66) 81-7811.
Hours open: 7:45 p.m.
Special Hours: 7:45 p.m. nightly, 2 p.m. and 7:45 p.m. weekends. Closed: Wed.

Back in the old days, Agua Caliente Racetrack was a favorite gathering spot for the Hollywood glamour crowd. It's not likely you'll spot too many celebs these days—nor any ponies. It's strictly greyhound racing these days. The dogs run nightly at 7:45 p.m., and at 2 p.m. on Saturdays and Sundays. Watch (and bet on) U.S. sports teams and horse races in the Foreign Book area. General admission is free but it's $5 for Turf Club seating (though a $5 betting voucher is included—such a deal).

Palacio Fronton

Avenida Revolucion at Calle 7, Tijuana, ☎ (66) 85-2524.

This fast-moving court game is sort of like handball, except players have a long, curved wicker basket strapped onto their wrists. The racy action takes place at the Moorish Palacio Fronton on Mondays and

Wednesdays, noon-6 p.m., and Thursdays through Saturdays 8 p.m.–
midnight. General Admission: $3-5.

South of the Border: For Kids

This is *much* better than the "people are starving in India" routine. The spoiled, vegetable-spitting little darlings can actually
see the starvation and degradation with their own eyes—witness
their Mexican peers toiling, begging—sick, lame and hungry.
Forget that high-priced shrink, mom and dad—Mexico (particularly TJ) is the ultimate attitude adjustment. This might not
work for teens (and many preteens), however—they'll get a
glimpse of cheap food and beer, parties and beaches, over-the-
counter drugs and one long siesta. They'll never go back to
school and get a job—they'll save a month's allowance and live
down here *forever*. On the other hand, that might be *your* goal.

Aside from that, most kids will be simply gaga over the festive
atmosphere and gaudy souvenirs (all of which you will buy). In
Tijuana, they might also enjoy **Mexitlan**—even if they're not interested in history, they'll like the scale models. More? Take
them to **Mundo Divertido** (Fun World) for rides and games, or
Museo de Cera for a waxed vision of Michael Jackson and Freddy
from *Nightmare on Elm Street*. At the **Cultural Center** the OMN-
IMAX theater and planetarium are interesting divertissements.

And, of course, you've got beaches and the blowhole.

Tijuana

Mundo Divertido

*2578 Jose M. Velasco, At Av. Paseo de los Heroes, Tijuana, ☎ (66) 34-
3214.*
Hours open: Noon–9 p.m.
Fun World will amuse the kids will miniature golf, bumper boats, a
mini-roller coaster and various games and activities. Prices for rides
and other amusements vary. Hours are 11 a.m.–10 p.m. on Saturdays
and Sundays.

Tours

Many visitors to Baja would rather leave the driving to someone else—not to mention the navigation, language problems,
red tape, and all that scary foreign stuff. If this is you, you're in
luck—a number of reputable companies run **guided tours** into TJ

and beyond. In addition, the various tourist agencies can help with **sportfishing** and **whale watching** excursions.

Baja

Baja California Tours ★★★
Baja, ☎ *(619) 454-7166.*
This company offers day tours by van to Tijuana and Ensenada, plus extended excursions throughout Baja Norte. Special interest tours can also be arranged (i.e. golf, art galleries, etc.).

Five Star Tours ★★★
Baja, ☎ *(619) 232-5049.*
Five Star buses will cart travelers from San Diego's Amtrak station to the center of TJ's Avenida Revolucion, several times each day (in either direction). Fare is $16 round-trip.

Gray Line ★★★
Baja, ☎ *(619) 491-0011.*
Gray Line's air-conditioned buses are reliable favorites for tours of TJ, plus extended packages to Ensenada and San Felipe. TJ tours run several times daily, 9 a.m.–6 p.m., $26, plus about another $10 if you want them to arrange lunch.

Events

Mexico forever seems to be one continual event. Fiestas, parties, weddings, baptisms, piñatas bursting all over the place. If a leaf drops, it's cause for celebration (and several days off work). This is why you come here—to have fun.

A few big sporting events draw the U.S. crowd—as spectators *and* participants. The annual **Rosarito-Ensenada 50 Mile Fun Bicycle Ride** takes place both in April and September, and the rugged **Score Baja 1000** is held over four days in November.

Ensenada

Score Baja 500 ★★★
Ensenada, ☎ *(310) 457-4823.*
This June event begins summer with a kick. The annual weekend race—with off-roading cars, motorcycles and trucks does a high-powered loop that begins and ends in Ensenada. Viewing is free (but not sedate).

Rosarito Beach

Rosarito-Ensenada 50-mile Fun Bicycle Ride ★★★
Rosarito Beach Hotel, Rosarito Beach, ☎ *(619) 583-3001.*
More than 8000 cyclists take part in Baja's Rosarito-to-Ensenada fun ride. Starting point is the Rosarito Beach Hotel (10 a.m.), moving south along the old highway to the Finish Line Fiesta in Ensenada. All ages and abilities are welcome to participate in the event held each April and September.

FIELDING'S EVERY-DAY'S-A-HOLIDAY-IN-MEXICO SELECT GUIDE

January 1	**New Year's Day**
February 24	**Flag Day**
March 21	**Benito Juarez' Birthday**
May 1	**Labor Day**
May 5	**El Cinco de Mayo**
September 15-16	**Independence Day**
October 12	**Día de la Raza**
November 1	**Presidential State of the Nation Address**
November 20	**Revolution Day**
December 12	**Feast of the Virgin of Guadalupe**

At Easter and Christmas, the feasts and fiestas last for weeks.

South of the Border: Music, Dance and Theater

Tijuana's **Cultural Center** is the venue for concerts, dance and theatrical performances. Lest you're focusing on mariachi music, think again—the Bolshoi Ballet and Mexican National Symphony are just two of the world-class acts that have performed here.

As for music, you're bound to hear some sort of jingle or jangle almost all the time—street musicians, plaza entertainment, boombox cassettes or your own olé dreams.

South of the Border: Nightlife

Author's Tip

Get rid of the t-shirts and shorts before a night out in Tijuana. The Mexicans get all gussied up and—as in New York or L.A.– dress codes are strictly enforced at discos. Wear your coolest, flashiest duds if you want to be included in the party scene.

Put on your red dress, baby. Discos are the hot ticket in TJ, as they are in every other Mexican city and resort town. The action doesn't even *begin* until around midnight. Most of the clubs are glitzy, glittery, trendy, sophisticated, dynamic and throbbing with sexual energy. Favorites in TJ are **Baby Rock**, **Hard Rock Cafe** and **Iguanas**. If discos aren't your thing, you'll also find **sports bars** and a midnight rodeo in the **Pueblo Amigo** center, and quieter entertainment at several larger hotels.

In **Rosarito Beach,** nightlife centers around the **Rosarito Beach Hotel,** with disco and live music and the Festival Plaza Hotel with a rickety ferris wheel and a bit more olé. A few bars nearby offer entertainment—though much of it is geared toward a *really* young crowd.

Many visitors wouldn't even *think* of leaving Mexico without getting down and drunk at **Hussong's,** Ensenada's notorious— and notoriously rowdy—cantina. Unless you're a college student or surfer, you'll probably prefer one of the hotel discos or lounges.

Ensenada

Hussong's Cantina ★★

Avenida Ruiz 113, Ensenada, near Lopez Mateos, ☎ *(617) 8-3210.*
Infamous Hussong's Cantina attracts a boisterous young crowd (surfers, sailors, coeds, etc,) into its SRO party machine. Other let-me-in's line up outside the door, awaiting their turn to party as soon as someone staggers out the door. Designated drivers get free soft drinks.

Rosarito Beach

Festival Plaza ★★★

Boulevard Benito Juarez 11, Rosarito Beach, ☎ *(661) 2-2950.*
This amusement park-style hotel is party central. Music is always blasting, locals are always disco dancing, and various concerts often take place on the outdoor stage. Besides all that, the hotel features a lounge, jazz club, various amusement attractions (beware the rickety Ferris wheel!), and a playground for the kids and/or the inebriated.

Papas and Beer ★★★

Boulevard Juarez, Rosarito Beach, ☎ *(661) 2-0343.*
This high-energy beachfront club, just north of the Rosarito Beach Hotel, is a casual environment for music, dancing, volleyball and hanging out. There's another (rowdier) location in Ensenada, on Avenida Ruiz near Hussong's.

Rene's ★

Boulevard Juarez, Rosarito Beach, ☎ *(661) 2-1020.*
Your all-around eclectic nightspot—mariachi bands, sports on widescreen TV and live dance bands to boot.

Rosarito Beach Hotel ★★★

Boulevard Juarez, Rosarito Beach, ☎ *(661) 2-0144.*
Choose from live sounds in the huge disco, or at the ocean-view bar. Fridays and Saturdays the evening Mexican Fiesta offers lively entertainment. Information in U.S., ☎ *(800) 343-8582.*

Tijuana

Baby Rock ★★★★

1482 Diego Rivera, Tijuana, in Zona Rio, ☎ (66) 84-0440.
Hours open: 9 p.m.–5 a.m.
Closed: Mon., Tue., Wed.

The fashion parade queues up early at this most trendy of rock-shaped discos for the chance to party the night away to hot light shows and pulsing beats. You won't even get inside the cave-like entrance unless you pass inspection at the door. Women get in free on Thursdays.

Hard Rock Cafe ★★

520 Avenida Revolucion, Tijuana, ☎ (66) 85-0206.
Hours open: 11 a.m.–2 a.m.

The usual Hard Rock Cafe day- and nightspot. Rock memorabilia, burgers and fries and irritating gringos. Live music Thursday through Sunday evenings. Is this what you came to TJ for?

Iguana's ★★★

Pueblo Amigo Center, Tijuana, ☎ (66) 82-4967.

A cutting edge, super-new wave, multi-level disco that's frequented by San Diegans (18–21) who are "underage" in their home town. Top concerts are booked here regularly, other nights it's dance music. A shuttle bus is available to transport swingles to and from the border. The club is open 8 p.m.–2 a.m. every night, and concerts begin at 10 p.m.

Rodeo de Media Noche ★★★

Pueblo Amigo, Tijuana, ☎ (66) 82-4967.

Thursday through Sunday nights you can view vaqueros riding their feisty beasts at the midnight rodeo, an inside arena complete with bleachers and other authentic rodeo accouterments. Other entertainment consists of a cocktail lounge, dance floor, country-western line dancing, and all the thrills one could expect from riding a mechanical bull (available to patrons after the "main event"). The midnight rodeo is on Thursday through Sunday. The action doesn't even get going until 10 p.m. or so, lasting until 2 a.m. Mondays through Thursdays, and 5 a.m. Fridays through Sundays.

Tia Juana Tilly's ★★★

701 Avenida Revolucion, Tijuana, ☎ (66) 85-6024.

Tia Juana Tilly's, for many Southern Californian partiers, is a reason to live. Located next to the Jai Alai Palace, the action over here includes standard Mexican meals plus a lively disco and bar that's open until midnight Sundays through Thursdays, until 3 a.m. on Fridays and Saturdays.

Yuppies Sport Cafe ★★

Paseo de los Heroes and Diego Rivera, Tijuana, Zona Rio, ☎ (66) 34-2324.

Would you ever, in a million anos, want to miss out on a place called Yuppies Sport Cafe? It's not alone—there are others nearby. Choose from a variety of entrées, if you wish, otherwise just down some brews and watch all the sports video action.

South of the Border: Shopping

Author's Tip

Bartering is part of the fun. It's SOP in Mexico and challenging for visitors. Hawkers at markets, street stalls, smaller arcade shops and on the street expect a "counter offer." Start about one-third less than the original asking price and then start bickering back and forth. Don't barter at department stores or the better shops—prices are nonnegotiable.

Tijuana's multitude of shops offer everything from clothing to handcrafted jewelry, leather goods and ceramics.

In tourist traps like TJ, you don't need to go to the shops—the shops come to *you*. Stand still, turn any corner, ride in your car—hawkers with wares will always be in your face. You'll be offered sombreros, huge piggy banks, armadillo purses, piñata bats, frogs on bicycles, and all manner of gawdy consumer horrors.

Shops and arcades are omnipresent. Tijuana's **Avenida Revolución** is choking with stores and stalls that offer everything from fine jewelry and imported perfume to low-class schlock. **Le Drug Store** is a steady favorite for cosmetics, perfumes and leather handbags. **Tolan,** across from the Jai Alai Palace, is one of the best craft shops with tin work, glassware, ceramics, wall hangings and such. At **Plaza Rio Tijuana,** across from the Cultural Center, you'll find more one-stop shopping (don't miss the bargain booze at **Comercial Mexicana). Plaza Fiesta,** across the street from Plaza Rio Tijuana, offers more boutiques and better shops and **Plaza de los Zapatos,** next door, is a two-level shoes-only shop. For those who just want to get their feet wet, Pueblo Amigo is but a tippy-toe across the border.

In Rosarito Beach, you can pick up crafts, pottery, jewlery, French perfume, weavings and furnishings at the shopping arcade near La Quinta del Mar Hotel. Bargain your brains out at the open-air **Mercado de Artesanias** arts-and-crafts market.

Shopping in Ensenada is centered on **Avenida Lopez Mateos,** in the tourist district—crafts, clothing, curios—it's all there.

FIELDING'S DID YOU THINK YOU COULD RUN AWAY FROM TAXES?

Not IRS, but IVA is your Mexican aggravation. It's the 10-percent sales tax added to almost everything, including your restaurant bill. That "IVA incluido," at the bottom of the check does not mean the tip has been taken care of–tack on another 15 percent!

South of the Border: Where to Stay

When staying over in Baja, keep in mind that this is *Mexico,* please—the accommodations may not be what you expect (or demand) back home. Housekeeping, furnishings, etc., might be a little lackluster in comparison. If you're visiting over a holiday, be sure to book a room in advance as Baja is a primo getaway choice for Southern Californians.

In TJ, **Grand Hotel Tijuana** is the best address, with **Hotel Lucerna, Villa Zaragoza Hotel** and **Hotel Real del Río** decent options. The

Rosarito Beach Hotel—for many romantics—is the only place to stay in Rosarito, though **Las Rocas Hotel and Suites** and **Residence Inn Marriott Real Del Mar** are two newer oceanfront choices. The **Festival Plaza** will suit those who don't mind unrestrained noise.

La Fonda, south of Rosarito, is an old favorite, though a little worn and very noisy—better to have that lobster dinner and move on. **Oasis Resort** is beach-resort lovely. In Ensenada, **Estero Beach Resort**, **Punta Morro**, **Las Rosas**, **San Nicolas Resort Hotel**, **El Cid Motor Hotel** and the ever-trusty **Ensenada Travelodge** should please most overnighters.

Hotels

Ensenada

Las Rosas $90–$130

On the Old Highway, Ensenada, North of city center, ☎ *(617) 4-4320, FAX: (617) 4-4595.*
Single: $90–$130. Double: $90–$130.
A contemporary pink property with marble-floored atrium lobby and green-glass ceiling. Accommodations are modern and well-furnished and all face the sea—some have private spas and fireplaces. If you care to leave the room there's a restaurant, cocktail lounge, pool, hot tub and jewelry shop. Amenities: Jacuzzi. 32 rooms. Credit Cards: A, MC, V.

Punta Morro $65–$125

Mexico Highway 1, Ensenada, Just north of Ensenada, ☎ *(800) 726-6426, (617) 8-3507, FAX: (617) 4-4490.*
Single: $65–$125. Double: $65–$125.
Off the main highway and away from the Ensenada-hustle, this three-story establishment offers rooms and suites, all with ocean-front terraces, some with fireplaces and kitchen facilities. The pool, hot tub, restaurant, and bar leave you practically sprawling in the waves. Bring your sweetie or your waterproof laptop. Amenities: Jacuzzi. 30 rooms. Credit Cards: MC, V.

San Nicolas Resort Hotel $50–$90

Avenida Lopez Mateos and Avenida Guadalupe, Ensenada, ☎ *(617) 6-1901, FAX: (617) 6-4930.*
Single: $50–$70. Double: $60–$90.
A huge sprawling resort with cheery ambience. Rooms feature folk-arty decor, balconies, air conditioning, TVs and phones. Narcissists should opt for a higher-priced suite (around $130) with mirrored ceilings, private hot tubs and separate living areas. Other features include two pools, spa, travel agency, gift shop, beauty salon, restaurant, bar and disco. Amenities: Jacuzzi. 143 rooms. Credit Cards: A, MC, V.

Rosarito Beach

Festival Plaza $50–$100

Boulevard Benito Juarez 11, Rosarito Beach, ☎ *(800) 453-8606, (661) 2-2950, FAX: (661) 2-0124.*
Single: $50–$100. Double: $50–$100.
Located next door to the Rosarito Beach Hotel, this eight-story, theme park-style, hotel-and-entertainment facility includes motel-type rooms, private casitas, a swimming pool, outdoor concert area, children's playground, a rickety ferris wheel, and what is billed as the

"world's largest tequila museum." Cartoons are on tap from the ubiquitous televisions and fake snakes will nip at your wobbly ankles. Noise, noise, noise, all the time. Your idea of home-away-from-home? Rooms are no-frills (though some have ocean-view balconies), while casitas offer separate living areas, private garages, and a bit more quiet. Restaurants, bars, and party action are right outside (or insiide) your door. There is also a dance club for those inclined. 120 rooms. Credit Cards: MC, V.

Las Rocas Hotel and Suites $50–$95   ★★★

Km 37 on the Old Highway, South of Rosarito Beach, ☎ *(661) 2-2140. Single: $50–$95. Double: $50–$95.*

The dramatic Hotel Las Rocas sits above the Pacific, all white with striking trim poised atop a cliff. Choose from spacious rooms or extra-luxurious suites. All accommodations have great ocean views and private terraces. Suites have fireplaces, wet bars, refrigerators and microwaves. The restaurant serves Continental and local cuisine in the evening, and a cafe with outdoor terrace is open for breakfast and lunch. Do your drinking at the palapa bar or the more intimate space with frequent piano music. Recreation is at the pool, spas or tennis court. Information in the U.S., ☎ *(619) 425-2682.* Amenities: tennis, Jacuzzi, sauna. 26 rooms. Credit Cards: A, MC, V.

Residence Inn Marriott Real del Mar $69–$169   ★★★

Off the toll road, at km 19.5, seven miles north of town center, Rosarito Beach, ☎ *(800) 331-3131, (661) 3-3401, FAX: 661-3-3677. Single: $69–$149. Double: $69–$169.*

Wouldn't you know one of the big U.S. names would set up shop? This newer all-suite hotel, seven miles north of Rosarito, overlooks the ocean and offers all the joys of Marriott's all-suite enterprise—separate living areas, kitchen facilities, plush furnishings, fireplaces and relaxing atmosphere. Guests have use of a golf course, pool, spa and exercise room but the dining room is only open 11 a.m.– 10 p.m. Stock the kitchen accordingly! Amenities: exercise room, Jacuzzi. 62 rooms. Credit Cards: A, DC, MC, V.

Rosarito Beach Hotel $60–$120   ★★★★

Boulevard Juarez, Rosarito Beach, At south end of town, ☎ *(800) 343-8582, (661) 2-0144, FAX: (661) 2-1176. Single: $60–$120. Double: $60–$120.*

This is still the landmark choice for romantics. Dating from the 1920s, the Rosarito Beach Hotel was *the* getaway for prohibition-shunning Americans, who could drink, bet and carouse in this fabulous seaside palace. Though a bit downtrodden from time to time, the place is still fabulous with its murals, tilework, stained glass, elegant public rooms and ballrooms. Try for a room in the older section of the hotel, rather than the more modern tower and low-risers—the originals feature colonial decor, beamed ceilings and hand-painted trim. Tower rooms feature air conditioning—though the ocean breezes should suffice. Hang out at Chabert's Steakhouse, the all-day Azteca Restaurant, oceanfront bar or weekend disco. Facilities are extensive—a full-service European spa in the converted 1920s mansion next door, Olympic-size pool, sauna, spa, gym, aerobics classes, beachfront playground, racquetball and tennis courts, miniature golf, shopping arcade, meeting facilities and free parking. Rates are often reduced for mid-week visitors, though expect to pay top peso for the ocean-view rooms. Amenities: tennis, health club, Jacuzzi, sauna, balcony or patio. 280 rooms. Credit Cards: MC, V.

Tijuana

Camino Real Tijuana $150–$150   ★★★★

Paseo de los Heroes 10305, Tijuana, ☎ *(800) 722-6466, (66) 33-4000, FAX: (66) 33-4001.*

Single: $150. Double: $150.

Opened in 1996, Camino Real Tijuana has added some distinctive hotel class to this occasionally unclassy city. Located in the relatively posh Zona del Rio, about 15 minutes from the Tijuana airport and the international border, this property offers cool style, warm colors, sophisticated service and efficient (in a scary sort-of-way) security. Guest rooms are large and exceptionally well-decorated. Facilities include a fine restaurant with international cuisine, a deli, two bars, a fitness center, business center, tobacco shop (Cuban cigars, anyone?), car rental agency, and 24-hour room service. Also available: Jacuzzi, business center, meeting facilities. Amenities: exercise room, sauna, business services. 250 rooms. Credit Cards: A, MC, V.

Grand Hotel Tijuana $72–$200   ★★★★

4558 Agua Caliente Boulevard, Tijuana, ☎ *(800) 472-6385, (66) 86-3300, FAX: 66-86-3639.*

Single: $72–$200. Double: $72–$200.

Formerly Hotel Fiesta Americana, the Grand Hotel is a TJ icon—two 22-story mirrored towers, next to the golf course and close to the racetrack. The Grand is the haunt of Tijuana's celebrities, visiting notables, wheeler-dealers, politicos and matadors—with all the associated pomp and glamour. Accommodations—air-conditioned and with phones and TVs—are the best in town, and the top four floors (Fiesta Grand Club) offer even classier rooms with sitting areas, king beds, concierge service and views of both the country clubs and slums. Facilities are unparallelled in TJ with fine dining restaurant, 24-hour cafe, weekend disco, lobby bar, round-the-clock room service, golf course access, tennis courts, heated pool, sauna, spa, meeting rooms and free underground parking. Amenities: tennis, Jacuzzi, sauna, club floor. 422 rooms. Credit Cards: Not Accepted. Credit Cards: DC, MC, V.

Holiday Inn Pueblo Amigo $60–$90   ★★★

Via Oriente 9211, Tijuana, At Pueblo Amigo, ☎ *(800) 465-4329, (66) 83-5030, FAX: (66) 83-5032.*

Single: $60. Double: $90.

This place looks so appallingly familiar, you might not even realize you've left the good, old USA. Not for the adventurous—or the spirited—visitor, nonetheless you'll feel secure with the name, logo, and guest rooms with mini-bars, direct-dial long-distance phones, and built-in purified water system. The location is convenient to most major sites (including the USA), and guests have use of lobby cafe, bar, fitness center, indoor pool, business and secretarial facilities. Amenities: exercise room, sauna. 108 rooms. Credit Cards: A, MC, V.

Hotel Lucerna   **$65–$85**   ★★

Avenida Paseo de los Heroes 10902, Tijuana, In Zona Rio, ☎ *(800) 582-3762, (66) 34-2000, FAX: 34-24-00.*
Single: $65–$75. Double: $75–$85.

Near the flashy discos in the Zona Rio, Hotel Lucerna is an interesting 80's-ish six-story property with good enough furnishings and decor, rooms with either brick patios or balconies, TVs and phones, plus a dinner-only French restaurant, two bars, nightly piano entertainment, summer poolside barbecues and a long swimming pool with a crossover bridge. Room service is available most of the day. Extra spacious suites run about $130. Amenities: balcony or patio. 168 rooms. Credit Cards: A, DC, MC, V.

Hotel Real del Rio   **$65–$85**   ★★

Calle Velasco 1409, Tijuana, In Zona Rio, ☎ *(66) 34-3100.*
Single: $65–$75. Double: $75–$85.

A welcome addition to the Tijuana hotel non-scene, Hotel Real del Rio, situated in the Zona Rio offers modern comfortable rooms, a restaurant/cafeteria, bar and a much-needed hodge-podge of cool amenities—satellite TV, hair dryer, safety locks, laptop plug-ins, voice mail, a business center, car- and cellular rental and travel agency. Amenities: business services. 103 rooms. Credit Cards: MC, V.

Motels

Ensenada

El Cid Motor Hotel   **$40–$60**   ★★

Avenida Lopez Mateos 993, Ensenada, ☎ *(617) 8-2401, FAX: (617) 8-3671.*
Single: $40–$50. Double: $50–$60.

A trusty Spanish-style motor inn with air-conditioned rooms, queen beds, TVs, radios, phones, some private balconies and a pool, dining room, coffee shop and cocktail lounge. Fishing trips can also be arranged. Credit Cards: MC, V.

Ensenada Travelodge   **$45–$70**   ★★

Avenida Blancarte 130, Ensenada, Near Avenida Lopez Mateos, ☎ *(800) 578-7878, (617) 8-1601, FAX: (617) 4-0005.*
Single: $45–$60. Double: $55–$70.

You usually know what you'll get from Travelodge—a decent family-oriented place to bed down. Air-conditioned rooms have TVs, movies, radios, phones and coffeemakers. Other staples are the pool, spa and enclosed parking. Amenities: Jacuzzi. 52 rooms. Credit Cards: A, MC, V.

Resorts

Estero Beach

Estero Beach Hotel Resort   **$40–$90**   ★★★

On Old Highway 1, eight miles south of Ensenada city center, Estero Beach, ☎ *(617) 6-6230, FAX: (617) 6-6925.*
Single: $40–$90. Double: $40–$90.

Just south of Ensenada, this family-friendly resort features adequate rooms, suites with kitchens, a private beach, fishing, swimming, boating (with boat rentals), water skiing, windsurfing, fishing, horseback-riding, tennis, a recreation room, archaeologocial museum and gift shop—also a restaurant and cocktail lounge. Amenities: tennis, horse-back riding. 115 rooms. Credit Cards: MC, V.

Rosarito Beach

Oasis Resort   **$40–$85**   ★ ★ ★

Km 40 on the Old Highway, South of Rosarito Beach, ☎ *(800) 462-7472, (661) 3-3255, FAX: (661) 3-3252.*
Single: $40–$75. Double: $50–$85.

A happy, friendly beachfront resort with a hotel section and RV park. Hotel suites have separate bedrooms with air conditioning, heat, minibars and TVs. Bring your own RV or rent one there. Guests tend to mingle and kick back at the restaurant, bar, games room, tennis courts, miniature golf course or at one of the pools (there's a children's pool, also). Amenities: tennis. 100 rooms. Credit Cards: MC, V.

South of the Border: Where to Dine

Señor Frog's in Tijuana is a lively spot for lunch or dinner.

In Tijuana you may be surprised by some of the excellent fine dining. On Avenida Revolución—where you'll find an endless stream of eateries—**La Costa** for seafood and **Chiki Jai** for Basque dishes. **Tia Juana Tilly's** and **Hard Rock Cafe** are—as you can probably gather from the times—tourist meccas. Steak-lovers should hit **El Rodeo,** where Revolución turns into Agua Caliente. Over in the Zona Rio, you'll find some of the trendier, more formal restaurants. **La Espadana** is a top pick for all-around dining, **La Spezia** offers elegant Italian/Mexican dishes, and **La Taberna Espanola** is everyone's favorite tapas bar. **La Lena**, over on Boulevard Agua Caliente is making gringo mouths water with its delectable grilled meats. The **Grand Bistrot Restaurante** in the Grand Hotel Tijuana features splendid Continental dishes and **Tour de France,** on the old road to Ensenada, is a fabulous French offering.

The **Rosarito Beach Hotel** has a good steakhouse, but **El Nido** is also a long-time favorite. Craving Chinese? Try **Dragon del Mar** (*expensive* for these parts!). Other restaurants are in Quinta Plaz or along Boulevard Juarez.

La Fonda Hotel, out on the old Ensenada Highway, is the all-time pick for your "lobster-dinner-in-Mexico" experience. In **Puerto Nuevo** you can choose from about 30 lobster spots. FYI, lobsters are priced according to their size—and may be from *Australia* between April and September (the Ensenada off-season).

El Rey Sol, in Ensenada, has been serving fine French cuisine since 1947. **La Embotelladora Vieja**, near the Santo Tomas winery, is the current buzz. For family dining, try **El Charro**, on Lopez Mateos—where you'll find many other options. Also, don't forget the **Fish Market** on the waterfront for fish tacos and seafood cocktails.

Ensenada

El Charro   **$$**   ★★

Avenida Lopez Mateos 475, Ensenada, ☎ (617) 8-3881.
Mexican cuisine. Specialties: grilled chickens, kid-friendly.
Lunch: 11 a.m.–2 a.m., entrées $4–$18.
Dinner: 11 a.m.–2 a.m., entrées $4–$18.
Bring the kids, feed them chicken, fries, tortillas and try to keep them from breaking the pinatas. This casual little diner has been in operation since 1956. Whole chickens rotate on window-facing spits, pinatas hang from the walls, the kids can't mess up the concrete floors (too much). Other treats are carne asada, guacamole and tortillas. Features: wine and beer only.

El Rey Sol   **$$$**   ★★★★

Lopez Mateos 475, Ensenada, ☎ (617) 8-1733.
French cuisine. Specialties: escargots, gourmet seafood, machaca.
Breakfast: 7:30 a.m.–noon, entrées $6–$14.
Lunch: Noon–5 p.m., entrées $10–$20.
Dinner: 5–10:30 p.m., entrées $14–$35.
The family-owned El Rey Sol has been famed for its chic cuisine, formal ambience and great service since its inception in 1947. The country French restaurant offers scrumptious French/Mexican cuisine—fresh fish and seafood in spectacular sauces, veggies grown at the owner's farm and some unusual Mexican touches. Lunch, before 2 p.m., offers special deals—an entrée, soup or salad, veggies and sorbet

for about $10. Breakfast-eaters can choose American, Mexican or French varieties. Jacket and tie requested for dinner. Reservations recommended. Credit Cards: V, MC, A.

Haliotis $ ★★
Av. Delante 179, Ensenada, ☎ *(617) 6-3720.*
Seafood cuisine. Specialties: Seafood grill.
Lunch: 12:30–10 p.m., entrées $5–$12.
Dinner: 12:30–10 p.m., entrées $5–$12.
Slightly off the beaten highway, locals flock to this spot for luscious seafood dishes. Lobster and abalone are both popular, as are the parrillada seafood grill (a combo plate with fish, shrimp, lobster, and octopus)and seafood soups. Features: late dining. Credit Cards: V, MC.

La Embotelladora Vieja $$$ ★★★★
Avenida Miramar 666, Ensenada, ☎ *(617) 4-0807.*
French cuisine. Specialties: Grilled lobster, wine sauces.
Lunch: Noon-11 p.m., entrées $12–$30.
Dinner: Noon-11 p.m., entrées $12–$30. Closed: Sun.

San Diegans schlep down here just for lunch. Located at the Santo Tomas winery, in a former aging room with cathedral ceilings, the country French setting is a perfect place for French a la Baja gourmet—pates, smoked tuna, grilled lobster, as well as poultry and meat dishes. The sauces are wine-laden nectars, and the wine list is comprised of about 150 international labels (including, of course, Santo Tomas vintages). Features: wine and beer only, late dining. Jacket requested. Reservations recommended. Credit Cards: V, MC.

Rosarito Beach
Dragon del Mar $$$ ★★
Boulevard Juarez 283, Rosarito Beach, ☎ *(661) 2-0604.*
Chinese cuisine.
Lunch: 11 a.m.–11 p.m., entrées $15–$20.
Dinner: 11 a.m.–11 p.m., entrées $15–$20.
Elegant surroundings for well-prepared and beautifully presented Chinese cuisine—not a tortilla in sight! A pianist plays most evenings. Credit Cards: V, MC.

El Nido $$ ★★
Boulevard Juarez 67, Rosarito Beach, ☎ *(661) 2-1430.*
Mexican cuisine. Specialties: Steak.
Lunch: 2–11 p.m., entrées $9–$18.
Dinner: 2–11 p.m., entrées $9–$18. Closed: Wed.
El Nido is one of Rosarito's oldest dining spots—the perfect dark wood and leather booth aura to gnaw on mesquite-grilled steaks. Features: late dining. Credit Cards: V, MC.

La Fonda $$ ★★★
Km 59 on the Old Highway, Rosarito Beach, .
Seafood cuisine. Specialties: Lobster dinner.
Lunch: 1 p.m.–midnight, entrées $10–$20.
Dinner: 1 p.m.–midnight, entrées $10–$20.
Many people go to Baja just for the chance to eat *the* lobster dinner at La Fonda, a semi-dilapidated beachfront hotel/restaurant south of Rosarito Beach. The bar is rowdy, margaritas are strong and the lobster dinner is still fab (non-lobster lovers can order steak, prime rib and Mexican specialties). Prepare for waits—painless while drinking

on the beachfront patio. Features: late dining. Reservations not accepted.

Tijuana

Chiki Jai   **$$**   ★★★

Avenida Revolucion 1042, Tijuana, ☎ (66) 85-4955.
Spanish cuisine. Specialties: squid in its own ink, crusty rolls with bleu cheese.
Lunch: 11:30 a.m.–4 p.m., entrées $6–$14.
Dinner: 4-9 p.m., entrées $8–$18. Closed: Wed.

This simple and unobtrusive cafe has long been a hit with the homesick Spanish jai alai set who gather for authentic Basque-style dishes. Squid in its own ink is a trademark dish, as are the crunch-in-your-ear crusty rolls served with bleu cheese. Chicken, paella, baked lamb, and shrimp are all goodies. Reservations not accepted.

El Rodeo   **$$**   ★★

Boulevard Salinas 1647, Tijuana, ☎ (66) 86-5640.
Mexican cuisine. Specialties: Steaks.
Lunch: 11 a.m.–4 p.m., entrées $10–$20.
Dinner: 4-11 p.m., entrées $10–$20.

Pick your cut of cow and it will be cooked at your table in this vaquero-esque beef-lovers haven. Meals are rounded up with appetizers, salad, beans, quesadilla and dessert. Credit Cards: V, MC.

El Taurino   **$$**   ★★★

Calle 6, 7531, off Revolution, Tijuana, ☎ (66) 85-7075.
Specialties: New York Steak, chicken, grilled quail and fish.
Lunch: 11 a.m.–midnight, entrées $5–$16.
Dinner: 11 a.m.–midnight prix fixe $5–$16.

Americans and other English-speakers are put at ease by the dapper maitre d' and the English-language menu. Both the setting and the beef are a cut above the ordinary schlock. Diners sit in comfy booths while eating huge portions of trademark New York steak as well as chicken, grilled quail, fish, and a number of shrimp preparations. Both food and service rate high with visitors. Features: late dining. Credit Cards: V, MC.

Hard Rock Cafe   **$$**   ★★

Avenida Revolucion 520, Tijuana, ☎ (66) 85-0206.
American cuisine. Specialties: Rock and roll memories.
Lunch: 11 a.m.– 2 a.m., entrées $4–$16.
Dinner: 11 a.m.–2 a.m., entrées $4–$16.

The perfect place for visitors who want to be in Mexico but eat in America—hey, even the Mexicans do it. Get your burgers, fries, just-like-home sandwiches plus rock-and-roll memorabilia. Bring back Hard Rock Cafe-Tijuana t-shirts for all your amigos. Families swamp in at lunch time and locals dig the weekend disco. Features: late dining. Reservations not accepted. Credit Cards: V, MC.

La Espadana   **$$**   ★★★

Avenida Sanchez Taboada 10813, Tijuana, ☎ (66) 34-1488.
Mexican cuisine. Specialties: baby back ribs, filet brochette.
Breakfast: 7:30–11 a.m., entrées $7.
Lunch: 11 a.m.–4 p.m., entrées $8–$16.
Dinner: 4–11 p.m., entrées $8–$16.

It looks like a mission inside and out (the name translates to 'bell tower'), the atmosphere is friendly, service quite good. Breakfasts are excellent, but the lunch and dinner menu is best—mesquite-grilled meats, chicken in mole, skewered filet steak, leg of lamb—and portions are HUGE. Try to save room for one of the homemade desserts. Features: late dining. Credit Cards: V, MC.

La Lena $$ ★★★

Boulevard Agua Caliente 11191, Tijuana, ☎ (66) 86-2920.
Lunch: 11 a.m.–midnight, entrées $5–$17.
Dinner: 11 a.m.–midnight, entrées $5–$17.
This spotless bright white dining room offers an open kitchen and grill which turn out delectable meats such as tender beef, chicken, and quail. Dinners include soup, salad, and made-just-for-you tortillas by the on-premises tortilla magician. Iron stomachs might want to go for the tripe. Another branch is located on Avenida Revolution, between Calles 4 and 5. Features: late dining. Credit Cards: V, MC, A.

La Spezia $$ ★★★

Paseo de los Heroes, Tijuana, ☎ (66) 34-2941.
Italian cuisine. Specialties: Mex-italian.
Lunch: 1 p.m.–1 a.m., entrées $7–$18.
Dinner: 1 p.m.–1 a.m., entrées $7–$18.
This elegant Mediterranean-style restaurant in the trendier-by-the-minuto Zona Rio features an Italian menu, but it's really 'Mex-italian'—pastas, seafood and other specialties with Mexican-ish flavorings and sauces. The service is superb, the bar super-luxe, the ambience thoroughly enchanting. Features: late dining.

La Taberna Espanola $$ ★★★

Paseo de los Heroes 1001, Tijuana, ☎ (66) 84-7562.
Spanish cuisine. Specialties: Tapas, ceviche, paella.
Lunch: 1 p.m.–midnight, entrées $4–$18.
Dinner: 1 p.m.–midnight, entrées $4–$18. Closed: Tue.
The local sophisticates line up and cram into the small tapas bar—even though the sawdust-covered floor makes a mess of their Gucci's and Ferragamos. The Spanish tapas are outstanding creative concoctions that can easily be made into a meal, though entrées are also well-prepared. Outdoor tables are set up for those who feel too knocked about inside. Features: late dining. Credit Cards: V, MC.

Tia Juana Tilly's $$$ ★★★

Avenida Revolucion 701, Tijuana, ☎ (66) 85-6024.
Mexican cuisine. Specialties: American tourists.
Lunch: 11 a.m.–4 p.m., entrées $8–$16.
Dinner: 4–11 p.m., entrées $12–$28.
One of the most happening spots south of the border. Locals as well as tourists swarm in for Mexican combination plates, interesting specialties and *lots* of party atmosphere and antics. The disco heats up on weekends. Credit Cards: V, MC.

Tour de France $$$ ★★★★

Gobernador Ibarra 252, Tijuana, ☎ (66) 81-75-42.
French cuisine. Specialties: pates, escargots.
Lunch: 1:30–10:30 p.m., entrées $7–$25.
Dinner: 1:30–10:30 p.m., entrées $7–$25. Closed: Sun.

A divine bit of France south of the border—run by the illustrious chef who opened Coronado's extraordinary 'Marius.' The cuisine is top-notch, particularly pates and escargots. Not everything is complicated and costly—bistro items, such as pizzas and sandwiches, can be ordered up until 6 p.m. After that it's the gourmet diet—delectable seafood and meats, delicate vegetables, dreamy desserts, an international wine list and superb service, to boot. Dinner is served until 11:30 on Fridays and Saturdays. Reservations recommended. Credit Cards: V, MC.

*"How about a discount for the little lady, pal, as your
way of saying thanks for the bailout?"*

Drawing by Ziegler; ©1995 The New Yorker Magazine, Inc.

SPORTS AGENDA

Rancho Bernardo Inn offers five golf courses and tennis.

San Diego sports get their own chapter. Yes, active ones, your favorite sport is right here—or at least nearby. Golf, tennis, fishing, swimming, surfing, water-skiing, jet-skiing, snow skiing, ballooning, gliding, volleyball, dancing atop a Steinway grand piano—it's all here. We've got more than 80 golf courses, 1200 tennis courts, designated jogging paths, marinas, piers, slopes, fishing holes—*everything*. And for those who just like to watch— plenty of voyeurism. Read the individual chapters for activities and sporting events specific to each region.

Golf Finder

San Diego County is greens-fiends paradise—some 83 courses, many of them public. Tee off almost any day of the year—overlooking the ocean or bay, from within a verdant valley or rolling across one of the scenic parks. Golfers of every level of expertise will find their perfect course.

Golfland USA hosts some of the country's top tournaments such as the **Mercedes Championships** at La Costa and the **Buick Invitational** at Torrey Pines.

If you're not quite at championship level, or just need to brush up your game, sign up for instruction with **Aviara Golf Academy by Kip Puterbaugh** (☎ *(619) 438-4539)*, or **THE School of Golf** (☎ *(800) 457-5568)*. To arrange tournaments, or individual or group tee times, contact **American Golf Corporation** (☎ *(619) 793-5416)*, **M&M Tee Times** (☎ *(619) 482-4637)*, **Play Around Golf** (☎ *(619) 573-0113*, **Preferred Golf Tours** (☎ *(619) 792-6556)*, or **San Diego Golf Events** (☎ *(619) 232-4707)*.

Carlsbad

Four Seasons Resort Aviara

7409 Batiquitos Drive, Carlsbad, North County, ☎ *(619) 929-0077.*
Practically by the time the first round had been played, the name "Aviara" was buzzing throughout the golf world. This Arnold Palmer-designed beauty (18 holes, par 72), sculpted across 500 acres overlooking the Pacific Ocean and Batiquitos Lagoon, combines challenge with aesthetics. The public course has greens fees ranging $105-$120 with cart (required), a pro shop, 32,000-square-foot clubhouse, restaurant (with view of the 18th hole) and—some day—the resort might actually be built.

La Costa Resort and Spa

Costa del Mar Road, Carlsbad, North County, ☎ *(619) 438-9111.*
Home of January's Mercedes Tournament of Champions, the PGA championship 36-hole, par 72 traditional course is a top golf destination. The private course has greens fees of about $110 plus cart fees and the amenities are superb—driving range, top-notch pro shop, golf school, restaurant, lounge—and a whole resort's worth of niceties.

Coronado

Coronado Golf Course

2000 Visalia Row, ☎ *(619) 435-3121.*
The course is right off the San Diego-Coronado Bay Bridge, along Glorietta Bay—18 holes, par 72 with eye-popping views of the bridge and bay from the back nine. Tree-lined fairways and wide greens—not to mention those views—make this a popular walking course. Greens fees run about $20, not including cart fee. A driving range, pro shop and restaurant are available.

Ensenada

Bajamar

77.5 Km on Mexico Route 1, South of Ensenada, ☎ *(800) 522-1516.*
Serious golfers will want to make the south-of-the-border pilgrimage to what is commonly referred to as the "Pebble Beach of Mexico." You've got stunning ocean views from the back nine and undulating greens on this challenging 18-hole, par 71, Scottish link course. Greens fees at this public course range $15-25, not including cart fee.

Facilities include a restaurant, pro shop, club rental and repair and villa accommodations.

Escondido

Pala Mesa Resort and Golf Course

2001 Old Highway 395, Escondido, Inland North County, ☎ *(619) 728-5881.*

Rolling, twisting terrain highlights this better-be-accurate 18-hole, par 72 public course. Challenge-lovers will take to the long narrow fairways. Greens fees are $55-$70, including cart. Amenities include pro shop, restaurant, lounge, club rental and repair, and resort lodging.

Welk Resort Center

8860 Lawrence Welk Drive, Escondido, Inland North County, ☎ *(619) 749-3225.*

This full-on scenic resort keeps golfers happy with a 36-hole, par 72 PGA championship course, as well as open-to-the-public The Oaks (a par three) and The Fountains (a 4100-yard exec course). Greens fees are $21-$35 (including cart) and amenities are extensive.

La Jolla

Torrey Pines Municipal Golf Course

11480 North Torrey Pines Road, La Jolla, North County, ☎ *(619) 452-3226.*

Probably every golfer in the world dreams of playing at Torrey Pines one day. Site of February's "Buick Invitational," the 36-hole, par 72 public course features spectacular ocean views from every hole, and a unique and challenging layout. The North Course is more scenic, while the South Course holds the most challenges. Do them both. Greens fees run $18-$50 (without cart) and amenities include an excellent pro shop, restaurant, lounge, equipment rental and adjacent lodging.

Oceanside

Oceanside Golf Course

825 Douglas Drive, Oceanside, North County, ☎ *(619) 433-1360.*

A popular 18-hole, par 72 public course with water traps, lighted driving range, pro shop, snack bar, cocktail lounge and $17-$22.50 greens fees (excluding cart).

Rancho Bernardo

Rancho Bernardo Inn and Country Club

17550 Bernardo Oaks Drive, Inland North County, ☎ *(619) 487-0700.*

Rancho Bernardo's 18-hole, par 72 championship public course features all kinds of delights—fast greens, just enough challenge to keep the game fun (sand traps, water hazards, lakes, waterfalls), plus a driving range, golf college, pro shop, restaurant (fabulous Sunday brunch) and greens fees around $65-$80, including carts.

Rancho Santa Fe

Morgan Run Country Club

4000 Concha del Golf, North County, ☎ *(619) 756-2471.*

Semi-private club with 27-hole, par 71 course, enough challenge for all levels of expertise, and beautiful scenery near the polo grounds. Greens fees run $50-$60, including cart, and facilities consist of pro shop, driving range, equipment rental, restaurant, lounge and lodging (golf packages available).

San Diego

Balboa Park Muncipal Golf Course

Golf Course Drive, At Balboa Park, ☎ *(619) 235-1184.*
Lovely scenic 18-hole, par 72 public course that drops to canyons and rises to mesas. Greens fees range $12-35 (not including carts), and facilities include a pro shop, restaurant, lounge and equipment rental and repair.

Carmel Mountain Ranch Country Club

14050 Carmel Ridge Road, East of downtown, ☎ *(619) 487-9224.*
This semi-private 18-hole, par 72 course is in a really boring suburban area—nonetheless it's ranked as one of California's top 20 public courses. Accuracy is critical. Greens fees range $45-65 (including cart) and there's a putting green, driving range, 20,000-square-foot clubhouse, restaurant and pro shop.

Eastlake Country Club

2375 Clubhouse Drive, South of downtown, ☎ *(619) 482-5757.*
This 18-hole, par 72 public course is a ways out of downtown but the rolling greens and water hazards make it fun and exciting for golfers of all levels. Greens fees range $44–$59, including cart, and a pro shop and restaurant are on hand.

Handlery Hotel and Country Club

950 Hotel Circle North, In Mission Valley, ☎ *(619) 298-0511.*
Semi-private U.S.G.A.-rated 27-hole course, with executive course, lighted driving range, two putting greens, lessons and all the requisite facilities. Greens fees vary.

Mission Bay Golf Course

2702 North Mission Bay Drive, Mission Bay Park, ☎ *(619) 490-3370.*
This 18-hole, par 58 executive course won't be the biggest challenge of your life but it's open to the public, has a driving range, club rentals, restaurant, is lit for night play—and sits on Mission Bay Park. Greens fees are $14-$16.50, for 18 holes; $9-$10, for nine holes.

Mt. Woodson Country Club

16422 North Woodson, East of San Diego, ☎ *(619) 788-3555.*
This semi-private club—open to the public—set in a wooded and mountainous area outside the city, offers an 18-hole, 71 par Landmark Signature course with interesting boulders, bridges, elevated tees and get-away-from-it-all scenery. Greens fees average $42-$60, including cart, plus there's a pro shop, restaurant and cocktail lounge.

Rancho San Diego Golf Course

3121 Willow Glen Road, East of downtown, ☎ *(619) 442-9891.*
A popular public course with lots of tree-lined fairways (good both for walking and tee-tests). Greens fees on the 36-hole, par 73 course range $30-35 (without cart), and there's a pro shop, equipment rental and restaurant on site.

Singing Hills Country Club

2007 Dehesa Road, East of downtown, ☎ *(619) 442-3425.*
Golf Digest raves about Singing Hills, so it probably warrants checking out. The semi-private club offers 36 championship holes plus an

executive course. The setting is superb—a lush resort hidden in a valley surrounded by small mountains. Greens fees range $29-$35, plus cart, and there's a pro shop, restaurant, lounge and lodging.

San Diego County Golf Courses

Listed are the longest hole (regulation), par and number of holes

Bernardo Heights Country Club

16066 Bernardo Heights Parkway
San Diego, CA 92128
☎ *(619) 487-4022*
508, 5, 18

Bonita Golf Course

5540 Sweetwater Road
Bonita, CA 92002
☎ *(619) 267-1103*
483, 5, 18

Carlton Oaks Country Club

9200 Ironwood Drive
Santee, CA 92071
☎ *(619) 448-4242*
500, 5, 18

Carmel Highland Doubletree Golf & Tennis Resort

14455 Penasquitos Drive
San Diego, CA 92129
☎ *(619) 672-9100*
501, 5, 18

Castle Creek Country Club

8797 Circle R Drive
Escondido, CA 92026
☎ *(619) 749-2422*
519, 5, 18

Chula Vista Muncipal Golf Course

4475 Bonita Road
Bonita, CA 92002
☎ *(619) 479-4141*
514, 5, 18

De Anza Country Club

509 Catalina Drive
Borrego Springs, CA 92004
☎ *(619) 767-5577*
532, 5, 18

Escondido Country Club

1800 West Country Club Lane
Escondido, CA 92026
☎ *(619) 746-4212*
482, 5, 18

Fairbanks Ranch Country Club

15150 San Dieguito Road
Rancho Santa Fe, CA 92067
☎ *(619) 259-8819*
519, 5, 18

Fallbrook Country Club

2757 Gird Road
Fallbrook, CA 92028
☎ *(619) 728-8334*
488, 5, 18

La Jolla Country Club

High Avenue Extension
La Jolla, CA 92038
☎ *(619) 454-2505*
531, 5, 18

Lake San Marcos Country Club

1750 San Pablo Drive
San Marcos, CA 92069
☎ *(619) 744-1310*
589, 5, 18

Lomas Santa Fe Country Club

Lomas Santa Fe Drive
Solana Beach, CA 92075
☎ *(619) 755-1547*
511, 5, 18

Marine Memorial Golf Course

Camp Pendleton
Oceanside, CA 92055
☎ *(619) 725-4756*
510, 5, 18

Meadow Lake Country Club

10333 Meadow Glen Way
Escondido, CA 92026
☎ *(619) 749-1620*
534, 5, 18

Miramar Memorial Golf Course

NAS Miramar
San Diego, CA 92145
☎ *(619) 537-4155*
510, 5, 18

Mission Trails Golf Course

7380 Golfcrest Place
San Diego, CA 92119
☎ *(619) 460-5400*
558, 5, 18

Navy Golf Course San Diego

Admiral Baker Road
San Diego, CA 92120
☎ *(619) 556-5520*
544, 5, 18

Pauma Valley Country Club

Highway 76
Pauma Valley, CA 92061
☎ *(619) 742-1230*
525, 5, 18

Rams Hill Country Club

1881 Rams Hill Road
Borrego Springs, CA 92004
☎ *(619) 767-5125*
518, 5, 18

Rancho Bernardo Golf Club

12280 Greens East Road
San Diego, CA 92128
☎ *(619) 487-1212*
510, 5, 18

Rancho Santa Fe Golf Club

La Granada
Rancho Santa Fe, CA 92067
☎ *(619) 756-3094*
587, 5, 18

Rancho Santa Fe Farms Country Club

Rancho Santa Fe, CA 92067
☎ *(619) 756-5884*
520, 5, 18

San Diego Country Club

88 L Street
Chula Vista, CA 92011
☎ *(619) 422-0108*
550, 5, 18

San Luis Rey Downs Country Club

31474 Golf Club Drive
Bonsall, CA 92003
☎ *(619) 758-9699*
558, 5, 18

San Vicente Country Club

24157 San Vicente Road
Ramona, CA 92065
☎ *(619) 789-3477*
516, 5, 18

Sea 'n Air Golf Course

NAS North Island
Coronado, Ca 92135
☎ *(619) 545-9659*
580, 5, 18

Shadowridge Country Club

1980 Gateway Drive
Vista, CA 92008
☎ *(619) 727-7706*
521, 5, 18

Stardust Country Club

950 Hotel Circle
San Diego, CA 92108
☎ *(619) 297-4796*
474, 5, 18

Steele Canyon Golf Course

3199 Stonefield Drive
Jamul, CA
☎ *(619) 441-6900*
533, 5, 27

Stoneridge Country Club

17166 Stoneridge Country Club Lane
Poway, CA 92064
☎ *(619) 487-2117*
518, 5, 18

Tijuana Country Club

Agua Caliente
Tijuana, Baja California
☎ *(619) 298-4105*
538, 5, 18

Vista Valley Country Club

29354 Vista Valley Drive
Vista, Ca 92038
☎ *(619) 758-5275*
548, 5, 18

Warner Springs Ranch

Highway 79
Warner Springs, CA 92086
☎ *(619) 782-3555*
515, 5, 18

Willowbrook Country Club

11905 Riverside Drive
Lakeside, CA 92040
☎ *(619) 561-1061*
510, 5, 36

Cycling

It's not quite as bad as China, but San Diego cyclists have a definite *presence*. Miles of coastline, gentle hills and rural communities—combined with all that great weather—keep the two- and three-wheelers happy. One of the most popular routes is **Old Highway 101,** with designated paths stretching from La Jolla to Oceanside and almost the entire distance hugs the coast. The bit from La Jolla to Torrey Pines Beach, along **North Torrey Pines**

Road, is somewhat of a killer grade—many cyclists end up walking their bikes up the hill. A noteworthy detour is up **Lomas Santa Fe Drive,** through Solana Beach into Rancho Santa Fe, where you can do a serene pedal around the exclusive community, then—depending on how adventurous and in-shape you are—keep going along the **Del Dios Highway** either to Lake Hodges or on to Escondido where you can bike your way right to the Wild Animal Park.

Other scenic routes (most of them flat) are around **Coronado** (you can take your bike on the ferry or bus), **Balboa Park, Mission Bay Park, the Embarcadero,** and along the **Mission Bay Boardwalk.** Visitors with ID and helmet can even tour around **Camp Pendleton.** And don't forget about the **velodrome** at Balboa Park.

Beware, though—you will probably be sharing the road with skateboarders, rollerbladers and whirling dervishes.

For route maps, bicycle bus routes and other information on the county's 500-plus miles of bike paths, contact **Commuter Computer** (☎ *(619) 231-2453)* or the **California Department of Transportation** (☎ *(619) 688-6699).*

Jogging and Rollerblading

Joggers and rollerbladers are everywhere—or so it seems. The city's estimated 170,000 **joggers** take to the same routes as the cyclists, except they can get a bit closer to the ocean. **Popular runs** include **Balboa Park, Mission Bay Park, along the Embarcadero, and parallel to the ocean on the cliffs at Del Mar.** They run in the bike paths, on the sidewalks, through median dividers— they run in the streets paying no mind to oncoming traffic as they continually monitor their pulses. They are sick people.

Rollerbladers also seem to fly from every hill and intersection, though **Mission Bay Park** and **Mission Bay Boardwalk** are their favorites.

Fish Finder

What's your pleasure—lake, ocean or pier? Pier fishing requires no license, otherwise any angler over the age of 16 needs the proper paperwork. Licenses are available at the **Department of Fish and Game** (☎ *(619) 467-4201)* or from most bait and tackle shops.

Catch bass, bluegill, catfish, trout or crappie at one of the well-stocked **inland lakes**—most of which offer boat rentals, bait and tackle shops, picnic areas and hiking trails. Some offer campgrounds, others prohibit public boat launching or body-contact watersports. Call ahead for the rules and regulations.

North County inland lakes: Dixon Lake, elevation 1045 ft. (☎ *(619) 741-4680);* Lake Hodges, elevation 314 ft. (☎ *(619) 465-3474);* Lake Poway, elevation 500 ft. (☎ *(619) 679-4383);* Lake Wohlford, elevation 1500 ft. (☎ *(619) 738-4346).*

San Diego area inland lakes: Lake Jennings, elevation 700 ft. (☎ *(619) 443-2510);* Lake Miramar, elevation 714 ft. (☎ *(619) 465-3474);* Lower Otay Lake, elevation 490 ft. (☎ *(619) 425-9587);* Murray Reservoir, elevation 350 ft. (☎ *(619) 465-3474);* Santee Lakes, elevation 350 ft. (☎ *(619) 448-2482);* San Vicente Lake, elevation 659 ft. (☎ *(619) 465-3474).*

Backcountry lakes: El Capitan Reservoir, elevation 750 ft. (☎ *(619) 465-3474);* Lake Cuyamaca, elevation 4620 ft. (☎ *(619) 765-0515);* Lake Henshaw, elevation 2727 ft. (☎ *(619) 782-3501);* Lake Morena, elevation 3200 ft. (☎ *(619) 478-5473);* Lake Sutherland, elevation 2058 ft. (☎ *(619) 668-2050).*

Ocean fishers who hanker for the deep sea—and some marlin, yellowtail, barracuda, black or white sea bass, bluefin tuna, bonito, halibut, swordfish, yellowtail or albacore—should sign up for a fishing expediton (best months are April through October). If you're staying at a large hotel or resort, these can be arranged painlessly—otherwise contact one of the companies directly. Operators that offer a variety of half-day, full-day or longer excursions include: **Fisherman's Landing** (☎ *(619) 221-8500)*, **H & M Sportfishing** (☎ *(619) 222-1144)*, **Helgren's Sportfishing** (☎ *(619) 722-2133)*, **Islandia Sportfishing** (☎ *(619) 222-1164)*, **Point Loma Sportfishing** (☎ *(619) 223-1627)*, and **Seaforth Boat Rentals** (☎ *(619) 223-7584).*

If you're a **surf fisher** you might reel in corbina, croaker, opaleye perch, rockfish or halibut. Public **fishing piers** are located at Oceanside, Ocean Beach, Shelter Island, and Crystal Pier in Pacific Beach.

If you're into **clam digging** (as many Southern Californians are) you can find not only clams, but scallops, mussels, grunion, lobster and abalone—inquire with the Department of Fish and Game about open seasons. Also keep in mind that a quarantine is in effect for mussels and clams, May through October. Best **clamming spots** are Silver Strand State Beach, Torrey Pines State Beach, and Border Field State Park (though that area is often contaminated). You might also give San Onofre State Beach a try if you're *really* into it.

Boating

Pleasure boats as well as competition craft (such as the now-gone America's Cup) have a number of protected waterways for their use. If you're staying at one of the Coronado, San Diego- or Mission Bay resort hotels, a variety of boats will be waiting at your back door. Aside from boating heaven **Mission Bay Park,** other on-the-water meccas include San Diego Bay's **Shelter and Harbor islands, Coronado's Glorietta Bay, Oceanside Harbor** and **Snug Harbor, in Carlsbad.**

If you have your own boat, pull in at one of the **marinas** listed in the Point Loma, Harbor Island and Shelter Island chapter. Otherwise rent a craft—everything from 14- to 27-foot sailboats, 20- to 27-foot offshore power boats, catamarans, canoes, kayaks or sailboards. Good resources include: **Club Nautico** (☎ *(619) 233-9311);* **Mission Bay Sportcenter** (☎ *(619) 488-1004);* **Seaforth Boat Rentals** (☎ *(619) 223-1681);* and **Coronado Boat Rentals** (☎ *(619) 437-1514).*

For **lake cruising,** check the "Fishing" section in this chapter. Alas, the America's Cup is gone, but boating enthusiasts should enjoy the **San Diego Crew Classic** and **Bayfair Unlimited Hydroplane Racing,** both held annually at Mission Bay Park.

Hang Gliding

San Diego offers several popular hang gliding spots.

Is it a bird? A plane? If it's hovering around the cliffs at Torrey Pines, it's most likely a hang glider just out for a bit of "look, ma, I can fly" recreation. The **Torrey Pines Glider Port** is world famous for its upward wind from the surf below as well as its absolutely spectacular vistas—the Pacific Ocean *and* naked people at Black's Beach below. Alas, peepers-in-the-name-of-sport, this glider port is more experienced pilots only and all fliers must have a rating card from the U.S. Hang Gliding Association. Contact the **Torrey Pines Hang Gliders Port** (☎ *(619) 452-9858)* for information about the port, renting gear or taking lessons.

Other favorite soaring areas are **Otay Mountain, Black Mountain** and **Mount Laguna.**

Horseback Riding

The horsey set has been somewhat thwarted by the high price of insurance for stables, though there are still enough facilities around to satisfy most riders. Beaches, countryside and mountain areas are all targeted for rides lasting a few hours through several days. Outfits to try include **Holidays on Horseback** (☎ *(619) 445-3997)*, **Bright Valley Farm** (☎ *(619) 670-1861)* and **Beachfront Horse Rentals** (☎ *(619) 428-4330).*

Colorful balloons fill the North County skies.

Ballooning

Does life get any better than floating suspended in a gondola basket from a seven-story high hot-air balloon? The glorious color parade takes to the North County skies (with the ideal combination of winds and open expanses) almost every sunrise and sunset—soaring quietly up to 3000 feet, a perfect altitude to take in the views stretching from San Clemente in the north down to Mexico. Balloonatics usually help set up and pack up their craft—with the crew's instructions, of course, and finish up the three-hour-or-so event (including flight) with champagne.

Balloon operators include: **A Adventure Flights, Inc.** (☎ *800-404-6359*)*;* **Skysurfer Balloon Company** (☎ *(619) 481-6800*)*;* and **Del Mar Balloons** (☎ *(619) 259-3115*)*.*

Diving

One of the country's most special (though hardly secret) skin- and scuba-diving spots is La Jolla's **Underwater Marine Preserve** at the cove (Coast Boulevard and Girard Avenue). This ecological preserve harbors a magnificent array of unique and colorful sea life. Due to the **dangerous rip currents,** it's best explored by experienced divers only.

Other popular diving spots are **Scripps Canyon** (between La Jolla Cove and Black's Beach)—where some areas drop to around 900 feet—as well as **Point Loma's Sunset Cliffs** (another strong riptide section),**Swami's Beach** near Encinitas, and the man-made reefs off **Silver Strand** and **Imperial beaches.**

For recorded info on beaches, weather, tides, and diving conditions, call Beach and Weather Report (☎ *(619) 221-8884*). For diving equipment and organized dives, try **The Diving Locker** (☎ *(619) 272-1120* or (☎ *(619) 755-6822,* North County), **Ocean Enterprises** (☎ *(619) 565-6054*), or **San Diego Divers Supply** (☎ *(619) 224-3439* or ☎ *(619) 459-2691,* La Jolla).

Gambling

You probably already know about the betting action at **Del Mar Racetrack, Agua Caliente Racetrack** and the jai alai **Fronton Palacio.** But were you aware that San Diego County has three full-on **casinos** on East County Indian reservations? The glitzy, mega-casinos have video poker machines, Indian blackjack, poker, off-track wagering, bingo, megabingo, live entertainment, cocktail service, 24-hour restaurants, and "800" numbers. For info and directions, call **Viejas** (☎ *800-YELL-BINGO*—don't count the letters), **Sycuan** (☎ *800-2-SYCUAN*) and **Barona** (☎ *800-227-UBET*). Note: no booze is sold or allowed at either Barona or Sycuan, but the casinos compensate by bringing in big-name entertainers.

Tennis and Other Racquets

As with golf, San Diego is the tennis player's died-and-gone-to-heaven dream—some 1200 private and public courts throughout the country combined with perfect weather. The **Toshiba Tennis Classic,** held at La Costa Resort and Spa is one of *the* events of the year.

If you're staying at one of the resorts or hotels with tennis facilities, you can backhand your brains out. Among the many choices are The Sheratons on Harbor Island, Kona Kai Continental Plaza Resort and Marina, Hyatt Regency San Diego, San Diego Marriott Hotel and Marina, The Westin at Horton Plaza, Hotel del Coronado, Le Meridien San Diego at Coronado, Bahia Resort Hotel, San Diego Hilton Beach and Tennis Resort, Dana Inn and Marina, Red Lion Hotel San Diego, Handlery Hotel and Country Club, San Diego Marriott Mission Valley, Hyatt Regency La Jolla, Radisson La Jolla Hotel, La Jolla Beach and Tennis Club, Sea Lodge at La Jolla Shores and The Inn at Rancho Santa Fe. The **Inn at Rancho Bernardo** and **Rancho Valencia Resort** are both renowned tennis-destination facilities. Though most of the courts are open only to guests, on a slow day several of the hotels will admit the peon public for a fee.

Morley Field, in Balboa Park (☎ *(619) 295-9278*, **La Jolla Recreation Center** (☎ *(619) 552-1658*), and **Robb Field,** in Ocean Beach (☎ *(619) 531-1563*) all offer public facilities—either free, or for a small fee. Also, most communities have **city parks** with tennis courts.

Racquetballers can play their game for free, most weekends, at **San Diego City College**, *1313 Twelfth Avenue, downtown* (☎ *(619) 230-2486*).

Skiing—Jet, Snow and Water

Jet-skiers can take off from many beaches as long as they quickly take off beyond the surf lines and don't linger near shore (check with the lifeguards). Calmer waters can be cruised at **Mission Bay Park** and Carlsbad's **Snug Harbor Marina** (☎ *(619) 434-3089*)—both places rent equipment. It's ditto for **water-skiers** at Mission Bay Park and Snug Harbor. For rentals at Mission Bay, contact **Seaforth Boat Rentals** (☎ *(619) 223-1681*). Bored with the water and feel like snow? You can hit many ski resorts in the **San Bernardino Mountains** in just a few-hours drive. Tops are **Snow Summit** (☎ *(909) 866-5766*), **Bear Mountain** (☎ *(909) 585-2517*), and **Snow Valley** (☎ *(909) 867-2751*).

Many of the local sporting goods stores rent equipment and hand out suggestions.

Insider Tip

If your schedule allows it, head for Mammoth Mountain. It's about an eight-hour drive, but the quality of snow and number of lifts and runs are astounding. Make reservations early for lodgings because it's extremely popular with local ski-sters during holiday periods. The resort is located at Interstate 395 in Mammoth Lakes (☎ 800-367-6572.)

Spas

Bones aching from all the activity? Or, is your idea of an action-packed day having a sauna, Swedish massage and seaweed facial? You can have the works—for a price—at **Coronado's Le Meridian** and the **Clarins Institut de Beaute** (☎ *(619) 435-3000*), **Del Mar's L'Auberge Del Mar Resort and Spa** (☎ *(619) 259-1515*), **Carlsbad's La Costa Resort and Spa** (☎ *(619) 438-9111*), **Escondido's Castle Creek Inn Resort and Spa** (☎ *(619) 751-8800*), or **Rosarito Beach's Casa Playa** (☎ *800-343-8582*). When you emerge, your toned body will glow and your sloughed skin will gleam. You will be hard, firm and 21 years old again.

Bellissima Day Spa (☎ *(619) 234-7722*), atop The Paladion downtown, offers beauty treatments lasting one-hour or one-day—a good respite from shopping or sightseeing.

Swimming

Many of the public beaches have **lifeguards** on duty—if you see a red flag waving at a lifeguard station, it's a warning that swimming is dangerous. Also, make sure you keep out of "surfing-only" areas—if the boards don't get you, the surfers might.

Popular **swimming beaches** include **Mission Bay Park, Pacific Beach, Ocean Beach, Mission Beach, Coronado Beach, Silver Strand State Beach, Imperial Beach** (without the raw sewage), **Windansea** (without the surf nazis), **La Jolla Shores, La Jolla Cove** (including the Children's Pool), Windansea, and most of the **North County** beaches.

Pool swimmers shouldn't miss the **Mission Bay Plunge** at Belmont Park (☎ *(619) 488-3110*). The public is also invited to swim at the **Downtown YMCA**, *500 West Broadway Avenue* (☎ *(619) 232-7451*), the **Copley Family YMCA**, *3901 Landis Street* (☎ *(619) 283-2251*), and the **Magdalena Ecke YMCA**, *200 Saxony Road, Encinitas* (☎ *(619) 942-9622*).

Surfing

It's Surf City year-round—though, some months, you might need a wetsuit. San Diego has its large share of "serious surfers" and, in some places (such as La Jolla's **Windansea**), newcomers and visitors might be psychologically—or physically—intimidated (or tortured). C'ést la vie—isn't the harrassment worth getting into "the California scene?"

See "Fielding's Handy Beach Guide" for the complete skinny on beaches. Basically, **beginners** should hang at **Mission and Pacific beaches, La Jolla Shores, Del Mar or Oceanside.** If you're on the **experienced** level, head for **Sunset Cliffs, La Jolla's Windansea, Black's Beach, or Swami's in Encinitas.**

A surfer tackles the waves at Rosarito Beach.

SAN DIEGO COUNTY SURF SHOPS

Almost anywhere along the coast, you'll find a selection of cool shops for boards, wetsuits, beachwear and accessories.

The Beach Co.	Oceanside	☎ *(619) 722-2578*
Carlsbad Pipelines	Carlsbad	☎ *(619) 729-4423*
Encinitas Surfboards	Encinitas	☎ *(619) 753-0506*
Five-forty	Solana Beach	☎ *(619) 481-5404*
Hansen's	Encinitas	☎ *(619) 753-6595*
Hobie Oceanside	Oceanside	☎ *(619) 433-4020*
Mitch's Surf Shop	La Jolla	☎ *(619) 459-5933*
Mitch's Surf Shop	Solana Beach	☎ *(619) 481-1354*
Offshore Surf Shop	Carlsbad	☎ *(619) 729-4934*
101 Sports	Leucadia	☎ *(619) 942-2088*
South Coast	Ocean Beach	☎ *(619) 223-7017*
South Coast Windansea	Pacific Beach	☎ *(619) 483-7660*
Sunset	Encinitas	☎ *(619) 753-6655*

Windsurfing

Windsurfing, sailboarding—call it what you will. Beginners should stick to calm waters like **Mission Bay Park** or Carlsbad's **Snug Harbor Marina**. Both places offer **rentals and instruction** through **Mission Bay Sportcenter** (☎ *(619) 488-1005*) or **San Diego Sailing Center** (☎ *(619) 488-0651*), both at Mission Bay Park, or—at Snug Harbor—**California Water Sports** (☎ *(619) 434-3089*).

Once you feel confident, you can head out into the blue yonder in **Del Mar or La Jolla**.

Spectator Sports

Lean back and relax—or sit forward and scream—at one or more of your favorite sports teams.

San Diego Jack Murphy Stadium is the game site for **Chargers football, Padres baseball, and college football at the Plymouth Holiday Bowl**. Intercollegiate **basketball** is played by the **San Diego State University Aztecs** in their Peterson Gym. Catch the **San Diego Sockers** indoor soccer matches at the **Sports Arena**.

Del Mar Racetrack is the place for in-season **thoroughbred racing** and you can catch the **greyhounds** at **Tijuana's Agua Caliente.** South of the border is also the spot for fast, fast, fast **jai alai** games at **Fronton Palacio**.

Golf and tennis tournaments are held at various locations throughout the county—most notably **Torrey Pines Municipal Golf Course** and **La Costa Resort and Spa**.

FIELDING'S BEST WALKS

Historical walks-in-the-past, coastal toes-in-the-sand, and rub-elbows-with-The-Beautiful-People strolls are all possible in San Diego County. More adventurous? Head to the hills—or desert—for some more vigorous hiking.

Balboa Park

One of the most perfect walks—especially on a Sunday afternoon. Visit museums and the zoo, eat junk food all day. Approximately 1400 acres of terrain allow your feet to experience everything from paved walkways to rugged canyon areas.

Cabrillo National Monument

Gorgeous drop-dead scenery from atop rugged cliffs, plus all that history to boot. The Bayside Trail is a two-mile trek through native shrubbery and Native American footprints.

FIELDING'S BEST WALKS

Coronado

    A lovely journey through and around the knock-out Hotel del Coronado. Continue along Ocean Boulevard to see some of the smashing turn-of-the-century homes—as well as seaside scenery.

Del Mar

    Parade around Del Mar Plaza in your New York-Sunday best. Cross over to L'Auberge and the short block to beachfront Seagrove Park.

Downtown

    You must do the historic **Gaslamp Quarter** (flat all the way), stopping in for a latte or cappuccino at every street corner. Pumped up? Keep walking to the Embarcadero and Seaport Village.

La Jolla

    Explore the village, especially Prospect Avenue—the so-called "Rodeo Drive of San Diego," including La Valencia Hotel. Go the short way to La Jolla Cove, and the newly remodelled San Diego Museum of Contemporary Art.

Mission Bay Park

    Scenic pathways, nooks and crannies, bays and coves *galore*.

Old Town State Historical Park

    A flat walk through San Diego's curvaceous beginnings.

Torrey Pines State Reserve

    Fabulous nature walks along a variety of trails—featuring clifftop views of the Pacific along with close-up views of the rare Torrey Pine tree and other native shrubs and plants.

Pacing back and forth

    In your hotel room, drapes drawn, TV on (picture only, no sound), popping Prozac and begging God to let you live here forever.

DAY TRIPS AND GETTING AWAY FROM SAN DIEGO

Anza Borrego Desert offers more than 700 miles of hiking trails.

You've seen it all—the non-glitz, the non-glitter. Now you want to see more. Of everything. This is life—you're never satisfied.

Anza Borrego Desert ★★★

Park Information ☎ (619) 767-4684

A 600,000-acre park that at first glance looks as though it had an atomic bomb dropped on it. Those who come expecting giant saguaros or Monument Valley will be disappointed, but if you take the time to look closely, you'll come to appreciate the gentle rhythms of the desert. Visitors in a hurry should stop at the interpretive center in Borrego Springs, then blast around the shimmering blacktop in search of scenery. Those with more time (and in better shape) can explore the more than 700 miles of hiking trails in search of waterfalls and oases, badlands, babbling streams and dramatic canyons. If you have a four-wheel-drive vehicle, take the dirt roads to the more remote regions of the park. There is even an arduous back door into Terwilliger to the north, along Coyote Canyon. One of the park's major attractions is the 600 species of wildflowers that bloom each year in February and March. Then, the winter rains unlock the desert's colorful secrets and a canvas of yellows, reds, pinks and blues extends over the landscape. Then, voila, it's gone until the next year. If you want to stay overnight, the Casa del Zorro is a famous—albeit expensive—choice for lodging. 180 miles roundtrip.

Big Bear   ★★★

Visitor Information ☎ *(909) 866-5877*

For San Diegans who want to hit the slopes FAST, the Big Bear area (rising to an elevation of 8600 feet) offers a variety of ski runs, chalets and the whole après-ski and family snowball number. In summer months, weekenders jam those chalets, lakes, hiking trails and quaintsy mountain village shops. The Rim of the World Highway is worth a drive, though in winter you might need chains.

Catalina Island   ★★★

Visitor Information Center ☎ *(310) 510-2500*

Santa Catalina Island sits about 22 miles across the Pacific Ocean from Los Angeles. Discovered by Juan Rodriguez Cabrillo in 1542, the island was later used as a hideout for pirates and smugglers. Somewhere along the line, the Wrigley family (chewing gum magnates) gained control of the island until 1972 when it was turned into a conservancy to protect the native habitat. These days it's a favorite getaway for families, honeymooners, boaters, divers and fishermen—and a great way to pretend you're on a remote island even when (on a rare) clear day, you can see Los Angeles with your bare eyes. Access to Catalina Island is by boat (approximately two hours from San Pedro, Long Beach or Newport Beach), or by plane or helicopter (much faster, but also more expensive—though there is direct service from San Diego). Once on the island, you can explore the main town of Avalon—checking out the famous Avalon Casino (formerly a popular dance hall), rent a bike and tour at your leisure, take one of the renowned glass-bottom boat rides, visit some wild buffalo (left behind after Cecil B. DeMille filmed *The Vanishing American* on the island in 1924), or take the 66-mile guided tour that includes the more countryish side of the island. Diving and fishing trips are also available, but should be booked out of San Pedro or Long Beach before departing. Overnight guests should consider one of Catalina's romantic B&Bs, priced from reasonable to "when will we ever do this again?" splurges. The island can be packed with those irritating Angelenos on weekends and during summer.

Death Valley   ★★

Furnace Creek Visitor Center ☎ *(619) 786-2331*

It is died-and-gone-to-hell HOT, here where the low-lying areas of the park average 116 degrees in July (and it has reached 134 degrees!). In the winter, however, temperatures drop to around 85 degrees, and the 3.3 acre national park becomes a weekend getaway for the adventurous, curious and/or rich. The money-is-no-object crowd lodges at Furnace Creek Inn, while the peons check into Furnace Creek Ranch. Birders, who flock here in late May to catch the spring migration, usually just camp out. The park is a geologist's dream with its tortured rock formations, salt pans and 700-foot sand dunes, 900-plus species of plants and trees (including 21 unique to Death Valley). Elevations go from 282 feet below sea level to 11,049 feet above, making for a really dazzling variety of landscapes.

Disneyland ★★★★

Information *(714) 781-4000*
How can you resist? If you have kids, you can't. If you're child-free, you'll probably go through the "I really just want to admire the technology" justification. Shut up and GO! Buy a pair of mouse ears and explore Adventureland, Tomorrowland, Mickey's Toontown, Main Street U.S.A. and Critter Country. We'll see you on the Matterhorn. We'll see you on the Mad Hatter's Tea Cups. We'll see you waiting in the mile-long line for the Indiana Jones ride. Sucker!

Joshua Tree ★★★

Visitor Center *(619) 367-7511*
The setting is sparse, which only makes the Joshua tree stand out more. The trees—members of the yucca family—grow up to 40 feet tall and can only be found in the high desert at elevations above 3000 feet. Keep in mind, this is not Palm Springs—no luxury resorts or pampering. Rather Joshua Tree is a haven for rock climbers, and a combo of dirt and paved roads will let you view a huge variety of geological formations and desert life (ocotillos, cactuses, palo verdes, pinon pines, smoke trees and—in spring— glorious blooming wildflowers). The park is open year-round.

DAY TRIPS AND GETTING
AWAY FROM SAN DIEGO

Mountain air, scenic views, antiques and apples make Julian a popular tourist stop.

Julian ★★★

Chamber of Commerce *(619) 765-1857*
This ramshackle collection of wooden houses in San Diego County was once a mining town—now it's a friendly tourist trap. Gold was discovered here in 1870 and some diehards are still working mines in

L.A. MUSEUMS

L.A. county has amassed an impressive collection of art. Scattered throughout the city is a broad range of museums housing art of different styles, origins and time periods.

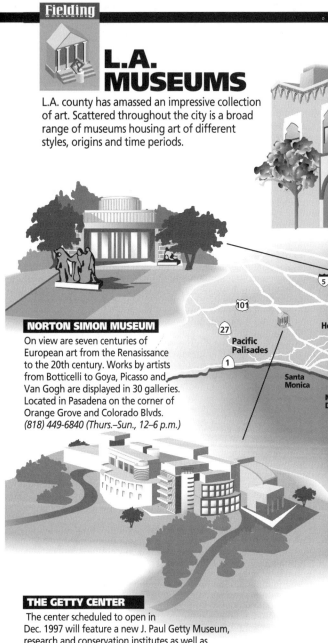

NORTON SIMON MUSEUM

On view are seven centuries of European art from the Renaissance to the 20th century. Works by artists from Botticelli to Goya, Picasso and Van Gogh are displayed in 30 galleries. Located in Pasadena on the corner of Orange Grove and Colorado Blvds. *(818) 449-6840 (Thurs.–Sun., 12–6 p.m.)*

THE GETTY CENTER

The center scheduled to open in Dec. 1997 will feature a new J. Paul Getty Museum, research and conservation institutes as well as educational and information centers plus a central garden. *1200 Getty Center Drive, near the 405 Fwy and Sepulveda Pass.* *(310) 440-7360.*

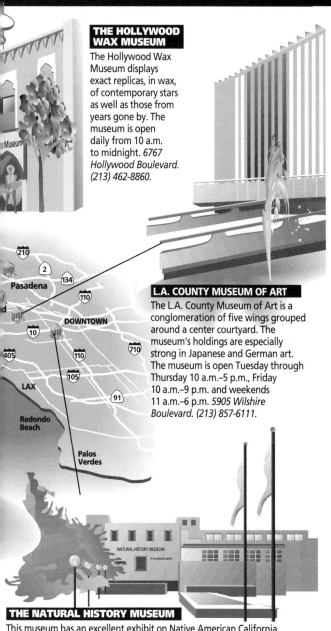

THE HOLLYWOOD WAX MUSEUM

The Hollywood Wax Museum displays exact replicas, in wax, of contemporary stars as well as those from years gone by. The museum is open daily from 10 a.m. to midnight. *6767 Hollywood Boulevard. (213) 462-8860.*

L.A. COUNTY MUSEUM OF ART

The L.A. County Museum of Art is a conglomeration of five wings grouped around a center courtyard. The museum's holdings are especially strong in Japanese and German art. The museum is open Tuesday through Thursday 10 a.m.–5 p.m., Friday 10 a.m.–9 p.m. and weekends 11 a.m.–6 p.m. *5905 Wilshire Boulevard. (213) 857-6111.*

DAY TRIPS AND GETTING AWAY FROM SAN DIEGO

THE NATURAL HISTORY MUSEUM

This museum has an excellent exhibit on Native American California History. With displays of dinosaurs, archeology, zoology and marine biology, it attracts the most visitors of any California museum. *900 Exposition Park, Tues.–Sun., 10 a.m.–5 p.m. (213) 744-3466.*

the mountains outside of town. At 4200 feet above sea level, Julian is perfect for winter frolics in the snow. Autumn, however, is the town's most popular season—when San Diegans snap up locally grown apples by the bushel, stuff their faces with homemade apple pie and schlep home jugs of cider for Halloween. Even if you hate apples, the mountain air and terrific views will make your trip worthwhile—also there are shopping ops for antique collectors. All roads in or out of town are quite scenic—Anza Borrego Desert to the east, lush agriculture to the west. Pretty, pretty, pretty. 120 miles roundtrip.

Laguna Beach ★★★

Visitor Information Center ☎ *(714) 497-9229*

This coastal resort is pretty as a picture postcard—steep hills rising above the Pacific Ocean, luxurious estates and picturesque cottages, and enough charm to tame a cobra. Long known as an artist's colony, Laguna's village is filled with galleries, cafes, restaurants, boutiques and craft shops. Between early July and late August people come from all over to catch the famed Sawdust Festival and Pageant of the Masters (the nightly pageant features real people masquerading as characters in famous paintings—anyone out there resemble the Mona Lisa?). The place is tops for a romantic interlude (for a special treat, spend the weekend at the Ritz-Carlton Laguna Niguel).

Los Angeles ★★★★★

See Fielding's L.A. Agenda

Yes, L.A. Yes, five stars. Prove me wrong. Hollywood, Malibu, Sunset and Vine, the museums, the beaches, the kitsch, the sleaze, the trends, the elegance, the ugliness, the cosmetic surgery... 200 miles roundtrip.

Palm Springs ★★★

Convention and Visitors Bureau ☎ *(619) 770-9000*

Punks and polyester used to make for an odd mix in this famous desert town, but today Palm Springs is a favorite winter weekend getaway for crowd- and smog-exhausted Angelenos. More than two million people spend at least one night in Palm Springs each year, with the more discriminating (and rich) choosing the famous resorts at La Quinta and Indian Wells. The tennis-and-golf crowd (there are more than 90 golf courses in the Coachella Valley and scads more tennis courts) is supplemented by the onslaught of college students on Spring Break, who usually hang in the cheapest accommodations and party-their-pants-off in the downtown area. If you want to get above the landscape (and don't have claustrophobia or vertigo), you might enjoy the 14-minute trip up the Palm Springs Aerial Tramway which heads up the mountain to an elevation of 8516 feet. Palm Springs' hotels and condos are nearly always full during winter, so make sure you have a reservation before departing. Summer is the time for cheap digs, but it's also inferno season. You might want to jaunt over to Joshua Tree while you're in the area.

San Juan Capistrano ★★★

It's not too far from the San Diego County line, and worthy of a journey to explore the beautiful Mission San Juan Capistrano (founded in 1776, and one of the most elaborate of the chain). The swallows, of course, are a big attraction and, if you're here at the right time, it's quite a sight. Since the late 1700s, the trusty birds have been flying up from Argentina on March 19th (St. Joseph's Day). They nest and split again on October 23rd.

Temecula   ★★★

Chamber of Commerce ☎ *(909) 676-5090*

Inland, at the San Diego County line, Temecula is the area's wine country. It's not Napa Valley—and certainly not the Rhone Valley—but some 11 wineries (most along Rancho California Road) produce whites, reds and rosés. The first grapevines were actually planted in the early 1800s by Franciscan missionaries, but then cattle ranching took over. Grape-growers gave it another try in 1968, and the first local wines were produced a few years later. Most of the wineries are family-owned and operated—expect lots of company on weekends. Tasters are welcome year-round though harvest time falls mid-August through September. Don't miss Old Town Temecula, with its pre-served turn-of-the-century buildings and storefronts. 120 miles roundtrip.

Temecula boasts 11 wineries plus a plethora of antique shops and historic buildings.

SAN DIEGO AGENDA

A submerged hippo delights visitors to Hippo Beach at the zoo.

One Day Agenda for San Diego

One day in San Diego. What to do? Well, certainly do **your hair** first, then do **downtown.** Mosey around the historic **Gaslamp Quarter,** stop *everywhere* for an espresso or latte (order it low-fat and no one will even know you're a tourist—try to curb the nasals and twangs). Head over to **the Embarcadero.** Watch the passing parade of ships and small craft. Do the **Seaport Village** thing. Back in the Gaslamp, eat lunch at the **Grant Grill,** then cross the street to **Horton Plaza** for your bring-back-home shopping (which *might* take up the entire day).

Get over to **Old Town** before dark. Join the walking tour and get into the spirit of San Diego's early times. Work off lunch by climbing to the top of **Presidio Park,** then roll back down. Walk through **Heritage Park** and go back into the historical park for a gadabout in **Bazaar del Mundo.** Time to eat again. Have dinner at one of the authentic restaurants—order the whole routine of combo plates, rice, beans, fresh guacamole, chips and salsa and wash it all down with pitchers of cerveza or margaritas—you'll be up all night. Head back into downtown—or wherever you're staying—and relax over a drink at one of the hotel lounges (the Hyatt Regency or Marriott are both good bets), an underground club, or artsy cafe—your choice.

Horton Plaza is a great choice for lunch, dinner and shopping.

Agenda for the 2nd Day of a 2-Day Trip

Start the day at the **half-price ticket booth** in front of Horton Plaza. Choose a **theatrical performance** for the evening. (Old Globe for traditionalists, Sledgehammer for the avant-garde.)

Definitely explore **Balboa Park.** Go to every one of the **museums**, visit artisans at work in Spanish Village, check out your favorite animals at **the zoo**, or saddle up in one of the antique hand-carved species on the **carousel** out front. Have lunch at the **Sculpture Garden Cafe**, **Cafe del Rey Morro**, or grab a hot dog from one of the vendors.

If you're not a museum or park person, kick in a **ferry ride** to **Coronado.** Explore the **Old Ferry Landing**—buy souvenirs or gifts and sip an espresso while staring back at the city. Take a taxi or the shuttle over to the **Hotel del Coronado.** Do the self-guided tour, and—if you're dressed for it—eat lunch in the **Crown Room.**

As you amble back to the ferry dock, stop at **Le Meridien** for drinks, views and a taste of France.

Over on the city side, you should have enough time for an early dinner in the Gaslamp Quarter and to make your **theatre performance.** By now you should have a feel for what area you feel happiest in—go back there for drinks, dessert and a little night music.

Agenda for the 3rd Day of a Three-day Trip

Make a choice—north or south (if you feel urbane and sporty, go north—derelict and devil-may-cares, point south).

If you're heading north, hit **Mission Bay Park** and spend the morning on a sport of choice. Do lunch at **Point Loma Seafoods** and then make a quick visit to **Cabrillo National Monument.** Continue up the coast—primp along **Prospect Street,** visit the **San Diego Museum of Contemporary Art** or stroll above **La Jolla Cove**, have a quick drink at the **Whaling Bar** in La Valencia Hotel, and scoot over to **Stephen Birch Aquarium-Museum**. Take North Torrey Pines Road past **Torrey Pines Golf Course** and **Torrey Pines State Reserve**—straight to **Del Mar Plaza** where you can rub elbows with the beautiful people (who most assuredly are not local Del Martians). Have a late supper at **Il Fornaio** before the short drive to Solana Beach and **Belly Up Tavern** to hear top blues, rock or salsa performers—the end to a perfect day.

Pointing south? Take the trolley and walk—or drive—across the border into **Mexico**. Kick yourself for not waiting to buy take-home gifts on the other side of the border and load up anyway on painted piggy banks, sombreros and straw animal figurines. If there's still time after your shopping and bargaining extravaganza, continue south to **Rosarito** or **Ensenada**. Stop for lobster dinner at **Puerto Nuevo**, return to TJ, **disco** all night, then come back into the U.S. and get on the plane with a margarita hangover and a foggy memory. Ole!

Special Agendas

Shopping Agenda

Horton Plaza is your first and maybe *only* stop—a Disneyland-ish maze of department stores, specialty shops, boutiques and souvenir outlets, with plenty of restaurants, cinemas, and a theater for wimps in need of a break. Fat wallets and window shoppers should cross the street to the **Palladion** for a few Tiffany baubles and several pair of Ferragamo shoes. Unique jewelry, shoe, and clothing shops are interspersed amongst the historic buildings of the Gaslamp Quarter. **Seaport Village**, commercial though it is, is still rife with interesting shopping-bag fillers and top-quality souvenirs. For take-homes with that south-of-the-border feel (without actually *going* over the border), head for **Old Town** and **Bazaar del Mundo**. The gift shops at any and all of the **museums** offer an abundance of quality items including books, cards, and one-of-a-kinds. **Mall maniacs** will definitely want to cruise the **Mission Valley** and **Fashion Valley** complexes. **University Towne Center** in the Golden Triangle area is an outdoor sort of mall with better shops, a bit of schlock, and SoCal ambiance. **Prospect** and **Girard** avenues, in "downtown" La Jolla, are lined with snazzy boutiques and galleries while farther north the **Del Mar Plaza** is *the* place to carry away classy acquisitions. Budget shoppers should cross the border into **Tijuana**, taxi over to **Avenida Revolution** and knock yourselves out (just be sure to ascertain if your purchases are in US$ or Mexican pesos—mucho *grande* difference!).

Bai Yun, a giant panda, has become a zoo favorite.

Kids Agenda

Doing San Diego with the kids is *easy*. They'll love the boats in the **harbor** (especially those big Navy destroyers!), and the carousel at **Seaport Village** is a sure winner. The **Children's Museum**, downtown, will last them (and you) for hours, days, months, their entire upbringing. All ages will be fascinated by just about every museum in **Balboa Park**, not to mention the park itself (and, don't forget, that includes the world-famous **zoo**). **Mission Bay Park** is another all-day, all-week , lifetime event—kite-flying, sailboats, Frisbee-throwing, swimming, softball—**Sea World!** **Belmont Park**, nearby, offers a beautiful hand-carved carousel, plus the big dipper and unique 175-foot-long plunge. Inland, the kids will spend many happy hours at the **Wild Animal Park**, while along the coast—hey, it's the **beach**!

Local Wannabe Agenda

You're here from Poughkeepsie or, *worse*, from Duluth! You're a *tourist*—that ugly word (like being the new kid on the block, or in elementary school). You want to look like you fit in. Okay, first—rip off your clothes, all or just part of them, head for the closest **beach** and get rid of some of that pasty-white covering. No time, hate the beach? One of the local **tanning salons** should suit you well. Do not take **public transportation**—drive around in a rental car (please not a Pontiac Grand Prix—dead giveaway), drive *everywhere*, spend most of your vacation or business trip searching for **parking places** or dumping the car with a **valet**. Eat all your meals during peak hours at one of the ubiquitous **trattorias** or **cucinas** in the **Gaslamp Quarter**. On weekends, or after normal business hours, rent a **bike**, **roller-skates**, **skateboard**, **roller blades**, put on skintight latex sportswear, sports bra and/or jock strap, and take to the specially designated lanes around the city, Balboa Park, or up the North County coast. Stop for freshly-squeezed **juice** or a **smoothie** on odd-numbered hours. On even-numbered hours, hit any **café**, plunk down on the **outdoor patio**, and order a *nonfat* **coffee** drink (use real sugar, however—caffeine is optional). Shower off the exercise (you *did* make sure to sweat, didn't you?), with some sort of **herbal body scrub** and **aroma therapy** concoction. Is it Friday or Saturday night? Put on some cool duds (short body-clinging cocktail dress for the women, something cool and Italian for the men). Try for a table at **Il Fornaio** in the **Del Mar Plaza** (book ahead, if possible and—if it's a warm night—request seating on the outdoor patio, very cool). Do not order anything with red meat, sip red wine with your meal, do not look your server in the eye, and *never* ask for advice. Still feel like a tourist? Get tattooed. Join the ravers or the Navy.

Night Owl's Agenda

Denny's, *two* locations—Mission Valley *and* Del Mar. *Whoopee!*

SAN DIEGO AGENDA

FIELDING'S PICKS FOR...

Hotels with the Best Ambience

Rank	Hotel	Phone	Price
1	**Rancho Bernardo Inn** *17550 Bernardo Oaks Drive* *San Diego*	☎ (619) 487-1611	$115–$255
2	**Welk Resort Center** *8860 Lawrence Welk Drive* *Escondido*	☎ (619) 749-3000	$100–$120
3	**L'Auberge Del Mar Resort and Spa** *1540 Camino del Mar* *Del Mar*	☎ (619) 259-1515	$165–$315
4	**La Jolla Marriott** *4240 La Jolla Village Drive* *San Diego*	☎ (619) 587-1414	$115–$135
5	**Sea Lodge** *8110 Camino del Oro* *La Jolla*	☎ (619) 459-8271	$109–$379
6	**Bed & Breakfast Inn at La Jolla** *7753 Draper Avenue* *La Jolla*	☎ (619) 456-2066	$85–$225
7	**Loew's Coronado Bay Resort** *4000 Coronado Bay Road* *Coronado*	☎ (619) 424-4000	$175–$225
8	**Bahia Resort Hotel** *988 West Mission Bay Drive* *San Diego*	☎ (619) 488-0551	$130–$220
9	**Catamaran Resort Hotel** *3999 Mission Bay Boulevard* *San Diego*	☎ (619) 488-1081	$140–$295

Hotels with the Best Ambience

Rank	Hotel	Phone	Price
10	**Sheratons on Harbor Island** *1380 Harbor Island Drive* *San Diego*	☎ (619) 291-2900	$180–$220

The Best Hotels for Honeymooners

Rank	Hotel	Phone	Price
1	**Rancho Bernardo Inn** *17550 Bernardo Oaks Drive* *San Diego*	☎ (619) 487-1611	$115–$255
2	**Rock Haus** *410 15th Street* *San Diego*	☎ (619) 481-3764	$75–$150
3	**Prospect Park Inn** *1110 Prospect Street* *San Diego*	☎ (619) 454-0133	$80–$145
4	**Sea Lodge** *8110 Camino del Oro* *San Diego*	☎ (619) 459-8271	$109–$379
5	**Colonial Inn** *910 Prospect Street* *San Diego*	☎ (619) 454-2181	$120–$220
6	**Hyatt Islandia** *1441 Quivira Road* *San Diego*	☎ (619) 224-1234	$109–$174
7	**Dana Inn & Marina** *1710 West Mission Bay Drive* *·San Diego*	☎ (619) 222-6440	$70–$130
8	**Bahia Resort Hotel** *988 West Mission Bay Drive* *San Diego*	☎ (619) 488-0551	$130–$220
9	**Catamaran Resort Hotel** *3999 Mission Bay Boulevard* *San Diego*	☎ (619) 488-1081	$140–$295
10	**Humphrey's Half Moon Inn** *2303 Shelter Island Drive* *San Diego*	☎ (619) 224-3411	$79–$169

The Most Relaxing Hotels

Rank	Hotel	Phone	Price
1	**Rancho Bernardo Inn** *17550 Bernardo Oaks Drive* *San Diego*	☎ **(619) 487-1611**	**$115–$255**
2	**Rancho Valencia Resort** *5921 Valencia Circle* *San Diego*	☎ **(619) 756-1123**	**$315–$450**
3	**Sheraton Grande Torrey Pines** *10950 North Torrey Pines Road* *San Diego*	☎ **(619) 558-1500**	**$175–$260**
4	**Sea Lodge** *8110 Camino del Oro* *San Diego*	☎ **(619) 459-8271**	**$109–$379**
5	**La Valencia** *1132 Prospect Avenue* *San Diego*	☎ **(619) 454-0771**	**$150–$300**
6	**Le Meridien San Diego** *2000 2nd Street* *San Diego*	☎ **(619) 435-3000**	**$165–$265**
7	**Hotel del Coronado** *1500 Orange Avenue* *San Diego*	☎ **(619) 435-6611**	**$160–$370**
8	**San Diego Princess Resort** *1404 West Vacation Road* *San Diego*	☎ **(619) 274-4630**	**$130–$195**
9	**San Diego Hilton Beach & Tennis Resort** *1775 East Mission Bay Drive* *San Diego*	☎ **(619) 276-4010**	**$135–$235**
10	**Las Rocas Hotel and Suites** *On the Old Highway, six miles* *south of Rosarito Beach* *San Diego*	☎ **(661) 2-2140**	**$60–$90**

The Most Romantic Hotels

Rank	Hotel	Phone	Price
1	**Rancho Valencia Resort** *5921 Valencia Circle* *San Diego*	☎ **(619) 756-1123**	**$315–$450**
2	**Sheraton Grande Torrey Pines** *10950 North Torrey Pines Road* *San Diego*	☎ **(619) 558-1500**	**$175–$260**

The Most Romantic Hotels

Rank	Hotel	Phone	Price
3	**La Valencia** *1132 Prospect Avenue* *San Diego*	☎ (619) 454-0771	$150–$300
4	**Le Meridien San Diego** *2000 2nd Street* *San Diego*	☎ (619) 435-3000	$165–$265
5	**Hotel del Coronado** *1500 Orange Avenue* *San Diego*	☎ (619) 435-6611	$160–$370
6	**San Diego Princess Resort** *1404 West Vacation Road* *San Diego*	☎ (619) 274-4630	$130–$195
7	**San Diego Hilton Beach & Tennis Resort** *1775 East Mission Bay Drive* *San Diego*	☎ (619) 276-4010	$135–$235
8	**Las Rocas Hotel and Suites** *On the Old Highway, six miles* *south of Rosarito Beach* *San Diego*	☎ (661) 2-2140	$60–$90
9	**Rosarito Beach Hotel** *Boulevard Juarez* *San Diego*	☎ (661) 2-1106	$60–$120
10	**Pelican Cove Inn** *320 Walnut Avenue* *San Diego*	☎ (619) 434-5995	$75–$175
11	**L'Auberge Del Mar Resort and Spa** *1540 Camino del Mar* *San Diego*	☎ (619) 259-1515	$165–$315
12	**Bed & Breakfast Inn at La Jolla** *7753 Draper Avenue* *San Diego*	☎ (619) 456-2066	$85–$225
13	**Loew's Coronado Bay Resort** *4000 Coronado Bay Road* *San Diego*	☎ (619) 424-4000	$175–$225
14	**Heritage Park Bed and Breakfast** *2470 Heritage Park Row* *San Diego*	☎ (619) 299-6832	$85–$200
15	**Horton Grand Hotel** *311 Island Avenue* *San Diego*	☎ (619) 544-1886	$130

Restaurants with the Best Ambience		
Rank	**Restaurant** **Phone**	**Price**
1	**Mille Fleurs** *6009 Paseo Delicias* *San Diego* ☎ (619) 756-3085	$18–$50
2	**El Bizcocho** *17550 Bernardo Oaks Drive* *San Diego* ☎ (619) 487-1611	$30–$45
3	**Cindy Black's** *5721 La Jolla Boulevard* *San Diego* ☎ (619) 456-6299	$21–$30
4	**Top O'The Cove** *1216 Prospect Street* *San Diego* ☎ (619) 454-7779	$9–$32
5	**George's at the Cove** *1250 Prospect Street* *San Diego* ☎ (619) 454-4244	$8–$26
6	**The Crown Room** *1500 Orange Avenue* *San Diego* ☎ (619) 435-6611	$12–$28
7	**Marius** *2000 2nd Street* *San Diego* ☎ (619) 435-3000	$39–$70
8	**The Belgian Lion** *2265 Bacon Street* *San Diego* ☎ (619) 223-2700	$20–$35
9	**Cafe Pacifica** *2414 San Diego Avenue* *San Diego* ☎ (619) 291-6666	$7–$25
10	**Mister A's** *2550 Fifth Avenue* *San Diego* ☎ (619) 239-1377	$7–$30

The Best Business Location Restaurants		
Rank	**Restaurant** **Phone**	**Price**
1	**Mister A's** *2550 Fifth Avenue* *San Diego* ☎ (619) 239-1377	$7–$30
2	**Putnam's** *910 Prospect Street* *San Diego* ☎ (619) 454-2181	$9–$26

The Best Business Location Restaurants

Rank	Restaurant	Phone	Price
3	**Cafe Japengo** *8960 University Center Lane* *San Diego*	☎ (619) 430-3355	$12–$28
4	**Monterey Whaling Company** *901 Camino del Rio South* *San Diego*	☎ (619) 543-9000	$6–$20
5	**Sally's** *1 Market Place* *San Diego*	☎ (619) 687-6080	$7–$20
6	**Ruth's Chris Steakhouse** *1355 North Harbor Drive* *San Diego*	☎ (619) 233-1422	$6–$23
7	**Old Columbia Brewery & Grill** *1157 Columbia Street* *San Diego*	☎ (619) 234-2739	$5–$14
8	**Sfuzzi** *340 Fifth Avenue* *San Diego*	☎ (619) 231-2323	$8–$18
9	**Hob Nob Hill** *2271 First Avenue* *San Diego*	☎ (619) 239-8176	$6–$14
10	**Trattoria La Strada** *702 Fifth Avenue* *San Diego*	☎ (619) 239-3400	$10–$28

The Most Romantic Restaurants

Rank	Restaurant	Phone	Price
1	**Mille Fleurs** *6009 Paseo Delicias* *San Diego*	☎ (619) 756-3085	$18–$50
2	**El Bizcocho** *17550 Bernardo Oaks Drive* *San Diego*	☎ (619) 487-1611	$30–$45
3	**Marine Room** *2000 Spindrift Drive* *San Diego*	☎ (619) 459-7722	$7–$30
4	**Top O'The Cove** *1216 Prospect Street* *San Diego*	☎ (619) 454-7779	$9–$32
5	**George's at the Cove** *1250 Prospect Street* *San Diego*	☎ (619) 454-4244	$8–$26
6	**The Crown Room** *1500 Orange Avenue* *San Diego*	☎ (619) 435-6611	$12–$28

The Most Romantic Restaurants

Rank	Restaurant	Phone	Price
7	**Marius** *2000 2nd Street* *San Diego*	☎ (619) 435-3000	$39–$70
8	**Thee Bungalow** *4996 West Point Loma Blvd.* *San Diego*	☎ (619) 224-2884	$10–$22
9	**La Embotelladora Vieja** *Avenida Miramar 666* *San Diego*	☎ (617) 4-0807	$12–$30
10	**Tourlas** *1540 Camino del Mar* *San Diego*	☎ (619) 259-1515	$14–$33

LIST OF ATTRACTIONS

Attraction	Rating	Pg.
Founder's Chapel, University of San Diego (1949)		105
Four Seasons Resort Aviara		286
Fritz Theater	★★★	67
G Lounge	★★	182
Garden Cabaret		109
Gaslamp Quarter Theatre	★★★	66
Gaslamp Quarter	★★	60
Gaslamp Quarter	★★★★★	44
Gold Coast Anchorage		157
Gourmet Lounge	★★★	111
Grant Grill	★★★★	71
Gray Line	★★★	269
Greek Festival	★★★	235
Green Circle Bar	★★	70
Grille at La Jolla	★★★	208
Guild Theatre (1912)		104
Guild Theatre		109
H&M Landing		159
Half Moon Marina		157
Hall of Champions	★★★	46
Hamel's Action Sports Center		178
Handlery Hotel and Country Club		288
Hansen's		244
Harbor Island West Marina		157
Hard Rock Cafe	★★	272
Hard Rock Cafe	★★★	208
Harley's House of Harleys		244
Haunted Museum of Man	★★★★	61
Heritage Park	★★★★	99
HGH Pro-Am Golf Classic	★★★	62
Hillcrest Cinemas		109
Hipodromo de Agua Caliente	★★★	267
Holiday Lights Walk	★★★	142
Hook, Line & Sinker		163
Hornblower/Invader Cruises	★★	60
Hornblower/Invader Cruises		159
Horsedrawn Carriage Tours		60
Hot Air Balloon Classic	★★★★	236
Hotel del Coronado	★★★	141
Humphrey's Concerts by the Bay	★★★★★	162
Hussong's Cantina	★★	271
Iguana's	★★★	272
Il Forno Bistro and Bar	★★	208
Imperial Beach		92
Improv	★★★★	183
Independence Day Celebration	★★★★	142
Intermezzo Lounge	★★	111

Attraction	Rating	Pg.
Marine Street Beach		91
Maritime Museum	★★★	49
Marriott Marina		157
Marston House Museum	★★	46
Mason Street School	★★	99
McP's Irish Pub and Grill	★★★	144
Meade House		139
Mercedes Championships	★★★★★	236
Mexican Village	★★	144
Mexitlan	★★★★	266
Milligan's Bar and Grill	★★	209
Mingei Museum of World Folk Art	★★★★	198
MiraCosta Theatre	★★	239
Mission Bay Golf Course		288
Mission Bay Park	★★★★★	174
Mission Bay Park		301
Mission Bay Sport Center		178
Mission Bay		92
Mission Beach		92
Mission San Antonio de Pala	★★★	228
Mission San Diego de Alcala (1769)		105
Mission San Diego de Alcala	★★★	101
Mission San Luis Rey de Francia	★★★	228
Mister O's Nightclub	★★★	111
Model Railroad Museum	★★★	58
Moose McGillycuddy's	★	183
Morely Field Sports Complex	★★★★★	51
Morgan Run Country Club		287
Mormon Battalion Visitors Center	★★★	99
Mother Goose Parade	★★★★	62
Mount Soledad	★★★	201
Mt. Woodson Country Club		288
Mundo Divertido	★★	268
Murder Mystery Dinner Theatre	★★★	109
Museo de Cera	★★	267
Museum of Contemporary Art	★★★	49
Museum of Man	★★★★	46
Museum of Photographic Arts	★★★★★	47
Museum of San Diego History		47
Mystery Cafe	★★★	67
NAS Miramar Air Show	★★★★★	205
Natural History Museum	★★★★	47
Naval Ships	★★	60
Neiman's Bar and Grille	★★★	241
North Coast Repertory Theatre	★★★	239
O'Hungry's	★★★	112
OB People's Natural Foods		191

LIST OF HOTELS

Hotel	Price	Rating	Pg.
Bahia Resort Hotel	$125–$325	★★★★	186
Bay Club Hotel & Marina	$110–$150	★★★★	164
Bed & Breakfast Inn at La Jolla	$85–$225	★★★★	210
Best Western Hacienda Hotel Old Town	$99–$119	★★★	118
Best Western Hanalei Hotel	$100–$160	★★★	116
Best Western Inn by the Sea	$95–$150	★★	213
Best Western Posada Inn	$72–$102	★★	165
Best Western Seven Seas	$49–$59	★★	119
Best Western Shelter Island Marina Inn	$89–$99	★★★	165
Camino Real Tijuana	$150–$150	★★★★	277
Carlsbad Inn Beach Resort	$140–$198	★★★	247
Catamaran Resort Hotel	$140–$325	★★★★	186
Colonial Inn	$120–$220	★★★	211
Dana Inn & Marina	$70–$130	★★★	186
Days Inn Hotel Circle	$55–$89	★	118
Del Mar Hilton	$75–$140	★★★	246
Doubletree Club Hotel Del Mar	$75–$125	★★	246
El Cid Motor Hotel	$40–$60	★★	278
Embassy Suites Hotel	$130–$190	★★★	75
Embassy Suites	$128–$188	★★★	211
Ensenada Travelodge	$45–$70	★★	278
Estero Beach Hotel Resort	$40–$90	★★★	278
Festival Plaza	$50–$100	★★★	275
Gaslamp Plaza Suites	$70–$180	★★	76
Glorietta Bay Inn	$89–$275	★★★	145
Grand Hotel Tijuana	$72–$200	★★★★	277
Handlery Hotel and Resort	$80–$150	★★★	116
Heritage Park Bed and Breakfast	$95–$150	★★★★	116
Holiday Inn Hotel Circle	$69–$99	★★	117
Holiday Inn on the Bay	$100–$100	★★	75
Holiday Inn Pueblo Amigo	$60–$90	★★★	277
Horton Grand Hotel	$80–$100	★★★	76
Hotel Circle Inn and Suites	$49–$89	★★	119
Hotel del Coronado	$169–$389	★★★★★	145
Hotel Lucerna	$65–$85	★★	278
Hotel Real del Rio	$65–$85	★★	278
Humphrey's Half Moon Inn	$99–$169	★★★	166
Hyatt Islandia	$115–$190	★★★	186
Hyatt Regency La Jolla	$125–$190	★★★★★	211
Hyatt Regency San Diego	$165–$230	★★★★	78
Kona Kai Continental Plaza Resort and Marina	$130–$500	★★★★	166
L'Auberge Del Mar Resort and Spa	$165–$315	★★★★	248
La Costa Hotel and Spa	$225–$420	★★★★	247

Hotel	Price	Rating	Pg.
La Jolla Marriott	$198–$198	★★★★	211
La Valencia	$165–$370	★★★★★	212
Las Rocas Hotel and Suites	$50–$95	★★★	276
Las Rosas	$90–$130	★★★	275
Le Meridien San Diego	$165–$265	★★★★★	144
Lexington Hotel and Suites	$79–$119	★★	166
Lodge at Torrey Pines	$85–$155	★★★	212
Loew's Coronado Bay Resort	$195–$245	★★★★	146
Oasis Resort	$40–$85	★★★	279
Ocean Park Inn	$85–$145	★★	185
Pacific Shores Inn	$58–$95	★★★	185
Pacific Terrace Inn	$135–$215	★★	185
Pelican Cove Inn	$85–$175	★★★	245
Prospect Park Inn	$85–$150	★★	213
Punta Morro	$65–$125	★★★	275
Quality Resort Mission Valley	$59–$69	★★★	120
Radisson Hotel San Diego	$89–$149	★★★	117
Radisson Inn Encinitas	$79–$105	★★	246
Ramada Hotel Old Town	$59–$89	★★	119
Ramada Inn	$75–$107	★★	247
Rancho Bernardo Inn	$115–$255	★★★★★	248
Rancho Valencia Resort	$335–$470	★★★★★	249
Red Lion Hotel	$89–$175	★★★	117
Residence Inn by Marriott	$95–$189	★★	214
Residence Inn Marriott Real del Mar	$69–$169	★★★	276
Rock Haus	$90–$150	★★★	245
Rosarito Beach Hotel	$60–$120	★★★★	276
San Diego Hilton Beach & Tennis Resort	$135–$235	★★★★★	187
San Diego Marriott Hotel & Marina	$185–$205	★★★★	78
San Diego Marriott Mission Valley	$109–$135	★★★	117
San Diego Mission Valley Hilton	$109–$179	★★★	118
San Diego Princess Resort	$130–$195	★★★★★	187
San Diego Yacht and Breakfast	$130–$245	★★★	165
San Nicolas Resort Hotel	$50–$90	★★	275
Sea Lodge	$109–$379	★★★★	214
Sheraton Grande Torrey Pines	$175–$260	★★★★★	213
Sheraton on Harbor Island	$180–$220	★★★★	164
Stratford Inn	$75–$150	★★	246
Town and Country Hotel	$85–$150	★★★★	118
Travelodge Hotel-Harbor Island	$79–$89	★★★	164
U.S. Grant Hotel	$80–$120	★★★★	76
Vacation Inn Old Town	$70–$115	★★★	119
Welk Resort Center	$110–$0	★★★★	248
Westgate Hotel	$165–$205	★★★★	78
Westin Horton Plaza	$160–$245	★★	77
Wyrdham Emerald Plaza	$140–$240	★★★★	77

LIST OF RESTAURANTS

Restaurant	Price	Rating	Pg.
94th Aero Squadron	$$$	★★★★	189
Alfonso's	$$	★★★	215
Alize	$$$	★★★★★	80
Anthony's Fish Grotto	$$	★★★★	85
Anthony's Star of the Sea	$$$	★★★★★	85
Athen's Market	$$$	★★★★	85
Azzura Point	$$$	★★★★	150
Baci's	$$$	★★★★	188
Barrymore	$$	★★★	124
Bayou Bar and Grill	$$	★★★★	81
Belgian Lion	$$$	★★★★★	189
Berta's Latin American Restaurant	$$	★★★	126
Billiard Gallery Sports Grill	$	★	254
Boathouse	$$$	★★★	167
Brigantine	$$$	★★★	147
Bully's North	$$$	★★★	250
Bungalow	$	★★★★	189
Busalacchi's	$$	★★★★	120
Cafe Beignet			113
Cafe Japengo	$$$	★★★★	215
Cafe Lulu	$	★★★	81
Cafe Pacifica	$$$	★★★★★	126
California Cuisine	$$	★★★★	120
Casa de Bandini	$$	★★★★	126
Casa de Pico	$$	★★★	127
Cecil's Cafe and Fish Market	$	★★★	189
Celadon	$$	★★★	121
Charley Brown's	$$$	★★★★	167
Chart House	$$$	★★★★	147
Chateau Orleans	$$	★★★★	190
Chez Loma	$$$	★★★★	147
Chicago Coffee Co., Inc.			113
Chiki Jai	$$	★★★	282
Chino	$$	★★★★	81
Cilantro's	$$$	★★★	250
Cindy Black's	$$$	★★★★★	216
Corvette Diner	$	★★★	121
Crest Cafe	$	★★	121
Croce's	$$	★★★	82
Crown Room	$$$	★★★★★	148
Daily's Fit & Fresh	$	★★	216
Dakota Grill and Spirits	$$	★★★★	82

Restaurant	Price	Rating	Pg.
De Medici	$$$	★★★★	86
Dobson's	$$$	★★★★	86
Dragon del Mar	$$$	★★	281
El Bizcocho	$$$	★★★★★	254
El Charro	$$	★★	280
El Nido	$$	★★	281
El Rey Sol	$$$	★★★★	280
El Rodeo	$$	★★	282
El Taurino	$$	★★★	282
Epazote	$$$	★★★	251
Espresso Roma			113
Extraordinary Desserts			113
Fairouz Cafe & Gallery	$$	★★★	168
Fidel's	$$	★★★	255
Filippi's Pizza Grotto	$$	★★★★	125
Fio's	$$	★★★★	82
Fish House Vera Cruz	$$	★★★	249
Fish Market	$$	★★★★	79
French Gourmet	$$	★★★	216
Garlix	$$	★★★	86
George's at the Cove	$$$	★★★★★	216
Grant Grill	$$$	★★★★	82
Haliotis	$	★★	281
Harbor House	$$$	★★★	88
Hard Rock Cafe	$$	★★	282
Harry's	$	★★★	217
Hob Nob Hill	$$	★★★★	86
Hops! Bistro & Brewery	$	★★★	215
Humphrey's	$$$	★★★★	169
Il Fornaio	$$$	★★★★	251
Indigo Grill	$$$	★★★★	125
Jake's Del Mar	$$	★★★	251
Jimmy Carter's Cafe	$	★★	122
Jimmy Wong's Golden Dragon	$	★★★★	122
Johnny Rocket's	$	★★	252
Kansas City Barbecue	$	★★★	89
Karinya Thai Cuisine	$$	★★★	190
Kim's Restaurant	$	★★	253
Kiva Grill	$$	★★★	217
Kiyo's Japanese Restaurant	$	★★★	83
La Embotelladora Vieja	$$$	★★★★	281
La Espadana	$$	★★★	282
La Fonda	$$	★★★	281
La Lena	$$	★★★	283
La Spezia	$$	★★★	283
La Taberna Espanola	$$	★★★	283
Lamont Street Grill	$$	★★★	190

Restaurant	Price	Rating	Pg.
Laurel	$$$	★★★★★	87
Manhattan	$$$	★★★	217
Marine Room	$$$	★★★★	217
Marius	$$$	★★★★★	148
Marrakesh	$$$	★★★	218
Miguel's Cocina	$	★★★	149
Mille Fleurs	$$$	★★★★★	254
Mister A's	$$$	★★★★★	122
Montana's American Grill	$$$	★★★★	123
Monterey Whaling Company	$$	★★	126
Neiman's	$	★★★	250
Nobu Japanese Restaurant	$$	★★★	254
Old Columbia Brewery & Grill	$$	★★★★	83
Old Spaghetti Factory	$	★★★	83
Old Town Mexican Cafe	$$	★★★★	127
Osteria Panevino	$$	★★★★	87
Pacifica Del Mar	$$$	★★★	252
Palenque	$$	★★★	190
Pamplemousse Grill	$$$	★★★★	252
Panda Inn	$$	★★★★	85
Pannikin Brockton Villa	$	★★★	218
Peohe's	$$$	★★★	149
Pizza Nova	$	★★★	168
Planet Hollywood	$	★★	87
Point Loma Seafoods	$	★★★★	168
Potato Shack Cafe	$	★★★	253
Primavera	$$$	★★★★	149
Prince of Wales Room	$$$	★★★★	149
Princess Pub and Grill	$	★★★	125
Putnam's	$$$	★★★	218
Quel Fromage			113
Quiig's Bar & Grill	$$	★★★★	189
Rainwater's	$$$	★★★★★	88
Red Sails Inn	$$	★★★★	168
Royal Thai Cuisine	$$	★★	219
Ruth's Chris Steakhouse	$$$	★★★★	80
Sally's	$$	★★★★	88
Sammy's California Woodfired Pizza	$	★★★	84
SamSon's Deli-Restaurant	$	★★★	219
Saska's Steak & Seafood	$$	★★★	188
Seau's: The Restaurant	$$	★★	88
Sfuzzi	$$	★★★★	84
Spices Thai Cafe	$$	★★★★	252
Spot	$$	★★	219
Sushi Ota	$$	★★★	191
Taste of Szechuan	$$	★★★	123
Taste of Thai	$$	★★★★	123

Restaurant	Price	Rating	Pg.
Thai Chada	$	★★★	123
Tia Juana Tilly's	$$$	★★★	283
Tip Top Meats	$	★★★	250
Tom Ham's Lighthouse	$$$	★★★★	167
Top O'The Cove	$$$	★★★★★	219
Tour de France	$$$	★★★★	283
Trattoria Acqua	$$	★★★	220
Trattoria La Strada	$$$	★★★★	84
Twiggs Tea and Coffee Company			113
Vegetarian Zone	$$	★★★	124
Venetian	$$	★★★	169
Vigilucci's	$$	★★★	253
When in Rome	$$$	★★★★	253
Yakitori II	$$	★★★	169
Yoshino's	$$	★★★	127

INDEX

Order Your Guide to Travel and Adventure

Title	Price	Title	Price
Fielding's Alaska Cruises and the Inside Passage	$18.95	Fielding's Indiana Jones Adventure and Survival Guide™	$15.95
Fielding's America West	$19.95	Fielding's Italy	$18.95
Fielding's Asia's Top Dive Sites	$19.95	Fielding's Kenya	$19.95
Fielding's Australia	$18.95	Fielding's Las Vegas Agenda	$16.95
Fielding's Bahamas	$16.95	Fielding's London Agenda	$14.95
Fielding's Baja California	$18.95	Fielding's Los Angeles	$16.95
Fielding's Bermuda	$16.95	Fielding's Mexico	$18.95
Fielding's Best and Worst	$19.95	Fielding's New Orleans Agenda	$16.95
Fielding's Birding Indonesia	$19.95	Fielding's New York Agenda	$16.95
Fielding's Borneo	$18.95	Fielding's New Zealand	$17.95
Fielding's Budget Europe	$18.95	Fielding's Paradors, Pousadas and Charming Villages	$18.95
Fielding's Caribbean	$19.95	Fielding's Paris Agenda	$14.95
Fielding's Caribbean Cruises	$18.95	Fielding's Portugal	$16.95
Fielding's Caribbean on a Budget	$18.95	Fielding's Rome Agenda	$16.95
Fielding's Diving Australia	$19.95	Fielding's San Diego Agenda	$14.95
Fielding's Diving Indonesia	$19.95	Fielding's Southeast Asia	$18.95
Fielding's Eastern Caribbean	$17.95	Fielding's Southern California Theme Parks	$18.95
Fielding's England including Ireland, Scotland and Wales	$18.95	Fielding's Southern Vietnam on Two Wheels	$15.95
Fielding's Europe	$19.95	Fielding's Spain	$18.95
Fielding's Europe 50th Anniversary	$24.95	Fielding's Surfing Australia	$19.95
Fielding's European Cruises	$18.95	Fielding's Surfing Indonesia	$19.95
Fielding's Far East	$18.95	Fielding's Sydney Agenda	$16.95
Fielding's France	$18.95	Fielding's Thailand, Cambodia, Laos and Myanmar	$18.95
Fielding's France: Loire Valley, Burgundy and the Best of French Culture	$16.95	Fielding's Travel Tools™	$15.95
Fielding's France: Normandy & Brittany	$16.95	Fielding's Vietnam including Cambodia and Laos	$19.95
Fielding's France: Provence and the Mediterranean	$16.95	Fielding's Walt Disney World and Orlando Area Theme Parks	$18.95
Fielding's Freewheelin' USA	$18.95	Fielding's Western Caribbean	$18.95
Fielding's Hawaii	$18.95	Fielding's The World's Most Dangerous Places™	$21.95
Fielding's Hot Spots: Travel in Harm's Way	$15.95	Fielding's Worldwide Cruises	$21.95

To place an order: call toll-free 1-800-FW-2-GUIDE
(VISA, MasterCard and American Express accepted)
or send your check or money order to:
Fielding Worldwide, Inc., 308 S. Catalina Avenue, Redondo Beach, CA 90277
http://www.fieldingtravel.com
Add $2.00 per book for shipping & handling (sorry, no COD's),
allow 2–6 weeks for delivery

Favorite People, Places
& Experiences

ADDRESS:	NOTES:

Name

Address

Telephone

Name

Address

Telephone

Name

Address

Telephone

Name

Address

Telephone

Name

Address

Telephone

Name

Address

Telephone

Name

Address

Telephone

NEW FIELDING WEAR!

Now that you own a Fielding travel guide, you have graduated from being a tourist to full-fledged traveler! Celebrate your elevated position by proudly wearing a heavy-duty, all-cotton shirt or cap, selected by our authors for their comfort and durability (and their ability to hide dirt).

Important Note: Fielding authors have field-tested these shirts and have found that they can be swapped for much more than their purchase price in free drinks at some of the world's hottest clubs and in-spots. They also make great gifts.

WORLD TOUR

Hit the hard road with a travel fashion statement for our times. Visit all 35 of Mr. D.P.'s favorite nasty spots (listed on the back), or just look like you're going to. This is the real McCoy, worn by mujahadeen, mercenaries, UN peacekeepers and the authors of Fielding's *The World's Most Dangerous Places*. Black, XL, heavy-duty 100% cotton. Made in the USA. $18.00.

LIVE DANGEROUSLY

A shirt that tells the world that within that high-mileage, overly educated body beats the heart of a true party animal. Only for adrenaline junkies, hardcore travelers and seekers of knowledge. Black, XL, heavy-duty 100% cotton. Made in the USA. $18.00.

MR. DP CAP

Fielding authors have field-tested the Mr. DP cap and found it can be swapped for much more than its purchase price in free drinks at some of the world's hottest clubs. Guaranteed to turn heads wherever you go. Made in U.S.A. washable cotton, sturdy bill, embroidered logo, one size fits all. $14.95.

Name:

Address:

City:

State: Zip:

Telephone:
Shirt Name:
Quantity:

For each item, add $4 shipping and handling. California residents add $1.50 sales tax. Allow 2 to 4 weeks for delivery.

Send check or money order with your order form to:

Fielding Worldwide, Inc.
308 South Catalina Avenue
Redondo Beach, CA 90277

or order your shirts by phone,:
1-800-FW-2-GUIDE
Visa, MC, AMex accepted

International Conversions

TEMPERATURE

To convert °F to °C, subtract 32 and divide by 1.8. To convert °C to °F, multiply by 1.8 and add 32.

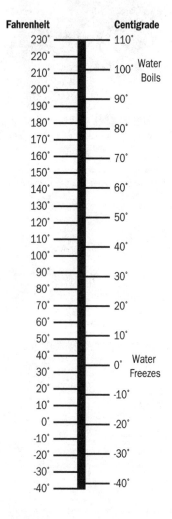

WEIGHTS & MEASURES

LENGTH

1 km	=	0.62 miles
1 mile	=	1.609 km
1 meter	=	1.0936 yards
1 meter	=	3.28 feet
1 yard	=	0.9144 meters
1 yard	=	3 feet
1 foot	=	30.48 centimeters
1 centimeter	=	0.39 inch
1 inch	=	2.54 centimeters

AREA

1 square km	=	0.3861 square miles
1 square mile	=	2.590 square km
1 hectare	=	2.47 acres
1 acre	=	0.405 hectare

VOLUME

1 cubic meter	=	1.307 cubic yards
1 cubic yard	=	0.765 cubic meter
1 cubic yard	=	27 cubic feet
1 cubic foot	=	0.028 cubic meter
1 cubic centimeter	=	0.061 cubic inch
1 cubic inch	=	16.387 cubic centimeters

CAPACITY

1 gallon	=	3.785 liters
1 quart	=	0.94635 liters
1 liter	=	1.057 quarts
1 pint	=	473 milliliters
1 fluid ounce	=	29.573 milliliters

MASS and WEIGHT

1 metric ton	=	1.102 short tons
1 metric ton	=	1000 kilograms
1 short ton	=	.90718 metric ton
1 long ton	=	1.016 metric tons
1 long ton	=	2240 pounds
1 pound	=	0.4536 kilograms
1 kilogram	=	2.2046 pounds
1 ounce	=	28.35 grams
1 gram	=	0.035 ounce
1 milligram	=	0.015 grain